Immigrant Voices

Immigrant Voices

NEW LIVES IN AMERICA,

1773–1986

Edited by

Thomas Dublin

University of Illinois Press

URBANA AND CHICAGO

© 1993 by Thomas Dublin
Manufactured in the United States of America
1   2   3   4   5   C   P   5   4   3   2   1

This book is printed on acid-free paper.

Library of Congress Cataloging-in-Publication Data

Immigrant voices : new lives in America : 1773–1986 / edited by Thomas
Dublin.
        p.   cm.
    Includes bibliographical references.
    ISBN 0-252-01769-2 (cloth : alk. paper). — ISBN 0-252-06290-6
(pbk. : alk. paper)
    1. United States—Emigration and immigration—History.
2. Immigrants—United States—Correspondence.   I. Dublin, Thomas,
1946–   .
JV6450.I553   1993
325.73—dc20   92-31748
                                                      CIP

*To the memory of my grandparents,
Louis and Augusta Salik Dublin, and my
mother, Louise Goldschmidt Dublin,
whose immigrant voices were shaping
influences in my life.*

Contents

Acknowledgments

This book had its genesis fifteen years ago when I first taught an undergraduate survey course on U.S. immigration at the University of California, San Diego. I was distressed at the limited choices of paperback books I might assign to beginning undergraduate students. Overview textbooks and analyses of immigration law and native-born attitudes toward immigrants predominated, making it difficult for students to get any sense of how immigrants perceived their own experiences.

I tried to address this limitation by finding immigrant first-person accounts that permitted students to hear immigrant voices. Initially, Europeans predominated, but over time, as the field of immigration history changed and as my own reading expanded, I discovered sources that spoke to the Asian and Latin American immigrant experience as well. The result of this fifteen-year journey is the reader offered here.

I have had a great deal of help as this book has evolved. First, my students at the University of California, San Diego, and the State University of New York at Binghamton have read and dissected most of the selections reprinted here, and their comments and papers have sharpened my appreciation of these accounts. Moreover, both of these institutions offered financial support at crucial junctures as the readings developed, for which I am grateful.

Graduate teaching assistants have offered numerous suggestions for possible assignments and helpful critiques of those I used in my courses. Several worked as summer research assistants, combing published sources for additional titles. Victoria Brown, Arthur McEvoy, Scott Nash, and Gerald Shenk stand out for special thanks. A number of colleagues directed me to sources that I have included here, and I want to thank Susan Glenn and Mary Lou Locke in particular.

Other colleagues have offered helpful comments and criticism as I wrote the general introduction and prepared commentary for the selections in this volume. This is a better book for the criticisms offered by Victoria Brown, John Higham, William Miller, Dorothee Schneider, Kathryn Kish Sklar, Philip Taylor, and an anonymous reader for the University of Illinois Press.

The preparation of an edited reader is a tortuous undertaking, and the support and encouragement of people at the University of Illinois Press have made all the difference. I thank Richard Wentworth for his faith in the project, Karen Hewitt for guiding the work through the publication process with care and competence, and Jane Mohraz for exemplary copyediting that went far beyond the usual concern for commas and danglers.

Finally, a host of publishers, libraries, and museums made possible the reprinting of the selections and illustrations in this reader. Publishers are listed below, and sources of illustrations are noted at appropriate places in the text. Thanks go also to Mae Galarza, Victor Laredo, Monica Sone, and Louise Wade. Anne Gibson and Margaret Pearce of the Cartography Lab at Clark University, prepared the maps of immigrant origins and destinations that appear in the introduction. Rochella Thorpe prepared the index with her customary care and intelligence. My thanks to all who have helped to bring this reader out of my individual classroom and into the wider reading public.

Permission to reprint the following is gratefully acknowledged:

Chapter 1. The John Harrower Diary, 1773–1776
Excerpts from "The Diary of John Harrower," *American Historical Review* 6 (1900): 65–107.

Chapter 2. The Hollingworth Family Letters, 1827–1830
Excerpts from Thomas W. Leavitt, ed., *The Hollingworth Letters: Technical Change in the Textile Industry* (Cambridge, Mass.: M.I.T. Press, 1969), pp. 5–9, 20–29, 36–39, 53–56, 87–89. Copyright © 1969 by M.I.T. Press; reprinted by permission of the publisher.

Chapter 3. The William and Sophie Frank Seyffardt Letters, 1851–1863
Excerpts from Louis F. Frank, comp., *German-American Pioneers in Wisconsin and Michigan: The Frank-Kerler Letters, 1849–1864*, trans. Margaret Wolff; ed. Harry H. Anderson (Milwaukee: Milwaukee County Historical Society, 1971), pp. 101, 104, 106, 116, 119–20, 131, 173–75, 224, 227, 232, 265, 288–90, 304, 319–20, 336–37, 343, 350, 409, 450–51, 518–19, 524, 544–45. Copyright © 1971 by the Milwaukee County Historical Society; reprinted by permission of the publisher.

Chapter 4. Rosa Cassettari: From Northern Italy to Chicago, 1884–1926
Excerpts from Marie Hall Ets, *Rosa: The Life of an Italian Immigrant* (Min-

neapolis: University of Minnesota Press, 1970), pp. 162–71, 178–95, 203–7, 223–24, 228–31, 234–35, 237–38. Copyright © 1970 by University of Minnesota Press; reprinted by permission of the publisher.

Chapter 5. Rose Gollup: From Russia to the Lower East Side in the 1890s
Excerpts from Rose Cohen, *Out of the Shadow* (New York: George H. Doran, 1918), pp. 13–16, 26, 29, 31–33, 41, 44–45, 47, 50–57, 60–65, 69–70, 73–74, 81–82, 84, 100–103, 108–12, 123–27.

Chapter 6. The Childhood of Mary Paik, 1905–1917
Excerpts from Mary Paik Lee, *Quiet Odyssey: A Pioneer Korean Woman in America*, ed. Sucheng Chan (Seattle: University of Washington Press, 1990), pp. 6–56: "My maternal grandparents . . .   the class never learned about the subject." Copyright © University of Washington Press, 1990; reprinted by permission of the publisher.

Chapter 7. The Galarza Family in the Mexican Revolution, 1910: From Mexico to Sacramento
Excerpts from Ernesto Galarza, *Barrio Boy* (South Bend: Notre Dame Press, 1971), pp. 7–17, 33–34, 57–58, 66–71, 194–212, 237–40. Copyright © 1971 by University of Notre Dame Press; reprinted by permission of the publisher.

Chapter 8. Kazuko Itoi: A Nisei Daughter's Story, 1925–1942
Excerpts from Monica Sone, *Nisei Daughter* (Boston: Little, Brown, 1953), pp. 3–15, 18–28, 109, 111–16, 145–51, 154–59, 165–66, 168–78. Copyright © 1953 by Monica Sone; reprinted by permission of Little, Brown and Company.

Chapter 9. Piri Thomas, Puerto Rican or Negro? Growing Up in East Harlem during World War II
Excerpts from Piri Thomas, *Down These Mean Streets* (New York: Alfred A. Knopf, 1967), pp. 18–21, 33–38, 86–91. Copyright © 1967 by Piri Thomas; reprinted by permission of Alfred A. Knopf, Inc.

Chapter 10. The Nguyen Family: From Vietnam to Chicago, 1975–1986
Excerpts from Al Santoli, *New Americans: An Oral History* (New York: Viking Penguin, 1988), pp. 105–27. Copyright © 1988 by Al Santoli; reprinted by permission of Viking Penguin, a division of Penguin Books USA, Inc.

Editorial Method

In assembling and editing the selections that follow, I have had in mind a general rather than a specialized audience. All the selections have been previously published and where diaries, letters, and oral history are concerned, they have benefited from the close attention of an editor well acquainted with the original, primary material.

In preparing brief introductions and explanatory footnotes to each selection, I have frequently drawn on the work of earlier editors. I have tried to provide adequate material to place the authors' lives in perspective and to place the selections within a broader context without unduly burdening readers with detail. In working with the editorial apparatus prepared for earlier editions of the selections, I have used some of the footnotes, deleted others, and added a fair number of my own. I have kept in mind the audience for this collection and have drawn on my own experience teaching many of these selections to undergraduates at the University of California, San Diego, and the State University of New York at Binghamton.

Occasionally, I have employed subheadings within selections. In some cases these subheadings were chapter titles in the original selections (as with *Nisei Daughter* and *Down These Mean Streets*); where I have employed subheadings of my own choosing, I have enclosed them in brackets. In addition, I have sometimes summarized portions of the narratives that I could not include in this edition. All such additions are marked and enclosed in brackets that distinguish them from text drawn from the original published sources. Finally, I have employed spaces between periods in ellipses that indicate where I have deleted material from the original; where ellipses appeared in the original source, there are no additional spaces.

Immigrant Voices

Introduction

————

Since independence the United States has been a nation of immigrants. In 1782 a French observer, Crèvecoeur, wrote optimistically in words that anticipated the later metaphor of the melting pot: "Here individuals of all races are melted into a new race of men."[1] A hundred years later Emma Lazarus penned the famous words that were later engraved on a plaque mounted on the pedestal of the Statue of Liberty: "Give me your tired, your poor, your huddled masses yearning to breathe free."[2] More recently, scholars have confirmed the centrality of immigrants in the nation's history. Oscar Handlin best summed up this view when he wrote in 1951, "Once I thought to write a history of the immigrants in America. Then I discovered that the immigrants *were* American History."[3]

So they are. Over the course of almost four centuries some 57 million men and women left their native lands—voluntarily and involuntarily—and came to what has become the United States. John Harrower and Mary Paik were two among those millions who crossed oceans to reach this nation's shores and make new lives for themselves. John Harrower left the Shetland Islands, just north of Scotland, a few years before the American Revolution; Mary Paik migrated from Korea in the first decade of the twentieth century. Neither was very different from other immigrants of similar backgrounds in these periods. What sets them apart from their fellow countrymen and women is that they wrote about their experiences and that John Harrower's diary and Mary Paik's memoir have survived to offer readers

1. J. Hector St. John de Crèvecoeur, *Letters from an American Farmer and Sketches of Eighteenth-Century America* (New York: Penguin Books, 1981; originally published in 1782), p. 70.

2. "The New Colossus," in *The Poems of Emma Lazarus*, vol. 1 (Boston: Houghton Mifflin, 1895), pp. 202–3.

3. *The Uprooted: The Epic Story of the Great Migrations that Made the American People* (New York: Grosset and Dunlap, 1951), p. 3.

today a glimpse of what the immigrant experience meant to them. Their stories are two of the ten first-person accounts of immigrants or their children that make up this volume. Taken together these sources provide a unique perspective on a crucial dimension of the building of the United States over the past two hundred years. They show us the remarkable range of peoples who contributed to the growth of this nation and offer views of how American society changed over time.

Before examining these individual accounts, we should consider the nature of immigration as a social process. Historians commonly distinguish between the first European settlers and the immigrants who came later and gained admission to an already existing society.[4] A second important distinction is between those who chose to come to the United States as immigrants and those who were brought here against their will as slaves. Both groups, however, were significant in the "peopling of America," as one historian has recently termed this broader process.[5] So, too, were the 80,000 Californios, Hispanos, and Tejanos—residents of the northern provinces of Mexico that were annexed by the United States with the conclusion of the Mexican War in the mid-nineteenth century.[6] Immigrants, slaves, and annexed colonial peoples have all shaped the development of the culture evident in the United States today.

The focus here is on immigrants—those who chose voluntarily, however coerced by circumstance, to come to the United States after initial European settlement. Some historians have stressed the different ethnic identities of successive groups of immigrants over time, describing them as waves of immigration. I am more struck by fundamental similarities over time—the similar motivations of immigrants and the processes of assimilation they experienced. The first-person accounts in this volume offer evidence of basic continuities in the immigrant experience over a period of two hundred years.

Still, to place these accounts in perspective, it is useful to keep in mind changes that occurred over time. Successive periods, for instance, have seen striking shifts in the size and composition of the immigrant flow. In the years of English colonial rule, somewhat more than 600,000 immigrants, primarily British, Irish, and German, came

4. John Higham, *Send These to Me: Immigrants in Urban America*, rev. ed. (Baltimore: Johns Hopkins University Press, 1984), p. 6.

5. Bernard Bailyn, *Voyagers to the West: A Passage in the Peopling of America on the Eve of the Revolution* (New York: Alfred A. Knopf, 1986).

6. Carlos E. Cortés, "Mexicans," in Stephan Thernstrom, ed., *Harvard Encyclopedia of American Ethnic Groups* (Cambridge, Mass.: Harvard University Press, 1980), pp. 698–99.

to these shores.[7] The numbers of immigrants grew dramatically during the century following independence. In the mid-nineteenth century Irish and German immigrants predominated, and southern and eastern Europeans were most numerous between 1890 and 1924. Immigration declined significantly during the four decades after 1924, as exclusionary federal legislation ended an era of almost unrestricted immigrant flow. Finally, in the past twenty-five years, Asian and Latin American immigration has increased markedly, adding to the ethnic diversity of the nation.

Immigration to the United States has been unique in the annals of world history in three respects. First, the numbers of immigrants entering the nation have dwarfed those of other countries. That has been the case from the start. Spanish and Portuguese immigration to Latin America, for instance, averaged about 3,500 annually over the first two centuries of colonial rule. In contrast, immigration to the British North American colonies averaged 5,000 annually throughout the seventeenth and eighteenth centuries, peaking at almost 15,000 annually in the fifteen years before the American Revolution.[8] Similar differences in the scale of immigration persisted into the nineteenth century. Between 1881 and 1910, for instance, more than 17.7 million immigrants entered the United States.[9] For Brazil and Argentina, the leading destinations among Latin American nations, comparable figures were only 2.4 and 2.1 million immigrants, respectively. Australia, also a nation of immigrants, admitted still fewer, with only 1.3 million immigrants during the half-century between 1852 and 1901. Although Australia's numbers skyrocketed in the years immediately before the outbreak of World War I, they reached an average of only 150,000 annually in the peak years 1911–13, compared with more than 1 million immigrants a year to the United States in the same period.[10]

7. Bailyn, *Voyagers to the West*, pp. 24–26. To these figures of immigrants we might add another 250,000–300,000 enslaved Africans brought to the British North American colonies. Philip D. Curtin, *The African Slave Trade: A Census* (Madison: University of Wisconsin Press, 1969), p. 72.

8. Bailyn, *Voyagers to the West*, pp. 24–26; Ida Altman and James Horn, eds., *"To Make America": European Emigration in the Early Modern Period* (Berkeley: University of California Press, 1991), esp. pp. 1–29.

9. Roger Daniels, *Coming to America: A History of Immigration and Ethnicity in American Life* (New York: HarperCollins, 1990), p. 124.

10. Frederick C. Luebke, *Germans in the New World: Essays in the History of Immigration* (Urbana: University of Illinois Press, 1990), p. 95; Samuel Baily and Franco Ramella, eds., *One Family, Two Worlds: An Italian Family's Correspondence across the Atlantic, 1901–1922* (New Brunswick, N.J.: Rutgers University Press, 1988), p. 19; Geoffrey Sher-

Second, the diversity of immigrants to the United States is unparalleled elsewhere. Canada, Australia, Argentina, and Brazil experienced migrant flows that at times represented larger shares of their populations than was the case for the United States, but only one or two (or at most three) ethnic groups predominated. In the United States, immigrants have been far more diverse, and over time there have been startling shifts among the nationalities constituting this flow. Finally, immigration to the United States has persisted for almost four hundred years, with more immigrants today than in most earlier periods. Immigration to the United States has been greater, more diverse, and longer lasting than that of any other nation.[11]

The diversity and scale of American immigration, in turn, have generated considerable controversy. As early as 1751, Benjamin Franklin decried the impact of German newcomers on the colony of Pennsylvania: "Why should the Palatine Boors be suffered to swarm into our Settlements, and by herding together establish their Language and Manners to the Exclusion of ours? Why should Pennsylvania, founded by the English, become a Colony of *Aliens,* who will shortly be so numerous as to Germanize us?"[12] Southern and eastern Europeans came under even harsher criticism as they entered the nation in growing numbers in the years after 1880. Consider an editorial in the *Philadelphia Inquirer* in 1891: "What kind of people are these new citizens? Some are honest men seeking a home. . . . Others will join the hordes of Huns and Poles in the coal regions, hive together in hovels, live on refuse, save 90 per cent of their earnings and work for wages upon which no responsible laborer could exist. Others will come from the scum of Italy and Sicily. . . . Others will be fresh from jails and prisons, brigands, outlaws, murderers. . . . Isn't there food for thought in the increasing number of immigrants?"[13] The influx of Latin American and Asian immigrants in recent years has prompted

---

ington, *Australia's Immigrants, 1788–1978* (Sydney: Allen and Unwin, 1980), p. 85; Walter F. Willcox, *International Migrations,* vol. 1 (New York: Gordon and Breach, 1969), p. 950.

11. Recent studies that have influenced the interpretation I am offering here include Daniels, *Coming to America;* and Alejandro Portes and Rubén G. Rumbaut, *Immigrant America: A Portrait* (Berkeley: University of California Press, 1990). For comparative immigration data similar to these offered here, see Higham, *Send These To Me,* pp. 13–17, 22–23.

12. *"Observations concerning the Increase of Mankind,"* in Leonard W. Labaree, ed., *The Papers of Benjamin Franklin,* vol. 4 (New Haven, Conn.: Yale University Press, 1961), p. 234, as quoted in Daniels, *Coming to America,* pp. 109–10.

13. Quoted in Stanley Feldstein and Lawrence Costello, eds., *The Ordeal of Assimilation: A Documentary History of the White Working Class* (New York: Anchor/Doubleday, 1974), p. 170.

renewed concerns. "I'm surrounded," complained one San Diego resident about her Indochinese neighbors in 1980. "They are lovely people, but I just don't feel at home since the refugees came here in swarms."[14] Since 1750 ambivalence and downright hostility have greeted America's immigrants.

Despite the opposition to specific groups of immigrants, Americans have had very positive feelings toward immigration in general. They have maintained something of a love affair with the idea of the United States as a haven for the oppressed around the world and with the immigrant success story. That individual immigrants have been able to make a new start in this country and achieve success and even great wealth is taken as a vindication of the superiority of the American economic and social system. Yet the picture that emerges from the myth of the immigrant success story is too rose-colored and stereotyped to illuminate this nation's history accurately. The character of immigration to the United States, the experiences of immigrants, and the responses of native-born Americans have been more varied than the stereotype allows. By surveying changes over the course of American history, we gain a broader picture, enabling us to place the narratives of individual immigrants in context.

Compared with later periods, immigration was extremely modest in the years before independence. An average of 5,000 individuals arrived annually in the British North American colonies that became the United States.[15] This figure includes free migrants, indentured servants and redemptioners, and African slaves. A variety of factors— some technological and economic, others social and political—converged to limit the number of immigrants. The size of ocean-going ships, the difficulties of resupplying settlements, imperial rivalries and periodic warfare, changing power relations among Puritans and Royalists in England, and changing attitudes within English governing circles as to the propriety of emigration all set limits on immigration in the colonial period.

Two major social groups, both drawn by the demand for agricultural labor, played leading roles in "peopling" the American colonies: indentured servants from the British Isles and African slaves.[16] Few En-

14. Rita Calvano, "They're 'Different': Race, Language Create Barriers," *Los Angeles Times*, Mar. 17, 1980.

15. Daniels, *Coming to America*, p. 30.

16. Russell Menard has made a good case for viewing this larger process as a "re-peopling" of the North American colonies depopulated of Native Americans by disease and warfare. See his essay, "Migration, Ethnicity, and the Rise of an Atlantic Economy: The

glish men or women had both the resources for and an interest in migrating to the American colonies as independent settlers in the seventeenth or eighteenth century. Migrants to Plymouth and Massachusetts Bay colonies were exceptions to this generalization, but they totaled only 20,000–30,000 at their peak between 1620 and 1642.[17] Many more seventeenth-century immigrants headed for the Chesapeake colonies as indentured servants, where an expanding tobacco-export economy created a strong demand for labor.

The Virginia Company, organizers of the colony at Jamestown, recruited "adventurers" to serve the company as laborers for seven years. The company's need to recruit laborers led it to improve the conditions under which adventurers served and to offer them land at the end of their terms of service. Out of this practice evolved the broader system of indentured servitude, by which more than 100,000 Britons immigrated to the Chesapeake colonies in the seventeenth century.[18]

Under the system of indentured servitude, a man or woman desiring to immigrate to the American colonies signed a contract, also known as an indenture, with an innkeeper or ship's captain in London, Bristol, or another British or Irish port. The contract obligated the signer to accept a period of service in the American colonies, commonly four or five years, in return for the Atlantic passage, food, clothing, and shelter during that period, and freedom dues (which varied from colony to colony) at the end of service.[19]

Re-Peopling of British America, 1600–1799," in Rudolph J. Vecoli and Suzanne M. Sinke, eds., A Century of European Migrations, 1830–1930 (Urbana: University of Illinois Press, 1991), pp. 58–77.

17. Virginia DeJohn Anderson, "Migrants and Motives: Religion and the Settlement of New England, 1630–1640," New England Quarterly 58 (1985): 339–83; David Cressy, Coming Over: Migration and Communication between England and New England in the Seventeenth Century (Cambridge: Cambridge University Press, 1987), pp. 63–73.

18. Richard S. Dunn, "Servants and Slaves: The Recruitment and Employment of Labor," in Jack P. Greene and J. R. Pole, eds., Colonial British America: Essays in the New History of the Early Modern Era (Baltimore: Johns Hopkins University Press, 1984), pp. 157–94; Wesley Frank Craven, White, Red, and Black: The Seventeenth-Century Virginian (Charlottesville: University Press of Virginia, 1971), chap. 1; Allan Kulikoff, Tobacco and Slaves: The Development of Southern Cultures in the Chesapeake, 1680–1800 (Chapel Hill: University of North Carolina Press, 1986), pp. 32, 39.

19. The most useful sources on indentured servitude are Abbot Emerson Smith, Colonists in Bondage: White Servitude and Convict Labor in America, 1607–1776 (Chapel Hill: University of North Carolina Press, 1947); Mildred Campbell, "Social Origins of Some Early Americans," in James Morton Smith, ed., Seventeenth-Century America: Essays in Colonial History (Chapel Hill: University of North Carolina Press, 1959), pp. 63–89; David Galenson, White Servitude in Colonial America: An Economic Analysis (New York: Cambridge University Press, 1981).

This practice was patterned after the English apprenticeship system, which customarily required a youngster to serve a master for a period of seven years in exchange for food, clothing, shelter, and training in the mysteries of a given trade. Migration abroad, while novel in terms of the distance involved, was simply an extension of internal migration from the countryside to cities, and between English cities, that had evolved in the sixteenth and seventeenth centuries. A young man or woman, faced with the prospect of extended unemployment, might well choose indentured service in Virginia or Pennsylvania.[20]

Before the last quarter of the seventeenth century, indentured servants provided Chesapeake planters with most of their agricultural labor force. After 1700, however, African slaves increasingly outnumbered English or Irish servants in the region's tobacco fields. Improved life expectancy made the purchase of slave labor more economical, and growing concerns about the place of former indentured servants in Chesapeake society gave planters second thoughts about their reliance on short-term servants.[21] Still, whether they came as servants in the seventeenth century or slaves in the eighteenth, immigrants to the Chesapeake colonies and the Carolinas were most commonly unfree when they landed in the New World.[22]

As slavery displaced indentured servitude in the tobacco colonies at the end of the seventeenth century, incoming servants were increasingly directed toward the middle colonies, with Philadelphia serving as the leading port of entry for Germans and Scotch-Irish in the eighteenth century. In this later period, the German servant trade gave rise to a significant innovation. Immigrants able to finance part of the cost of transportation were brought to the New World and given the opportunity to secure the final portion of their payment upon arrival. If unable to pay the entire cost of their (or their family's) transportation, they could redeem the unpaid portion by accepting a term of service proportional to the remaining debt. These individuals were known as redemptioners, and this practice was widespread among German immigrants to Philadelphia in the eighteenth century.[23]

20. This is precisely the framework in which Bernard Bailyn explores British immigration to the North American colonies; see *The Peopling of British North America: An Introduction* (New York: Alfred A. Knopf, 1986), pp. 20–25.

21. For the classic statement of growing concern about the place of indentured servants after the end of their terms of service, see Edmund Morgan, *American Slavery, American Freedom: The Ordeal of Colonial Virginia* (New York: W. W. Norton, 1975).

22. Kulikoff, *Tobacco and Slaves*, pp. 37–43, offers a useful discussion of the transition from reliance on indentured servants to reliance on slaves.

23. Marianne S. Wokeck, "The Experience of Indentured Servants from Germany and Ireland: Guaranteed Employment, Educational Opportunity, or Last Resort?" *The Report: A Journal of German-American History* 40 (1986): 61–63.

While evidence is sketchy, it appears that indentured servants and re-demptioners constituted a majority of Philadelphia immigrants before 1800. Demand remained evenly divided, with about half of the new-comers serving out their terms in Philadelphia city and county and half working as farm laborers in outlying districts. Servants, however, never accounted for as large a proportion of the population in the middle colonies as they had earlier in the Chesapeake. On the eve of the American Revolution, unfree servants made up only 5–6 percent of Philadelphia's population, compared with 40 percent in the Chesa-peake in the first half of the seventeenth century.[24]

As the thirteen colonies united, first under the Articles of Confed-eration and then under the Constitution, the federal government implemented new immigration policies.[25] Federal policy set no sig-nificant limitations on European immigration, but the formal closing of the African slave trade in 1808 did reduce one major source of new-comers. European immigration returned to prewar levels in the first three decades after independence, averaging about 7,500 annually.[26] As in the colonial period, immigrants from the British Isles and Ger-many continued to predominate. European events—wars, interrup-tions of international commerce, and the ups and downs of economic cycles—played a more significant role in the level of immigration than did American developments in this period.

The century beginning in 1820 marks the period of greatest migra-tion in world history. More than 33 million European immigrants came to the United States in these years, representing almost 60 per-cent of all immigration in the nation's history. Another 22 million Eu-ropeans migrated elsewhere in the world during the same period—to Australia, Canada, Argentina, Brazil, and South Africa, among other destinations.[27] About 2.4 million Chinese migrated to Southeast Asia, Hawaii, and the Western Hemisphere between 1840 and 1900, of whom 300,000 entered the United States.[28] Finally, more than 3 mil-lion Canadians immigrated to the United States between 1830 and

24. Farley Grubb, "Immigrant Servant Labor: The Occupational and Geographic Dis-tribution in the Late Eighteenth-Century Mid-Atlantic Economy," *Social Science History* 9 (1985): 249–75; Dunn, "Servants and Slaves," pp. 159–60.

25. William S. Bernard, "Immigration: History of U.S. Policy," in Thernstrom, ed., *Har-vard Encyclopedia*, p. 488.

26. Maldwyn Allen Jones, *American Immigration* (Chicago: University of Chicago Press, 1960), p. 65.

27. Daniels, *Coming to America*, p. 23; Leonard Dinnerstein and David M. Reimers, *Ethnic Americans: A History of Immigration*, 3d ed. (New York: Harper and Row, 1988), p. 16.

28. H. M. Lai, "Chinese," in Thernstrom, ed., *Harvard Encyclopedia*, p. 218.

1900.[29] The world saw migration on a scale not experienced before or since.

Economic, social, and political forces contributed to a geographical mobility unparalleled in any earlier period. Historians typically divide these forces into two groups. Those operating within sending countries, propelling migrants outward, as it were, are known as push factors. Developments within specific receiving nations attracting a portion of the immigrant stream are called pull factors. Both sets are crucial to understanding the shifting paths of migrant flows over time.

The push factors have a certain logical priority and have been well explored for the nineteenth-century flood of European emigrants. A population explosion rocked Europe in this century and disrupted the equilibrium between economic resources and population. Population growth began in northern and western Europe—in the British Isles, Germany, and Scandinavia—where migration peaked between 1850 and the 1880s. Beginning in 1880, the combined effect of economic development and declining birthrates in these nations led to declines in migrant outflow, and Italy, Austria-Hungary, and Russia became the new centers of European emigration.[30]

As in earlier periods, economic change and dislocation promoted considerable rural-urban and interurban migration within regions that sent large numbers of emigrants overseas. The mechanization of weaving and knitting in the north of England, for instance, left tens of thousands of handworkers unemployed and contributed to a dramatic increase in migration from the region. Enclosure and the mechanization of agriculture had similar devastating consequences on rural employment and fueled emigration as well.[31] Emigration represented the logical extension of national developments on an international scale. Rural residents first moved to burgeoning cities in search of employment, and when these opportunities proved inadequate, overseas prospects beckoned.[32]

Socioeconomic developments and natural disasters reinforced one another to promote migration at unprecedented levels. Ireland stands

29. Alan A. Brookes, "Canadians, British," in Thernstrom, ed., *Harvard Encyclopedia*, pp. 191–97; Jacques Rouillard, *Ah les États! Les travailleurs Canadiens-français dans l'industrie textile de la Nouvelle-Angleterre d'après le témoinage des derniers migrants* (Montreal: Boréal Express, 1985), pp. 11, 77.

30. A useful survey of these interrelated developments is offered by John Bodnar, *The Transplanted: A History of Immigrants in Urban America* (Bloomington: Indiana University Press, 1985), chap. 1.

31. Philip Taylor, *The Distant Magnet: European Emigration to the U.S.A.* (New York: Harper and Row, 1971), pp. 55–56.

32. Bodnar, *The Transplanted*, pp. 43–45.

out as the extreme case. An exploitative landlord-tenant system imposed by English rule and successive seasons of potato blight in the 1840s left the nation decimated. Emigration cost Ireland a fourth of its population between 1845 and 1855; starvation and disease took another eighth. On average, 210,000 Irish departed annually for England, Canada, or the United States during that decade.[33] German emigration was almost as great as Irish emigration in this period, but the German population base was far larger, and nothing like the wholesale starvation evident in Ireland was repeated in the German states.[34] Between them, the Germans and the Irish accounted for about 70 percent of the 4.3 million immigrants who came to the United States between 1840 and 1860. The rate of immigration at midcentury dwarfed that of earlier periods; it was almost thirty times greater than in the first decades after independence.[35]

Finally, the precarious position of religious and ethnic minorities made these groups much more likely than the dominant majorities to emigrate when economic difficulties surfaced. Poles in Prussia, Slavs in the Austro-Hungarian Empire, Jews in Russia, and religious dissenters from Norway and Sweden figured prominently in the heightened European emigration of the late nineteenth and early twentieth centuries.[36]

Push factors predisposed certain groups of Europeans to emigrate, but pull factors directed the flow toward the United States. Economic development and its accompanying demand for labor proved a powerful magnet for Europeans anxious about their futures. The prospects for work in urban construction, on canals and railroads, in textile mills, and as urban domestic servants drew the first Irish to these shores. With cities growing at a feverish pace and a revolution in transportation knitting the continent into a single national market, there was plenty of work for the newcomers. The wages of the first to arrive found their way back to families at home through remittances or prepaid tickets that fueled the continuing flow of immigrants. For Germans and Scandinavians, who came with greater resources, the

33. Kerby A. Miller, *Emigrants and Exiles: Ireland and the Irish Exodus in North America* (New York: Oxford University Press, 1985), pp. 286, 291.

34. Walter D. Kamphoefner, Wolfgang Helbich, and Ulrike Sommer, eds., *News from the Land of Freedom: German Immigrants Write Home* (Ithaca, N.Y.: Cornell University Press, 1991), pp. 1–11.

35. Dinnerstein and Reimers, *Ethnic Americans*, p. 16; Jones, *American Immigration*, p. 65.

36. Bodnar, *The Transplanted*, pp. 48–49; Taylor, *The Distant Magnet*, pp. 31, 57–58.

existence of uncultivated lands in the Midwest and West and public policies promoting settlement created opportunities for land ownership far beyond prospects in their native lands.[37]

The pull factors were equally significant for another group of immigrants in this period—Chinese immigrants to the West Coast. The Chinese ideogram for California, translated literally as "Golden Mountain," reflects the lure of gold that attracted Chinese across the Pacific. Although Chinese immigration constituted only about 3–4 percent of the overall flow in the decades between 1850 and 1882, this immigration was more significant than its 300,000 total might suggest. Concentrated in one geographical region, Chinese immigration played a crucial role in the economic development of California and the Far West. Chinese were essential to the emergence of mining, agriculture, and railroads, three sectors of increasing importance in the national economy in this period.[38] Moreover, the presence of the Chinese sparked a nativist movement on the West Coast and led to the eventual passage of the 1882 Chinese Exclusion Act, the first major piece of federal immigration-restriction legislation in the nation's history.[39] Chinese exclusion, limited initially to a ten-year period, was renewed in 1892, made permanent in 1902, and extended in 1924 to permit the exclusion of Asian immigrants generally under the provisions of the Johnson-Reid Act. Not until 1965 did Congress fully erase the racial criteria for the admission of immigrants that were introduced with the Chinese Exclusion Act.[40]

Congress could deny admission to certain groups, such as the Chinese, by legislative fiat, but it could not control the ethnic makeup of most of those seeking entrance into the United States. Between 1882 and 1907 there was a pronounced shift in the national origins of European immigrants. At the beginning of this period, Britons, Germans, and Scandinavians still composed almost two-thirds of the entering immigrants. By 1907, Austro-Hungarians, Italians, and Russian

37. Advertising efforts of private transportation companies and various state and local governments provided another important pull factor. See Taylor, *The Distant Magnet*, pp. 70–84.

38. Roger Daniels, *Asian America: Chinese and Japanese in the United States since 1850* (Seattle: University of Washington Press, 1988), esp. chaps. 1–2.

39. The fullest treatment of the anti-Chinese movement is found in Alexander Saxton, *The Indispensable Enemy: Labor and the Anti-Chinese Movement in California* (Berkeley: University of California Press, 1971).

40. Bernard, "Immigration," pp. 490–95; Sucheng Chan, ed., *Entry Denied: Exclusion and the Chinese Community in America, 1882–1943* (Philadelphia: Temple University Press, 1991).

Jews predominated, accounting for 69 percent of immigrants recorded at ports of entry.[41]

The same sort of developments operating in northern and western Europe a generation or two earlier stimulated migration from eastern and southern Europe at the turn of the century. Rapid population growth, increasing fragmentation of landholdings, the impact of capitalist economic development on traditional occupations, discrimination against religious and ethnic minorities, and the movement of population to cities from the countryside characterized regions from which large numbers of these new immigrants came.

The experiences of southern and eastern European immigrants in the United States, however, contrasted sharply with those of their predecessors. Improvements in ocean-going transport reduced the time, cost, and risk of migration and encouraged far more return migration than had been common earlier.[42] Urbanization and industrialization had transformed the American social and economic landscape since mid-century, and immigrants in the early twentieth century were directed much more exclusively to American cities than had been the case previously. Moreover, since very few came from England, Ireland, or Scotland, language and cultural barriers were greater. Finally, entering into more crowded cities with declining opportunities, new immigrants faced harsher nativist hostility to their presence than had been common for Irish, German, and British immigrants.

This hostility bore fruit in a movement to restrict and reshape immigration. In 1917 Congress passed (over President Woodrow Wilson's veto) a literacy requirement that excluded those who were not literate in their native languages. In 1919 massive raids organized by Attorney General A. Mitchell Palmer led to deportations of resident aliens active in radical political organizations. Then, in 1921 and 1924, Congress passed successive immigration restriction laws. Ultimately, they set a quota for legal immigration at a level of 150,000 annually, a figure about one-seventh of the average annual number of entrants in the decade before the outbreak of World War I. Equally important, the 1924 act established a framework of national origins quotas that made it relatively easy for northern and western Europeans to be admitted but far more difficult for individuals from countries

41. Taylor, *The Distant Magnet*, p. 63. Polish and other eastern Europeans were prominent in this migration, but the political division of Europe in the pre–World War I era meant that they were typically recorded at ports of entry or in censuses according to the nationality of their rulers, be they German, Russian, or Austro-Hungarian.

42. Bodnar, *The Transplanted*, pp. 53–54; Vecoli and Sinke, eds., *Century of European Migrations*, part 4.

in southern and eastern Europe. Moreover, Asian immigrants were excluded entirely by the legislation that extended the ban on Chinese immigrants to other nations in the region. Only Filipinos, because of their territorial status, were permitted entry, although after 1934 this loophole disappeared with the setting of a token annual quota of fifty immigrants from the Philippines.[43]

Just as pressures grew to restrict and reshape European and Asian immigration, new sources for immigrants developed in the Western Hemisphere. Mexican immigration to the American Southwest emerged after 1910 in a setting very different from the settings of European or Asian immigrants on either the East or West Coast. Prior to 1850, of course, what became the Southwest consisted of the northern provinces of Mexico. Spanish settlement there began in the late sixteenth century, and a hybrid caste society drew on both Indian and Spanish cultural sources. In a reversal of the common immigrant experience, it was the old-stock Hispanic residents of the region who had to acculturate and the Anglo newcomers who shaped the newly emerging dominant culture.[44]

By the turn of the nineteenth century this process of cultural reshaping had been largely completed as far as the dominant social institutions in the region were concerned. Still, a substantial and long-standing Hispanic cultural tradition persisted among native-born Californians, Texans, and New Mexicans, and when Mexican immigration accelerated in 1910, that culture shaped the immigrant experience in unique ways. The pressure to conform to Anglo culture was certainly strong, but the existence of an established Hispanic community permitted the newcomers to accommodate to a rather different set of cultural standards as well. As Mario T. Garcia expressed this contradiction, "Mexican Americans are both an old and a new ethnic group."[45]

The upsurge in Mexican immigration developed just as the United States was entering a period of renewed nativism. Restrictive legislation and the impact of the Great Depression and World War II combined to curtail immigration drastically in the years between 1930

43. Daniels, *Coming to America*, pp. 278–84; Bernard, "Immigration," esp. table 1, p. 493; Higham, *Send These to Me*, pp. 52–56.

44. Leonard Pitt, *The Decline of the Californios: A Social History of the Spanish-speaking Californians, 1846–1890* (Berkeley: University of California Press, 1966); Sarah Deutsch, *No Separate Refuge: Culture, Class, and Gender on an Anglo-Hispanic Frontier in the American Southwest* (New York: Oxford University Press, 1987).

45. Mario T. Garcia, *Mexican Americans: Leadership, Ideology, and Identity, 1930–1960* (New Haven, Conn.: Yale University Press, 1989), p. 1.

and 1950. Immigration in these decades was lower than it had been since 1840. Immigration from within the Western Hemisphere—unrestricted by the 1924 Johnson-Reid Act—came to predominate over European immigration. Mexican immigration was a significant component of this new flow, as was a renewed stream of Canadian immigrants in the 1920s.[46]

Even with declining immigration, racial antagonisms fueled nativist attacks on specific ethnic groups. Once again California led the way with a series of laws restricting Asian immigrants from owning land or leasing farms. Growing labor organization and strike activity among Mexican farmworkers and growing unemployment in urban centers contributed to a significant rise in deportations during the Great Depression, which reversed the flow of Mexican immigrants. Finally, in the aftermath of Pearl Harbor, the federal government, under considerable pressure from West Coast elected officials, established internment camps for more than 100,000 Japanese and Japanese Americans residing in Arizona, California, Oregon, and Washington. The racial criteria already inscribed in American immigration policy since 1924 were all too evident in the blanket policy of internment implemented by the War Department in the spring of 1942.[47]

After World War II the restrictionist impulse receded, though the federal government moved only grudgingly against the discriminatory system established in the 1920s. A number of factors contributed to this process. First, Hitler and Germany's wartime atrocities gave racism a bad name. Furthermore, the continued existence of a national origins quota system hampered U.S. government efforts to exercise leadership in the Third World. The first cracks appeared in 1952, when Congress passed the McCarran-Walter Act, which allowed Asian immigrants to become naturalized citizens and provided token quotas that admitted 2,000 Asian-Pacific immigrants annually.

Still, racial and ethnic barriers to immigration remained strong as the McCarran-Walter Act continued to enforce unequal national quo-

46. As Mexican numbers increased, administrative efforts proceeded to stem the immigrant flow that was otherwise not restricted by the 1921 and 1924 federal legislation. Higham, *Send These to Me*, pp. 56–57.

47. H. Brett Melendy, "California's Discrimination against Filipinos, 1927–1935," in Roger Daniels and Spencer C. Olin, Jr., eds., *Racism in California: A Reader in the History of Oppression* (New York: Macmillan, 1972), pp. 141–51; Cletus E. Daniel, *Bitter Harvest: A History of California Farmworkers, 1870–1941* (Berkeley: University of California Press, 1981), chap. 4; Abraham Hoffman, "Stimulus to Repatriation: The 1931 Federal Deportation Drive and the Los Angeles Mexican Community," in Norris Hundley, ed., *The Chicano* (Santa Barbara, Calif.: Clio Books, 1975), pp. 109–23; Roger Daniels, *Concentration Camps USA: Japanese Americans and World War II* (Hinsdale, Ill.: Dryden Press, 1971).

tas based on 1924 legislation. The major opening for increased immigration in the postwar period came from the admission of refugees and displaced persons from war-torn Europe. The emergence of a national refugee policy institutionalized the notion of the United States as a haven from overseas oppression.[48] Over time cold war foreign policy considerations came to dominate American refugee policy as Congress permitted substantial numbers of immigrants from Hungary after 1956 and Cuba after 1960 as non-quota refugees from Communism. Discriminatory differences among national quotas were finally abolished in 1965, after which a 20,000 limit was set for quota immigration from any single country. Overall immigration inched up only slowly after 1965, as reform legislation set hemispheric immigration ceilings of 170,000 for Europe, Asia, and Africa, and 120,000 for the Western Hemisphere.[49]

Nonetheless, 1965 marked a turning point in the history of American immigration policy and a repudiation of the restrictive and discriminatory practices of four decades. With the disappearance of national quotas favoring immigration from northwestern Europe, there was a dramatic shift in the composition of immigrants to the United States. Latin Americans and Asians came to dominate the new mix. Moreover, provision for the admission of non-quota immigrants and periodic revisions upward of quota limits have resulted in steadily increasing numbers of immigrants. From an average of 330,000 annually in the 1960s, the numbers grew to almost 450,000 each year in the 1970s and to 600,000 annually in the 1980s. The "Golden Door," while not entirely open, is clearly much wider today than any time since the passage of restrictive legislation in the years between 1917 and 1924.[50]

Who are these newest immigrants to this country? According to statistics from the U.S. Immigration and Naturalization Service, Asians and Latin Americans constitute almost 45 and 40 percent, respectively, of legal immigrants and refugees who entered the United States in 1986. Leading national groups in the current migration

48. Jacques Vernant, *The Refugee in the Post-war World* (New Haven, Conn.: Yale University Press, 1953), pp. 473–541. For recent analysis of contemporary refugee issues, see "Refugees and the Asylum Dilemma in the West," a special issue of *Journal of Policy History* 4, no. 1 (1992). My thanks to John Higham for reminding me of the importance of these policy developments in the postwar period.

49. David M. Reimers, *Still the Golden Door: The Third World Comes to America* (New York: Columbia University Press, 1985), pp. 20–22, 81–82.

50. Dinnerstein and Reimers, *Ethnic Americans*, p. 210; Daniels, *Coming to America*, p. 404.

flow include Filipinos, Koreans, Vietnamese, Mexicans, Cubans, and Dominicans.[51]

Individual motivations for Asian and Latin American immigrants today are similar to those of European immigrants a century ago, but the economic and political world in which this migration occurs has changed dramatically. Economic opportunity, for the migrants themselves and for their children, undoubtedly looms large in the minds of immigrants today. While we may use historical hindsight and view the succeeding waves of European immigration between 1820 and 1920 as temporary responses to economic and social dislocations resulting from the first stage of capitalist industrialization, it is more difficult to explain contemporary immigration in entirely parallel terms. In part this difficulty is inherent in any attempt to offer historical explanations of contemporary events. We cannot see into the future, and we have difficulty achieving sufficient distance to analyze current developments. Still, most Third World countries that are the sources for contemporary immigrants to the United States are not experiencing significant economic development.[52] Immigration today results from the tremendous difference in standards of living between the United States and poorer nations linked to the United States economically or politically. The continuing lack of economic development in the Third World in recent decades suggests that today's high levels of immigration are unlikely to be reduced in the near future.[53] Currently, both the supply of immigrants and the demand for their services in the U.S. economy are high; one wonders, however, how long these two conditions will hold and how long today's relatively open-door policy will persist.

Recent legislative developments underscore this uncertainty. The passage of the Simpson-Mazzoli bill in 1986 confirmed the federal government's simultaneous commitment to increased immigration, on the one hand, and to increasingly strict enforcement of the nation's immigration laws, on the other. Increasing numbers of illegal immigrants reside in the United States, without the protections of mini-

51. Leonard Dinnerstein, Roger L. Nichols, and David M. Reimers, *Natives and Strangers: Blacks, Indians, and Immigrants in America*, 2d ed. (New York: Oxford University Press, 1990), pp. 268–69; Portes and Rumbaut, *Immigrant America*, chap. 1.

52. Korea stands out as an exception to this generalization. Among the other leading sending nations, however, continuing lack of economic development is the norm. These nations include Mexico, the Philippines, Cuba, India, China, the Dominican Republic, and Vietnam. For the relative shares of immigrants from each of these nations, see Portes and Rumbaut, *Immigrant America*, p. 40.

53. Portes and Rumbaut, *Immigrant America*, chap. 1.

mum wages, social security, unemployment insurance, or other benefits that U.S. citizens and legal resident aliens enjoy. How the nation will respond to continuing worldwide immigrant flows from Latin America, Asia, Eastern Europe, and Russia that far exceed limits set by the United States and European receiving nations remains to be seen. Whether the United States will continue to open its doors to the "tempest-tost" of succeeding generations or instead will retreat within the walls of a fortress America will have a profound effect on both this country and the rest of the world.

The recent resurgence of immigration and the growing concern about federal immigration policy have revived interest in the history of immigrants to the United States. Archival collections have expanded; new scholarly journals have appeared.[54] Historians have shifted from an earlier focus on immigration policies and attitudes of the dominant majority to an examination of the experiences and attitudes of immigrants themselves. Particularly revealing are the insights that have emerged from studying the experiences of specific groups of immigrants both in their countries of origin and in the United States. A new generation of ethnic historians, equipped with the requisite language and quantitative skills, has explored the cultural as well as structural dimensions of the immigrant experience.[55]

The recent emphasis on the lived experiences of immigrants in the United States has fostered a new interest in the writings of immigrants themselves.[56] First-person accounts, whether diaries, letters, or reminiscences, remain the historian's chief source of evidence on the cultural values, beliefs, and attitudes of immigrants. While analyses of marriage and birth registers, port lists, ships' manifests, and federal manuscript censuses of populations have permitted historians to ex-

54. In particular, the Immigration History Research Center at the University of Minnesota and the Balch Institute in Philadelphia have emerged as national institutions promoting the growing interest in immigration and ethnic history. The *Journal of American Ethnic History*, first published in 1981, reflects the expanding scholarly interest in the field.

55. Two pioneering works focusing on the attitudes of the dominant majority that are still worth examining are Ray Allen Billington, *The Protestant Crusade, 1800–1860: A Study of the Origins of American Nativism* (New York: Macmillan, 1938); and John Higham, *Strangers in the Land: Patterns of American Nativism, 1860–1925* (New Brunswick, N.J.: Rutgers University Press, 1955). Examples of work in the new mold include Josef J. Barton, *Peasants and Strangers: Italians, Rumanians, and Slovaks in an American City, 1890–1950* (Cambridge, Mass.: Harvard University Press, 1975); Dino Cinel, *From Italy to San Francisco: The Immigrant Experience* (Stanford, Calif.: Stanford University Press, 1982); Walter D. Kamphoefner, *The Westfalians: From Germany to Missouri* (Princeton: N.J.: Princeton University Press, 1987); and Miller, *Emigrants and Exiles*. For an excellent summary of recent trends in immigration history, see Vecoli and Sinke, eds., *Century of European Migrations*.

56. See the bibliography of first-person immigrant accounts at the end of this volume.

plore structural dimensions of the immigrant experience, these quantitative sources offer only oblique views of the collective consciousness of immigrants. Historians still read individual first-person accounts and painstakingly attempt to synthesize varied materials and perspectives into an understanding of the larger social group. Questions of representativeness and bias always loom large in the evaluation of such sources, but they remain a rich source for understanding the attitudes and experiences of immigrants.

FIRST-PERSON ACCOUNTS

A variety of factors has influenced the selection of first-person accounts for this volume. The number of immigrants from different backgrounds, their levels of literacy, the passage of time, and the work of historians have affected the number of surviving accounts for different ethnic groups. The largest array of such sources survives for European immigrants in the period 1880–1920. There are far fewer first-person accounts for the seventeenth and eighteenth centuries because few immigrants in that period had literacy skills and so much time passed before historians began looking for and preserving such sources. Among Asian Americans, the paucity of such sources reflects the relatively smaller number of immigrants, their educational limitations, and, until recently, the lack of interest and language skills among historians.

Two of the selections excerpted here were written by children of immigrants, and a few comments about their relevance may be useful. Given the large number of immigrants of different backgrounds, the incompleteness of their assimilation within a uniform culture, and continuing immigration, the distinctiveness of immigrants to the United States did not disappear with the arrival of an American-born generation. Differences in language and religion commonly persisted beyond the immigrant generation. Racial differences continued to distinguish many of the children of immigrants from the dominant white majority. Moreover, the second generation was typically more numerous than the first and over time came to dominate ethnic communities. An appreciation of the influence of immigrants in American life and of conflicts within ethnic groups is therefore possible only when we take into account the experiences of the children of immigrants. These concerns have led me to include narratives written by both immigrants and their children.[57]

57. For useful discussions of these issues, see William Petersen, Michael Novak, and Philip Gleason, *Concepts of Ethnicity* (Cambridge, Mass.: Harvard University Press, 1982).

In addition, I have made a conscious effort to include the writings of immigrant men *and* women in this collection. Six of the ten accounts are written entirely (or primarily) by men; four are written by women. Until the 1980s it was relatively common to analyze the male immigrant experience only and to treat that experience as if it stood for the immigrant experience more broadly. Historians now understand that immigrant men and women had distinctly different experiences. Far more men than women, for instance, immigrated alone and earned money for a period of time before sending for their families or returning to their homelands to marry. Women were more likely to immigrate with family or join family in the United States and thus to experience this country first within a family context. Cultural continuities between the Old World and the New World are much more evident when we take into account the experiences of women as well as men.

Despite the unrepresentativeness of surviving first-person accounts, I have attempted to select examples that reflect the diversity of American immigrants and changes in their experiences over time. Where there is a relative abundance of surviving material for a particular time period or ethnic group, I have chosen a specific document to represent that period and group.[58] I also have selected sources that offer insights into the everyday lives of immigrants and the relations between particular immigrant groups and the larger society. Finally, I have tried to find strong voices that speak to central issues of the immigrant experience and reach beyond a particular ethnic group or moment in time. There is much we can learn from these varied accounts of diverse immigrants and ethnic Americans, whose combined aspirations and experiences have shaped the contours of this nation's history.[59]

58. On final review, I sense the particular selections may underplay the experience of the male immigrant who set out alone to earn enough money to return home and improve his position or to bring other family members over later. For the period 1880–1920, when this practice was quite common, I have chosen selections by two women, Rose Gollup and Rosa Cassettari, who joined a father and a husband, respectively. We only know about the experiences of the earlier male migrants in these families through female eyes. Still, in the selections as a whole, male voices are evident, and it is possible to consider how male and female experiences and attitudes differed.

59. Primary historical sources are, of course, not the only kind of sources that speak to ethnic cultural issues. Fiction is another source that is increasingly being used to address questions similar to those posed in this volume. For useful guides to ethnic literatures of interest, see Wesley Brown and Amy Ling, eds., *Imagining America: Stories from the Promised Land* (New York: Persea Books, 1991); Joyce Antler, ed., *America and I: Short Stories by American Jewish Women Writers* (Boston: Beacon Press, 1990); and Jeffrey Paul Chan, Frank Chin, Lawson Fusao Inada, and Shawn Wong, eds., *The Big Aiiieeeee!: An Anthology of Chinese American and Japanese American Literature* (Seattle: University of Washington Press, 1992).

From the letters, diaries, and reminiscences of a limited number of individuals we can discern larger group patterns. As immigration historian Rudolph Vecoli noted in his introduction to one of the life stories excerpted here, "*Rosa* stands as a personal document against which we can test certain ideas regarding the immigrant experience. While quantitative analysis may provide answers to certain questions, there are qualitative inquiries which numbers cannot satisfy. Subjective states of mind cannot be inferred with confidence from such 'objective data.' "[60]

From first-person sources, for instance, we gain a sense of the range of factors that motivated immigrants to give up the familiar and venture to a new land. John Harrower, whose diary leads off this collection, left his wife and children in the Shetland Islands, north of Scotland, because of economic difficulties in December 1773. Despite three months of searching, Harrower found no work in Scotland or London and no ships heading to Holland. Reduced to his last shilling, he signed up as an indentured servant bound for Virginia. An economic depression disrupted the regular flow of Harrower's life and led him to the dramatic step he finally took.

Economic dislocation continued to fuel immigration. Fifty years after Harrower left his home, members of the Hollingworth family in the Huddersfield district in the north of England reacted similarly to a depression that hit the woolen industry in the mid-1820s. Two sons, Jabez and Joseph, emigrated first in December 1826, and they were joined a year later by the rest of their family. The Hollingworths settled in central Massachusetts and continued for at least a decade to work in the rural woolen factories of that region. Surviving letters that they wrote to kin in England and elsewhere in the United States offer us glimpses of their accommodation to a new life in this country.

War and revolution have also commonly set off large-scale immigration. Among the immigrants featured in the excerpts that follow, the families of Ernesto Galarza, Mary Paik, and Trong Nguyen found their lives transformed by such conflicts. The Mexican Revolution upset that nation's countryside after 1910 and loosened the bonds that tied families to their native homes; hundreds of thousands of immigrants (many like the Galarzas) headed from the countryside to the city, then northward, and finally to the United States to start new lives beyond the reach of Mexico's contending armies. So, too, the Japanese occupation of Korea in 1905 uprooted Mary Paik's family and led to a

---

60. Marie Hall Ets, *Rosa: The Life of an Italian Immigrant* (Minneapolis: University of Minnesota Press, 1970), p. x.

Routes of European American Writers

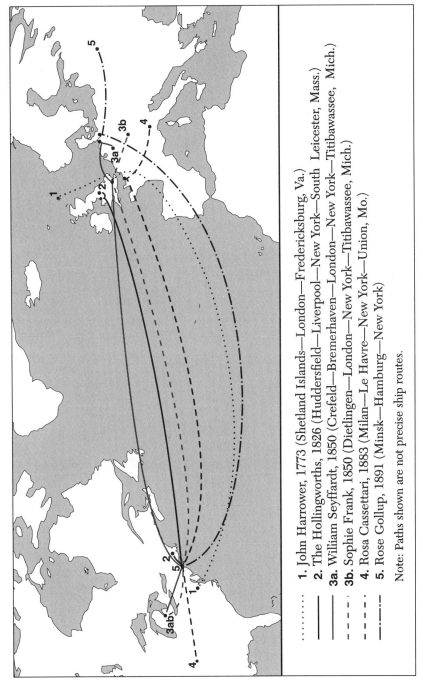

1. John Harrower, 1773 (Shetland Islands—London—Fredericksburg, Va.)

2. The Hollingworths, 1826 (Huddersfield—Liverpool—New York—South Leicester, Mass.)

3a. William Seyffardt, 1850 (Crefeld—Bremerhaven—London—New York—Titibawassee, Mich.)

3b. Sophie Frank, 1850 (Dietlingen—London—New York—Titibawassee, Mich.)

4. Rosa Cassettari, 1883 (Milan—Le Havre—New York—Union, Mo.)

5. Rose Gollup, 1891 (Minsk—Hamburg—New York)

Note: Paths shown are not precise ship routes.

journey to Hawaii and then California, a story told in her autobiography, *Quiet Odyssey,* excerpted here. Finally, the French and American wars in Indochina disrupted the fabric of society in Vietnam, Laos, and Cambodia and resulted in the massive refugee flows evident since 1975. The experience of the Nguyen family in Vietnam and Chicago is simply one story among the hundreds of thousands that might be told about this most recent immigrant wave.

Just as these stories reveal common motivations and predisposing events that promoted immigration to the United States, so too they reflect common aspects of immigrants' experiences in this country. Cultural differences, poverty, the discriminatory attitudes of older-stock Americans, and immigrants' needs for mutual social and economic support led immigrants to cluster together and rely on one another during their first years in the United States. Evidence of such patterns abounds in the letters and reminiscences reprinted here. German immigrants in Michigan clustered together to such an extent that two years after immigrating Sophie Frank Seyffardt still had not learned much English. Koreans in southern California fifty years later lived near one another and attended religious services together. Sometimes they had no choice since many white Californians refused to welcome them into their neighborhoods or churches. Ernesto Galarza also found that in Sacramento differences between the "lower part of town" and the "upper part" had nothing to do with topography. When Kazuko Itoi's mother tried to rent a beachfront apartment in Seattle one summer to aid the convalescence of a daughter suffering from tuberculosis, she found the neighborhood closed to Asian families. Finally, ethnic enclaves often served to ease the adjustment process for immigrants, as is evident in the experience of the Nguyen family in Chicago's "Little Saigon" in the past decade. Whether from choice or in self-defense, immigrants typically learned to rely on one another as they began to make their way in their adopted land.

First-person accounts, while often chronicling the long-term success of immigrants in adjusting to life in the United States, also reveal their conflict with native-born Americans. There is little overt ethnic conflict evident in the earlier accounts reprinted here—those of John Harrower, the Hollingworths, and the Seyffardts—which represent the experiences of Britons and Germans who arrived in a period in which immigrants from northwestern Europe predominated. Yet as the ethnic diversity of immigrants increased after 1880, so too did ethnic conflict. Rose Gollup Cohen described in graphic terms the election-night attacks on Russian Jews that were commonplace in New York City in the 1890s. When Mary Paik and her family landed in San

Birthplaces and Routes of Asian American and Hispanic American Writers

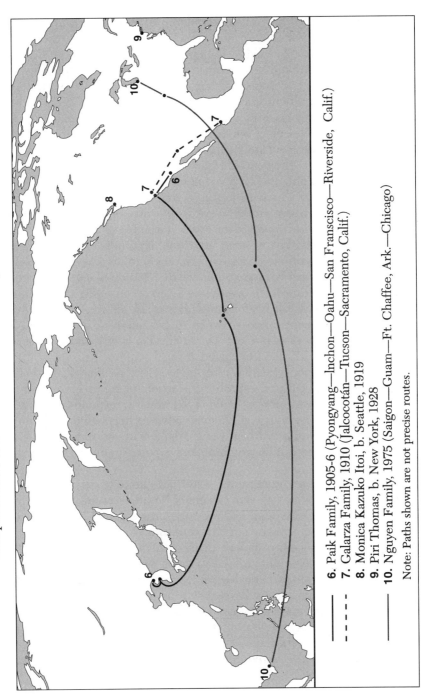

6. Paik Family, 1905-6 (Pyongyang—Inchon—Oahu—San Franscisco—Riverside, Calif.)

7. Galarza Family, 1910 (Jalcocotán—Tucson—Sacramento, Calif.)

8. Monica Kazuko Itoi, b. Seattle, 1919

9. Piri Thomas, b. New York, 1928

10. Nguyen Family, 1975 (Saigon—Guam—Ft. Chaffee, Ark.—Chicago)

Note: Paths shown are not precise routes.

Francisco in 1906, they encountered the fury of an organized anti-Asian movement, including considerable harassment by the white schoolchildren in Riverside, California. So, too, Ernesto Galarza faced the repeated taunts of classmates in Sacramento schools, despite the evident efforts of some teachers to mold their diverse students into a tolerant, multicultural body. Piri Thomas, son of Puerto Ricans growing up in East Harlem in the 1940s, suffered repeated attacks by an Italian-American gang when his family moved onto an "Italian" block. Finally, the Itoi family experienced racial discrimination at two crucial moments in the years chronicled in *Nisei Daughter:* first, when the family could not rent an apartment along the beach because the neighborhood was closed to Japanese Americans; and second, when all Japanese Americans on the West Coast were required to report for evacuation and internment after Pearl Harbor.

Not all the conflict evident in these accounts arose from the immigrant-native divide. Within immigrant families different attitudes and expectations across generations were a source of significant conflict. Joseph Hollingworth wrote one letter to an uncle complaining that his father took all his earnings. He asked his uncle to find him work in Poughkeepsie and to write to his father so that he might "break the bands of opression" by leaving his family and joining his uncle. Similarly, Kazuko Itoi chafed at the discipline instilled in a Japanese cultural school weekday afternoons. Her parents felt their children needed the cultural exposure the school offered; their daughter was too much the American "child of Skidrow" to respond favorably to this kind of socialization. Piri Thomas's adolescent rebellion led him to leave his family in suburban Long Island and move back to East Harlem, where he felt he would be less exposed to the racial barbs of white society.

Conflict among immigrants was not limited to that cross-generational conflict. The experiences of Rosa Cassettari are revealing in this regard. On arriving in New York City, she and her fellow immigrants were set upon by a fellow countryman, who put them up in his hotel for three days before placing them on the train for Missouri—a train they might have taken the first day they were in the city had their countryman been less concerned about the profits he derived from their prolonged hotel stay. Finally, Rosa's life in a Missouri mining camp was marked by continuous conflict with an abusive husband that eventually led her to take her children and run away to Chicago. Old World expectations of women were commonly eroded by experiences in the United States, and conflict among immigrants across gender lines was frequently the result.

In addition, first-person narratives often reveal conflicts within immigrants themselves. The longer John Harrower lived in Virginia the more he identified as an American, but his separation from his wife and children in the Shetland Islands made it impossible for him to make a complete transition. The Hollingworths wrote disparagingly about the English factory system, but they vacillated between idealistic visions of life as rural cultivators and the very real prospects that woolen factories offered in New England. Rosa Cassettari was caught between devotion to the Italian ideals she learned as a child and newer values that emerged out of her experience in the United States. It was not easy for her to leave her husband, and for a considerable period she accepted the Catholic church's condemnation of her divorce. Only gradually did Rosa accept the life she had made for herself in Chicago and move beyond an acceptance of her subordination to a violent and unloving husband. Finally, Piri Thomas struggled to accept his dark complexion that proved such a barrier to acceptance in the wider American society.

The themes of ethnic conflict and immigration assimilation that emerge repeatedly in these first-person accounts remain as vital in the United States today as they were for Benjamin Franklin and John Harrower in colonial America. For a period of four decades—between 1924 and 1965—the nation lost confidence in its ability to cope with an influx of newcomers and turned its back on its immigrant past. In the last quarter century, however, older values and a renewed self-confidence have reasserted themselves. Since the abolition of national quotas in 1965, the annual flow of immigrants has shot up, and the range of ethnic and racial groups represented has broadened. The United States once again plays a leading role in worldwide immigration. Yet the acceptance of ethnic diversity is not complete. Political and racial considerations still warp our refugee policies, as evident in the experience of Central American and Haitian immigrants. Moreover, opposition to the growing number of Asian Americans suggests that nativism has a continuing place in American life. Finally, the conflict over multiculturalism in higher education in the United States today reflects a European-centered view of American culture.[61]

61. "Suit Attacks Policy of Keeping Aliens in Texas," *New York Times*, Jan. 7, 1989; "For Haitians, a Risky Voyage to the Land of Inequity," *New York Times*, July 16, 1991; "Refugees Match Wits with Uncle Sam," *New York Times*, Dec. 8, 1991; "Violent Incidents against Asian Americans Seen as Part of Racist Pattern," *New York Times*, Aug. 31, 1985; "Harvard Cleared in Inquiry on Bias," *New York Times*, Oct. 7, 1990. For contrasting perspectives on multiculturalism in higher education, see Henry Louis Gates, Jr., "Whose Culture Is It, Anyway," *New York Times*, May 4, 1991; and Donald Kagan, "Western Values Are Central," *New York Times*, May 4, 1991.

There is no denying the multiracial and multicultural character of American society today. Nor can one deny the conflict and suffering that the building of such a culture has entailed. Such diversity involves risks; it may, for instance, promote ethnic nationalisms of the sort that threaten to tear apart Eastern Europe. Yet the ethnic diversity of the United States also presents this nation with rich possibilities. In accepting immigration as a fundamental and enduring aspect of American life, we at once acknowledge and accept the altered character of national life that such immigration has wrought and the prospect of continuing change that renewed immigration entails. To accept the contributions of generations of immigrants in the making of this nation is to accept the ongoing process of cultural change that is our nation's future.

ONE

The John Harrower Diary, 1773–1776

The diary of John Harrower offers a remarkable early account of an immigrant to the British North American colonies. Like the majority of British immigrants to the American colonies, Harrower had to sign away his freedom to finance his ocean crossing.

Poverty and desperation led him to leave his native Shetland Islands in December 1773. The first third of the diary traces his southward wanderings. He traveled first to Scotland, seeking work or, failing that, passage to Holland. Since no ships were departing for Holland, he took coastal vessels to Newcastle and then Portsmouth. He walked the final eighty miles to London, where he desperately sought employment. Finally, down to his last shilling, Harrower signed up as a servant on a vessel bound for America. Only in this roundabout way did this Shetland Islander down on his luck find himself enroute to Virginia.

Like many immigrants who have left accounts, Harrower was far from a typical indentured servant. His literacy set him apart from his comrades, and even before the ship, the *Planter,* had left the Thames, its master had sought Harrower's aid against disgruntled servants.[1] During the trip, he helped the master in numerous ways, caring for the sick and keeping up the ship's journals. Just before the vessel landed, Harrower copied the names and occupations of all servants.

Once settled in Virginia, Harrower enjoyed a variety of privileges that distinguished him from fellow servants. First of all, he worked only occasionally in the fields. Hired by William Daingerfield as a

---

1. An analysis of the register of the *Planter* revealed seventy-one male indentured servants aboard the ship, forty-two from London and vicinity and the others from more distant locales. See Bernard Bailyn, *Voyagers to the West: A Passage in the Peopling of America on the Eve of the Revolution* (New York: Alfred A. Knopf, 1986), p. 277.

tutor for his children, he was treated more as a member of the family than as a servant. Moreover, he was encouraged to teach other children in the area and was permitted to negotiate payment from their families. These earnings and the gifts he received from the parents of his pupils set him apart from the typical indentured servant in tidewater Virginia.

Despite these differences, we can see elements of the archetypical immigrant experience in Harrower's diary. Aboard the *Planter* and in Virginia he sought out fellow Scotsmen and information about events back home. He complained in one letter of the difficulty he had in speaking "high English." As a Shetlander, he was something of an outsider in Virginia society, despite the good treatment accorded him because of his education and skills.

Over the course of the diary, we see the process of assimilation at work in Harrower's life. Harrower's attitudes toward the colonial struggle for independence, for instance, shifted over time. By the end of his diary, it is clear that he intended to bring his family over and to see his wife an "American" like himself. His diary offers a view of the Americanization process that is repeated in later immigrant accounts.

Munday, 6th Decr 1773. This morning I left my house[2] and family at 4 OClock in order to travel in search of business and imediatly went on board a sloop ready to saile for Leith, Oconachie M^r[3] and at 5 OClock he sailed Accordingly with the wind at N.   At this time I am Master of no more Cash but 8½d and stockins[4] &c. to the amount of £3 st^r[5] or thereabout, a small value indeed to traviel with.[6]

Munday, 27th.   Wind at S. E. with heavy rain. Both the Smacks[7] in the River yet. This evening it being St John's night the Free Masons made a very grand procession through the high street. . . .

2. At Lerwick, in the Shetland Islands, north of Scotland.

3. M^r: abbreviation for master (as in a ship's captain). A man name Oconachie was the master of the vessel Harrower took to Scotland. Leith is a Scottish port adjacent to Edinburgh; see the map, "John Harrower's Journey from the Shetland Islands, 1773."

4. D: abbreviation for pence (as in sixpence). Shetland stockings were famous and already an important article of export. Harrower brought along stockings to sell as he traveled.

5. Pounds sterling as distinguished from pounds Scots, the common currency in Shetland.

6. Finding a fisherman willing to take him ashore at Montrose, Harrower then walked to Dundee, where he remained from December 13 to December 29. Failing to find passage to Holland, he agreed to take a vessel to Newcastle.

7. Smacks: small sailing vessels.

John Harrower's journey from the Shetland Islands, 1773. (Courtesy of the Colonial Williamsburg Foundation)

Tuesday, 28th. Wind at E. fine weather. this day I once thought of engaging with the M.ʳ of the Elizabeth Brigantine bound for North Carolina but the thoughts of being so far from my family prevented me. at noon the wind came all round to the N. V.[8] and then Mr. began to make ready as fast as possible for sailing.

Wednesday, 29th. At 2 AM left my Loging having been here 16 days and my method of living was as follows Vizt[9] for Breackfast ½d. worth of bread ½d. worth of Cheese and a bottle of ale at 1d. For dinner ½d. worth of bread, ½d. worth of Broath, 1d. worth of Meat and a bottle of ale at 1d. and the same for supper as for breackfast, and 1d. a night for my bedd. On leaving my logings at the time above mentioned I went onb.ᵈ[10] the sloop Williams, Wm. Bell M.ʳ, for Newcastle,[11] and he imediatly hauled out of the harbour and made saile with the Wind at N. N. V. At 9 pm was obliged to ly too for the tide on Tynemouth bar. at midnight bore away for the Bar and got weel over it.

Thursday, 30th. At 1 AM we passed by shiels[12] and went up the River Tyne, and at 2 AM made fast to Newcastle Key, we having been no more than 24 hours from Dundee here 3 of which we lay too. At 9 AM I went ashore to Newcastle in Comp.ʸ with M.ʳ Bell and 5 others who were passangers along with me, and after drinking a English poynt[13] of ale a piece I enquired at the Pilots and others if there was any Vessel presently at Newcastle bound for Holland but found there was none. At same time was informed that Sunderland was a more proper place to look out for a ship bound there. . . .

Munday, 3ᵈ Jan.ʸ, 1774.[14]   This day snowing very hard, Wind at N. N. E. At 9 AM went out to see if I cou'd sell any stockins, but returned again at 10 AM without selling any. . . . Just now I am Master of no more Cash than 1s. 1½d. . . . I traviled the Town untill 2 PM in which time I sold three pair of stockins for four shillings and four pence, which was eight pence less than they cost me in Zetland.[15] I then returned home and bought 1d. worth of bread 1d. worth

8. N. V.: N.W., or northwest. Harrower frequently substitutes a V for a W, and the reader will have to transpose the letters on occasion.

9. Vizt (Or Viz.ᵗ): used as we would a use a colon.

10. Onb.ᵈ: onboard.

11. Newcastle: English port city in the Northeast, located on River Tyne, very near Shields, also mentioned.

12. Shields.

13. Poynt: pint.

14. Harrower pens this entry at Sunderland, where no ships for Holland were to be found because the ice in the Dutch rivers precluded the voyage.

15. Zetland: Shetland.

of cheese and 1d. worth of small beer which served me for dinner and supper.

Wednesday, 5th. Wind and weather as yesterday.   this afternoon I hear of a Brigantine[16] called the Nancy ready load for Holland, and that she always used that trade.

Thursday, 6th. Wind at S. and a verry gentle thaw.   at 8 AM I went to Warmouth[17] and spacke with Mr. George Lacen [?] Com[r][18] of the Nancy Brigantine, who informed me, that he himself was not sure where he was to go, But that I might speacke to M[r] John Taylor the Owner which I immediatly did and he told me, that if the Rivers was open the Nancy would go to Holland, if not probably to London, and that I was extreamly welcome to my passage. I then waited on Mr. Lacen and aquanted him of the same, and imediatly put my trunk and bundle on board. . . .

Freiday, 7th. Got out of bedd at 6 AM this morning.   at 8 AM went.   at 9 AM they began to haul out of the harbour and came to an Anchor in the Roads at 10 AM and lay in the road untill four keels of Coals was put on board, each keel being Twenty Tun, and they were all Onb[d] by half an houre past noon. At 1 pm got under saile with the wind at N. B. E.[19] with a verry high sea runing, a great deall of which she shipped all this afternoon.   steered until midnight S. S. E.[20]

Wednesday, 12th. This morning fine clear weather but hard frost. I waited onb[d] untill three pm for Cap[t] Lacoers [?] returning. But when I found he did not I left a letter of thanks to him for his favours shown me, for he would take no passage money from me, Besides that he used me like a Brother making me sleep and eat with himself; I then went ashore and immediately set out for London with no more cash in my pocket [but] 1s. 8½d. St[r] I pray, May God provide more for me and for all who are in strait. Immediatly as I left Portsmouth I fell into Comp[y] and conversaition on the road to whome I sold two pair of stockins 4/6d. it being the price they cost me in Zetland. I traveled four Miles this afternoon and lodged all night at Post doun[21] bridge and the House had a Battery of Twelve Canon round it.   here I supped on eight Oisters and 1d. and ½ worth of Bread, with a poynt

16. Brigantine: a kind of boat.
17. Monk Wearmouth, opposite Sunderland.
18. Com[r]: commander.
19. North by east.
20. From this time until noon of the eleventh, the brigantine sailed along the English coast, finally coming to anchor at Portsmouth, where the captain went ashore to sell his coal and where Harrower vainly sought passage to Holland.
21. Portsdown.

of strong and a poynt of small beer which [cost] me 3d., being in all
4½d. for supper, here I paid 3d. for my bedd, and it was warmed with
a warming pan, this being the first time I ever seed it done.

Thursday, 13th.   Wind at E. so thick that I could not see above 100
yards distance. I crossed over Post doun hill and Breackfast at
Handen,[22] and after crossing a large barren Common of that name I
dinned at Petersfield and then Got as far as Raik in the County of Sussex where I staid all night, having traviled twenty miles this [day]
which is more than I did expect carring my Box and Bundle on my
back; They have for firing[23] here, nothing but a kind [of] heath like
flaws.[24]   at this place I paid 3d. for my bedd, My diet being all the
old storry, Bread, Cheese and beer, and I had a Rush Candle to light
me to bedd.

Freiday, 14th.   This morning I sold in my lodgings sundry articles
to the amount of 18/9d. St[r] [25] which Articles cost me £1.5/6 St[r]. So
that necessity obliged me to lose 6/9d. . . .[26]

Sunday, 16th.   This day after breackfast and read[g] some Chapters
on a Newtestament I found in my room. . . . Here I hade an extream
good dinner in Publick, for sixpence.   in the Afternoon I took a Walk
and seed round this place a great many fine Houses and gardens most
of them belonging to Londoners.

[*Tuesday*], *18th.*   This day I got to London and was like a blind man
without a guide, not knowing where to go being freindless and having
no more money but fifteen shillings and eight pence farthing a small
sum to enter London with ; But I trust in the mercys of God who is a
rich provider and am hopefull before it is done some way will cast up
for me. I took up my lodging at the old ship Tavern in little Hermitage
street,[27] Mr. George Newton being the landlord, but in Prison for
debt at present.

Wednesday, 19th.   This day I shifted[28] my cloaths and put on a
clean Ruffled Shirt, clean Britches and waistcoat and my Brown Coat,
I not having any other cloaths on ever since I left Lerwick but my blew
Jacket and Bigg Coat above it and a plain shirt. At 11 AM I called to

22. Horndean.

23. For firing: for burning.

24. Flax.

25. 18/9d. St[r].: 18 shillings, 9 pence sterling—a bit less than one pound (20 shillings
equaled a pound; 12 pence equaled a shilling).

26. Harrower then walked on by way of Godalming and Guilford to Epsom, where he
spent Sunday.

27. In Wapping, near the London docks.

28. Shifted: changed (clothes).

see Cap.! Perry, but was told he would not be at home untill 5 pm. Having eat nothing for 24 houres, I dinned in my Lodging this day which cost me 1/2 St.ʳ. After dinner I took a walk with the mate of a ship a Scotsman. . . .

A 5 pm called again at Cap.! Perrys and the first face I saw was Willie Holcraw of Coningsburgh[29] who I found staid here as a servant, and while I was speacking to him, Cap.! Perry came home and he immediatly knew me, and desired me to walk in which I did, and after sitting some time and drinking some tea, I called Cap.! Perry aside and made my Intentions known to him, at same time begged his advice and assistance ; He told me he hardly thought there would be any Business got for me in London. But told me to call on him at the Jamacia Coffee House to morrow at Change time.[30] I then went home. and soon went to Bedd.

Thursday, 20th. This morning breackfast at home and paid 6d. for it. At noon called at the Jamacia Coffee House and soon after seed Cap.! Perry and waited here and Change untill 3 pm but no appearance of any Business for me. the time I was in the Coffee house I drank 3ds. worth of punch, and I was obliged to make it serve me for Dinner. at night I hade ½d. worth of bread and 1d. of Cheese and a poynt of Porter for supper it being all I cou'd afford.

Freiday, 21st. This morning I seed an advertisement for Bookeepers and Clerks to go to a Gentlemen [at] Philadelphia. I went as it directed to N.º 1 in Catharine Court princes street, but when I came there I was told they were served. I then waited again on Cap.! Perry untill after 3 pm But to no purpose. I this day offered to go steward of a ship bound to Maryland but could not get the birth. This day I was 3 or 4 miles through London and seed S.! Paul's Church, the Bank of England where I seed the gold lying in heaps, I also seed Summerst house,[31] Gild hall, Drury Lane, Covingarden,[32] Adelphus Buildings and several other pleaces. I then returnd and near my lodgings I dinned at an eating house and hade 4d. worth of roast Beiff 1d. worth of bread and a poynt of small beer, in all 5½d.

Saturday, 22d. This morning I seed an advertisement in the Publick ledger for a Messenger to a publick Lodge, Sallery 15/St.ʳ per week and another advertisement for an under Clerk to a Merch.! to

29. Or Cunningsburgh, a village about eight miles south of Lerwick.

30. Change time: time of the exchange, when merchants gather in a public house for drinks and discussion of business.

31. Somerset House, not the modern building but its predecessor, the old mansion of the Protector Somerset.

32. Covent Garden.

both which I wrote answers and went to the places apointed, and found at each place more than a dozen of Letters before me, so that I hade litle expectation that way they being all weel aquanted and I a stranger. . . .

Sunday, 23d. This morning I drank some purle[33] for breackfast and then I took a walk in the forenoon through severall streets, and at 1 pm I returned to the eating house I hade formerly been at and dinned which cost me 6½ today having hade 1d. worth of pudding more than I formerly hade. In the afternoon I went to a Methodists meeting. the Text was in the V Chap : Mathew and the 20th Verse. After sermon I came home and being solitary in my room I made the following Verses which I insert on the other side of this leaf.

> Now at London in a garret room I am,
> here frendless and forsaken ;
> But from the Lord my help will come,
> Who trusts in him are not mistaken.

> When freinds on earth do faint and faile,
> And upon you their backs do turn ;
> O Truly seek the Lord, and he will
> Them comfort that do murn.

> I'll unto God my prayer make,
> to him my case make known ;
> And hopes he will for Jesus sake,
> Provide for me and soon.

Munday, 24th. This morning I wrote six tickets to give to shipmasters at Change seeking a steward's birth onb[d] some ship, but could not get a birth. I also wrote a petition in generall to any Merch[t] or Tradesman setting forth my present situation, and the way in which I hade been brought up and where I hade served and in what station, at same time offering to serve any for the bare suport of life fore some time. But all to no effect, for all places here at present are intierly carried by freinds and Intrest, And many Hundreds are sterving for want of employment, and many good people are begging.

Tuesday, 25th. Having heard last night that John Ross sloop was come from Zetland, I took a Boat this morning and went onboard her and seed him and Robert Irvine. And then I hade the happiness to hear that my wife and Childrein were all well on the 3[d] In[st] it being the day they left Bressaysound.[34] The rest of this day I was employed

33. Purle: a liquor made by adding herbs to ale or beer.

34. The 3[d] In[st] noted here refers to the third of this month, January. Bressaysound is the harbor of Lerwick.

in presenting the Petition I hade drawn up on the 24th Ins[t] to severall Merch[ts] and others and doing all I cou'd to get into business of some kind near home but all to no effect.

Wednesday, 26th. This day I being reduced to the last shilling I hade was obliged to engage to go to Virginia for four years as a schoolmaster for Bedd, Board, washing and five pound during the whole time. I have also wrote my wife this day a particular Acco[t] of every thing that has happned to me since I left her untill this date ; At 3 pm this day I went on board the Snow Planter Cap[t] Bowers Com[r] for Virginia now lying at Ratliff Cross, and imediatly as I came Onb[d] I rec[d][35] my Hammock and Bedding.   at 4 pm came Alex[r] Steuart onb[d] the same Ship.   he was Simbisters Serv[t][36] and had only left Zetland about three weeks before me.   we were a good deall surprised to meet w[t][37] on another in this place.

Thursday, 27th. This day ranie weather.   the ships crew imployed in rigging the ship under the Direction of the mate and I was imployed in getting my Hammock slung.   at 2 pm came onb[d] Alex[r] Burnet nephew to Mr. Francis Farquharson writter in Edinburgh and one Samuel Mitchell a Cooper from Yorkshire and both entred into the berth and Mace[38] with Stewart and me.

Saturday, 29th. This day came on b[d] Alex[r] Kennedy a young man from Edinb[r] who hade been a Master Cooper there and a Glasgow Man by trade a Barber both which we took into our Mace, which compleated it being five Scotsmen and one Yorkshireman, and was always called the Scots mace, And the Cap[t] told me he was from the Toun of Aberbothick in Scotland, but th[t] he [had] not been there since he was fifteen years of age but hade been always in the Virginia trade which I was verry glad to hear.

Munday, 31st. This day I went ashore and bought a penknife, a paper Book, and some paper and pens and came on board to Dinner. It is surprising to see the N[o] of good tradesmen[39] of all kinds, th[t] come onb[d] every day.

Freiday, February 4th. This day at 7 AM unmoored from Ratliffcross and fell down the river with the tide there being no wind. . . .

---

35. Rec[d]: received.

36. Alexander Stewart was a servant of John Bruce Stewart of Symbister and Bigton, an important proprietor in the south of Shetland. Gilbert Goudie, ed., *Diary of the Reverend John Mill, Minister of the Parishes of Dunrossness, Sandwick and Cunningsburgh in Shetland, 1740–1803* (Edinburgh: Scottish Historical Society, 1889), pp. 22, 151.

37. W[t]: with.

38. Mace: mess, a group that ate together on board ship.

39. Artisans.

Sunday, 6th.   At 7 AM got under way with a fair wind and clear w.ʳ⁴⁰ and at 11 AM came to an anchor off Gravesend and immediatly the Merchᵗ came onboard and a Doctor and clerk with him and while the Clerk was filling up the Indentures the doctor search'd every servᵗ to see that they were sound when . . . seventy five were Intend⁴¹ to Capᵗ Bowres for four Years.

Munday, 7th.   This forenoon imployed in getting in provisions and water.   at 4 pm put a servant ashore extreamly bade in a fever, and then got under saile for Virginia with seventy Servants on board all indented to serve four years there at their differint Occoupations my-self being one of the Number and Indented for a Clerk and Bookeeper, But when I arrived there I cou'd get no such birth as will appear in the place.⁴² At pm we came to an anchor at the nore it blow-ing and snowing verry hard.

Tuesday, 8th.   At 5 AM made saile from the Nore with the wind at W. N. W. Clear weather and blowing hard.   at 2 pm got off a Pillot from Deall to take our River Pillot ashore for which Boat Capᵗ Bowers paid one and a half Guineas, and after buying some Gin here we stood streight to sea Under Close R. T. sails⁴³ and our fore saile, a verry high sea running all this day.

Sunday, 13th.   Wind at V. B. S.⁴⁴   squally weather. Eight saile more at anchor in Company wᵗ us. At noon the Indented servants was like to mutiny against the Capᵗ for putting them to Allowance of bread and Mate,⁴⁵ but it was soon quelled, Our mace not joyning with the rest.   in the afternoon he went ashore, But before he left the Ship he called me and begged I wou'd stand by the Mate if there arose any disturbance among the rest of the servants.

Saturday, 26th.   Wind at N. B. E.   fine moderate weather.   got up Yd.ˢ and Topmasts.   at 10 AM The Capᵗ went ashore to get more fresh provisions, at 4 pm he came onb.ᵈ from Portsmouth with Bread, Beiff Pork and Water and then imediatly got under sale and stood out to sea. At this time we hade three men sick onb.ᵈ one with the flux,

---

40. W.ʳ: water.

41. Intend: indented. This was the formal process by which servants signed indentures and any who were sick were taken off the ship before it headed out to sea.

42. This and the entry of May 25 below show that the entries through May 25 were not in the absolute sense contemporary; but a passage in a letter, under August 7, 1774, seems to indicate that daily notes were taken.

43. Close-reefed topsails.

44. West by south.

45. Mate: meat.

one with the fever and Ego,[46] and one frost bitt in his feet. At 11 pm the wind came all round to the N. V. Blowing verry hard.   at Midnight close reefd the topsails.

Sunday, 27th.   Wind at N. V.   at 4 AM Tack'd ship. At same time the man who was bade with the flux was found dead in his hammock.   at 8 he was sewed up in it and at 9 AM he was burried in the sea after reading the service of the Dead over him, which was done by the Mate.

Freiday, March 11th.   Wind weather and course as yesterday. this forenoon clear but verry squally like.   at 4 pm stowed the Main-topsail and at 7 pm stowed fore Top saile and close reefd the Main saile and scuded under it. The wind blowing excessive hard and a verry high sea running still from the westward.   at 8 pm was oblidged to batten down both fore and main hatches, and a little after I really think there was the odest shene[47] betwixt decks that ever I heard or seed. There was some sleeping, some spewing, . . . some daming, some Blasting their leggs and thighs, some their liver, lungs, lights and eyes, And for to make the shene the odder, some curs'd Father, Mother, Sister, and Brother.

Saturday, 12th.   Wind weather and course as before.   we are now past the skirts of the Bay of Biscay and entred into the Atlantick Ocean, going at the rate of 8 knots per houre.

Sunday, 13th.   Wind at S. S. E.   course V. B. S.   at 11 AM Moderate weather.   let out all reefs.   at noon in Latitude 44 North per observation. This afternoon got most of sick and ailing to deck the number of which I cannot really now ascertain. But I thank God I have as yet kept my health weel. At 3 pm there was two servants put in Irons for wanting other than what was served. But they were soon released on their asking pardon and promising to behave better.

Sunday, 27th.   Wind, weather, and course as yesterday.   at 8 AM got up all hammocks and the sick likways they being now in number about 37, there being th[ree] sick in our mace Viz.: Stewart, Burnet, and the Yorkshire Cooper.   at noon we all betwixt decks cleand out, and washed with wineggar.[48]

Thursday, 31st.   Wind weather and course as before. The sick are now increased to the number of fifty betwixt decks, besides three in the steerage Viz.: two seamen and a passanger.

46. Ego: ague. Notice how long the ship's departure has been delayed by unfavorable winds.

47. Shene: scene.

48. Winnegar: vinegar.

Sunday, April 3d.   Wind weather and course as before. Last night Alex.ʳ Stewart was so high in the fever that I sat up with him all night, and Burnet and the Cooper are still verry bad, but not so high as Stewart. This day the Cap.ᵗ ordered some Cock and hen to be killed and fresh broth made for the sick.

Munday, 4th.   Wind weather and course still as before and jogging on from 4 to 6 knots at an average per houre.   at 5 pm I was oblidged to get Stewart blister'd and sat up again all night with him, having become his nurse for Country sake he being the first in the Mace that was taken ill, and I was not sure how soon it might be my own fate. But thank God I am as yet well and hearty. This night I supped on a dish called Scratchplatters.   it is made of biscuits broack small and soacked in water until they are soft, and then Winegar, oile, salt, and Onions cut small put to it, and supped with spoons.

Wednesday, 6th.   . . . I have wore no Britches nor stockins since we got into the trade winds[49] only a pair of long trousers down to my buckles. And this day having put on a shorter pair untill my longest pair was wash'd, I got both my Ancles burned by the sun, it is so verry hot here.

Tuesday, 19th.   . . . This day I brought up M.ʳ Jones[50] Journall for five days back, also Cap.ᵗ Bowers Journall for four days back and at same time begged me to mark the Logg Book and ordred that Whoever hade the charge of watch to aquant me what the ship went per Logg &c.

Thursday, 21st.   This morning a young lad, one of the serv.ᵗˢ being verry ill with the Fever and Ague, he begged me to apply to Mr. Jones the Cheif Mate, and told me he cou'd give him something that would cure him. . . .

Freiday, 22d.   This day I was seased with a sever Cold and Aching in my bones, but I thank God I am weel car'd for and has every thing sent me from the Cabin I can desire.

Wednesday, 27th.   This morning I am fairly got the better of my cold and the Aching in my bones and am able to stir about. . . . At 7 pm we made Cape Henry[51] and the Coast plain. we then highesed[52] our flagg for a Pillot Boat and at pm we hade four Pillot boats[53] along

49. Latitude this day was 27°37′ north. On the tenth day they were near Barbados.

50. James Jones, chief mate, then sick. The captain had Harrower help bring the ship's journals up to date.

51. Cape Henry: the southern tip of the Virginia side of the entrance to Chesapeake Bay. See the accompanying map, "John Harrower's Route to Belvidera."

52. Highesed: raised.

53. Pillot boat: small boat used to bring on board a local pilot familiar with the Virginia coast. The captain subsequently employed another pilot to navigate the Rappahannock River.

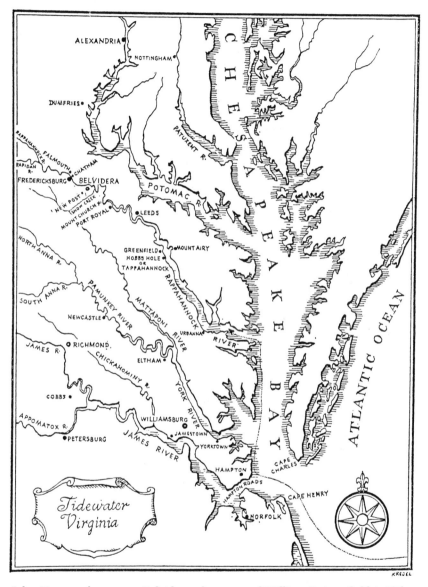

John Harrower's route to Belvidera, the estate of William Daingerfield in Tidewater Virginia, 1774. (Courtesy of the Colonial Williamsburg Foundation)

side and Cap.[t] Bowrs took one M.[r] Cooper who brought us within the Capes, and to an Anchor at 10 pm where we lay all night.

Thursday, 28th. At 7 AM the Pillot wegh'd Anchor and wrought the ship up to Hampton Roads[54] where we came to an Anchor at 10 AM. This morning I was employ'd in Making out a Clean list of the servants names and Business and age, and how soon I was done[55] Cap.[t] Bowers went ashore in the Pillot boat to Hamton on Elizabeth river. we have some goods to put out before we leave this place. at night, a deal of Thunder, lightning and rain.

Monday, May 2d. Wind as before, fine fair warm weather. got out the rest of the goods that was for Hampton. at 2 pm the Cap.[t] Carried five serv[ts] ashore to Hampton in order to sell their Indentures, But returned again at Midnight with[out] selling any more but one Boat Builder. he brought onb.[d] with him four Barrells Virginia Pork and one Puncheon D.[o] [56] rum, and 3 live hogs.

Tuesday, 3d. Wind at W. N. W. fine moderate weather. at 6 AM weigh'd Anchor from Hampton Roads, and stood out to sea untill we made the Entry of Rappahannock river, which we did at 10 AM, proceeding up the same for Fredericksburgh. at 6 pm came to an anchor at Arrabanna.[57]

Freiday, 6th. Wind as before. at 4 AM got under saile and stood up the river and at 9 AM passed by the Town of Hobshole[58] and let it on our Larboard hand as we did the Town of Arrabanna. at Hobshole there was five Glasgow ships and an English Brigantine lying. at 2 pm we passed by Leedstown[59] on our Starboard hand where there was a ship from London lying with Convicts.[60] at night came to anchor about 6 Miles above Leedstown. . . .

Tuesday, 10th. At 2 AM weigh'd and stood up with the tide, came to an anchor at 6 AM and lay untill Do. 8 when we weigh'd with a fair wind and got to our Moorings at 6 pm at the Toun of Fredericksburgh.

54. Hampton Roads: the entrance to the James River.

55. As soon as I was done.

56. D.[o] means ditto. In this context, it would refer to Virginia rum. A puncheon was a large cask.

57. Urbanna, in Middlesex County, only a short distance up the Rappahannock River.

58. Hobb's Hole, in Richmond County.

59. Leeds, in Westmoreland County.

60. It was a common practice to commute the sentences of English criminals in exchange for transportation to the colonies and a period of seven or fourteen years of indentured service. The Virginia House of Burgesses passed laws limiting such practice, but the English privy council routinely overruled the colonists' efforts. See A. Roger Ekirch, *Bound for America: The Transportation of British Convicts to the Colonies, 1718–1775* (New York: Oxford University Press, 1987).

Wednesday, 11th. At 10 AM Both Coopers and the Barber from our Mace went ashore upon tryall. At night one Daniel Turner a serv.^t returned onb^d from Liberty so drunk that he abused the Capt and chief Mate and Boatswan to a verry high degree, which made to be horse whip.^t put in Irons and thumb screwed[61] on houre afterward he was unthumbscrewed, taken out of the Irons, but then he was hand cuffed, and gagged all night.

Thursday, 12th. All hands quite on board this day. Turner ungagged But continoued in handcuffs.

Freiday, 13th. This forenoon put ashore here what bale goods we hade remaining onboard. in the afternoon Mr. Burnet, Stewart and myself went ashore on liberty to take a walk and see the Toun, who's principal street is about half an English Mile long. . . . In this Toun the Church, the Counsell house, the Tolbooth the Gallows and the Pillory are all within 130 yd.^s of each other. The Market house is a large brick Building a litle way from the Church. here we drank some Bottles of beer of their own brewing and some bottles of Cyder for which we paid 3½ per bottle of each. returned on board in the evening. Turner still in handcuffs.

Munday, 16th. This day severalls came onb.^d to purchase serv.^ts Indentures and among them there was two Soul drivers. they are men who make it their business to go onb.^d all ships who have in either Servants or Convicts and buy sometimes the whole and sometimes a parcell of them as they can agree, and then they drive them through the Country like a parcell of Sheep untill they can sell them to advantage, but all went away without buying any.

Tuesday, 17th. This day Mr Anderson the Merch.^t sent for me into the [cabin] and verry genteely told me that on my recomendations he would do his outmost to get me settled as a Clerk or bookeeper if not as a schoolmaster which last he told me he thought wou'd turn out more to my advantage upon being settled in a good famely.

The ships crew and servants employed in getting ashore all the cask out of the hould, no sales th.^s day.

Wednesday, 18th. This day the ships crew and servants imployed in getting out the ballast and unrigging the ship. One Cooper, one Blacksmith and one Shoemaker were settled with Masters this day.

Thursday, 19th. One Farmer's time sold and one Cabinet Maker on tryall.

Saturday, 21st. This day one Mr Cowly a man 'twixt fifty and sixty years of age, a serv.^t, also three sons of his their ages from eight to fourteen were all settled with one McDonald a Scotchman.

---

61. Thumb screwed: punishment for a servant's returning to ship drunk.

Munday, 23d. This morning a great number of Gentlemen and Ladies driving into Town it being an annuall Fair[62] day and tomorrow the day of the Horse races.   at 11 AM M.ʳ Anderson begged to settle as a schoolmaster with a friend of his one Colonel Daingerfield[63] and told me he was to be in Town tomorrow, or perhaps tonight, and how soon he came he shou'd aquant me.   at same time all the rest of the servants were ordred ashore to a tent at Fredericksb.ᵍ and severall of their Indentures were then sold.   about 4 pm I was brought to Colonel Daingerfield, when we imediatly agreed and my Indenture for four years was then delivered him and he was to send for me the next day.   at same time ordred to get all my dirty Cloaths of every kind washed at his expense in Toun ; at night he sent me five shillings onb.ᵈ by Cap.ᵗ Bowers to keep my pocket.

Tuesday, 24th. This morning I left the Ship at 6 AM having been sixteen weeks and six days on board her. I hade for Breackfast after I came ashore one Chappin[64] sweet milk for which I paid 3½ Cur.ʸ. . . .

Wednesday, 25th. I Lodged in a Tavern last night and paid 7½ for my Bedd and 7½ for my breackfast.   this morning a verry heavy rain until 11 AM. Then I rec.ᵈ my Linens &c. all clean washed and packing every thing up I went onboard the ship and Bought this Book for which I paid 18d. St.ʳ.[65] I also bought a small Divinity book called the Christian Monitor and a spelling book, both at 7½ and an Arithmetick at 1/6d. all for my Acco.ᵗ.

Thursday, 26th. This day at noon the Colonel sent a Black with a cuple of Horses for me and soon after I set out on Horseback and aravied at his seat of Belvidera about 3 pm and after I hade dined the Colonel took me to a neat little house at the upper end of an Avenue of planting at 500 yd.ˢ from the Main house, where I was to keep the school, and Lodge myself in it.

This place is verry pleasantly situated on the Banks of the River Rappahannock about seven miles below the Toun of Fredericksburgh and the school's right above the Warff so that I can stand in the door and pitch a stone onboard of any ship or Boat going up or coming doun the river.

---

62. By law fairs were held at Fredericksburg twice a year for the sale of "cattle, victuals, provisions, goods, wares and merchandizes."

63. Col. William Daingerfield of Belvidera employed John Harrower for his entire period in Virginia.

64. A Scottish measure, about equivalent to an American quart.

65. "This Book" refers to a bound volume in which Harrower kept his journal. He evidently had recorded earlier entries elsewhere and copied them after this date into the new volume.

Freiday, 27th. This morning about 8 AM the Colonel delivered his three sons to my Charge to teach them to read write and figure.   his oldest son Edwin 10 years of age, intred into two syllables in the spelling book, Bathourest [Bathurst] his second son six years of age in the Alphabete and William his third son 4 years of age does not know the letters.   he has likeways a Daughter whose name is Hanna Basset   Years of age. Soon after we were all sent for to breackfast to which we hade tea, Bread, Butter and cold meat and there was at table the Colonel, his Lady, his Children, the housekeeper and myself. At 11 AM the Colonel and his Lady went some where to pay a visite, he upon horseback and she in her Charriot. At 2 pm I dined with the Housekeeper the Children and a stranger Lady.   at 6 pm I left school, and then I eat plenty of fine strawberries, but they neither drink Tea in the afternoon nor eat any supper here for the most part. My school Houres is from 6 to 8 in the morning, in the forenoon from 9 to 12 and from 3 to 6 in the afternoon.

Sunday, 29th. There is no church nearer Belvidera than Fredericksburgh, and for want of a sadle I was oblidged to stay at home all day and when I was alone in the school I thought on the following verses.

Ist.

In Virginia now I am, at Belvidera settled,
but may they ever mercy find, who hade the cause
that I am from my sweet wife seperated
And Oblidged to leave my Infant Children Fatherless.

2^{d}.

As a schoolmaster, I am here ;
And must for four years, remain so ;
May I indeavour the Lord to fear,
And always his commands do.

3^{d}.

For in Gods strength I do rely,
that he at his appointed time,
Will bring me back my family,
if I his precepts do but mind.

4th.

O May my God provide for them,
Who unto me are near and dear ;
tho they afar off me are from
O Jesus keep them in thy fear.

5th.

Do thou enable me to labour,
and my fortune do thou mind ;
that what I get by thy favour,
I to my family may send.

6th.

O Lord my God do thou them save
from dangers and from death
And may they food and rayment have
and for the same may thankfull be while they have breath. . . .

After dinner I took a walk about a Miles distance from the house
along the highway, and by the road side seed a Corn Mill and another
pretty house called Snow Creek belonging to the Colonel.

Tuesday, 31st. This day there was about fifty white Ewes and
Lambs feeding 'twix the main house and the school door and so tame
that they wou'd come and look in at the door and see what we was
doing.   the lambs here are as large at this date as in Zetland at
Michelsmass, being of the english bread.

Wednesday, June 1st. This day there was prayers in all the
Churches in Virginia on Acco^t of the disagreement at present betwixt
great Brittain and her Colonies in North America, On Acco^t of their
not agreeing to pay a duty on Tea laid on them by the british parliment
and the Bostonians destroying a Quantity of Tea belonging to the British East India Comp^y in 1773.[66]

Freiday, 3d. This day I eat green pease at dinner, this being the
last of them this season here.

Wednesday, 8th. This day I eat plenty of fine ripe Cherries
brought out of the woods this morning by the Colonel.

Freiday, 10th. Rec^d two pair fine new brown thread stockins. Below is an Inventory of the Cloaths &c I brought to Belvidera with me
Viz.

One Superfine Brown Cloath Coat full mounted.[67]
One D° vest Coat.
One floored silk D°
One fine marsyled D°
One Brown Duffel D°

66. The fast-day was decreed by the Virginia House of Burgesses to show support for
Massachusetts after the Boston Tea Party.

67. To help in reading Harrower's list below, recall that D° means ditto. Also, floored
means flowered; marsyled means Marseilles; and Osenburgh means Osnaburg, a kind of
coarse linen.

One pair new black Stockins Britches
One pair new Doe skin D°
One pair flannen Drawers.
One pair Osenburgh D°
Six Ruffled Shirts
five plain white D°
One Cheque D°
One Blue Cloath Jacket
Seven Musline Stocks
One Black silk Cravate
One pair Ribbed Cotton Stockins   ⎧ Severall other
Ten pair worsted D°   ⎪ Articles besides
One new Hat and one D° Wigg.   ⎬ what are here
Five pocket Napkins.   ⎪ mentioned but
two hand Towels   ⎪ are too tedeous
two pair Trousers   ⎩ to mention.
One pair Shoes ; with Pinchback shoe, stock and
knee buckles.
One trunk, with fine lock and hinges.

Saturday, 11th. At 9 AM left the school and went a fishing on the
River with the Colonel his eldest [Son] and another Gentleman in two
Canoes, Mrs. Dangerfield another Lady and the other two boys mett
us at Snow Creek in the Chair at 2 pm when we all dined on fish under
a tree.

Sunday, 12th. This day at Church at Fredericksburgh and at same
time settled a Correspondance at Glasgow for getting letters from
home, by their being put under cover to Messrs. Anderson and Hors-
burgh Merch.ts in D° and the expence charged to Mr. Glassel[68] Merch.t
in Fredericksb.g Virginia.

Tuesday, 14th. This morning entred to school William Pattie son
to John Pattie wright, and Salley Evens daughter to Thomas Evens
Planter. This day I wrote my wife a particular Acco.t of all my transactions since I wrote her from London 26.th Jan.y last, the Coppy of
which I have by me.[69]

Thursday, 16th. This eveng the Colonel told me he hade about
400 Acres of land in wheat and as much in Indian Corn every year
and that he comonly exported about 3600 bushels of wheat every
year besides serving his own Family. But that he did not expect to

68. John Glassell was a Scotsman who came to Fredericksburg and became a prominent
merchant there. Harrower had arranged with this local merchant to send letters home and
have expenses charged to his account.

69. See its text under August 7, below.

have above the one half th^s year owing to a strong frost they had in Aprile last.

Freiday, 17th. This day rec^d two pair new Rushia drill britches and two new short Coats of Brown Holland.

Munday, 20th. This morning entred to school Philip and Dorothea Edge's Children of Mr Benjaman Edge Planter. Same day Colonel Dangerfield began to cut down his wheat, which they do with a syth.[70]

Tuesday, 21st. This day Mr Samuel Edge Planter came to me and begged me to take a son of his to school who was both deaf and dum, and I consented to try what I cou'd do with him.

Thursday, 23d. This day entred to school John Edge son to the above named Mr Sam: Edge. he is a lad about 14 years of age and is both deaf and dum.[71]

Saturday, 25th. This afternoon I went and took a walk in the wheat field and under a tree I filled all my pockets of as fine walnuts as ever I eat, But so hard shell that I was oblidged to have a hammer to breack them.

Sunday, 26th. After Breackfast I took a walk 3 Miles to Mr. Edge's, the dum lad's fathers where I dined and drank some grogg and returned home in the afternoon. at night I had a small Congregation of Negroes, learng their Catechisim and hearing me read to them.

Sunday, July 3d. At home all the forenoon, in the afternoon went to see One Mr. Richards an Overseer and his wife where I eat plenty of honney out of the Comb, it being taken out of a Beehive in a tree in the woods last night.

Freiday, 8th. After school houres I went two Miles to see the Taylor who made my Cloaths he being a Brittoner but married to a Buckskine,[72] and I found his wife and Daughters drinking tea, at which I joyned them, The Taylor not being at home.

Tuesday, 12th. Sold the spelling book that I bought Onb^d the Planter 25th May last, and got the same money for it that I paid for the Christian Monitor and it.

Saturday, 16th. This afternoon the Colonel finished the cutting down of His wheat which cost of wages to hired people £23: 10 Curr^y[73] besides their victualls and drink.

70. Syth: scythe.

71. John Edge may have been the first deaf-mute instructed in America. For subsequent details of Harrower's experiment, see the entries of July 19 and 25, 1774, March 18 and May 20, 1775, and his letter of December 6, 1774.

72. Buckskine: American.

73. Curr^y: abbreviation for currency—meaning Virginia money as opposed to English sterling. Worth 80 percent of English money.

Munday, 18th. This morning entred to School Lewis Richards. Same day I put on a pair of new shoes made in Fredericksburgh of English calf leather the price of them 12/6 Cur.ʸ. Same day gave one pair of old worsted stockins for 22 foot of Gum plank 10 Inch broad and one thick to make me a Chest.

Tuesday, 19th. On Freiday 15ᵗʰ Insᵗ John Edge the Dumb lad left the school at 6 pm and has not returned since.

Wednesday, 20th. On Munday, 4ᵗʰ Insᵗ at 6 pm William Pattie left the school and has not returned since.

Munday, 25th. Nothing remarkable. Jnᵒ Edge returnᵈ to school.

Sunday, August 7th. This afternoon meeting accidentaly with a Gentleman here who was on his way to London I wrote my wife a few lines by him having wrote her fully 14ᵗʰ June last but having omitted to insert the Coppy in it's proper place I now do it here before I insert the coppy of my second Letter to her from this country.

Belvidera 14ᵗʰ June 1774.

My Dearest Life

I wrote you from London on Wednesday 26ᵗʰ Janʸ last which Im hopefull came safe to hand, and found you and my dear Infants in perfect health, and am hopefull this will find both you and them in the same state, As I am at present and have been I bless God since I left you. You will remember when I wrote you last, I informed you that I was to go for Baltimore in Maryland, But I altred my design in that and came here it being a more healthy pleace. I sailed from London on Freiday the 4ᵗʰ Febʸ last, and arrived in Hampton roads in Virginia on the 27 April, having been a Month of the time at Spithead in England. As to particulars of our Voyage &ᶜᵃ it would take up too much room here to insert it. But I have a Journal of every days transactions and remarcable Occurances since the morning I left you which will be amusing to you when please God we are spared to meet, for I design to see and prepare a way for you all in this Country how soon I am able.—I shall now aquant you wᵗ my situation in this Country. I am now settled with on Colonel Wᵐ Dangerfield Esqʳ of Belvidera, on the Banks of the River Rappahannock about 160 miles from the Capes or sea mouth, and seven Miles below the Toun of Fredericksburgh. My business is to teach his Children to read write and figure, Edwin his oldest son about 8 years of [age] Bathurest his second 6 years of age and William his youngest son 4 years of age. he has also a Daughter whose name is Hanna Basset. I came to this place on Thursday 26ᵗʰ May and next morning I received his three sons into my

charge to teach, the two youngest boys I got in A:B:C. and the oldest
Just begun to syllab and I have now the two youngest spelling and the
oldest reading. I am obliged to teach in the English method which was
a little aquard[74] to me at first but now quite easy. I am also obliged to
talk english the best I can, for Lady Dangerfield speacks nothing but
high english, and the Colonel hade his Education in England and is a
verry smart Man.[75] As to my agreement it is as follows Viz.! I am
obliged to continue with Col! Dangerfield for four years if he insists
on it, and for teaching his own children I have Bed, Board, washing
and all kind of Cloaths during the above time, and for what schoolars
I can get more than his Children I have five shillings currency per
Quarter for each of them, which is equall to four shillings sterling, and
I expect ten or twelve to school next week, for after I hade been here
eight days and my abilities and my behavior sufficiently tried, the
Colonel rode through the neighbouring Gentlemen and Planters in
order to procure scollars for me, so that I hope in a short time to make
something of it. And as I have no Occasion to spend a farthing on myself every shill.g I make shall be carefully remitted you, for your support and my Dear Infants. But I must be some time here before any
thing can be done, for you know every thing must have a beginning.

As to my living I eat at their own table, and our witualls are all
Dressed in the English taste.   we have for Breackfast either Coffie or
Jaculate,[76] and warm Loaf bread of the best floor, we have also at table
warm loaf bread of Indian corn, which is extreamly good but we use
the floor bread always at breackfast.   for Dinner smoack'd bacon or
what we cal pork ham is a standing dish either warm or cold.   when
warm we have greens with it, and when cold we have sparrow grass.
we have also either warm roast pigg, Lamb, Ducks, or chickens, green
pease or any thing else they fancy. As for Tea there is none drunk by
any in this Government since 1.st June last, nor will they buy a 2ds
worth of any kind of east India goods, which is owing to the difference
at present betwixt the Parliment of great Britton and the North Americans about laying a tax on the tea ; and I'm afraid if the Parliment do
not give it over it will cause a total revolt as all the North Americans
are determined to stand by one another, and resolute on it that they
will not submit. I have the news paper sent me to school regularly
every week by the Col!—Our family consists of the Col! his Lady and

74. Aquard: awkward.
75. Shetland Islanders still spoke a dialect with strong traces of Norse influence so it was
often difficult for Harrower to understand or speak the "high English" spoken by the
Daingerfields. See George Low, A Tour through the Islands of Orkney and Shetland (Kirk-
wall, Orkney: W. Peace, 1879).
76. Chocolate, or what we would call cocoa.

four Children a housekeeper an Overseer and myself all white. But
how many blacks young and old the Lord only knows for I belive there
is about thirty that works every day in the field besides the servants
about the house ; such as Gardner, livery men and pages, Cooks,
washer and dresser, sewster and waiting girle. They wash here the
whitest that ever I seed for they first Boyle all the Cloaths with soap,
and then wash them, and I may put on clean linen every day if I
please. My school is a neate little House 20 foot long and 12 foot wide
and it stands by itself at the end of an Avenue of planting about as far
from the main house as Rob.[t] Forbes's[77] is from the burn, and there
comes a bonny black bairn every morning to clean it out and make my
bed, for I sleep in it by myself. I have a verry fine feather bed under
me, and a pair of sheets, a thin fold of a Blanket and a Cotton bed
spread is all my bed cloaths, and I find them just enough.   as for
myself I supose you wou'd scarce know me now, there being nothing
either brown, blew, or black about me but the head and feet, I being
Dressed in short cloath Coat, vest Coat, and britches all made of
white cotton without any lyning and thread stockins and wearing my
own hair curled round like a wigg.   at present a suite of Cloaths costs
five and twenty shillings here of making which I really think verry high.
    . . . I thank God I want for nothing that is necessary, But it brings
tears from my eyes to think of you and my infants when at the same
time it is not in my power at present to help you. But how soon I am
able you may depend upon it. I have litle else to say at present ; only
may the great God who governs all things wisely suport you and my
Infants, and guide and direct you in all your ways.
    . . . Pray write me verry particularly how it is with you and my D.[r]
Infants, likeways any thing that is remarcable in the Country. I shall
conclude this with offering my Comp.[ts78] to all enquiring freinds if I
have any and my sinceer prayers both evening and morn.[g] for you and
my Children. My Blessing to you all, is all at present from my Dearest
Jewell your ever aff.[te] Husband untill Death. Signed, John Harrower.
    Addressed, To Mrs. John Harrower in Lerwick, Zetland

2.[d] Letter from Virginia.

Belvidera 7 Aug.[t] 1774.

My Dearest Life
    I wrote you verry fully 14.th June last to which I refer you it being
verry full, but meeting Accidentally Just now with a Gentleman

77. The reference here is to an acquaintance of Harrower back in Lerwick. Harrower's
wife would undoubtedly have understood the comparison he makes here.
    78. Comp.[ts]: compliments.

bound to London, I have just time to write you a few lines while he is at Dinner to let you know that I am still in good health I thank God for it, and am hopefull this will find you and my Dr Infants the same. . . .

. . . I have Just time to aquant you that I am settled here as a Schoolmaster and can really say with great truth that I never lived a genteel regulare life untill now. I shall write you again soon verry fully and untill then I am with my blessing to you my Dear and my Dear Infants Your ever Aff^te husb^d untill death—Signed—John Harrower.

Adressed, To Mrs. John Harrower, Lerwick, Zetland.

Tuesday, August 16th.   Expecting a visit of one M^r. Kennedy an Edinburgher, a Cooper now in Fredericksburgh, I this day sent to Toun for a Quart of the Best Vestindia Rum which cost me Eighteen pence Virginia Currancy.

Wednesday, 17th.   This evening entred to school Thomas Brooks M^r. Spotswoods[79] carpenter in order to learn Writing and Arithmetick at nights and on Sundays.[80]

Freiday, 19th.   This day at noon Col^l. Willm. Daingerfield finished his wheat harvest by getting the last of it brought home and stacked.

Sunday, 21st.   At home teaching Brooks. Nothing remarcable.

Munday, 22d.   This afternoon Col^l. Daingerfield begun to sow wheat again for the next years crope. They sow their wheat here in the field where there Indian Corn is growing and plough it into the ground, so that the corn and wheat both Occupy the ground from this date untill January next and then the Corn is cut down.

Tuesday, 23d.   This day at noon was finished at one of Col^l. Daingerfields Barns a new Machine for beating out of wheat.   it is a circle of 60 feet diameter in the center of which their is a paul [pole?] fixed in the ground from which there goes three beams that reach the outer edge of the great circle and betwixt the outer ends of them are fixed four rollers, each roller having 320 spokes in it, they are 6 feet long, vizt. the rollers, and goes round upon a floor of 3 Inch plank of 7 feet long from the outer edge of the great circle and round the outer ends of the floor plank there is a thin plank upon it's edge and round the inner edge the same which keeps in the wheat.   the Machine is drawn round by 4 Horses and beats out 100 Bushels of wheat every day. It was begun 1st instant.

Sunday, 28th.   At home all day teaching Brooks.

79. Presumably Alexander Spotswood of Newport, grandson of a Virginia governor.
80. Notice Harrower's willingness to work (and earn money) on the sabbath.

Sunday, September 11th. D?. teaching Brooks. at 1 pm came M.ʳ Kennedy from Fredericksburgh here to see me and after we had dined we ended the Quart of Rum I Bought 16.ᵗʰ Last M?..

Tuesday, October 4th. Went to Fredericksb.ᵍ and seed a Horse Race for a Hundred Guineas, Gained by M.ʳ Fitchews Horse.

Wednesday, 5th. This day a Horse race at Fredericksburg for Fifty pound, and it was gain'd by a Horse belonging to Col.ˡ Tailo.

Thursday, 6th. This day a Horse race at Fredericksburg for Fifty pound, and it was gained by a Horse belonging to M.ʳ Fitchew.

Freiday, 7th. The race this day at Fredericksburg for Fifty pound was gained again by another Horse belonging to M.ʳ Fitchew.

Saturday, 8th. This day the races at Fredericksburg was finished and this night finishes the Puppet shows, roape dancings &c, which has continowed every night this week in town. I only seed the purse of a Hundred Guineas run for, and that day I hade the Misfortune to have my Horse, saddle and bridle stole from me, while I was doing some business in town. And I never could hear, nor get any intelligence of either of them again.

Sunday, 23d. At church but there was no sermon only prayers. This day I carried home a Westcoat with a silver sprig through a strip'd white satine and Padasoy silk, which I had formerly bought made as it was being nothing worse than new for 8/6 Virginia Currancy, and a Brass Inkholder with a penknife in it bought at 1/6 C.ʸ.

Monday, 31st. This morning two Carpenters was put to new weather board my house on the outside with featherage plank, and to new plaster it on the Inside with shell lime.

Tuesday, November 1st. This day Col.ˡ William Daingerfield finished sowing his Wheat, having sown in all this year 160½ bushels. This day I eat extream good green Pease they being the second croap this season. In the afternoon they began to gather new corn and bro.ᵗ home 8 Ba.ˡˡˢ [81] at night from 1000 Corn hills.

Sunday, 27th. This day at Church and heard Sermon by Mr. Muree[82] his text was in Hebrews 13.ᵗʰ Chap : and 18.ᵗʰ verse. Bought a hanging lock for my Chest at 7½ Currancy.

Rec.ᵈ from Colonel Daingerfield New Coat and veastcoat of Claret couler'd Duffel.

Tuesday, December 6th. Wrote home—3d letter from Virginia.

---

81. Barrels.
82. Rev. James Marye was rector of St. George's Parish from 1767 to 1780. He was the son of Rev. James Marye, a Huguenot refugee.

Belvidera 6th Decr. 1774.

My Dearest Life,

Since my aravil here I wrote you 14th June and 7th Augt last to both which I shall partly refer you. I now rite you with a shaking hand and a feeling heart to enqair of your and my Dr Infants welfare, this being the return of the day of the year on which I was obliged to leave you and my Dr Infants early in the morning which day will be ever remembred by me with tears untill it shall please God to grant us all a happy meeting again. I trust in the mercies of a good God this will find you and my Dr Infants in perfect health as I am and have been ever since I came here, for neither the heat in summer nor what I have as yet felt of the cold in winter gives me the least uneasiness I thank God for it. About 20 days ago I only laid aside my summer dress, and put on a suit of new Claret Coulerd Duffle neatly mounted but no lyning in the Coat only faced in the breasts. I wrote you in my first letter, that I was designed Please God to prepare a way for you and my Infants in this Country ; And I begg youll give me your thoughts fully upon it, in your first letter after receipt of this with respect to your moving here. If you do your method must be thus ; Take your Passage to Leith, from thence go to Glasgow and from that to Greenock where you will ship for this country. But this you are not to attemp untill I have your thoughts upon it and I send you a recomendation to a Merch^t in Glasgow and cash to bear your expences. I have as yet only ten scollars One of which is both Deaff and Dumb and his Father pays me ten shilling per Quarter for him he has been now five M^{os} [83] with [me] and I have brought him tolerably well and understands it so far, that he can write mostly for anything he wants and understands the value of every figure and can work single addition a little.   he is about fourteen years of age. Another of them is a young man a house Carpenter who attends me every night with candle light and every Sunday that I don't go to Church for which he pays me fourty shillings a year. He is Carpenter for a gentleman who lives two miles from me and has Thirty pound a year, free bedd and board.

The Col^{ls} Children comes on pretty well.   the Eldest is now reading verry distinctly in the Psalter according to the Church of England and the other two boys ready to enter into it ; the Col^l. and his Lady being extreamly well satisfied w^t my Conduct in every respect ; On 31st Jully last Mrs Daingerfield was deliv^d of a fourth son who is now

83. M^{os}: months.

my nameson. I am now verry inpatient to hear from you and I [beg]
of you not to slip a Packqut without writting me.[84] . . .

You no doubt have heard of the present disturb.[s] Betwixt Great Britain and the Collonys in N. America, Owing to severall Acts of Parliment latly made greatly infringing the rights and Liberties of the
Americans, and in order to enforce these Acts, The Harbour and Toun
of Boston are at present blockt up by a fleet and armie under the
Command of Gen.[l] Gage. The Americans are determined to Act with
Caution and prudence in this affair, and at same time are resolved not
to lose an inch of their rights or liberties, nor to submit to these Acts.
And in order to enforce a repeal of them, A Generall Congress was
held at Philadelphia by Delegates from the following Provinces Viz.[t]
New Hampshire, Massachusetts Bay, Rode Island and Providence
Plantations, Connicticut, New York, New Jersey, Pennsylvania, The
Countys of Newcastle, Kent, and Sussex on Delewar, Maryland, Virginia, North Carolina, and South Carolina. The Delegates were chosen from the Houses of Burges of each of the above Collonys and met
on the 5th Sept.[r] last and continued sitting untill the last of Oct.[r85] And
it is resolved that they will allow no goods to be imported into America
from Great Britain, Ireland, or any of the Islands thereto belonging a[ft]
the 1[th] Ins[t86]   Nor will they export from America to Great Britain or
Ireland or any of the Islands thereto belonging any goods after the 1[st]
Dec.[r] 1775 during which time any that are indebted to Great Britain
may pay up their ballances. Ma[n]y and pretty are the resolves of August Assembly, but room wou'd fail me here to insert them. By the
Congress the Bostonians are desired not to leave the Toun nor to give
any offence to Gen.[l] Gage or the troops under his Command, But if he
or they offers to commit the least Hostielyties in order to enforce any
to the Obedience of these Acts, they are to repel force by force and
the Bostonians can raise in their Collony in 24 Hours warning ods of
60 M men[87] well disiplined and all readdy provided w.[t] arms and amu-
nition. And the resolves of the Congress every one of the above Collonys and each man in every Collony are determined to abide by. And
it is my oppinion that the laboring part and poor of Boston are as well
supplied at present by controbutions sent free to them from the other

84. Harrower is advising his wife not to let a packet ship sail without sending him a response to his letter.

85. The reference here is to the First Continental Congress, whose actions Harrower followed in newspapers.

86. 1.st Ins.[t]: first of this month.

87. 60 M undoubtedly means 60,000.

Collonys as when their trade was oppen. Mr Daingerfield this year for
his own hand gives them fifty Bushels of wheat and One Hundred
Bushels of Indian Corn, By which ye may Judge of the rest.[88]

The 19th August last, Mr Daingerfield finished his wheat hearvest
and began to plow and sow wheat again for the next crop . . . and after
sowing 260 Bushels finished it in the 1st of Nov.^r.   they are now gathering Indian Corn of which he will have better than 4000 bushels 3000
of which he will Use for his Nigers and horses, the rest for sale ; so
much for American and Plantation news the Veracity of which you
may depend upon and may show the same to any of your freinds or
well wishers. . . .

. . . Pray my Dearest let me know what my Dr Boys and Girle are
doing. I hope Jock and George are still at school and I begg of you
to strain every nerve to keep them at it untill I am able to assist
you, for he who has got education will always gain Bread and to
spare, and that in a genteel way in some place or other of the World.
I supose Betts is at home with yourself, but pray keep her tight to
her seam and stockin and any other Housold affairs that her years
are capable of and do not bring her up to Idleness or play or going
about from house to house which is the first inlet in any of the sex to
laziness and vice. Send me an Acco.^t of their Ages from the Bible
which ye may do verry short by saying Jo : Born ——— day Nov. 1762
Geo : Born &c.^{ca}

I yet hope please God, if I am spared, some time to make you a
Virginian Lady among the woods of America which is by far more
pleasent than the roaring of the raging seas round abo't Zetland, And
yet to make you eat more wheat Bread in your old age than what you
have done in your Youth. But this I must do by carefullness, industry
and a Close Application to Business, which ye may take notice of in
this letter I am doing Sunday as well as Saturday nor will I slip an honest method nor an hour whereby I can gain a penny for yours and my
own advantage.

There grows here plenty of extream fine Cotton which after being
pict clean and readdy for the cards is sold at a shilling the pound ; and
I have at this time a great high Girl Carline as Black as the . . . spinning some for me for which I must pay her three shillings the pound
for spinning it for she must do it on nights or on Sunday for any thing
I know notwithstanding she's the Millers wife on the next plantation.
But Im determined to have a webb of Cotton Cloath According to my
own mind, of which I hope you and my infants shall yet wear apart ;

88. Virginians made substantial contributions to assist the Bostonians in this period.

I cou'd write to you for a week for it gives me pleaser while I am writting to you, But as room fails me I must conclude with offering my good wishes to your Broth.^{r}, M.^{r} and Mrs Vance, M.^{r} and Mrs Forbes and Mr Ferguson[89] if deserving at your hand with my Comp.^{ts} to all who asks for me. And my sinceer prayers to God for you and my Dr Children and belive me to be ever while I have breath, My Dearest Jewell, your Aff.^{te} husb.^{d} till death. Signed J. H. Addressed to Mrs John Harrower in Lerwick Zetland By Edinburgh, North Britain. . . .

Wednesday, 14th. This day Mr Daingerfield hade 35 Hoggs Killed weighting at an average about 150 lb. and they are to serve for salt Beacon untill the return of next year this time. all the Hams and Shoulders are cured with salt peter. Sold ½ doz.^{n} horn Buttons at 3¾.

Tuesday, 20th. last night I dreamt that my wife came to me here, and told me she had sent Johnnie and Bettie to Deall to stay and left George in the house with M. J. the servant.[90]

Sunday, 25th. Christmas day, stayed at home all day along w.^{t} the Overseer and Childreen because I hade no saddle to go to the Church with. In the morning the Col.^{l} Ordred up to school two Bottles of the best Rum and some suggar for me.

Munday, 26th. This forenoon the Col.^{l} wou'd have me to take his saddle and ride to Toun and Amuse myself, and when I was going gave me Six Shillings for pocket money. I went to Toun and Dined in a private house and after buying 1½ Doz.^{n} Mother of Pearle buttons for my white morsyld Vest I return'd home in the evening.

Tuesday, 27th. St. Johns day. This day a Grand Lodge in Toun,[91] And the whole went to Church in their Clothing and heard sermon.

Thursday, 29th. I began to keep school. . . .

Tuesday, January 10th, 1775. This day Thos Brooks who has atten[d]ed ever night and on Sundays left school being obliged to go 40 miles up the country to work. at same time he gave me an order on Col.^{l} Daingerfield for £1. 10. 8. Curr.^{y} of which £1. 5. 2 was for teaching him.

89. These are all prominent Lerwick friends of John and Ann Harrower. James Vance was married to Barbara Craigie, Ann Harrower's sister, and William Ferguson was the brother-in-law of James Craigie, Ann Harrower's brother.

90. Deall is a village north of Lerwick. Johnnie, Bettie, and George are Harrower's children.

91. Always a day of special festivity at Fredericksburg, ending in a ball at the Sun Rise Tavern.

Saturday, 21st. Some time ago I having got a present of piece of Lead coul.^d Cloath from Miss Lucy Gaines⁹² I got made in a Vest by Kidbeck the Taylor for which I have this day paid him 3/ 1½ Cur.^y.

Sunday, 22nd. This day at Church in Town and heard Mr Maree preach Text 2.^d Cor.^s 4 Chap : and 18.th Verse.

Tuesday, 31st. 1 pm yesterday Ja.^s and Wm Porters, sons of Mr William Porter Merch.^t in Fredericksb.^g came here to School.

Tuesday, February 14th. This day the Col.^l on finding more wheat left among the straw then should be blamed Mr Lewis the Overseer for his carelessness, upon which Mr Lewis seem'd verry much enraged for being spoke to and verry sawcily threw up all the keys he hade in charge and went off ; upon which the Col.^l sent for me and delivered me the keys of the Barn and begged I would assist him in his business untill he got another Overseer.

[Wednesday], 15th. This morning the Col.^l sent to scholl for me, and begg'd me to go to Snowcreek Barn and deliver the wheat that was there first to the Vessel who was come to receive the whole of it. She was a schooner of 120 Tun M.^{rs} name Jno Lurtey.

Tuesday, 21st. Empl.^d as Yesterday. This day the Col.^l engaged a young man for an Overseer Whose name is Anthony Fraser.

Thursday, 23d. This day finised trading out wheat,⁹³ also deliv.^d the last of it having delivered One thousand five hundred Bushels and 240 Bushels formerly deliv.^d by Mr Lewis which with 260 Bushels sown makes 2000 Bushels besides serving the Famely and some bushels sold to people who works on the plantation.

Munday, 27th. This day Mr Fraser came here and entred to take his charge as Overseer, and he is to have his bed in the school along with me.   he appears to be a verry quiet young man and has hade a tolerable education.   his Grandfather came from Scotland. . . .

Saturday, [March] 25th. At noon went to Newport to see Mr Martin Heely schoolmaster to Mr Spotswood's Children, and after Dinner I spent the afternoon with him in conversation and hearing him play the Fiddle. He also made a Niger come and play on an Instrument call'd a Barrafou. The body of it is an oblong box with the mouth up and stands on four sticks put in bottom, and cross the [top] is laid 11 lose sticks upon [which] he beats.

Sunday, 26th.   9 AM Set out on horseback for Mount Church in Caroline County in Company with Mr Richards, Mrs Richards, M.^r

---

92. The housekeeper for the Daingerfields.

93. Trading: read as treading. Horses tread on the wheat to separate grains from chaff—an early form of threshing.

Martin Heely, M.ʳ Anthony Frazer and Miss Lucy Gaines. And heard
M.ʳ Waugh preach his text being the 1.ˢᵗ V. of the 12.ᵗʰ Chapter of Ec-
clesiastes. After which we all returned to M.ʳ Richard before 3 pm
where we dined and spent the afternoon. From Belvidera to Mount
Church is 10 Miles.

Saturday, April 1st.   At 6 pm M.ʳ Martin Heely schoolmaster at
Newport for M.ʳ Spotswoods Children came her to pay me a Visite and
staid with me all night.

Sunday, 9th.   This day a good number of Company dined here
among which was M.ʳ and M.ʳˢ Porter from Town, who heard their eldest son read and seemed verry well pleased with his performance
since he came to me ; Myself at home all day.

Freiday, 14th.   This being good Freiday, I broke up school for Eas-
ter Holly day, and the Col.ˡˢ three sons went to Town with M.ʳ Porter's
two sons this forenoon I went a money hunting[94] but catc'd none.

Saturday, 15th.   This forenoon I went a Money Hunting again an
other way but hade no better success then yesterday. This afternoon
M.ʳ Frazer went up the Country to see his Mother and friends, and I
give out corn for him, untill he returns again.

Munday, 17th.   At 8 AM I rode to Town in order to see the boys and
Amuse myself fore some hours. On my Aravel in Town the first thing
I got to do was to dictate and write a love letter from M.ʳ Anderson, to
one Peggie Dewar at the Howse of M.ʳ John Mitchel at the Wilder-
ness. After that I went to M.ʳ John Glassell's store to enquire for letters
from home but found none ; here I mett with the Col.ˡ who gave me two
pair brown thread stockins for my summers wear. At 2 pm I dined
with him in M.ʳ Porters, and soon after Returned home.

Thursday, 20th.   This morning all the boys came to school again at
their Usual hour. On tuesday last was missed out of the pasture a
breeding mare.   search being made fore her by the Overseer he
found this afternoon the Neiger fellow who hade rode her off and after
riding her about 24 Miles from the Plantation turned her loose in
the high road.   he is a Blacksmith by trade and belongs to and works
at a Plantation of M.ʳ Corbins, and after he had confessed the fact
M.ʳ Frazer ower Overseer stript him to the [skin] and gave him 39
laches with Hickry switches that being the highest the Law allows at
one Wheeping.

Munday, 24th.   This morning the Col.ˡ began to have his Indian
Corn planted. . . . Some are now done planting of corn.   last night
Mr. Frazer found the Mare that was rode off and brought her home.

---

94. Money hunting: bill collecting. Harrower was trying to get paid for his teaching.

Freiday, 28th. This day by an express from Boston we are informed of an engagement betwixt the British troops and the Bostonians, in which the former were repuls'd with loss, but no particulars as yet.[95]

Saturday, 29th. This day there was at Fredricksburgh about 600 men under Arms composed of the independent companys of severall Counties. they designed to have Marched to Williamsburg and to have made the Governor deliver back some poweder he caused to be Clandestinlly carried off, but was prevented by an express from the speacker with advice that the Governor was readdy to give it up on ten minutes warning.

Wednesday, May 3d. This day the Col! bought and rec^d ten bushels of Span^s Salt for ten bushels Indian Corn. at noon the Col^ls Nigers finised planting Indian Corn having planted about 300 Acres of land, which took about 25 Bushels of sead.

Saturday, 6th. This afternoon I planted 41 hills of grownd with Cotton seed.

Sunday, 7th. At 2 houses this day seeking money that was owing me but got none.

Munday, 8th. This morning I planted 22 Hills of grownd with Water Mellon and Mush Mellon Seed. This afternoon I eat ripe strawberries.

Saturday, 20th. This day I wrote [a] letter to Sam! Edge for Twenty shillings that has been due me since the 25th Novr 1774. . . .

This afternoon I was invited to a Gentlemans house in order to eat plenty of ripe Cherries.

Sunday, 21st. This day I hade sent me a present from Mrs Porter in Fred^g two silk Vestcoats and two pair cotton britches all of them having been but verry little wore by Mr Porter.

Saturday, 27th. This afternoon I rode to Town and bought at Mr Porters Store 2 handkerchiefs and one Yd Bedd Tyke[96] at 2/2d Curr^y being all 5/2d Curr^y. At same time rec^d a letter from my Wife dated 1st March 1775. It came under cover to Mr John Glassell Merch^t in Toun and cost me 1/3d Curr^y. At same time rec^d from Thos Anderson a pair of new Shoes on the Col^ls Acco^t.

Saturday, June 3d. At 9 AM Mr Porter's two son's was sent for and they went to Toun to keep Whitsuntide holliday.

Wednesday, 7th. Began to keep school again.

95. The reference here is to the battles of Lexington and Concord on April 19.
96. One yard of bed-ticking.

Freiday, 16th. This day at 9 AM Col? Daingerfield set out for his Q.[97] down the Country at Chickahommanie to receive his Cash for the last years of produce of said plantation from John Miller his Overseer there.

Sunday, 18th. This day at 10 AM went to John Pattie's and rec.d 6/ for teaching his William ¼ of a year and from [thence] to Thomas Evans's and rec.d 20/ for teaching his Daught.r Sarah for One Year.

Saturday, July 1st. At noon I went to Frederick.g and bought 15 bigg Double Guilt buttons at 4/9 One hank silk twist at 1/ and one ounce brown thread at 6d. my pocket expence this day 1/ . I returned home an houre before sun down.

Freiday, 7th. This day at sunset Col? Daingerfield finished cutting down 260 Bushels sowing of wheat in fifteen days with seven Cradlers and it was done in 6 days less time than 203 bushels sowing was last Harvest and with fewer hands. For this Harvest his money payments to Out labourers is reduced no less than £18.4 6d. lower than it was last and at same time the Wheat better put up all which is chiefly owing to the Activity of Anthony Frazer the present Overseer.

Saturday, 8th. This moring began to bring Wheat to the Barn with two Carts Six Oxen in the One and three Horses in the Other.

Sunday, 16th. This day I went to Church in Toun and heard sermon preached by one M.r Murray his text was Mat : 6.th and 24.th V. I was no pocket expence this day.

Wednesday, 19th. This day I was informed that M.rs Daingerfield had made a Complaint upon me to the Col? for not waiting after Breackfast and dinner (sometimes) in order to take the Children along with me to scholl ; I imagine she has a grudge against me since the middle of Feb.y last the reason was, that one night in the Nursery I wheep'd Billie for crying for nothing and she came in and carried him out from me. Some nights after he got into the same humour and his Papa The Col? hearing him call'ed me and Asked why I cou'd hear him do so and not correct him for it ; Upon that I told him how M.rs Daingerfield had behaved when I did correct him. At that he was angry w.t her.

Saturday, 22d. On Saturd.y 13 Ins.t some words happned betwixt John M.cDearmand and the Col? about John's not being expedecious enough About stacking and requiring too many hands to attend him upon which John left the work immedeatly and has not returned

97. Q.r: quarter. Large plantations in Virginia were commonly divided into quarters. Slaves and an overseer resided on particular parcels of land, often at some distance from the master's house on the home plantation.

since. And by the Acco^{ts} in my hands I find the Col^o is in Johns debt
£9. 10. 9 Virg^a Currancy.

Sunday, 23d.   Mrs Porter having been here all night from Town ; I
this day after breackfast brought all the boys with their books into the
passage to the Col^o who heard each of them read and was highly
pleased with their performance. Mrs Porter likeways told that her sons
did me great honour ; as well as the rest.

Wednesday, 26th.   This day at noon was finished the bringing hom
and stacking the Col^{os} Wheat having 18 Stacks of 100 Bushels each by
Computation besides a Large Barn fill'd up to the roof. It was brought
home this year in 15 days less time than it was last year. I this day ate
Watermelon of my own planting it being the first I ate this season.

Wednesday, August 2d.   Yesterday the Col^o Began to Sow Wheat
for the ensewing croop. This day came to School Wm John and Lucy
Patties, and are to pay conform to the time they Attend.   expecting
a Visit of Mr Kenedy sent to Town for a bottle of Vest India Rum which
cost me 1/3 Currancy.

Tuesday, 22d.   This morning the Col^o began to trade out wheat in
the Yard with horses which is done in the following manner Viz^t They
take wheat from the stack and spreads it about eight foot broad in a
large circle, and with as many horses as they have they ride upon it
round and round and 3 or 4 men keep always turning and stirring it up,
and by this method they with 10 or 12 horses will trade out 100 Bushels in a day.   where they trade Just now is 300 feet Circumference.

Munday, 28th.   Coppy of my 4th Letter wrote this day to my wife.

My Dearest Life
Your most agreeable favours I rec^d 27th May last, which was dated
1st March, And you may belive me it gave me the greatest satisfaction
I have hade for twelve months past to hear from your own hand that
you my Dearest Jewell and my sweet Infants are and has been in a
good state of health since I left you, As I still am and has been for the
above time, For which we have all great reason to render all due
praise to that ever Glorious Being who wisely governs and directs all
our Acctions ; And may he for the sake of him who suffered on the
Cross for all sinners continoue to protect and direct you and all that
conserns us for the better. I would have wrote you sooner after the
recept of yours, had I not been waiting an Answer to a verry long letter I wrote 6th Decr last which I find had not come to your hand when
you wrote me but am hopefull it has long before now and an Answer
to it on its way here. When you write me I intreat you to do it on a

sheet of the largest post paper you can get and leave no waste room in it, as the postage is no more than if it was three lines on ¼ sheet. And sure I am you can find subject enough to fill a sheet of paper as you well know that whatever comes from your hand must be agreeable. . . .

I begg you to advise with your Brother on that paragraph of my last letter with respect to your moving here, and I have likeways now begged him to write me his thoughts on the same subject, so that I expect you will both write me fully on recept of this, and I begg you to put him in mind of it. I have also wrote him to be assisting to you, untill such time as the ports are oppen for trade betwixt Britain and the Collonies and the disputes made up betwixt them, for untill that is done there is no such thing as remitting money or goods from any part of America to Britain, which gives me a good deall of trouble on your Acc.ᵗ of which your Broth.ʳ can more fully inform you of, As also of the engagements that has been betwixt the British troops and the forces of the united Collonies before Boston as room wou'd faill me here to do it. As to M.ʳ Forbes pray make my Compt.ˢ to him and spouse and tell him from me that I make no doubt from the information I have of his making good bread in this Country for that a Journaman Bricklayer here has no less than five shillings a day Currancy which is equall to four Shillings St.ʳ. And I am aquanted with an Undertaker in that branch of business who is now set down on good Estate and rides in his Chair every day. But if he was to come over he must resolve to give closs application to business and keep from drinking. About 7 months ago a Gentleman in Fredericksb.ᵍ hade his two sons taken from the high school there and put under my care for which he pays me £5 a year. He is an English man himself and his Lady from Edinburgh,[98] and I have the pleasure to have given the parents such satisfaction that I hade sent me in a present two silk vestcoats and two pair of britches ready to put on for changes in summer. I observe my Dear Dogg George writes me his name at the foot of your letter, But I am surprized that you take no notice of Jack and Bettie. But I hope you will not faill to be more particular about them in your next, and give my blessing to them all and tell them from me that I hope they will be obedient to you in every respect and mind their books. Before I get things brought to a bearing was any vessell by chance to put into Bressaysound[99] bound for any part of Virginia or for Pawtomack river which divides this Collony from Maryland,[100] I

98. These two are Mr. and Mrs. Porter.
99. The harbor of Lerwick.
100. The reference here is to the Potomac River.

wou'd have you at all events Make your Brother apply for your Passage
with the Children and a servant and imediatly dispose of every article
in the house your Feather Bedds Bedding and Cloaths excepted, and
if any money to spare lay it out in Linen ;[101] and write me imediatly on
your Aravell here by post and I shou'd soon be with you. May God
grant that such a cast may happen to you. I must now conclude by
offering my Compt.s to M.r and M.r.s Vance, and all who enquires for me
in a friendly way, with my blessing to you my sweet life and my Dear
Infants is all at present from, My Dearest Jewell, your ever affectionate Husband while—Signed J. H.

Belvidera 28th Aug.t 1775. Addressed to M.r.s John Harrower in Lerwick, Zetland, by Edinburgh, North Britain.[102] . . .

Saturday, September 2d.   At noon rode to Town and delivered two
letters to Mr. Henry Mitchell, One for my wife and one for her
Brother Cap.t James Craigie After which I retur.d home by sundown.

Wednesday, 6th.   This day I was informed by M.r Frazer that M.r.s
Daingerfield talking to them of me that morning about some Glue dis-
resptfully calld me Old Harrower by which and her behaveiour to myself I find her grudge continous tho she has not courage to say any
thing to myself well knowing she has [no] foundation to go upon.

Sunday, 10th.   This day came Dick a Serv.t belonging to M.r Anderson from Toun and a Comerade of his to see me and Brought me a pair
new shoes and a pair for M.r Frazer also a Bottle Vest India Rum which
we drank in school in Company with M.r Frazer.

Munday, 11th.   This day sent my letter to wife to Fredericksb.g by
M.r Frazer and gave him 1/6 to give with it at the post office as Postage
to New York. But M.r Brown my friend the Clark told M.r Frazer he
wou'd send it home free for me by a Ship going to saile.

Friday, 15th.   Wrote my 5th Letter this day from Virginia, This being the Coppy.

My Dearest Life, Yours of the 12th May last I received 2.d Ins.t immediatly after sending off one for you and one for your Aff.tt brother
dated 28th last M.o Both which will come to your Hand I imagine at the
same time that this will as I am obliged to send this to New York by

101. Linen was one of the chief articles of domestic manufacture and export from Shetland in the eighteenth century.

102. Excluded here is a letter Harrower wrote the same day to his wife's brother, James
Craigie. He explained his reasons for leaving Lerwick and asked for Craigie's help in assisting the migration of his wife and children.

post in order to come to London by the Pacquet, There being no more Opportunities from this Collony to Glasgow this season, by reason that the Nonimportation and Nonexportation Acts of the Continental Congress now takes place and will continue untill the disputes betwixt Great Britain and the Colonys be settled. And I intreat you imediatly on receipt of this letter to wait on your Brother and show it to him, and he will more fully inform you of these Matters than room will permit me to do here, As my principal Design of writing you this so soon after my last is to make you as easy as possible I can, both with respect to my not sending for you and making you a remittance. As to the first of these I cou'd not be certain if you wou'd come to this Country or not untill I rec^d your last letter. But as I find by it you are satisfied to come here, you may believe me nothing in this world can give me equall satisfaction to my having you and my Dr Infants with me. As a proof of which I have ever signified the same in my letters to your brother. And I now declare unto you as I sinceerly write from my heart before God, that I will how soon I am able point out the way to you how you may get here, and at same time make you what remittance I can in order to Assist you on your way. But you must consider this as I hade not a shilling in my pocket when I left you It must take me some time befor I can be able to make you a remittance. Therefore I even pray you for Gods sake to have patience and keep up your heart and no means let that fail you : For be asured the time is not Longer to you than me, And the National disputes and the stopage of trade betwixt this and the Mother Country if not soon settled will of course make the time longer as your bro^r will inform you. As to your Jocks upon me with respect to my getting a Virginian Lady it is the least in all my thoughts and am determined to leave that Jobb for you by aiding your sons with your advice to them in their choise of wifes among the Virginian Ladys : For I am resolved (as at first) to do as much for you as God is pleased to put in my power.

I am glad you are moved to a place of the Toun, as you say agreeable to your own disposition. . . . At same time it gives me great satisfaction to hear the Children are all well, and that Jock is still at Walls.[103] I hope he is now making some progress in his Education, and am hopefull George will do the same. As for Betts Im not afraid of her considering whose hands she is under. I have nothing further to add at present only I again begg of you to keep a good heart and do the best you can untill it please God to enable me to assist you and for aught I

---

103. Jock is a nickname for Harrower's son John. Walls is located on the west of the island of Mainland, about ten miles from Lerwick.

think you shall hear no more from me untill I be able to remitt you either more or less.

My Compliments and sinceer good wishes to your Brother M.[r] Craigie, his spouse and Family likeways my Comp.[ts] to M[r] and M[rs] Vance, and all others wh[o] may enquire for me in a friendly way ; with my sinceer love and prayers to God for you my Dearest Jewell and Children is all at present from your ever Aff.[tt] Husb.[d] signed J. H. Belvidera 15.th Sept.[r] 1775. Addressed to M.[rs] John Harrower in Lerwick Zetland by the New York Packet to London and by Edin.[r] North Britain.

Thursday, 28th.   This morning I rec.[d] from Benjamin Edge by the hand of his daughter two Dollars, one half and one Quarter Dollar being in all sixteen shillings and Sixpence in part payment for teaching his son and daughter. Same day I seed a Comp.[y] of 70 Men belonging to one of the Regiments of Regullars raised here for the defence of the rights and liberties of this Coll.[y] in particular and of North America in Generall. They were on their March to Williamsburg.

Thursday, October 12th.   Company here last night Viz.[t] Old M.[rs] Waller, her son and his wife and at school there M.[r] Heely Schoolmaster and M.[r] Brooks Carpenter and they w.[t] M.[r] Frazer and myself played whist and danced untill 12 OClock, M.[r] Heely the Fidle and dancing. We drank one bottle of rum in time. M.[r] Frazer verry sick after they went home.

Munday, 16th.   This morning 3 men went to work to break, swingle and heckle flax[104] and one woman to spin in order to make course linnen for shirts to the Nigers, This being the first of the kind that was made on the plantation. And before this year there has been little or no linnen made in the Colony.

Tuesday, 17th.   Two women spining wool on the bigg wheel and one woman spinning flax on the little wheel all designed for the Nigers.

Munday, 23d.   One Frieday last I lent to Miss Lucy one pair of my shoes to spin with. This day General Washintons Lady dined here, As did her son and Daug.[r] in Law, M.[rs] Spotswood, M.[rs] Campbell, M.[rs] Dansie, Miss Washington and Miss Dandrige, They being all of the highes Rank and fortunes of any in this Colony.

Saturday, 28th.   Last night came here to school M.[r] Heely and Tho.[s] Brooks in order to spend the evening. . . .

104. Flax is a fibrous plant grown to be made into cloth. The stems have long fibers that are broken, swingled, and hackled—all hand operations—in successive steps and then spun into linen yarn.

Thursday, November 9th. Upon Thursday 2^d Ins^t there was a Camp Marked out close at the back of the school for a Batalion of 500 private men besides officers and they imediatly began to erect tents for the same.[105] . . .

Sunday, 12th. This day a great number of company from Toun and Country to see the Camp four of which (Gentlemen) paid me a visite which put me to 1/3 expence for a bottle of rum. at noon by Accident one of the Captains tents was set on fire and all consumed but none of things of any Acco^t Lost.

Munday, 13th. This forenoon the Col^l sent a waggon Load of Turnups and Pitatoes to the Camp as a present for all the men.

Tuesday, 14th. All the minute-men in the Camp employed learning their exercise.

Wednesday, 15th. This morning I drank a small dram of rum made thick with brown suggar for the cold, it being the first dram I have drunk since I lived on the Plantation.

Thursday, 16th. The soldiers at muster.[106]

Freiday, 17th. The soldiers at D^o., and I left of going into the Nursery and taking charge of the children out of school.

Wednesday, 29th. This day the camp was brocke up and the whole Batallion dismissed. . . .

Saturday, December 2d. At noon went to Toun and seed two Companys of regulars from the Ohio among which was one real Indian. he was of a Yelow couler short brod faced and rather flat nosed, and long course black [hair] quite streight. he spoke verry good english. I staid in Toun all night and slept at Mr Andersons ; I bought from Mr Porter a black Silk Handkerchief at 5/.

Sunday, 3d. After breackfast I went and found out Miss Molly White and left with her cloth to make me two winter Stocks[107] and a stock to make them by. Dined in Toun, came home in the afternoon. . . .

Wednesday, January 10th, 1776. This day we hade the Confirmation of Norfolk being reduced to ashes by the Men of War and British Troops under Command of Lord Dunmore. It was the Largest Toun in the Collony and a place of great Trade, it being situated a little within the Capes. Severall Women and Child^n are killed.

---

105. An ordinance of the July Convention had provided for twenty days' drill on the part of the minutemen of each group of counties. The minutemen of the district composed of Caroline, Spotsylvania, King George, and Stafford counties numbered 500.

106. Soldiers at muster: on parade, at exercise.

107. Stocks: a kind of close-fitting neckcloth worn by men.

Saturday, 13th.   After 12 O Clock I went six Miles into the Forrest to one Daniel Dempsies to see if they wou'd spin three pound of Cotton to run 8 yds per lb., ⅔ of it belonging to Miss Lucy Gaines for a goun and ⅓ belonging to myself for Vestcoats, which they ag.ᵈ ¹⁰⁸ to do if I carried the cotton there on Saturd.ʸ 27.ᵗʰ Ins.ᵗ . . . .

Munday, 15th.   Miss Lucy spinning my croop of Cotton at night after her work is done ; to make me a pair of gloves.

Wednesday, 17th.   This evening Miss Lucy came to school with M.ʳ Frazer and me, and finished my croop of Cotton by winding it, after its being doubled and twisted the whole consisting of two ounces.

Tuesday, 23d.   This day I entred Edwin into the Latin Gramer.

Saturday, 27th.   After 12 pm I went to the forrest to the house of Daniel Dempsies and carried with me three pound of pick'd Cotton two of which belongs to Miss Lucy Gaines and one to me, which his wife has agreed to spin to run 8 Yd.ˢ per lb., I paing her five shillings per lb. for spinning it and it is to be done by the end of May next.

Tuesday, March 5th.   This morning Bathurest Daingerfield got don reading through the Bible and the Newtestament, and began to learn to write 15 Ult.º¹⁰⁹ I gave them Holyday this Afternoon.

Saturday, April 20th.   At noon I asked the Col.ˢ for a bottle of rum as I expected two Countrymen to see me tomorrow, which he verry cheerfully gave and desired me to ask him for one any time I wanted it and told me to take them to the Howse to dinner with me.   in the afternoon he, his Lady, and Daughter went over the river to M.ʳ Jones's in King George County.

Tuesday, 23d.   At noon rode to Town, got the Newspapers and settled with M.ʳ Porter for teaching his two sons 12 M.ºˢ when he verry genteely allowed me £6 for them, besides a present of two silk vests and two pair of Nankeen Breeches last summer and a Gallon of rum at Christenmass, both he and M.ʳˢ Porter being extreamly well satisfied with what I hade don to them.

Wednesday, 24th.   General Muster of all the County Malitia in Town today.   at Breackfast the Col.º desired me to go and see it if I pleased, But being in town yesterday I chose to stay to day with my boys.

Sunday, 28th.   this day came here to pay me a visit M.ʳ Reid from Mansfield and M.ʳ Scott from Toun and dined with me in the great house by the Col.ºˢ order, and after we hade spent the afternoon verry agreeably together they returned home in the evening.

108. Ag.ᵈ: agreed.
109. 15 Ult.º: the fifteenth of the previous month.

Sunday, May 5th.   Early this morning I went to M.ʳ McCalley's and entred his oldest son (about 8 years of age) to writting, stayed there all day and rode his horse home in the evening. The Col.º went to Newport and dinned there.

Tuesday, 7th.   Billie ended reading through his Bible.

Thursday, 9th.   After dinner I took the boys with me to Massaponacks Briges to see 56 prisoners that was taken at the late battle in North Carolina,[110] among them was a great many Emigrants from Scotland who were all officers. I talked with several of them from Ross Sh.ʳ and the Isle of Sky.

Freiday, 17th.   Gen.ˡˡ Fast by order of the Congress. I went to Church in Toun but no sarmon.   dined at M.ʳ McAlleys and came home in the evening. The Col.º and his lady at Mount C.ʰ.

Munday, 27th.   At 9 AM I went to M.ʳ McAlleys and staid teaching his Son and sister untill dark and then rode home bringing with me 1½ Yd. Linen for summer breeches. . . .

Saturday, [June] 8th.   At noon I went to M.ʳˢ Bataile's and entred two of her Daughters to writting, Viz. Miss Sallie and Miss Betty and continoued teaching them until night, when I agreed to attend them every Saturday afternoon and every other Sunday from this date until 8.ᵗʰ June 1777 (If it please God to spare me) for four pound Virginia currancy.

Sunday, 9th.   After breackfast I rode to M.ʳ McAlleys and teach'd his son to write untill 4 pm and then came home in the evening.

Freiday, 14th.   At noon Went to Jn.º McDearmons and had 6 Yd.ˢ stript Cotton warped for 2 Veastcoats and two handkerchiefs all prepared at my own expence.

Wednesday, 19th.   At noon went to snow creek and the boys and dined at the spring on Barbaque and fish. At 5 pm I went to M.ʳˢ Battaile and teac'd until ½ an hour past 7.

Wednesday, 26th.   At 5 pm I went to M.ʳ Becks and had a short Coat cut out of cotton cloth wove Jeans. I bought the cotton and paid for spinning it at the rate of 2/6 per lb. and one shilling per Yd. for weaving.

Sunday, July 7th.   This morning I rode to Mansfield and breackfast with M.ʳ Reid and stayed and dined with him and in the afternoon he and I rode to see the Rowgallies[111] that was building where we met with M.ʳ Anderson and Jacob Whitely and went to Town with them to Whitelys where we Joyned in Comp.ʸ with M.ʳ Wright and one M.ʳ

---

110. These were Tory prisoners taken in the Battle of Moore's Creek Bridge, February 27, 1776.

111. Rowgallies: row galleys to be used for defense on the Rappahannock River.

Bruce from King George.   about 11 pm we brock up and every one
went to his own home as I did.

Wednesday, 10th.   At 6 pm went to Mrs Battaile's and teach'd untill
sunset and then return'd home and soon after hea[r]d a great many
guns fired towards Toun.   about 12 pm the Col? Despatched Anth^y.
Frazer there to see what was the cause of [it] who returned, and informed him that there was great rejoicings in Toun on Acco^t of the
Congress having declared the 13 United Colonys of North America
Independent of the Crown of great Britain.[112]

Thursday, 25th.   I imployed this morn^g and forenoon getting Lead
off Snowcreek house.

John Harrower's diary trails off in July 1776, leaving numerous
unanswered questions. Did he succeed in bringing his wife and children to Virginia? Did he return to the Shetlands after his indenture
term was over? While the diary offers no clues, surviving correspondence provides sad answers.

Harrower died in April 1777, before he completed his indenture, of
an unidentified illness. A letter from Ann Harrower to William
Daingerfield indicates that Harrower's master had written her of his
death.[113] Harrower had managed in three years to save 70£ to bring
his family over to America, but he died before he was able to fulfill his
earnest wish. In the end, despite the evident advantages he enjoyed
compared with other indentured servants, John Harrower died apart
from his family in a strange land to which he had been driven by poverty and desperation. He shared more than he might have liked with
other immigrants to the British North American colonies in the eighteenth century.

112. This is the first news Harrower recorded of the Declaration of Independence, recently signed in Philadelphia.

113. Edward Miles Riley, ed., *The Journal of John Harrower: An Indentured Servant in
the Colony of Virginia, 1773–1776.* (Williamsburg, Va.: Colonial Williamsburg, 1963), ap-
pendix 1, pp. 164–65.

TWO

The Hollingworth Family Letters, 1827–1830

After independence the ethnic composition of immigrants to the United States did not change significantly until the 1830s, and in the 1820s British and Irish together constituted more than two-thirds of newcomers entering American ports.[1] Change was evident, however, as indentured servitude declined and with it the earlier preponderance of single males in the immigrant flow. Increasingly, whole families migrated, either together or sequentially.

One such family that was reunited on the American side of the Atlantic Ocean was the family of George and Betsey Hollingworth, originally from Huddersfield in the north of England. Two sons, Jabez and John, came first and settled in central Massachusetts, where they found employment in woolen mills, work they had done before immigrating. The two Hollingworths were soon joined by their parents, a sister, and other brothers. The letters—written primarily by one of the sons, Joseph—tell the story of a close-knit kin group, whose members worked together to provide for the family as a whole.

Like many other English immigrants in the early nineteenth century, the Hollingworths responded to the disruptions accompanying the dramatic expansion of the textile industry after 1790. Handloom weavers found their crafts undermined by the adoption of the power loom, while factory textile workers found themselves extremely vulnerable to cyclical fluctuations in the economy. Both groups migrated in substantial numbers to New England and Philadelphia, the two centers of the American textile industry in the first half of the nineteenth century.[2]

1. Leonard Dinnerstein and David M. Reimers, *Ethnic Americans: A History of Immigration*, 3d ed. (New York: Harper and Row, 1988), pp. 206–7.

2. Charlotte Erickson, "Who Were the English Emigrants in the 1820s and 1830s? A Preliminary Analysis," unpublished paper, 1977; David J. Jeremy, *Transatlantic Industrial Revolution: The Diffusion of Textile Technologies between Britain and America, 1790–1830s* (Cambridge, Mass.: M.I.T. Press, 1981), chaps. 8, 9.

The letters expressed a strong distaste for the English factory system, and at one point family members scouted some land in western New York, where they hoped to establish a utopian community along the lines of those pioneered by Robert Owen at New Lanark in Scotland. In the end, however, they remained in central Massachusetts and northern Connecticut, where they leased a woolen factory for a period of years. They did not escape the factory system, but they did become relatively independent, operating their own factory for a time instead of working for others. Their factory failed, however, revealing the precariousness of small entrepreneurs in the early industrial revolution.

The Hollingworth letters offer evidence of a family economy in operation, where all family members contributed to family needs as perceived by the patriarch, George Hollingworth. The family economy was not without friction, however. Son Joseph complained to an uncle (in his letter of November 7, 1829) that despite having worked considerable overtime in the mill, he had gotten only two dollars of his earnings for his own use. Joseph Hollingworth felt his father imposed upon him, but he did not have the nerve to confront him directly. In this letter we gain a rare glimpse into the immigrant family economy in the early factory system and the intergenerational conflict that remained common a century later when eastern and southern Europeans predominated in American immigrant communities.

JOHN HOLLINGWORTH TO WILLIAM RAWCLIFF

South Leicester April 1st 1827

Dear Uncle

I take the opportunity of writing to you to let you know that my Brother Jabez and I are in a good state of health at present and that we are doing all that lays in our power to accomplish the objects that induced us to leave Old England to brave the dangers of the Atlantic Ocean and to come to America that is to provide an happy asylum for our kindred our friends and ourselves, and it is our firm opinion that it will be best to form ourselves into a system after the manner of Robert Owen's plan,[3] that is to form ourselves into a society in common to

3. Robert Owen (1771–1858), after initiating reforms at his cotton mills in New Lanark, Scotland, had come to America in 1825 with his son, Robert Dale Owen, to establish a communal society at New Harmony, Indiana. When John Hollingworth was writing this letter, the Owens were about to conclude that the experiment at New Harmony was a failure. *Dictionary of National Biography*, vols. 7, 14.

help and assist each other and to have one common stock for it is the unatural ideas of thine and mine that produces all the evils of tyranny slavery poverty and oppression of the present day. My Brother Jabez, Cousins George and James Hollingworth Joseph Kenyon and I have made a contract for a parcel of land consisting of 200 Acres together with a house and other nessasaryes and there is 24 Acres of it cleared. All situated in the Township of Yorkshire in the County of Chataraugus in the State of New York within 40 Miles of the Town of Buffalo which is situated on the head of the great Westren Canal.[4] The farm has two public roads crossing each other at right Angles and runing on the east and north sides of the farm. There is also a water privelege on the same and with your assistance we think of erecting a small Factory at some futer period. There is also a branch of the Westren Canal in agitation to come within 2½ miles of the same place. Now we should wish you, my Father, my Uncle John Hollingworth and my Uncle John Kenyon to meet together and discus the subject form such plans as you think most proper and assist each other to utmost of your power for

Take this maxim old and young
Friendship and union makes us strong.

I should earnestly wish you to acceed to our plans and to fall in cooperative with us. . . .

. . . It is our intention to each of us to do all that lays in our power to accomplish our object and to keep regular accounts of our expences and when we get setteled to make a fair calculation and see what one has expended more than another so that they may have Intrest according to the money expended and the remainder to be divided equally amongest the members of the Community yearly which they may put in again as stock.[5] As to myself I still am working in the Card Room at Slubing and if all be well I intend to remaine at the same work till we have accomplished our undertaking and by that means I may be usefull at some future time in the same business.[6] My Brother Jabez is

4. Westren Canal: Erie Canal.

5. These plans for a cooperative farm south of the Erie Canal did not materialize, and the Hollingworths remained at work in woolen mills in central Massachusetts and northern Connecticut.

6. The carding machine, or "card" (hence "card room"), consisted of one large and several small water-powered cylinders clothed with thousands of short, protruding wires that separated and straightened the fibers. The process produced short rolls of wool as long as the card was wide. These rolls were prepared for spinning by piecing them together and drawing them out on a hand-powered slubbing billy. While a boy pieced the rolls together at the feed end of the billy, John Hollingworth would manipulate the carriage of the billy to twist and draw out the rolls into a continuous strand known as roving.

still working in the Machine Shop[7] but I expect we shall send him together with another of our company who may be geting the least
wages to the farm to be prepareing for the reception of us all which I
hope will not be long before we be there and then I hope the following
lines from Doctor Watts will be applicable to us[8]

> Blest are the sons of peace,
> Whose hearts and hopes are one,
> Whose kind designs to serve and please
> Thro' all their actions run. . . .

Give my tender love to my Wife and tell her that although she may yet
be in England through a peice of Villany that has been practiced upon
me that I have not forgot her, and that she must make herself as content as she possiabley can as I hope we shall not be long before we see
one another again in a place where we shall be free from the oppression of the Manufactureing System.

> I remaine with respect your most
> Affectionate Nephew John Hollingworth

Send me word how my little Mary and William are and how you
all are.[9]

N.B.   If you should approve of our plan I would advise you to loose
no time in disposeing of your property and to come to this country and
to do all that layes your power to assist the persons mentioned in this
letter likewise. Write imeadeately and let me know your mind on the
recipt of this.

> [To] Mr William Rawcliffe
> Oldfield near Honly
> Yorkshire

Joseph Hollingworth to William and Nancy Rawcliff

South Leicester. Tuesday Morning May 20th. 1828

Dear Uncle and Dear Aunt
I'm very glad to say

7. Probably in the machine shop that was part of the same mill in which John was
employed.

8. Like thousands of other Dissenters' children in the nineteenth century, the Hollingworths were raised on Isaac Watts (1674–1748), Congregational minister, hymn writer, and
poet. John Hollingworth apparently had a copy of Watts's *Psalms, Hymns, and Spiritual
Songs*, including these verses, which are excerpts from P. M. Dalston's "The Blessings of
Friendship."

9. Mary and William are probably John Hollingworth's young children. His wife and the
children came to the United States within a year. See letter of May 20, 1828, below.

That your kind letter I received
On the fifteenth day of May.

It was Dated March 25th We was short of provision on board the ship or at least it was not the right sort. We had plenty of buisquit enough for 3 voyages. We could not eat it. I believe I ate as much of it myself as all the rest. I contrived to pound it in a bag (made of sail cloth for the purpose) and made it into Pudings. That was the only way we could eat it. We bought 20 lb. of flour in addition to what we had when you left. Some of our provision was good but we had some not fit to eat. We ate the good first and we had finished a great part in the first 4 weeks. Our potatoes would have lasted out pretty well had it not been for a set of dishonest rascals. I mean the paddys.[10] We had nearly 1 third stolen, but it will take to much of my time and paper to give you every particular relating to this circumstance. Sufice it to say that should you ever come to America or have to buy provision for any body that is coming O BEWARE of BECKET! That Infernal wrech who when he could subsist no longer by riding his own country-men in Irland came over to Liverpool to impose on my Honest Countrymen who are flying from the wrath to come and going to seek an asylum in a country where that Villanous BECKET would be brought to Justice.[11] The most appropriate punishment that could be inflicted on that imposter would be to confine him in the Middle of the Atlantic Ocean in old Isaac Hicks and feed him on his own Biskit and stinking water but to conclude, O Beware of Becket.

I saw Joseph Hirst when I was at Poughkeepsie. He was a Spiner at Wadsworth's Factory. He was the only man that I have seen wear Breeches in America.[12] I had no particular conversation with him. He asked me some Questions and I answered them. I have forgot what they were. My Mother told him that his Wife was badly situated that she wanted to come to America and soon. By what he said then and by what another person told me, on whose word I can rely, I got to understand that he has no intention for sending for his wife. Mary Hollingworth knew her Grandfather when she first saw him here. She did not know me at first but when I began to ask her about the Oldfield she could recolect both you and your Daughter Mary-Ann. She says if Aunt Nancy was here she would say "Thank you mam" and give

10. Paddys: negative term for the Irish.

11. Becket was apparently an Irishman who sold provisions in Liverpool and cheated unsuspecting English emigrants.

12. Breeches: short trousers reaching just below the knee, unlike longer pants commonly worn in the United States.

her a cent for the frock. She goes to school and seldom failes to bring
home a ticket for reward of . . . I don't know what reason Jack-o-
Micks has to give such a bad acount of America. I dare say he'll not
find a Factory in England where the workmen will subcribe him
Mony to send him back to America. I would scorn say anything about
such a Black-Gard as Haddock for I don't calculate of fighting him
with my hands but should not mind doing it with my tongue provided he would not tell so many Infernal lies. William Perken knows
very little about America or the American Manufactory. He only
came from New York to this place and I believe took the same rout
back-again. 'Tis true that they work on sundays here. Bro' Jbz.[13]
has to work every 2 or 3 sundays in the factory repairing macheniry
and doing such work as can not be conveniently done on other days.
Bro. James is a spiner and he was ordered by the Bos spiner one
sunday afternoon in the Church while attending Devine Service to
go spin that evening soon as the church service ended, but he neither woad nor did obey. I had to go tenter the second sunday after
I began work and was ordered to go again but I did not obey and I
have not been on a sunday since.[14] The Factory system is the caus
of this.

> I hate to see a factory stand
> In any part of the k[n]own land
> To me it talks of wickedness
> Of Families that's in destress
> Of Tyrany and much extortion
> And of slavery a portion
> I wish that I no more might see
> Another woollen Factory.

John says he will write you in a few weeks. Jbz. says he would write
again but that he has told you all he knows, he has nothing to wright,
you must excuse him. My Mother was a little sea sick on our voyage
but it cured her leg. Sister H[annah] was never sick at all but she
could not walk when we landed. Mother likes country "vary weel" but
she has got disapointed she has got more work than ever [in] this a
land of labour. Sister H. knew her Father as soon as she saw him. He
took her into his arms and she would not leave him for several hours.
On the 2nd of March Miss Hollingworth was brought to bed of an

---

13. Bro' Jbz.: Brother Jabez Hollingworth.

14. Tentering is one of the finishing processes. At the time, woolen cloth was held in
place on a frame (by tenterhooks) for drying outdoors; since it was stretched, the cloth dried
without wrinkles and to a uniform width. Asa Ellis, *The Country Dyer's Assistant* (Brook-
field, Mass.: E. Merriam, 1798), p. 109.

Anglo-yankee.[15] The Black Cloth which you sent Capt Barnet came here in Feb.ʸ. It was 12 yds long. You must write when you get this and tell me how you get along with regard to your soar hole and other matters relating to that concern and you oblige your Inteligent

Joseph Hollingworth. . . .

P.S.   When you this letter have reciev'd
      Its contents read and all believ'd
      Then put it in your Chest
      Don't let each Busibody view
      What I have writ tho' all is true
      They would begin to Jest.—J.H. . . .

GEORGE HOLLINGWORTH TO WILLIAM RAWCLIFF

South Leicester June 28ᵗʰ 1828

Dear Brother

I have long had an intention of writing to you and giving you all the information respecting this Country I possably could, but has hitherto been detered by a perplexed mind, for which neglect I must beg your pardon. I must begin by informing you that we are all at present in good health with the exception of Son John who has not been well for these few weeks past, but perhaps is now a little better. With respect to the Weather they say the past Winter as been verry mild. At any rate it has been very fare from being insuportable. I have experienced colder Weather in England then I have yet done in America. The truth is that it will freeze ten times as quick and ten times harder then it will do in England and yet will not feel any colder. With respect to our Summer Weather it has hitherto been verry pleasant. It has been uniformly warm with now and then an hotter day. We are almost all-ways at these times favioured with a clear and pure atmosphere and an exhillerating breeze which enables us to sustain the heat of the day with verry little inconveniance. The prospect of the Country at this time is beautifull behond discription, the Woods and Fields orna-mented with beautiful Flowering Shrubs of almost every discription such as are considered rare ornaments in your Gentlemen's Gardens in England. Vegetation here growes most rapidly and luxuerantly. You would be surprised to see the uncultivated state of the Land and see the abundance that it will produce conected with the little labour that

15. Brought to bed of an Anglo-yankee: went into labor. Miss Hollingworth is actually John Hollingworth's wife. Her daughter, Elizabeth, is an "Anglo-Yankee" in the sense that she is of English parentage but American birth.

is bestowed. We have planted about half a Road[16] of Potatoes in verry rough Ground without any manure and they say they will grow verry well. Whether they will or not is yet to prove. Of this I am certain that had they been planted in like manner and with as little labour in your part of England that they would produce nothing. We have made a verry neat little Garden attached to our house in which we have now growing cucumbers Melons, Squash, various kinds of Beans such as is not known in your Country, Carriots Lettuce Parsley Beets Marygolds Sweet Williams Saffron Sage Hysop and various other things all of which we are raising from the Seeds. The uncultivated land even the Road Sides produces abundance of Red and White Clover and are excellant good Pasturage. . . .

. . . We all live together in a double House.[17] We have plenty of room. The House contains 8 Rooms besides a Celler under the whole. We pay 60 Dollars a year Rent. Geo. Mellor James Hollingworth and & J. Kenyon Boards with us. Son James is a Filling Spiner viz. a bobing Spiner and can earn 8 or 9 dollars per week.[18] Son John has been a little time a Condenced Spiner. This is a new meserable business for making money. He is now a Slubber which is a fare better Job. He will make better then a dollir a day.[19] Son Joseph has been a Gigger every since he came at only 15½ dollars per Month. As the Job was a new one to him and one I wished him to learn I was not particular about wages at first, but now has he has got an expert hand I am thinking of asking for more wages not less then 20 dollars per month.[20] Edwin is a Warp Winder or Spooler winder for the Warping Machine at 1½ dollars per Week.[21] I am intending to have his wages advanced

16. Half a Road: probably half a rood, a unit of area equal to about half an acre.

17. Two-family houses were commonly built by millowners in southern Massachusetts, Connecticut, and Rhode Island to house the families of their workers. Rural mills in southern New England typically employed families able to contribute several family members to the mill work force in contrast to practice in northern New England, where young, single, native-born women predominated.

18. Son James was probably spinning filling (i.e., weft) yarn. This could also explain the term *bobbin spinner*, since weft yarn was wound onto bobbins that fit into the loom shuttles. Abraham Rees, "Woollen Manufacture," in *The Cyclopedia: Or Universal Dictionary of Arts, Sciences and Literature*, vol. 40 (Philadelphia: Samuel F. Bradford, 1822).

19. As a slubber, John would have been operating a hand-powered slubbing billy, which took the output from the carding machine and joined pieces together into a continuous roving.

20. Gigging is a finishing process in which the surface fibers of woven cloth are brushed and raised. See Andrew Ure, *A Dictionary of Arts, Manufactures, and Mines . . . To Which Is Appended a Supplement of Recent Improvements to the Present Time* (New York: D. Appleton, 1845), p. 1325.

21. As a warp winder, Edwin was responsible for transferring yarn from small spindle bobbins to larger spools that fitted in the warping creel (a rack for holding the spools). In the

also.[22] There is not much in America I dislike [excep]ting the too general conduct of Emigrants, and the Factory Sistem which Sistem I hate with a perfect hatered as being only calculated to create bad feelings bad principles and bad practices. I must inform you of a disapointment I have experienced namely when I set off or rather was forced or driven off by Family and circumstances, I was fully perswaided to believe that my nearest Relatives viz Brothers & Sisters would Speedily follow after me, but now that I am in America how woefully I am undeceived by recent letters which have been received in which the writers state their relinquishment of an intention to come to this Country, and courting their Sons to return by flatterying accounts of the flimsy prosperity of Old England. These circumstances fully determines me never to trust to either Person or circumstance any more, nor will I try to perswaid any person against his mind to come to this Country. If any person is inclined to come from principle (and none else are fit to come) I will most willingly give them the best information I am able. I particularly request you to write as soon as possable and therein declare your Intention whether you will come to America or not.[23] If you should come it would be of no practical use to send you any money to England. But should you finelly determine to Stop in Old England then we will send you some Money as soon as possable. While I am writing Sons James and Joseph are Fishing in the Factory dam which is a Pond of Water containing A surface of 40 or 50 acrs. Son John's Wife was brought to bed some Months since of a verry fine daughter which they call Elizebeth—We all unite in our Special Regards to you and your Wife—and am D.ʳ Bro.[24]

Yours affectionately
Geo. Hollingworth

---

next step of the production process hundreds of warp threads were wound parallel to one another around a cylindrical warp beam in preparation for the weaving operation.

22. The language here suggests that George Hollingworth was responsible for the contracts under which his children worked and that he probably received their pay, practices common to smaller mills in southern New England in this period. The family may well have rented their home from the mill and purchased supplies at a company store. Rent and store purchases would have been charged to a family account and mill earnings credited. Once a year the account would have been settled and George Hollingworth would have received any balance in his favor.

23. William Rawcliff and his wife did immigrate to the United States and lived in Poughkeepsie, New York. See letter of November 7, 1829, below.

24. Actually, William Rawcliff was George Hollingworth's brother-in-law. See Thomas W. Leavitt, ed., *The Hollingworth Letters: Technical Change in the Textile Industry, 1826–1837* (Cambridge, Mass.: M.I.T. Press, 1969), "Genealogical Chart," pp. 110–11.

If you think proper you may lett my Brother John see this Letter.
I had forgot to mention son Jabez. He is working in the machine Shop
at 25 dollars per month.

JOSEPH HOLLINGWORTH TO WILLIAM AND NANCY RAWCLIFF

N°.4.   South Leicester, Dec^{br}. 7th. (One year old My New
                                              Birth Day. [1828][25]

Respected Aunt & Uncle
      In England I've left, both relations and friends,
      Whome I respect more, than just for my ends;
      For If I did not, than no more would I write,
      Since they are far from me, and out of my sight
Don't be astonished at my writing N°. 4. before I have received N°.
3. from you. One reason is this, viz. that this day being the 1st Aniver-
sary of my landing in America I wanted to celebrate it by writing a
Letter. Father sent you a letter many a months since but has had no
answer. I am afraid you did not get it. Bro. John sent you a letter 3
weeks ago (by Joseph Brook who is returning to England) wherin he
states "that he & James Hollingworth was going to take a small Man-
ufactorien place in Herkimer County, New York."[26] But they have not
taken the place on acount of the Owner wanting too much Rent. At
present they are working at Winstead in Conecticut.[27] Joshua Smith
is at the same place. If you write to Bro. John you must not Direct
to any place but South Leicester untill you have had another letter
from him. . . .

    I have lived in America exactly one year. I have seen all the Sea-
sons and must confess that I prefer the American weather far before
the English. I have never seen in this Country a Beggar such as I
used Daily to see in England, nor a tax gatherer with his <u>Red Book</u>[28]
<u>as Impudent as the D-v-l, taking the last penny out of the poor</u>
<u>Mans Pocket.</u> In this country are no Lords, nor Dukes, nor Counts,
nor Marquises, nor Earls, no Royal Family to support nor no King.

    25. Joseph Hollingworth numbered his letters, though not all are reprinted here. He
wrote this letter on the first anniversary of his arrival in the United States, December 7, 1827.

    26. Herkimer County is just east of Utica, along the Erie Canal in western New York.

    27. Winsted, Connecticut, was a village inside the township of Winchester, northwest of
Hartford. The Hollingworths may have worked for Alfred French, who made woolen broad-
cloth there. The village also included a dye-products dealer and a manufacturer of woolen
machinery. *The American Advertising Directory For Manufactures and Dealers in American Goods* (New York: Jocelyn, Darling, 1831), p. 147.

    28. Red Book: account book of an English tax collector.

South view of Winsted, Connecticut, circa 1838, a mill village where John and James Hollingworth worked. (From John Warner Barber, *Connecticut Historical Collections* [New Haven, Conn.: Durrie and Peck, 1838], p. 503)

The "President of the United States" is the highest Titled fellow in this Country. He is chosen by the People, out of the People; holds his station four years, and if not rechosen he is no more than the rest of the People. The President when he makes a speech does not begin with "My Lords and Gentlemen" but with "Fellow Citizens." When we came from Poughkeepsie to this place we stopped the first night at Amenia [N.Y.]. I was astonished to see the Driver lose the Horses off and leave the waggon by the road side. I spoke to Bro. John and told him I thout our goods would be stolen. He answered "No Danger." If I had not been well tired I believe I should not have slept that Night for fear, but I no ocasion to fear, for our goods was as safe as when locked up in the yard at Manchester, and all the journey thro' we never put our waggon under cover, but always left it in the road or street (or where ever it happened to be) all night to the Mercy of the Theives, if any there were. We have no lock to our doors, we never mak them fast at night. This helps to confirm the truth of some of my old English Poetry

> A land where tyrany is no more
> Where we can all be free
> And men without a lock to th' door
> Sleeps in tranquility

N.B.   There is the Factory Sistem which breeds a kind of petty Tyrany but ere long will be leveled as low as its supporters I Hope.

Give my respects to Old Haigh and tell him if you please that my Father has no occasion to hawk Nuts in America as every body can have them for gathering in this Country. Neither is he bound to carry Mes.^{rs.} Haighs wet Peices[29] up Mirylane on his Back nor to go Roast himself in their stove every Sunday morning for Nothing. I have got a New Hat which cost 5 dollars and three quarters. I have a pair of Boots making which will be 4 dollars and an half. I am still working in the Gig Room at 17 $ per month.[30] Father has been writing a letter for 6 months together to William Lockwood. He has not yet finished. It is to be so large, and so compleat with information, but I guess it will be like the Mountain in Labour, it may bring forth a Mouse. The more I live in this Country the better I like it. . . .

. . . You must excuse my Brothers James and Jabez for not writing as they are both deeply engaged in Sparking.[31] Jabez Sparks a yankee

---

29. Carry Mesrs. Haighs wet Peices: apparently a reference to work George Hollingworth had done in England. He may have been required to carry wet pieces of woolen cloth to be blocked and dried by a hot stove on Sunday mornings.

30. This wage represents a slight raise from the figure of $15.50 per month noted by Joseph's father in the previous letter.

31. Courting—or, in a twentieth-century sense, dating.

Girl James Sparks a Saddleworth Girl,[32] and on the 25th of Nov^{br}. Joseph Kenyon took two English Girls to a Ball.

We are all in good Health at present hoping you are the same. Jabez & James are a little tickled at what I have Just written So I will conclude.

> I Remain your most Inteligent Affectionate & well Wishing Nephew
> Joseph Hollingworth. . . .

JOSEPH HOLLINGWORTH TO WILLIAM AND NANCY RAWCLIFF

South Leicester Nov^{br}. 7th 1829 Saturday evening.

Dear Aunt, and Uncle.

I write this letter INCOGNITO, I therefore desire you to keep it to your selves. I shall state a few of my grieveances in a brief manner. I should have told you somthing of it when you was here, but I thought it best not to trouble you then; besides I had no oppertunity. You well know how things went on in our Family in England, with regard to me, that I was always the BAD LAD,&c. Were I to enumerate all the evils that has been practised against me in this country, I might fill sheets upon sheets; but I forbear. Let a few suffice. You know how James and I was clothed when we left England; he had 3 or 4 good suits, & I only one, besides my old clothes, which was wore out when I got here. I had to take one of James's old coats, which has been my every-day coat ever scince; and which I have got on this present moment. I did not have any new cloths till last June, (Hat Boots & satinet trousers excepted,) and might not have had any to this day; but I told them [in] plain terms, that if they did not get me some I would look out for myself. Last winter, I had to work a good deal of overtime at Nights; had I refused the whole Family might have lost their work: so I calculated to have the overtime wages for myself. It amounted to nearly five Dollars. I have succeeded in getting 2 dol^{rs} ONLY! which is all the pocket money I have had in this country! I might have overlooked all these circumstances, at least a little longer, had not one, transpired, of a diabolical nature. We have a new Family Bible, and I thought to make it a practice, every Night, to read the lessons. . . . I did so, 3 or 4 nights when Lo, and Behold! last Tuesday night, when I got redy to read my lesson, James had locked up the Bible, which he called his; and refused to let me have it, because it was too good to be used! (Turn over

---

32. The Saddleworth district was located in the north of England, in the wool manufacturing region from which the Hollingworths came.

> In days of old, the word of God,
> By Monks, and Friars, was read o'er;
> But now, a selfish PEDDY-NOD,
> Has lock'd it up within his Draw'r.

This is too much for me, to have the Family Bible locked up; in a Land of Liberty and Freedom. Nor can I bear all their frumps and scornings, to be called a selfish Devil when I ask for the money which I earned when they sleeped in their beds; and ever and anon, to be told, that it is not my own Coat that I wear. I say, I can not bear it. I will not bear it. It is too much for mortal man.

> I am no Cat, I am no Dog,
> I am no Ox, I am no Hog,
> I am not either Sheep or Cow,
> Or any beast, that I should bow
> To their proud wills, or haughty minds;
> Which are as various as the winds:
> But I'm a mortal man by birth,
> Am born to live upon the earth;
> O'er other men I wan no sway,
> But want my rights as well as they.

But after all, I do not wish to Ab[s]cond clandestinely; far, very [far] from my idea, to become a tramp. I wish to live among relations and friends. Will you acquiesce in a plan that I have formed, and give me a little assistance in changing my situation. My plan is this, that you, on the receipt of this letter, procure me some work at Poughkeepsie (any kind of work that I can do, I shall not be exact at first) and then write to my Father, to request him to let me come, without giving him any knowlege, or even insinuating, that you have had a letter from me. By this means I should leave them in a friendly manner, and they would find me money for the Journey. If you will thus assist me in time of tribulation, you will lay me under the greatest obligations possible; but should you refuse me; then write to me immediately, that I may know to use some other plan. For I am determined to break the bands of opression this once, let what will be the consequence. Whatever way you determin to do, I hope you will make no delay; for I shall wait with unceasing anxiety, till I see the result of this letter. I Still Remain,

Dear Aunt and Uncle;
Your Affectionate Nephew,
Joseph Hollingworth

P.S. We are all in good health. The wedding has not yet taken place, nor does it seem to be any nearer. The Factory will stop as soon as the stock is worked up. Some of the spinners has already done and cleared; all our folks expects to have done this this month. It is said that all Englishmen will have leave this place; work is very scarce in this part, and when a man gets out of employ tis hard for him to get in again. J.H. . . .

Joseph Hollingworth to William and Nancy Rawcliff

Muddy Brook Pond Factory,
Woodstock, Connecticut Sept. 5th 1830[33]

D—evolve on me the pleasant task,
E—ach time, to answer what you ask;
A—nd in return for favours done,
R—elate how things are going on.

A—ssisted by a power devine,
U—nveiled before me truth shall shine:
N—ature's grand works may all decay;
T—ruth shall endure to endless day.

A—nd now I take my pen in Hand,
N—ot doubting but you'll understand;
D—esiring, that you wont mistake,
U—nknown, the errors I may make.

N—ow tho' to distant lands we've roved,
C—an we forget those whome Loved;
L—ove, the great source of all our weal,
E—nlightens every mind with Zeal.

I recieved yours of June 20th on the 5th of July. which gave me great sattisfaction. The reason that I did not write sooner is this, Bro. John had written to you Just before I got yours giving you a description of this place, and also desiring you to write to Joseph Haigh, so I concluded not to write then lest you should have letters coming in to thick. Bro. James and Wife lives with Father and family at Southbridge. Mother says she should like to have come over to see you but that she could not well be spared. You want to know what work I have. Well, when I came to Southbrigdde at first there was no work for me

---

33. After the previous letter, Joseph moved to Woodstock, Connecticut, where he worked for his brothers John and Jabez and cousin James Hollingworth, who had leased a factory for the manufacture of satinet, a fabric combining cotton and woolen yarns and having a satinlike surface. After the last letter, sister Hannah died, and brother James got married.

Globe Village, Southbridge, Massachusetts, 1822 (oil painting by Francis Alexander). Joseph Hollingworth worked at a mill in Globe Village in November 1830.

at my old business, so Mr Sayles set me to work with my Father at the warping macheen.[34] I worked 5 weeks when I thought it time to ask what wages I should have. The reply was NOTHING! that having the chance to learn a fresh trade was thought a Just compensation for my verry valuable services. The result of which was, that I got into a Jackass' fit. Father then took the warping and spooling by the Job. He and Edwin worked at spooling and I at warping untill I got weary of the work. I then came here to work, when Mr Sayles sent for me back, as he wished to hire me to work in the fulling Room for a few days. I went back and worked 21 days for 12 dollars. And finaly I came here again, and am going to do the Napping, Shearing and pressing, when the work is ready. Mary Kenyon has had the misfortun to lose the forefinger of the right Hand.[35] She was weaving on a power loom. She put her finger where it had no business, and so the loom in return snapped it of between the first and second Joints. . . .

And now for a description of this place. It is situated in the township of Woodstock in the "land of steady habits" alias Con^ct about 4 miles south of Southbridge and about 16 from South Leicester alias Clapville. This place contains about 3 acers more or less on which is the Factory, consisting of two buildings Joined together, each 3 stories high, a dye house, a wood shed a Barn, and seven houses or tenements, together with another building divided into 4 sheds with a larger chamber over, which may be used as dry house. In the Factory are 3 carding machiens, 2 billys, 4 Jennys, 13 broad hand looms, 4 new satinet power looms, 1 fulling stock called a poacher, 1 picker, 2 broad shears, 1 press, 1 dye kettle, 1 satinet Napper and 2 shears which we have had to buy, and several other things. There is a most excelent watter weel, an over shot weel the best I ever saw.[36] It is suplied with watter from a larg pond called the Muddy Brook pond, although the watter is as clear and as soft as any other. They have hired this place for $500 a year, for 3 years but will have to Quit any time the owners think fit at 12 months notice. The owners are now determined to sell it without delay. They ask 6000 $ and will not take less. There

34. Willard Sayles was a principal in Tiffany, Sayles and Hitchcock, the Boston selling agents for the Hamilton Woolen Company in Southbridge, who employed George Hollingworth and leased the failed mill at Woodstock to Joseph's brothers and cousin. The warping machine at which Joseph worked unwound warp yarns from large spools and wound them in parallel fashion on a warp beam for weaving.

35. Mary Kenyon was a cousin of Joseph Hollingworth. See Leavitt, ed., *The Hollingworth Letters*, pp. 110–11.

36. The overshot water wheel was filled from the top; the force and weight of the water entering the buckets moved the wheel that turned the drive shaft. Oliver Evans, *The Young Mill-Wright and Miller's Guide* (Philadelphia: Carey and Lea, 1829), plates 13–16.

is a party of Yankees wants to buy, but they say they will give our folks the first chance and make the payment easy. Joseph Haig, Father, Brothers John, Jabez, & Jame and Cousin James have determined to buy rather than quit the place. The interest of the money will not be so much as the rent. Joseph Haigh & family arived here last Wedensday and I believe are verry much pleased with the place.[37]

If you could make it convenient to come over, and see us, and the place I should be very glad. . . .

[letter unsigned]

37. Despite the effort to interest other kin to join in the purchase of the Muddy Brook Factory, the Hollingworths apparently did not purchase the factory at the end of their three-year lease. John and Joseph Hollingworth remained in Woodstock but did not operate the factory in later years. Leavitt, ed., *The Hollingworth Letters*, p. xxv.

THREE

The William and Sophie Frank Seyffardt Letters, 1851–1863

Almost 1.4 million Germans entered the United States between 1840 and 1860, constituting about a third of all immigrants in these decades. Many German immigrants settled in eastern cities, such as New York and Philadelphia, but a large number moved on to states bordering the Great Lakes, particularly Michigan, Illinois, and Wisconsin. Among those Germans were William Seyffardt and Sophie Frank, who immigrated separately in 1850 and were married in Titibawassee, Michigan, in June 1852.

These two immigrants came from well-off families. Ludwig Seyffardt was a retired businessman when his son William emigrated in 1851. Sophie's father, John Henry Frank, was a rural pastor of the Evangelical church in a village in Baden in southern Germany. Ludwig Seyffardt supported his son's purchase of land and the building of a mill in Michigan. John Henry Frank paid for the passage of three children to the United States and probably supported the purchase of the farm in Titibawassee, worked jointly by Edward Barck and August Frank.[1]

The Seyffardt letters open a window to the German immigrant community of the antebellum period. The letters reveal networks of German settlements throughout the Midwest—such as the towns of Frankenmuth, Frankentrost, and Frankenlust in Michigan—and a support system whereby kin, friends, and neighbors offered sociability and mutual assistance to their fellow countrymen and women. Young men and women lived with married couples when they first arrived, and through networks of family and in-laws, they met their future business partners and spouses.

1. Louis F. Frank, comp., *German-American Pioneers in Wisconsin and Michigan: The Frank-Kerler Letters, 1849–1864*, trans. Margaret Wolff, ed. Harry H. Anderson (Milwaukee, Wis.: Milwaukee County Historical Society, 1971), pp. xii, xiv, 3–4, 51.

William and Sophie Frank Seyffardt. (Courtesy of the Milwaukee County Historical Society)

Germans brought more resources with them or were better able to draw on family back home than most other immigrants of the period. As these letters make clear, it took a sizable investment for a German family to set itself up on a midwestern farm. Luckily, William Seyffardt was able to draw on his father back in Crefeld for the necessary funds or credit, first to expand his farm and later to set up a grist and sawmill.

More so than other sets of letters, the Seyffardt letters reveal the gendered lives of immigrants. William Seyffardt busied himself with farm and mill matters, taking periodic trips to buy supplies, equipment, and machinery. He was the member of the family with extensive contact with Yankee neighbors, whether in conducting mill business or as a participant in periodic elections. He followed developments in the American economy and politics, and we can trace his steady Americanization over the course of his correspondence. Sophie, in contrast, was tied much more closely to home and family. In her letters to both sets of parents back in Germany, she reported on her children's development, the family's health, and her responsibility for a large work crew while the grist mill was under construction. Hers was a narrower world than her husband's, more confined within the family and a circle of German-American kin and friends.

1851

51)[2]   WILLIAM SEYFFARDT TO HIS PARENTS

Titibawassee, October 1

I visited several German settlements on horseback. About 4 miles from Frankentrost[3] I became lost, and in the growing darkness, was thrown from the horse by a branch. I found lodging in Frankentrost where an inn-keeper let himself be paid well for weak coffee and yard-long prayers. The next morning I was received in a friendly way by Mr. Veenfliet in Sheboyonon. After two days, I rode home by way of the friendly settlement at Frankenmuth. There are social gatherings

2. The Seyffardt letters excerpted here were numbered when originally collected and published, and I have employed the same system to permit locating these letters within the larger collection. The headings are also taken from that source. Note that William Seyffardt was writing to his father and stepmother, as his own mother died in 1833. See Frank, comp., *German-American Pioneers*, p. 52.

3. Frankentrost was one of the several German settlements established in Saginaw County, Michigan, during the late 1840s.

at Titibawassee on Sundays in which Count Salms and a Hungarian
Baron von Espenberg, an excellent musician, participate in target
shooting, etc. A daughter was born to the Roeser family, at which time
I made a trip to the doctor, 25 miles away. At this time I killed a deer,
using a piece of board to stun it. Two large bears were killed by Indians. My plan is to buy a 100–160 acre farm, and I therefore ask for
a loan of $3,000.

1852

56)   WILLIAM SEYFFARDT TO HIS FATHER

Titibawassee, January 10

At this time I can give no report about buying, but am busy looking,
for one must not make a lot of noise when one wishes to buy at a low
price. Wellington Farm has been my residence since I came here. It
is leased by G. Roeser for 5 years for $350. Our Sunday get-togethers
with indispensible dancing and target shooting angered only a few
Yankees and German old-Lutheran pietists, the participants, however, were well pleased. I was out of sorts for a week for my horse fell
on me, but nevertheless I could carry an 80-pound deer home 1½
miles. Christmas eve was at Roeser's with punch, cake and whist[4] for
the neighbors.

William Seyffardt

1852

58)   WILLIAM SEYFFARDT TO HIS FATHER

Saginaw, February 17

On this date I have purchased Wellington's farm for $1160. I will
build a suitable house next year. The farm consists of 67 acres, 45
clear, is the nicest location along the river, and recognized as such.
From Roeser, who had rented the farm, I received a team of horses
with harness for $105 and eight tons of hay for $80, also a lean-to shed
for $30. Household goods, $20. Not to forget 3 cows ($36), 7 pigs, etc.

William Seyffardt

As concerns thoughts of marriage, I merely mentioned them to
Louis, because it is necessary for a farmer to have a wife, and to be

---

4. Whist: a popular card game.

frank, the choice here is small. But I would 10-times sooner not have a wife than an uncultured or frivolous one.

Your William

1852

67)   WILLIAM SEYFFARDT TO HIS PARENTS

Titibawassee, March 30

I have important news to tell you, namely my engagement to Sophie Frank. The father of my bride-to-be is a minister at Dietlingen and may come over here this year. I became acquainted with my Sophie on the farm of Barck and Frank. To praise her good qualities is not the thing for a bridegroom to do, but I will get a dear good wife. I would prefer bringing her to you but the ocean prohibits that. I have learned the value of a home only since I own a farm. I cannot tell you how happy I am not to be so alone in America any more, and I am convinced that you will have no opposition to this marriage. The wedding date is set for the end of June. My farm is 67 acres, 40 cleared, 20 acres of meadow, which pays with the high prices of hay ($10 a ton). I have 2 horses, 2 cows, 7 pigs and 30 hens. I took over the equipment from Roeser.

1852

74)   PASTOR FRANK TO HIS DAUGHTER SOPHIE

Dietlingen, May 15

You ask us as parents, to give our permission to your engagement, but we do not really know to whom? For you and the law-educated brother-in-law do not say what the first name of your future husband is. Besides, one writes Seiffarth, another Seuffahrt, still another Seifard—the formalities and the personalities must first be correct. Of course, before this letter gets to you and yours or one of the other lazy people's gets to us, it will be fall before our permission and our blessing come to you. But fortunately the matter has been helped by a more sensible person than you are, as the following letter of April 28, from Crefeld says: Just now I received the surprising and pleasing news that my son William, etc.—Good, now we know that he, the dear fiance, is called William. The letter was signed L. Seyffardt, so William Seyffardt born February 1829, related to the bride in the

9999⅔ degree is financially free, was vaccinated in Germany (result, strong pustules), good heart, and nice farm, right by the river. But away with jesting.

That was a cordial letter of Mr. S's—we greeted each other as brothers, and upon his request I told him about Sophie and the other members of the family. The letter left for Crefeld on May 8, where twice I was quartered as commander of 24 men in April, 1814, playing no unimportant role. If the world would not be ungrateful my name would be found not in metal, but in pumpernickel, which grows well there. Dear Sophie, we give you our parental blessing for your union. May your marriage be not only a happy and peaceful one in the eyes of the world, but also a Christian one in the full sense of the word. You have the blessing of your parents and your parents-in-law, so that by agreeing to this peace is promised you in your marriage. Remain a good Christian and you will remain a good wife. We agree with you, that the wedding shall be on June 26, mother's birthday. In this respect we will leave everything up to you. You will have enough to do in your future home and I would gladly help you; but I think that Henry will often come and make many things easier for you. Mr. Seyffardt in Crefeld has invited us to spend several days with them on our way to America—I have promised to do so in case we take that route. You can consider it something pleasant that your husband has horses for as the wife of an American farmer you will be able to hold your head higher than our city women and rightly so. But I ask you not to let your good husband be too conscious of the fact that you belong to the rural women—did not Barck tell him anything about that? Now, farewell our bride Sophie, when you read this you will perhaps be a farmer's wife already. The best of wishes for your well-being and for that of your bridegroom, to whom all of us send greetings, stir within the heart of

your father

1852
85) Sophie Seyffardt to the Parents of William Seyffardt

Titibawassee, July 5

Now at last, after the wedding is past and I am united with my William forever, I get to greet you and to tell you how happy I feel being your daughter. Because of obstacles, the wedding had to be postponed until June 26, and since Roesers moved out before this day, William had to cook for himself for five weeks. I often felt sorry for him, when, tired from his work and bathed in sweat, he would stand at the stove and prepare his dinner. As a result of this he often caught a cold. The wedding was celebrated with only the family present. We were also sad that father and mother could not stand at our side. William did everything to make the most favorable impression. Everything was brightened, the windows cleaned, the room was whitewashed, and even the garden was prepared. We are happy together and my housekeeping gives me great pleasure.

I am adding my thanks for the valuable gift. William bought me a ladies' saddle with it and now we ride together on the farm. At first I was afraid, but William gave me a very gentle horse—maybe a bit too calm, as William who rode at my side had to help with his foot at times. From our two cows I get 8 pounds of butter weekly, but from the 40 hens in the coop, I get only one egg every other day. That is unpleasant since, with a lack of fresh meat, one is limited to a flour diet. The mosquitoes this summer were very kind, but still bother us enough. Since yesterday we have 8 men cutting wood for the barn. William exerts himself so much at it that I am worried about him because of the great heat. It is questionable if my parents will ever come, for the trip is being postponed from year to year. The older they get, the harder the trip will be. Cheer us often with letters for it is one of the greatest pleasures to get mail from our dear ones.

1852
123)   SOPHIE SEYFFARDT TO THE SEYFFARDT PARENTS

Titibawassee, October 16

When my last letter was sent I believed William to be free of all fever, but it returned after 14 days and weakened him very much. Added to that was a cholera attack, and you can imagine my fear and fright. The attack lasted from 2 a.m. until 12 noon. I am glad that Mr. Schlegel is a help to William. Our nearest German neighbors is a family named Vasold from Thueringen. They live diagonally across the creek, so near that we can talk to each other. The family consists of a daughter and five grown sons. One daughter is married to William Roeser. The nearest neighbors on our side are Yankees, quite friendly, obliging people. Unfortunately, I have so much trouble with English that I cannot say a decent sentence. Not only does it give me a headache, but William laughs at me on top of it. The farm of Gustav Roeser is a half mile from us, we often go there as they are the kind of neighbors that anyone could wish for. A young couple lives just below our farm; the husband is 18, the wife 15. The woman lived in a barrel in the open before they built a hut. Two families, the Bernhards from Frankfurt, and the Liskows from Pomerania, live some distance from us, six miles along the way to Saginaw. Count Solms of Austria lives three miles farther. When we visit them, we pick up Barcks with our horses for they have only oxen. Tomorrow I will ride with William to Saginaw, and will stay overnight there in order to go to church the next day. There are only 20 of our 70 chicks left as a result of the cold. The cabbage, which William planted when a bridegroom, bore such nice heads as I never saw in Germany. We are waiting for Indian summer, but it looks as though it will snow today. Winter is not unpleasant to me—it is so nice to sit in a warm room.

1852

124)   WILLIAM SEYFFARDT TO HIS PARENTS

Titibawassee, October 17

The three Roeser brothers are living in three houses upward along the river. Otto Roeser (law student), the hunter, runs a bachelor's hall and sometimes supplies us with deer meat. I have shot nothing recently and Schlegel (traveling salesman) with a residual south-German stoutness, tells us, mostly panting, that the deer ran through the river faster than it was possible for him to run. I consoled him and myself for better days. . . .

Tomorrow will be the first German meeting concerning County affairs, and I hope that the Germans will take a more active part than I have had the opportunity to observe up till now. The Presidential election is approaching and the Democratic and Whig newspapers are attacking each other like biting dogs. I have not been converted to either of these parties. The Whigs have spent a lot of money and are flooding the country with brochures, and with pictures of the invincible General Scott, who through the conquest of splintered Mexico is on a level with the first generals of Europe?!! There is no mention of administrative virtues. The Democrats have set up Pirie [Franklin Pierce], but their statement of principle is so undemocratic (for protection of slavery) that a free-minded person can not agree with them.[5]

5. The Democrats won the presidency in the 1852 election, with Franklin Pierce defeating Winfield Scott by more than 200,000 votes. Seyffardt's anti-Democratic views made it almost inevitable that he would join the ranks of the Republican party after its formation in

As far as the land is concerned which I intend to buy, I have my eye on two pieces of 80 acres each. They are to cost $2½ and $5 per acre respectively, but I will inquire further.

I ask you to tell Moritz that the no. 5 key on my accordion is broken, and that the nickle silver given to me by Band is no good. Maybe he can find out what the trouble is.

I am concerned about the beetles,[6] as there are few to be had. In any case, there are fewer here than in Pennsylvania.

1853

187)   WILLIAM SEYFFARDT TO HIS PARENTS

Titibawassee, August 15

Many thanks for the congratulations on the birth of our little one.[7] She is gaining well, is very dear, and sleeps from evening until morning. She smiles by day, and is friendly, so that she is the darling of the German as well as the Yankee neighbors. We had our pictures taken recently. I will send beetles and daguerrotypes[8] soon. It was a busy summer for us as we were building a house. The house will cost $370, the stone cellar $130. We hope to move in by November. On August 10, I drew $210 on Curtis & Co. as the remainder of my credit in New York. We had frightful heat recently, 38 R. [117°F.] in the sun. We are slimming down as a result of the heat and work. I do not know whether I have written about our carriage, the main parts of which are the wheels and axle of the rental wagon. Now the bold decision has been made to set an elegant box upon the manure wheels. I am the mailman for two miles around so I may become Postmaster in time. Barck has bought a horse now, too, so now we can get together more often.[9] Now comes the lovely autumn with its cool nights, when one can feel like living again.

------

the mid-1850s. His later letters, particularly during election years, contain considerable political commentary.

6. Seyffardt may have desired beetles to control insects, which otherwise would have damaged his crops.

7. Mathilde Seyffardt was born April 16, 1853, in Titibawassee and would thus have been four months old at the time this letter was written. She shared her name with both William's deceased mother and Sophie's younger sister. In subsequent letters, the Seyffardts usually refer to her as Tilde.

8. Daguerrotype: an early kind of photograph.

9. Edward Barck was a brother-in-law of Sophie Seyffardt and a good friend of William.

1853
191)   SOPHIE SEYFFARDT TO THE
                    [SEYFFARDT] PARENTS IN CREFELD

Titibawassee, August 19

Our little one gives us much joy, she is becoming so aware, pulls her
father's beard already, but she makes a lot of work for me. I would like
to devote myself to her more, but my household makes too many demands upon me. For the past three weeks I have had the oldest
daughter of my sister here. Bertha is only eight years old, but she
helps quite a bit. The poor things have to start working so young and
cannot enjoy their youth. It is so dry this summer that we get hardly
enough garden vegetables for our own use. The rest of the harvest,
however, is good. The heat this summer is almost unbearable, many
thunderstorms but no cooling. Our brother Ernst will visit us for several weeks next month, which I am looking forward to with happy anticipation. He is working as a mechanic in Louisville and earns $12 a
week. Best regards to Louis, Henry and Moritz.[10] Continue loving
your daughter

Sophie

1853
196)   WILLIAM SEYFFARDT TO HIS PARENTS

Titibawassee, October 2

We went through hard times, but it is better now. Our Mathilde
had whooping cough of the worst kind for 8-9 weeks. Also Sophie is
coughing hard, but I still do only when I get up. This cough was common here and attacked all the farmers. It was necessary to hire the
wife of Deibel, our laborer, during our sickness, and together they receive $140 annually. In order to make up the wages, it is absolutely
necessary to put the farm on a larger footing. I must have more land
under all circumstances. Prices of products will rise, since we will get
6–8 saw-mills in the county. One is being built 2½ miles below me.
Our prices now are [per bushel]: wheat $1¼, rye $1, barley $1, oats
$.50, Indian corn $.75, potatoes $.50, hay $10 a ton. All of these items
are rising in price. But if I have to pay $140 wages and have further
help with the harvest, and have only 6-7 acres of winter grain I cannot

10. These were William Seyffardt's brothers. Louis was two years older than William, and
the others younger. Frank, comp., *German-American Pioneers*, p. 52.

get along, although I made so much noise that I had to make do on the income from my farm. My intention is to buy 40–80 acres of adjoining land and clear my farm. My harvest this year is 20 tons of hay, 60 bushels rye, 130 bushels potatoes, 70 bushels of Indian corn, 11 bushels buckwheat, 6 bushels apples, vegetables, etc. I am requesting father to ask for $500 credit for me in New York. I was always opposed to large farms before, but when one constantly keeps hired help, one must have work for them.

Your William

1854

234)   WILLIAM SEYFFARDT TO HIS MOTHER IN CREFELD

Titibawassee, February 8

Having just returned from a trip to Detroit, I will tell about it. I had looked around for some other way to make a living, for we Americans happen to be very materialistic. Since we could not get grain ground for months without going 20–30 miles, I thought that I could start a small mill, as my neighbors would come to me if I could grind halfway well. So I went to Detroit with horse and sled. On the first day I went by way of Saginaw, 12 miles, and Flint, 36 miles. Since it was thawing hard, I took a wagon. I could not sleep at night, as there was a ball in the hotel. I left the next morning at nine and arrived in Pontiac at 1:30. From there I took the train (2 hours) to Detroit. The next morning in a severe snowstorm, I went on an inspection and by evening I had decided on a mill and a horse power of two horses—the mill $100, H.P. $128. . . . I was away for 8 days, for the first time since our marriage, and Sophie shouted so that it could be heard a mile away and Tilde stretched her arms out toward me. I have already earned 20 cts. today—I get one-tenth. The horses have to get used to the horse power, for the ground runs away from under their feet. The mill grinds 4–5 bushels wheat, rye and corn per hour. Since there was a great secret about Ernst's engagement, everyone was afraid to write, but we were very glad about the news. The Dietling Mathilde does not seem to care much about writing either.[11] I include greetings to Moritz.

Your William

11. Ernst Julius Seyffardt, William's younger brother, married Mathilde Frank, Sophie's younger sister. The new couple did not emigrate, however, so the Seyffardt and Frank families were joined on both sides of the Atlantic.

262)   SOPHIE SEYFFARDT TO THE PARENTS IN CREFELD

Titibawassee, March [no date]

. . . [We are sending] A deerskin for the parents, shot by William and sewed by me. You will see that it comes out of the primeval forest, since the colors of the wool do not match at all, I had no selection in Saginaw. Four pairs of moccasins, worked by Indians, for Louis, Ernst, Mathilde and Moritz [Seyffardt]. 8 boxes filled with maple sugar, also Indian work. The ornamentation on them is of porcupine quills.
An American hat for Mathilde.
A bottle of beetles for uncles Emil and Henry.
A turtle, humming bird and an Indian arrowhead, which are found in clearings, for Henry.
A small bottle of syrup, cooked from maple sap.
A daguerreotype and a wreath of American wintergreen.

Sophie

The two broken antlers are from a Virginia deer. They often get to be 4–5 times as heavy, but often large deer have very small antlers, as I noticed on a big buck which wanted to go through the river at my home. He did not go all the way in. Maybe it will interest Moritz as an ardent hunter.

William S.

1854
264)   WILLIAM SEYFFARDT TO HIS FATHER

Titibawassee, April 28

First, I want to announce that I have bought 40 acres of very good land across from mine. I paid $100 for it, and am connecting it to the mill with a ferry. I decided to go East to buy my machinery, and went to Rochester, N.Y., by way of Detroit, Canada, and the Suspension Bridge (Niagara Falls). The steam engine has 10 horse power and is arranged so that the power can be used in two ways so that if grinding grain does not pay, I will saw wood. This is definitely more profitable. My 9 days' trip cost me $30. The machine, with everything that went with it, cost $2135. There will be 99,000,000 feet of lumber cut this year on the Saginaw and branch streams and 400 ships will be needed to transport it.

I have most of the building material and bricks in place. The freight was lower because of the snow. The mill will be between our house and the river, so that the grain can come by land or water. It is being said that there will be a village here soon. It is 6 miles from here to Amelith and 9 miles to Frankenlust, both German Settlements, and we are negotiating for the building of a road from Amelith to here.

The whole thing amounts to more than I had expected, and I am sorry to have to get so much money from Germany where it is so well invested by you, but I am forced, dear father, to ask for further credit of $500, for I do not like to use a stranger's money. Next January 1, I will receive the rest of the money ($200), which August Frank has from me. How can I express my thanks to you for all the love and goodness which you are continually showing me. Just now in anticipation of all the horrors Europe faces, and which may also shake America, I think of all my loved ones with trepidation. But do not forget, dear father, that there are hearts beating on the other side of the big water, in a country which is younger and more firm than shaky old Europe, who will do their duty with happy hearts. Now farewell, greet dear mother and brother and sisters.

From your faithful son William

1854

280)   SOPHIE SEYFFARDT TO WILLIAM SEYFFARDT'S PARENTS

Titibawassee, August 18

I ask you to overlook the first long interruption in our correspondence, for the building of the mill took all of our time. Things are pretty topsy-turvy here, as we had 9–14 men regularly every day and there were headaches in the kitchen-department, as you, dear mother, can imagine. Our farm is as though transformed. It used to be so quiet, and now it is so lively, but I must admit that I miss the pleasant farm life very much. We finally received your package. Sincere thanks for the ring from William's sainted mother. I will save it as a sacred keepsake. Mathilde takes great pleasure in her fat boy [doll]. I will save the pretty garment until she is older and more sensible. She is not well just now, as she is teething. Barck is in agreement to start a little store here, and all that remains is to sell the farm. We would have them near us then and Barck would not have to work so hard. It was an awfully hot summer, 105° F. in the shade. To you, dear parents, most sincere kisses from your

faithful daughter Sophie

1855

295)   SOPHIE SEYFFARDT TO THE
          [FRANK] PARENTS IN DIETLINGEN

Titibawassee, January 7

We hope and wish that you have entered the new year cheerfully, but it was very quiet here. William and I sat quietly at home with our maid and hired man, with left-over springerle[12] and a glass of punch, because for certain reasons we could not get to Barck's.[13] Christmas, in contrast, was very jolly. Thilde stood enchanted before all the lights. Barck made a nice doll house for her, from Karl Scheuermann she got tin dishes, I received a wall basket from Richard, and from my Willi a large sheet on which were enumerated all the things that I was to get. I knitted a woolen jacket for him.

Feb. 23. You can see by the date that my letter has been started long ago, but our little Marie came in the meantime. The news of this you should have from Crefeld by now. The little one is lively and thriving.

William has written that Barck is here, and we will see how the business will go. You, dear mother, would laugh to see how he makes packs of sugar and coffee instead of legal papers, as before. William had much trouble in the mill, and the profits all went for repairs. Ernst's business does not seem to be doing very well, I feel very sorry for him, and wish that he were near us. You will be surprised, dear mother, that I went sled-riding with my little one three times already, although she is only six weeks old. American children get used to everything right away. The little one has dark hair and it seems to me that she has a Frank-face. Now farewell! Write real soon and be heartily kissed by your faithful daughter

Sophie

12. Springerle: Christmas biscuit or cookie.

13. Sophie's sister, Christiane (Nane), was married to Edward Barck, and the Barck family also lived in Titibawassee. Sophie immigrated with her sister and brother-in-law in 1850. The Barcks and Seyffardts remained close, as numerous references in the letters make clear.

1855

296) WILLIAM SEYFFARDT TO HIS PARENTS

Titibawassee, January 17

On January 13, at nine o'clock at night, we were presented with a little, healthy, 7¾ pound girl, who will be given the name of Marie Auguste.

We laughed, father, that you believed that Sophie takes care of the boiler. She only looks out the window to see if steam comes out of the safety-valve, for this shows whether there is more than 80 pounds of steam pressure. Since my engineer, through his carelessness, cost me so much money, in addition to $30 and board and room monthly, I run the machine myself, and find out that my miller stole from me and pocketed the money while I was absent. I chased [him] away, raved, even reached for the gun, the good friend of the backwoodsman. After calm deliberation, I now have an honest miller for $20, Emil Scheuermann is fireman for $15, a man on the farm $12, a girl $1-1¼ a week, W. Seyffardt with undetermined salary as overseer. That my mill is considered worthwhile by speculators is shown by the fact that a N[ew] Y[ork] company made offers to me. Since I cannot have the mill insured, I would sell the whole thing for $15,000, especially since I have too much gall for a miller. You dear father, think that we are saving in the wrong place by having too little help. It is an old story that where the pay is the highest the work is the poorest, because everyone wants to be a gentleman. In the present bad time for N. York and other large cities there is enough work here. Above us there are 120–150 oxen and 500 men working on 5–6 rivers which flow into the Saginaw. Today, the 22nd of January, the first worthwhile snow in 5 weeks and everyone is jubilant.

Your William

1855

314) WILLIAM SEYFFARDT TO HIS PARENTS

Titibawassee, May 2

On March 30 I took about 4500 pounds of mill stones on the ice 16 miles from Saginaw to here with two teams. On April 2, I attended Town Meeting, also across the ice [river], and the ticket which was hatched in Barck's store and called dutch ticket completely knocked out the old officers who had eaten at the public trough. Otto Roeser is now justice of the peace. Little Marie is sitting next to me and swinging her feet, so that I can hardly write. There is a small steam boat traveling the river now and I will have it deliver iron from the mill. Barck has rented his farm this year, gets hay for half, the rest for ⅓. He also wants to sell his cattle and invest the proceeds in the store.

314A)   SOPHIE SEYFFARDT TO THE
                    [SEYFFARDT] PARENTS IN CREFELD

[May 2, 1855]

I am interrupting William's letter because Marie is sleeping right now. We are very happy about the news, especially about the hopes of the dear couple. At Barck's there will also be a little one this summer. Mathilde is suffering much with fever because of the quick temperature changes. We thank you sincerely that you, dear mother, are so busy sewing clothes for our little ones, and are happy for them. We are expecting the doctor this week, who will vaccinate the children, I am worried about Mathilde, who often is not well. Little Marie is very lively and a pretty child. Most sincere greetings from your sincerely loving daughter

Sophie

1856
325)   SOPHIE SEYFFARDT TO THE
                    [SEYFFARDT] PARENTS IN CREFELD

Titibawassee, January 10

We celebrated a merry Christmas at Barck's and drove down with the children and Jacobine. The four Scheuermanns were there also, and happiness showed in the eyes of the three brothers to have their sister Emma here also. Yes, they glorified the occasion with a little keg of beer, which Barck and Mr. Jaexen [Jackson] rolled two miles along the snow. Afterward we danced, as William may not go anywhere without his accordion. Jacobine's box finally arrived, and she wept for joy when she saw it. What joy it was to see the pretty clothes for our children and the beautiful collar for me. What work for you, dear mother! Accept our heartfelt thanks for everything. The gold items will be saved until the girls are able to appreciate the value of the keepsakes from their sainted grandmother. We will make a flower bed with father's flower seeds. The mill is doing very well and William has much work. Our Marie will be a year old next Sunday, and she is a strong child but has no teeth yet. Louis [Seyffardt] should be back from England by now and his bride should be happy. Please tell us the day of the wedding. We had 20° [Reamur?—13° F] of cold for a week and could hardly get the room warm. Sincerest kisses from your

faithful daughter Sophie

1856

331)   WILLIAM SEYFFARDT TO HIS PARENTS

Titibawassee, May 15

A big letter-writing day today, and our Tilde has said: Papa, are you writing to Germany? I would like to know what her idea of Germany is. The little one says quite a bit already. She is very comical and is beginning to climb as recklessly as Tilde. We have a post office now and our address is Post Office Jay, Saginaw Co., Mich. The mail is delivered by a coach, which travels between Saginaw and Midland[14] twice a week. We also have a blacksmith shop, so now our village consists of two homes, three barns, one hotel and one pig sty. I did not include the mill and post office.

As soon as I can, I will buy another quarter section (160 acres). I have done pretty well until now, and I think that prospects are very good. I believe that I wrote to you that I had sold an acre for $50. 400,000,000 feet of fir planks were taken out of Michigan last year, (120,000,000 of it in the Saginaw valley). Average price was $12 per 1,000 feet. It is very cold at present, and we are expecting frost every night. Apple blossoms are ready to open and all trees are filled. All of the peaches froze in northern Michigan last year, and I will not plant any more trees.

Your loving son William

1856

332)   SOPHIE SEYFFARDT TO THE
              [SEYFFARDT] PARENTS IN CREFELD

Titibawassee, May 15

We were very glad about the good news. How robust the dear grandfather must be that he can do things at the age of 81. It is getting

14. Midland, Michigan, is on the Titibawassee River about fifteen miles northwest of Saginaw.

pretty here now. Everything is getting green, so that one feels good after the long winter. I have sown the flower seed, dear father, and am looking forward to the flowers like a child. We even started an asparagus bed 3 years ago, and it has finger-thick asparagus already this year. So we are introducing the German vegetables little by little, while the American lives on cake, meat and potatoes all year. There will be variety in Crefeld, with weddings and baptisms. We will gladly celebrate with them if we know the exact days. Dear Mathilde undoubtedly has her hands full getting the wardrobe nicely in order.

Your sincerely loving daughter

Sophie

1859
395) WILLIAM SEYFFARDT TO THE
[FRANK] PARENTS IN DIETLINGEN

Titibawassee, September 18[15]

For the first time in 8 years there is quite a bit of fever, especially along the rivers. The ground pants for rain, and the plowed land is dusty as ashes. Business is slow, flour is 2½ cts. a pound, and boards can hardly be sold. Sophie is not very lucky with her poultry, for a neighboring dog devoured eggs and young poultry by the dozen. You will be interested to know that we started a Titibawassee quartette. We meet every Saturday and Wednesday from 8 until 11 or 12. At present we are very eager for the trip of the big steamer, The Great Eastern.[16] I would like to see it. We will soon have to get ready for winter. When there is sledding, the winter is very charming. The Seyffardt family has a good sled and Willi drives and crows mightily.[17] It is a good thing my horses are steady. Now farewell and greet Foersters heartily. Your

W. Seyffardt

15. This letter is written during a deep depression that hit the United States between 1857 and 1860. Urban unemployment soared, and agricultural prices skidded. As a miller, Seyffardt felt the bad times acutely.

16. Seyffardt is probably referring to the maiden voyage of the trans-Atlantic steamer *The Great Eastern*. Built in 1858 in England, it was 680 feet long and had a gross weight of 18,915 tons. Until early in the twentieth century, it was the largest vessel afloat.

17. Willi was William and Sophie's third child, age three when this letter was written.

1859

396)   SOPHIE SEYFFARDT TO HER PARENTS

Titibawassee, September 18

It is on my mind every day that I have not written to you for such a long time, but sicknesses will be my excuse, and I am so tired evenings that I just cannot write. William has the fever again and Louis also. Nane often gives me her girls, for girls here are hard to get.[18] The summer brought pleasant variety, the visit of our brothers and then the engagement of Ernst. They were happy days, but too short. Ernst is a happy bridegroom.[19] He wants to come on the 20th of October to take his Emma home. It is painful for us that the wedding will take place in Saginaw, for we two sisters would have enjoyed nothing more than to have our brother's wedding here. We do not say anything about it and will go to please Ernst, who, of course, has to adjust to his wife. With the exception of potatoes and vegetables our harvest is pretty good, and we have to live on cereal foods now. Pigeons are overabundant, William caught them on the stubbles with a net, 61 at one time. We ate them every day and gave many away. Jacobine and Susanne want to enclose letters, too. Susanne had a little girl in July and Jacobine is expecting, too. Now farewell, and a sincere kiss from your

Sophie

1860

432)   WILLIAM SEYFFARDT TO HIS PARENTS,
BROTHERS AND SISTERS

Titibawassee, December 24

After very good business in my mill this winter and the prospect, that by spring I would be out of the hole, we were frightened out of our sleep by the blood-red glow from our burning mill at 4:30 on the morning of the 20th. In the space of 15 minutes there was no hope of saving anything, for the flames drove us from doors and windows. In

18. Nane Frank Barck was Sophie's sister. Her oldest daughters, Bertha and Marie, would have been fourteen and thirteen, respectively, certainly old enough to be helpful around the Seyffardt household. Frank., comp., *German-American Pioneers*, pp. 5, 35.

19. Ernst Frank was Sophie's youngest brother. He immigrated a year after she did and established himself as a successful optician in Milwaukee. He married Emma Scheuermann, a niece of Edward Barck, in October 1859. Frank, comp., *German-American Pioneers*, pp. 44–47.

half an hour everything was but a heap of rubble. We had to work
hard to save our home. Over 10,000 square feet of boards were
dragged out of the fire and 10 barrels of flour for me and 40–50 sacks
of flour for the customers. Besides the mill, we lost 600 bushels of
grain and about 40–50,000 square feet of boards, everything we
owned besides the farm. You can imagine that Sophie was very upset;
she worked and sacrificed, to keep things together and to save, and
now—but what good does it do! Now we must keep our heads.—In
this, our time of great need, our friends have proved themselves. As
our well being is of concern to you, I will tell you how I stand. First,
I am announcing that we will start rebuilding today.

Mortgage on the place...............................	$ 700.00
Obligations to creditors............................	1200.00
Credit for the new building	1100.00
	$3000.00

A very large debt!
The loss has not touched me as much as the sincere sympathy
manifest on all sides. The loss of the mill is considered a public
misfortune, but the people within a radius of several miles want to re-
build for me, I have only to furnish the boards and shingles. This is a
great help and in 6 weeks we can start working again. The machine
was damaged very little, the boiler not at all. The sawmill, which has
not brought in anything for me will go by the way, one less danger of
fire. The fire started because of the extreme carelessness of the fireman. When I think of our mill and work, I could almost despair. After
having been helped so strongly by dear father 2 times, it was with a
certain feeling of self-assurance that I wrote in my last letter that I
would be rid of my greatest worry by next spring. But, head up! The
battle shall be waged again for wife and 5 children. Sincere greetings
and kisses

Your faithful son and brother William Seyffardt

1862

512)   WILLIAM SEYFFARDT TO HIS FATHER

Post Office Jay, Saginaw, May 16

To my grief I saw from your letter of April 12, that you take me for
a thoughtless person who cannot be advised or helped. If I would not
have so much elasticity I would have given in long ago to all the vex-
ations. But what hits me hardest is that you misjudge me. My obli-

gations to you are burdensome to me; therefore I have exchanged 90 acres here for 120 in Saginaw. Believe me, we have deprived ourselves until we were able to make things a bit comfortable for ourselves. It is understandable that we have bad times as a result of the War, but the land is good and wood is always needed. As far as building in Saginaw is concerned, there is time and you need not worry. . . .

To your concern about my change of occupation and my not being a merchant, I must say that while I had mills I was primarily a merchant. It is enough that as a result of the destruction of that which I had worked so hard to get, my pride received the hardest blow. Not having the mills insured was a mistake which I made years ago, and I did not have the funds to remedy it. I am determined now to accept any work which I can do from my property at Saginaw. I have no intention of making a complete change. You cannot understand why Schmitz offered me the partnership?[20] The offer according to prospects here is very good. Schmitz is one of my best friends and needs someone in the business on whom he can depend when he travels. Now farewell and be assured that my circumstances, even though not in order at present, are on the way to becoming satisfactory, and that I will start nothing which could endanger them. Be sincerely greeted by your

grateful son Wm. Seyffardt

1862
520)   WILLIAM SEYFFARDT TO HIS FATHER

Post Office Jay, Saginaw, October 28

I would have written sooner but was kept from it by the uncertainty, which still exists, as to whether I will be inducted into the army. But it is high time to congratulate you on your birthday, the 18th of November, and to wish you many more and cheerful days in the bosom of your family. After the war has dragged on for 20 months with superhuman sacrifices, the Democrats have tried, step by step, to replace the wonderful successes of the Administration so that the sovereign people of the North will become shoe shiners for the South. It seems as though the majority only counts when the Democrats have it. Saginaw is going ahead rapidly, and prospects are exceeding the

20. Seyffardt did not accept this offer of a business partnership and sixteen months later was expressing regret over his decision. He did move to Saginaw, though, and by 1863 had established a hardware store that he ran until his death. Frank, comp., *German-American Pioneers*, pp. 43, 544.

keenest expectations. Wood, which sold for $1.50 last year, sells for $2.00, and fabulous gains are made in the salt works. A barrel of salt costs the manufacturer 60 cts., but it costs $3.00 wholesale for cooking salt and $4.00 for coarse salt (produced by evaporation). Woodland has gone up in value 25% in the last two weeks. Farm produce does not keep up with the enormous increase in wholesale groceries and dry goods. At present I am a butcher, but my butchering is confined to three large oxen. I sell a quarter @ 3½ cts. a pound. We had a letter from August Frank last week telling us that he is doing a brilliant business.[21] He suggests that we drop farming after the war. I do not know if he knows our Saginaw situation well. I will correspond with him regarding it, because he is good at figures. Sophie is so busy with her big household that she has asked me to send her sincere congratulations and best wishes to dear mother. I am having hopes again of being able to embrace you some time.

Your faithful son Wm. Seyffardt

1863
540)   SOPHIE SEYFFARDT TO PASTOR FRANK

Saginaw, November 9

It is a long time since I have written to you and I reproach myself, but time flies with all of the work I have. We left the farm in May and moved to Saginaw, but were hardly here for several weeks when Louis and Soepherle became ill with scarlet fever. After that our little Ernst, who after a hard struggle, succumbed to the illness.[22] Oh, it was a hard blow to lose the dear child and I often have such a great longing for our little darling, but he is better off with God than with us. Nane and I were in Bay City several times this summer. Ernst's business is pretty good, and he has paid back quite a bit already. Unfortunately he was drafted but he hopes to become free. If it is not the case, August wrote that he would give him the money to buy himself free.[23] Babo also is in Bay City and he is a pleasant man. He will start a bil-

21. This is Sophie's brother, August Frank, who had become a very successful dry-goods merchant in Milwaukee. Frank, comp., *German-American Pioneers*, pp. 34–40.

22. The three children noted here are Louis (b. 1858), Sophie (b. 1860), and Ernst (b. 1862, d. 1863). *Soepherle* is German for "little Sophie."

23. During the Civil War men could buy exemption from military service by paying for a substitute. August Frank seems to have offered to help his brother Ernst buy his way out of the draft.

liard parlor and is rooming with Ernst. We are sending pictures of ourselves with music teacher Zeller, who will be going to Stuttgart. The children look good, and also William is pretty good, but not I. Our Little Soepherle would not sit still, and that is why there is no picture of her. Now I will close, make us glad again soon with a letter. Be sincerely kissed by your faithful daughter

Sophie

FOUR

Rosa Cassettari: From Northern Italy to Chicago, 1884-1926

*R*osa is the story of a northern Italian immigrant to the United States in the last decades of the nineteenth century. It is the auto- biography of Rosa Cassettari as told to a social worker, Marie Hall Ets, at the Chicago Commons, a social settlement where she worked as a cleaning woman.[1] Rosa was evidently a fine storyteller, and the head of the settlement, Dr. Graham Taylor, encouraged her by ar- ranging meetings at which she described her life. Marie Hall Ets re- alized the significance of Cassettari's life and took down the stories she told.

The result was *Rosa*, offering a remarkable portrait of the child- hood, emigration, and American experiences of an Italian immigrant. Rosa grew up in a silkmaking town Ets called Bugiarno (actually Cug- giono, near Milan), and her account offers a detailed description of her experiences as a child worker unwinding silk from cocoons in a silk mill—a *filanda*.

We watch her grow up and become interested in young men around her, and we see her foster mother arrange her marriage to an older man for her own "protection." Her story is rich in insights into the socialization of a young woman in northern Italy in the 1870s and 1880s. The account excerpted here begins in 1884, just as Rosa was preparing to leave her young son with her foster mother and emigrate to join her husband, who was working in the iron mines of southwest Missouri.

1. Marie Hall Ets, *Rosa: The Life of an Italian Immigrant* (Minneapolis: University of Minnesota Press, 1970). Ets used the name Cavalleri to mask the author's identity; her real name becomes evident in newspaper clippings in the Marie Hall Ets Collection, folder 19, Immigration History Research Center, St. Paul, Minn. See also Louise C. Wade, *Graham Taylor: Pioneer for Social Justice, 1851–1938* (Chicago: University of Chicago Press, 1964), p. 124.

Rosa was a sharp observer of character and was sensitive to cultural differences between the United States and her native Italy. Her account offers a rich portrait of the cultural change she underwent and yet makes clear the ways she put her traditional culture to good use in a new setting. Rosa never earned much money, and life was a continual struggle; yet hers was very much a "success" story, the story of one immigrant's struggle to reconcile her old world upbringing and new world circumstances. Marie Hall Ets captured for posterity Rosa's strength and her humanity, and our appreciation of the broader meaning of Italian immigration is immeasurably enriched by this account.

[THE TRIP TO AMERICA]

The day came when we had to go and everyone was in the square saying good-bye. I had my Francesco in my arms. I was kissing his lips and kissing his cheeks and kissing his eyes. Maybe I would never see him again! It wasn't fair! He was *my* baby! Why should Mamma Lena keep him? But then Pep was calling and Mamma Lena took Francesco away and Zia Teresa was helping me onto the bus and handing up the bundles.[2]

"But Rosa, don't be so sad!" It was the other Rosa and Zia Maria in the station in Milan, kissing me good-bye and patting my shoulder. "It is wonderful to go to America even if you don't want to go to Santino.[3] You will get smart in America. And in America you will not be so poor."

Then Paris and we were being crowded into a train for Havre.[4] We were so crowded we couldn't move, but my *paesani*[5] were just laughing. "Who cares?" they laughed. "On our way to America! On our way to be millionaires!"

Day after day in Havre we were leaving the lodging house and standing down on the docks waiting for a ship to take us. But always

---

2. Francesco: Rosa's son, whom she left behind in Italy with her foster mother, Mamma Lena, when she went to the United States. Pep, who accompanied Rosa to the United States, was the brother of Mamma Lena.

3. Santino: Rosa's husband who had been working in iron mines in Missouri and had sent Rosa a prepaid ticket to enable her to join him. Rosa's foster mother, Mamma Lena, arranged the marriage when Rosa had shown affection for a young man Mamma Lena did not like.

4. Havre: short for Le Havre, French port city on the English Channel.

5. *Paesani:* fellow Italians, countrymen and women.

the ship was full before it came our turn. "O Madonna!" I prayed.
"Don't ever let there be room! Don't ever let there be room!"

But here, on the sixth day we came on. We were almost the last
ones. There was just one young French girl after us. She was with her
mother and her sister, but when the mother and sister tried to follow,
the *marinaro*[6] at the gate said, "No more! Come on the next boat!"
And that poor family was screaming and crying. But the *marinaro*
wouldn't let the girl off and wouldn't let the mother and sister on. He
said, "You'll meet in New York. Meet in New York."

All us poor people had to go down through a hole to the bottom of
the ship. There was a big dark room down there with rows of wooden
shelves all around where we were going to sleep—the Italian, the
German, the Polish, the Swede, the French—every kind. And in that
time the third class on the boat was not like now. The girls and women
and the men had to sleep all together in the same room. The men and
girls had to sleep even in the same bed with only those little half-
boards up between to keep us from rolling together. But I was lucky.
I had two girls sleeping next to me. When the dinner bell rang we
were all standing in line holding the tin plates we had to buy in Havre,
waiting for soup and bread.

"Oh, I'm so scared!" Emilia kept saying and she kept looking at the
little picture she carried in her blouse. "I'm so scared!"

"Don't be scared, Emilia," I told her. "That young man looks nice in
his picture."

"But I don't know him," she said. "I was only seven years old when
he went away."

"Look at *me*," said the comical Francesca with her crooked teeth.
"I'm going to marry a man I've never seen in my life. And he's not
Lombardo-he's *Toscano*.[7] But I'm not afraid."

Of course Francesca was not afraid. "Crazy Francesca" they called
her at the silk mill. She was so happy she was going to America and
going to get married that she didn't care who the man was.

On the fourth day a terrible storm came. The sky grew black and
the ocean came over the deck. Sailors started running everywhere,
fastening this and fastening that and giving orders. Us poor people
had to go below and that little door to the deck was fastened down. We
had no light and no air and everyone got sick where we were. We
were like rats trapped in a hole, holding onto the posts and onto the
iron frames to keep from rolling around. Why had I worried about

6. *Marinaro:* sailor.
7. *Lombardo:* native of Lombardy; *Toscano:* native of neighboring Tuscany.

Santino? We were never going to come to America after all! We were going to the bottom of the sea!

But after three days the ship stopped rolling. That door to the deck was opened and some sailors came down and carried out two who had died and others too sick to walk. Me and all my *paesani* climbed out without help and stood in line at the wash-house, breathing fresh air and filling our basins with water. Then we were out on the narrow deck washing ourselves and our clothes—some of us women and girls standing like a wall around the others so the men couldn't see us.

Another time there was fog—so much fog that we couldn't see the masts and we couldn't see the ocean. The engine stopped and the sails were tied down and a horn that shook the whole boat started blowing. All day and all night that horn was blowing. No one could sleep so no one went to bed. One man had a concertina and the ones who knew how to dance were dancing to entertain the others. Me, I was the best one. There was no one there to scold me and tell me what to do so I danced with all my *paesani* who knew how. Then I even danced with some of the Polish and the French. We were like floating on a cloud in the middle of nowhere and when I was dancing I forgot for a little while that I was the wife of Santino going to him in America. But on the third day the fog left, the sails came out, the engine started, and the ship was going again.

Sometimes when I was walking on the steerage deck with Giorgio—the little boy of one woman from Bugiarno[8] who was all-the-way sea-sick—I would look back and see the rich people sitting on the higher decks with nice awnings to protect them from the cinders and sun, and I would listen to their strange languages and their laughing. The rich always knew where they were going and what they were going to do. The rich didn't have to be afraid like us poor.

Then one day we could see land! Me and my *paesani* stood and watched the hills and the land come nearer. Other poor people, dressed in their best clothes and loaded down with bundles, crowded around. *America!* The country where everyone could find work! Where wages were so high no one had to go hungry! Where all men were free and equal and where even the poor could own land! But now we were so near it seemed too much to believe. Everyone stood silent—like in prayer. Big sea gulls landed on the deck and screamed and flew away.

Then we were entering the harbor. The land came so near we could almost reach out and touch it. "Look!" said one of the *paesani*. "Green

8. Bugiarno: fictional name of Rosa's hometown, near Milan in northern Italy.

View of steerage, as seen from the first-class deck, 1905. (From Edward A. Steiner, *On the Trail of the Immigrant* [New York: Fleming H. Revell, 1906], p. 10)

grass and green trees and white sand—just like in the old country!"
The others laughed—loud, not regular laughs—so that Pep wouldn't
know that they too had expected things to be different. When we
came through that narrow place and into the real harbor everyone was
holding their breath. Me too. There were boats going everywhere—
all sizes and all kinds. There were smoke chimneys smoking and white
sails and flags waving and new paint shining. Some boats had bands
playing on their decks and all of them were tooting their horns to us
and leaving white trails in the water behind them.

"There!" said Pep, raising his hand in greeting. "There it is! *New
York!*"

The tall buildings crowding down to the water looked like the cardboard scenery we had in our plays at the *istituto*.[9]

"Oh I'm so scared!" said Emilia again. "How can I know that man I
am going to marry? And what if he doesn't meet me?"

Us other women and girls were going to meet our husbands, or the
men to marry, in the iron mine in Missouri. Only the man to marry
Emilia lived in New York and was meeting her here. He didn't work
in the mines. He played a trumpet and had his own band.

"Look," said Pep. "Brooklyn Bridge! Just opened this year with fire-
works and everything."[10]

"And there's Castle Garden."[11]

"Castle Garden! Which? Which is Castle Garden?"

Castle Garden! Castle Garden was the gate to the new land. Everyone wanted to see. But the ship was being pulled off to one side—
away from the strange round building.

"Don't get scared," said Pep. "We go just to the pier up the river.
Then a government boat brings us back."

Doctors had come on the ship and ordered us inside to examine our
eyes and our vaccinations. One old man who couldn't talk and two
girls with sore eyes were being sent back to the old country. "O Madonna, make them send me back too!" I prayed. "Don't make me go
to Santino!"

About two hours later me and my *paesani* were back at Castle Garden on a government boat, bumping the dock and following Pep
across a boardwalk and leaving our bundles with some officers. I

9. *Istituto:* orphanage where Rosa lived for three years and worked in a silk mill.

10. The Brooklyn Bridge was completed in 1883, permitting us to date Rosa's arrival in
New York City.

11. Castle Garden: depot on the southern tip of Manhattan where immigrants were pro-
cessed beginning in 1855. The more famous reception center on Ellis Island was completed
in 1892.

wanted to hold onto my bottles of oil—they might get broken—but the officers made me leave those too. Then one by one we went through a narrow door into Castle Garden. The inside was a big, dark room full of dust, with fingers of light coming down from the ceiling. That room was already crowded with poor people from earlier boats sitting on benches and on railings and on the floor. And to one side were a few old tables where food was being sold. Down the center between two railings high-up men were sitting on stools at high desks. And we had to walk in line between those two railings and pass them.

"What is your name? Where do you come from? Where are you going?"

Those men knew all the languages and could tell just by looking what country we come from.

After Pep, it was my turn.

"Cristoforo, Rosa. From Lombardy. To the iron mine in Missouri."

Emilia was holding me by the skirt, so I stayed a little behind to help her. "Gruffiano, Emilia. From San Paola. What *signore?* You don't know San Paola?"

"She's from Lombardy too," I said. "But she's going to stay in New York."

"And do you know the man I am going to marry, *signore?*" asked Emilia. "See, here's his picture. He has to meet me in Castle Garden. But how can I know him? He plays the *tromba* and owns his own band."

"Get your baggage and come back. Wait by the visitors' door—there at the left. Your name will be called. All right. Move on!"

There were two other decks—one for railroad tickets and one for American money—but we *Lombardi* had ours already so we went back for our bundles. But I couldn't find my straw-covered bottles. Everybody was trying to help me find them. Then an inspector man came. "What's all the commotion?" he asked. "Oh, so those bottles belonged to her? Well ask her," he said to the interpreter. "Ask her what that stuff was? Was it poison?"

When Pep told him he said, "Well tell her her bottles are in the bottom of the ocean! Tell her that's what she gets for bringing such nasty stuff into America! It made us all sick!"[12]

My *paesani* looked at their feet or at the ground and hurried back into the building. Then they busted out laughing. That was a good one! That was really a good one! And even I had to laugh. I was bro-

---

12. Rosa had brought mustard seed oil sealed up in wine bottles. The immigration officers discovered too late that the bottles were not for drinking.

kenhearted to lose my good oil but it was funny anyway—how Mamma Lena's nice wine bottles had fooled those men in gold braid.

We *Lombardi* put down our bundles and sat on the floor near the visitors' door. At last after all the new immigrants had been checked, an officer at the door started calling the names. "Gruffiano, Emilia" was the first one.

"*Presente! Presente!*" shouted Pep jumping to his feet and waving his hands. But Emilia was so scared I had to pull her up and drag her along after him.

At the door the officer called the name again and let us pass. Then here came up a young man. He was dressed—O Madonna!— like the president of the United States! White gloves and a cane and a diamond pin in his tie. Emilia tried to run away but Pep pulled her back. "*Non è vero! Non è vero!* It's not true!" she kept saying.

"But it *is* true!" the young man laughed. "Look at me, Emilia! Don't you remember Carlo who used to play the *tromba* in San Paola when you were a little girl?" And he pulled her out from behind us and took her in his arms and kissed her. (In America a man can kiss the girl he is going to marry!) "But I never thought you would come like this," he said, holding her off a little and looking at her headkerchief and full skirt. "I'm afraid to look. Did you come in the wooden soles too?"

"No," said Emilia, speaking to him for the first time. "My mother bought me real shoes to come to America!" And she was lifting her feet to show him.

"She looks just the same as when she was seven years old," the young man said to Pep, and he was happy and laughing. "But I'm going to take her up Broad Street and buy her some American clothes before I take her home."

I was glad for Emilia that she was going to marry that nice young man, but why couldn't something like this ever happen to me?

Other visitors were called. Some families separated at Havre found each other again and were happy. But that nice young French girl, she was there all alone—nobody could find her mother and her sister. I don't think they ever found each other again.

When the gate was opened men wearing badges came running in, going to the different people. One dressed-up man with a cane and waxed mustache came to us. "*Buon giorno, paesani! Benvenuto!* Welcome to America! Welcome to the new country!" He was speaking Italian and English too and putting out his hand to shake hands with Pep. We other *paesani* looked on in wonder. A high man like that shaking hands with the poor! This was America for sure!

"I heard your talk and knew you were my *paesani*. I came to help you. You have the railroad tickets and the American money?"

"*Si, signore,*" said Pep and we all showed our tickets and our money.

Then Pep asked about the women's chests that had come on an earlier ship. "Leave it to me," said our new friend. "Leave it to me, your *paesano*, Bartini. I will find them and send them to Union. And in three days when your train goes I will put you on myself so you won't go wrong."

"Three days! But no, *signore!* We want to go today."

"My dear man," laughed Bartini, "you're lucky I found you. There's no train to Missouri for three days. But don't worry! Bartini will take care of everything. You can come and eat and sleep in my hotel, comfortable and nice, and in three days I will take you and put you on the right train."

And in three days he did put us on the train but he took all our money first, about thirteen dollars each one. He left us not even a crust of bread for our journey. And we didn't even guess that he was fooling us.

The American people on the train were sorry when they saw we had nothing to eat and they were trying to give us some of their food. But Pep said no. He was too proud to take it. Me, I would have taken it quick enough. But I couldn't after Pep said no—even with that little Giorgio crying with his face in my lap. Those American people were dressed up nice—the ladies had hats and everything—but they were riding the same class with us poor—all equal and free together.

"Look, Giorgio," I said, to make him forget his pains. "Horses and cows just like in *Italia*. But here there are no shepherds to watch every blade of grass they eat. Here they can go all around and eat what they want."

At last we were in the station in St. Louis changing trains for Union. We were sick for food but everyone was awake now—everyone excited. Domiana[13] could scarcely wait to see her husband, Masino. And Francesca—"Crazy Francesca"—was trying to find out from Pep what kind of a man was waiting to marry her. All the *paesani* were laughing, but not me. Me, I was hiding my rosary in my hand and kissing the cross and trembling inside. "O Madonna," I prayed, "You've got to help me! That man is my husband—I must do what he wants, to not offend God and offend You! But You've got to help me!"

Then the conductor was calling, "Union! Union!" And everybody was picking up bundles and pushing to the windows. There was a little

13. Domiana: a neighbor and friend of Rosa.

wooden station ahead and beside it were all our *paesani* from the iron mine with two wagons with horses to meet us.

"Look, Rosa, the one with white teeth and black mustache, he's my cousin, Gionin.[14] I think the young man beside him is the one I'm going to marry!"

"He looks nice, Francesca," I said.

I thought maybe Santino didn't come, or maybe I'd forgotten what he looked like. But then I saw him—a little back from the others—just as I remembered him.

Pep, a bundle on his back, was getting off first—laughing and excited—proud that he had brought us new *paesani* all the way from the old country.

"*Benvenuto*, Pep! *Benvenuto, paesani! Benvenuto!* But *Gesu Maria!* Why those three days doing nothing in New York?"

"Bartini said there were no trains for three days."

"No trains for three days! There come two trains every day to Missouri. Wait till we can get our hands on Bartini! But forget it now. Now we are all together. Just a little ride through the woods and you are in your new home. And in camp there is plenty to eat. Can a girl as beautiful as Rosa help cook it?"

It was like a *festa*. Everybody in their best clothes and everybody talking and laughing.

Francesca's cousin Gionin was introducing Francesca to the man she was going to marry, but they didn't know what to say. They just stood there getting red and red. Masino, the husband of Domiana, was laughing and crying at the same time, hugging Domiana, then taking Giorgio in his arms and kissing him. Without looking I could see Santino still back at one side eying me with his half-closed eyes. He did not come to me and I did not go to him. Instead I stood there talking and laughing with the *paesani* who had come to meet us— mostly young men I had known in Bugiarno. Twelve of them were going to eat in my house. I was to cook for them. "But I don't know how to cook!"

"*Per l'amore di Dio*, don't worry about that. We will teach you!"

"Watch close the way we are going, Rosa." It was Gionin, the cousin of Francesca. He was sitting next to me on the wagon. "You will be walking back here every two or three days to get groceries and ask for mail." He was not *Lombardo* like the others—he and his friend were *Toscani*. I had to listen careful to understand his words. But his talk

14. Gionin: a boarder in Rosa's household. Later he helped her run away to Chicago, and after she obtained a divorce, Rosa and Gionin were married.

sounded nice and so respectful. "Here in America they have the courthouse and the jail on the square, in place of a church."

The old *paesani* were all asking questions at once of the new ones. They wanted to know about this one and that one and all that had happened in Bugiarno since they went away. Only Santino said nothing. I could see him out of the corner of my eye sitting up near the driver watching me. But somehow I was not so afraid with Gionin beside me. And Gionin was one of the twelve going to eat in my house.

After two or three miles the wagons came out from the woods and there, below, was the iron mine and the camp. Down there there were no trees and no grass—just some shacks made of boards and some railroad tracks. The sun was going down behind the hills and a few miners with picks and sledgehammers were coming out from a tunnel. Other men down in an open place were wheeling away their tools in wheelbarrows. The new *paesani* grew silent—as if they had expected something else—as if they were no longer sure they were going to be millionaires. And me, looking up to see which shack Gionin was pointing to, met the eyes of Santino. . . .

[LIFE IN A MISSOURI MINING CAMP]

Domiana was bigger than me. Her baby was coming first. "And what are we going to do way off here in the mining camp with no doctor, no midwife—no one—to help us?" asked Domiana. "My husband, he's all the time drunk now. He gets the whiskey from those American men and he's all the time drunk. Masino is kind—he's not cruel like Santino—but how can he help me when he's drunk?" Then she told me I must listen and if I hear her knocking on the wall in the night I must come.

"It's no good for me to come, Domiana," I said. "I don't know how babies are born. I was three days without my senses when I had my Francesco."

"Never mind if you don't know, Rosa. You come and I will tell you what to do. You come and help me then I'll help you when yours comes."

I almost died when my first baby was born and I had two doctors and Mamma Lena and Zia Teresa besides. What was I going to do this time? And how was I going to help Domiana? Domiana said that the husband planted a seed in his wife and it was from that seed that babies grew. I never knew before where the babies came from but it sounded probably true. But even a seed couldn't grow into something alive unless God and the Madonna made it.

And sure enough, one night in the middle of the night there came the knocking on the wall. I sat up and saw a light coming through the cracks in the wall. The knocking came again. "Hail Mary Mother of God pray for us now and in the hour of our death!" I prayed as I climbed out of bed, put a skirt over my chemise, and went out my door and into Domiana's. The lamp was smoking but I could see Masino drunk on the floor. And there on the bed by Domiana was the new baby already born, but it was attached to Domiana with a funny twisted cord. It was kicking its arms and legs and crying with all its might. I was afraid to go in—afraid to go near.

"Don't be scared, Rosa!" Domiana called. "Bring the scissors and string from the table."

I went in and picked up the scissors and string and took them to her.

"Tie the string around the cord near the baby's stomach. Then take the scissors and cut off the cord."

"Oh no, Domiana! I can't! I'm afraid. I will kill you!"

When I didn't do what Domiana said she began crying and praying. So then I started to pray too. And suddenly the Madonna gave me courage. Even if it killed Domiana I must do what she said.

Domiana didn't die—she didn't even feel it when I cut the cord. The Madonna is wise. The Madonna knew all about such things. So then I brought warm water from the reservoir and bathed the baby's skin like Domiana told me and bound him up in the clothes Domiana had ready and laid him on the bed beside her. And there the first light of the morning was coming in through the window.

"*Grazie*, Rosa! *Grazie!* I can take care of the rest myself. But before you go wake up that drunk husband of mine."

So I went there and pushed Masino with my foot. "Wake up, you old drunk!" I said. "Wake up! You ought to be ashamed—lying there drunk and your wife having a new baby all alone! You're the father of another nice little boy!"

That poor man—he was not like Santino—he loved his wife and his babies. But he was all the time drunk.

"Get up and build a fire in the stove and make coffee. Then you can stay awake and help your wife and that new baby.

So after I helped her that night Domiana told me, "Now if I'm here, Rosa, when your baby comes I'm going to help you. But if I have to leave, you know what to do anyhow. You do like I showed you."

And sure enough, right after Domiana had her baby, the iron mine in Union started laying off men and Masino was one of the first to go. And because some of the other men were going to a new iron mine in Michigan, Masino was going there too. Domiana had to go with him.

So poor me, I was going to be there all by myself! I was so scared I
didn't know what I was going to do when the worst came! I almost
died when my first baby was born with two doctors—two professors.
This time I thought I would die for sure—all alone by myself. But
what could I do?

So it was Monday morning and I was trying to do my washing. I
always washed the men's clothes Monday morning. But when I tried
to hang them up I couldn't. I couldn't. When I first felt those terrible
pains I thought I was near the end, so I prepared the string and the
scissors ready on the table. Then I got so sick I thought I had come to
the end of my life! I went in and grabbed hold of the table and I
couldn't let go. I stayed there holding onto that table. "O Madonna,
pray God to forgive my sins. But don't let me die anyway! Don't let
me or my baby die!"

"Rosa! Rosa!"

Who was calling? Where was I? What had happened? I opened my
eyes and slowly I remembered. I was on the floor in my house. My
baby had been born. I had tied the cord and cut it, the way Domiana
showed me, but then everything had turned black. The baby was lying
there with no cover—nothing. But it must be alive. I heard it cry.

"Rosa! Rosa!"

Then I knew from the voice and from the way she said "Rosa" that
it was the German farmer lady from on the hill—Mis' Quigley. Probably Mis' Quigley had guessed something had happened when she
didn't see the clothes on the line. I wanted to speak to her but before
I could lift my head Mis' Quigley had run away. What could I do? I
tried to sit up but I fell back. My poor baby was lying naked on the
boards! Everything turned black again.

The next thing I knew old Angelina was leaning over me talking in
Italian. Mis' Quigley hadn't deserted me after all—God bless her! She
had only run off to get Angelina.

"Santa Maria, Rosa! You cut the cord and tied it yourself? Why
didn't you send your husband to tell me when you felt the pains? Oh,
the poor baby!" And Angelina was picking up the baby and wrapping
it gently in her apron. "But he's too little! He was born too soon! What
did you do, Rosa? You carried the heavy tubs of water and made your
baby come too soon? You're all right yourself, Rosa? You'll be all right
if I fix the baby first and then come back to you?"

Angelina bathed the baby and banded him up nice, and then she
helped me get clean and back onto the bed beside him. But then
Angelina had to run to her cooking. "When your husband comes,"

she said, "tell him to fix you a bowl of warm water with the bread and butter in. That's what the women like best when they have the baby born."

I lay listening. When I heard the hammering of the picks stop I knew the men would be coming to eat and there was nothing prepared. What could I do? I tried, but I couldn't get up. Santino came in first—the others had gone off to their own shacks to get washed. He stood still in the other room for a minute or two. Then he came to the door and looked in. I knew he was angry because there was nothing prepared. I trembled and put my arm around the baby. But he didn't come in. He just stood there looking at the baby as if he was afraid.

I was hungry and so thirsty. Maybe if I had something to eat I could get up. I remembered what Angelina had told me so I asked Santino if he will bring me a bowl of warm water from the reservoir with bread and butter in it.

He didn't answer at first. Then he started swearing and told me if I wanted something to eat to get up and get it myself.

Gionin and some of the others had come in and were standing near the door. How glad Gionin would be to get me whatever I wanted! But I knew he couldn't with Santino there watching. Instead he and one or two others made the meal themselves. Then he went early away and sent his cousin Francesca back and Francesca gave me something to eat.

The next morning, as soon as Santino and the others who worked in the tunnel had gone, Gionin came in himself with a big bowl of warm milk and bread and butter. He smiled down into my eyes, then lifted the corner of the blanket. And as he stood there looking his own face puckered and grew red—just like the baby's.

"He was born too young," I told him. "I don't know if he can live. If he dies before he's baptized he can never go to heaven. Gionin, you and Francesca be the godparents and take him to the priest and have him baptized before he can die."

"Yes, Rosa, I will be glad. Right away tonight after work."

On the second morning I was up doing the work as always. My baby was still weak—I didn't know whether he would live or die—but thanks to Gionin he had been baptized. And he had the name Domenico after Don Domenic. For sure the spirit of Don Domenic would help him if he died.

Gionin was watching the baby as much as I was. All the men who ate in my house, except Santino, were watching and hoping he could live. But Gionin most of all. Gionin was loving that baby more than a father. He even made him a cradle out of boards and when it was finished he brought a big pillow and put the baby in and the baby went right to sleep. Santino watched with the others. He said nothing but I could tell that he didn't like it that Gionin was loving that baby so much.

"But Rosa," said Miss Mabel the first time I went to the store with the baby. "Why didn't you tell me? I thought you looked kind of fat—but those full skirts and chemises! I never even guessed! What did you do, Rosa, with no doctor and no one to help you?"

I could not understand all that Miss Mabel said but I could understand that Miss Mabel was surprised—and sorry too—that she had not known so she could help. Sure, I had wanted to tell Miss Mabel but I had been ashamed. In the old country a woman not married is not supposed to know about such things.

"Oh, how sweet, Rosa! How nice! Let me hold him!"

As the baby grew stronger his crying grew louder. His crying angered Santino. He would shout at him to keep still. Then angered still more that the baby did not obey would go to the cradle and slap him. One evening the baby was crying harder than ever. I held him as long as I could but then had to put him down while I cleared the table and washed the dishes. The men sat on, playing cards. Now and then Santino swore and shouted at the baby to shut up. He was losing at the game and he was angry. Finally he slammed the money he owed on the table and swearing, he lifted his leg over the bench. I saw his eyes on the cradle. Dropping the dish I was drying I made a dash for the baby, grabbing him up just in time—just before Santino could reach him—and ran to the corner.

Since he couldn't get at the baby Santino struck out at me. He struck me several blows on my head, then he struck my back. The men at the table sat silent, watching. They still did not move or speak when Santino finally turned and faced them. Maddened by their disapproving silence Santino stalked across the room, snatched his hat from the nail, and went out.

I came from the corner and watched. He was going off up the road to Union—going to spend the night with Annie. I turned back to the room. Most of the men still sat at the table. But Gionin had risen and was going toward the stove. What was he doing—taking the big bread knife from the rack? Suddenly I dropped the baby in the cradle and ran to Gionin.

"No, Gionin! No!" I said, grabbing his arm and reaching for the knife.

"Let me go!" said Gionin, trying to shake me off. "Let me go! I am going to kill that man for you, Rosa! I am going to kill him!"

"No, Gionin, no! You mustn't even say such a thing! It's a sin just to think it! God lets him live—we've got to take it, that's all. Do you want to sit in jail the rest of your life? They could even put you on the rope! No, Gionin! No!" And I burst out crying.

"If I can kill that man for you first, Rosa, I will gladly sit in jail the rest of my life!"

"No, Gionin, no! To kill a man is a terrible sin! God will make you burn in hell forever and ever!"

Finally Gionin let me take the knife and went and sat down at the table, burying his head in his hands. I stood looking at him for a little, then putting the knife back in the rack I went and picked up the crying baby. I walked back and forth for a while then I sat down on the bench at the end of the room and gave the baby my breast.

The men at the table collected their cards and one by one got up and took their hats and went out.

The baby fell asleep and I put him back in the cradle. Then I turned down the light in the lamp and sat down at the table across from Gionin.

Gionin ran his fingers through his thick black hair several times before he looked up. "*Gesu Maria Giuseppe*, Rosa! I can't stand it to see anymore! I can't stand it! If I stay here and see anymore there is going to be trouble, that's all! Something is going to happen!"

"Then better you leave, Gionin. Better you go somewhere else to eat, so you don't see. Go to Francesca's."

For a long time Gionin did not answer. When at last he spoke, I could hardly hear him. It was like he spoke only to himself. "Yes," he said. "Yes. If you don't want me to fight with that man, Rosa, it's better that I go." And holding his hands out to show there was nothing he could do he got up, took his hat, and went out.

And so Gionin went from my house. But every Sunday morning I was with him when we walked the tracks to go to church. I walked with the women and he walked with the men, but we were together anyway. And we were listening together when the priest sang the beautiful Latin words of the mass.

[A Return Trip to Bugiarno]

One day when I went in to the little store and post office in Union they told me there was a letter for me. It was from Mamma Lena. Mamma Lena didn't write it—she couldn't write—but she had somebody write it for her. In the letter she said that she was getting old and sick and that I must come back and get Francesco. She said she had all my wages from America and a little besides to pay for the trip.

Oh, I was happy when I thought I could get back my Francesco! But would Santino let me go? I had to wait till he came home from the mine at night to ask him.

"Yes!" he said. "Just what I want! I don't trust the men that go back. You go there and get all my money from the bank. I am going to buy a business of my own and get rich." But he didn't tell me what the business was.

All the men and the girls in the camp were excited when they heard I was going back to Bugiarno. And one old man, Lorenzo, he asked to go with me. Lorenzo was sick with the consumption and the doctor said it would be nice if he could go home to die.

Enrico, the boss of the mine, found out how and when we could go and he bought the tickets and wrote it all down. Then came the Sunday to go and Gionin and all my *paesani* went on the wagon to Union to say good-bye at the train. Miss Mabel and Mr. Miller were there too. But not Santino. Santino, like always on Sunday, was at Freddy's saloon with Annie and those other women.

"You be careful of my little godchild, Rosa," said Gionin as he lifted Domenico up to me on the train. "Don't let anything happen to him. And bring him soon back."

Gionin talked only of Domenico but I knew from the way his eyes were looking into mine that he was thinking of me too.

When the trainman called, "All aboard!" Lorenzo rushed in to the window and stood there waving back with tears running down his old cheeks. When the train went around a bend we could no more see our *paesani* but Lorenzo still stood there.

I put Domenico on the seat, then pulled the hat pins out of my hat and took it off.

"A hat is no good for a poor woman with a baby and satchels and bundles," I said, holding the hat up for Lorenzo to see. I had to say something to make him forget his sad parting. "I never had a hat before, but I thought it would be nice to be wearing a hat when I come back from America. Then that rascal Cicco, Nick's little dog, found it on the table and chewed up all the feathers."

"You look beautiful in a hat, Rosa," said Lorenzo. He wiped his nose and cheeks with the back of his hand and sat down across from me. "You will look nice coming home in a hat."

I stuffed the hat into one of my bundles and put on my head-kerchief. No need to bother with the hat till I got off the *tramvai*[15] in Bugiarno.

15. *Tramvai:* streetcar.

But would we ever get to Bugiarno? I had learned more English in two or three years than anyone else in camp. But would anyone but Miss Mabel and Mr. Miller and Enrico understand me? And would I understand their answers? If we got on the wrong train in St. Louis we would go to the other end of America. But Enrico had been good. He had taught me the things I must say.

I was shaking and shivering when we came out in the station in St. Louis, but I just smiled at Lorenzo and marched up to the man at the gate: "Please will you tell me where to get the train to New York?"

"The train to New York? In one hour it goes." The officer held up one finger and took out his watch and showed me. Then he motioned to one of the long seats. "You sit down and wait there and I will tell you when it is time."

"Thank you, *signore*. Thank you."

Think of that! I had talked English to a strange man and he had understood me. Lorenzo was looking at me like I was something wonderful. So then I started watching the clock and counting the minutes. But that minute hand moved so slow that I thought the clock must be wrong. So I went back to the man by the gate—I wasn't afraid at all. In America the poor can talk to anyone and ask what they want to know.

"Yes, yes," the man said. "I didn't forget you. It's still early. But if you are nervous you can go and stand over there by the gate and wait. That train outside is the train to New York."

So me and Domenico and Lorenzo were the first ones to go through. And before we climbed on I asked again, "Is this the train to New York?"

"Yes," said the trainman. "Yes. This is where you go." And he even took us in and showed us the seats to sit on.

So there was no mistake. We were going right. There was nothing more to worry about until we came to the end of the line. And we didn't have to worry about where in New York we must stay overnight for Enrico had it written down on a paper so all those men from the lodging houses couldn't cheat us.

In the lodging house Lorenzo slept in the big room for men and me and Domenico in the smaller room for women. And the next morning we were ready and down in the waiting room hours before it was time for the man from the lodging house to take us to the pier. So we got there all right. And, thanks to the Madonna, on this ship all the women in the third class went in one room and all the men in another. And because I had some extra money in the pocket of my underskirt I gave some to the *marinaro* and made him understand it was for water every day to drink and to keep the baby clean. We were only allowed some water to drink with our meals. Most of the other women were French nuns and they were all the time playing with Domenico. They loved Domenico. (But coming back, on this trip too, all the men and the women had to sleep in the same room and even in the same beds.)

Italia! We were in Italy again! I could talk to everyone! And I wasn't afraid now that I came from America. "Will you please help me with my little boy?" I said to the trainman as we changed trains in Turin. I didn't really need help but I wanted to ask for something.

"*Ma si, signora*," said the trainman politely, taking Domenico while I climbed up with my bundles.

"*Grazie, signore. Grazie molte!*"

Lorenzo had climbed on first and was looking out the window. His old hat was pulled down over his eyes, but I could tell by the stiff way he sat on the board seat how excited he was. And I was excited too. Now we were so near, it was hard to wait to see my Francesco. And Mamma Lena. And Zia Teresa. And Toni. And Remo? Would I see Remo? He had been so brokenhearted when I was married to Santino that he had signed for another three years in the *militario*.[16] Maybe he would not know that I was in Bugiarno—or could not come if he did.

Nearly all the poor people in Bugiarno were there waiting in the square when we got off the *tramvai* Sunday morning. Some of those young men that used to like me even went up on top of the church tower to see me get off the *tramvai*. Two of the old women who came to help me with my bundles reached out and touched my skirt and kissed my hand. They had known me ever since I was a little girl saying the Latin prayers for them in their courts. But now because I came from America and was wearing a hat and new shoes they thought I was something wonderful.

Then I saw Mamma Lena and Zia Teresa at one side with a little boy between them. That little boy must be my Francesco! I ran and threw my arms around him and kissed him. But he pushed me away.

"Give him time, Rosa," said Zia Teresa. "He was only a baby when you went away. You will have to get acquainted all over again."

But by the time we passed through the gate to the old *palazzo*[17] I had Francesco's hand in mine and was swinging it back and forth, and

16. *Militario:* army.
17. *Palazzo:* city hall.

he was half smiling at me. Sure it wouldn't take us long to get acquainted, me and my Francesco!

The big dark *osteria* smelled just as it always had—the same smell of men and of sour wine and of cabbage soup and of the chickens in the coop. A few of the guards who lived on the court had already come in and were sitting at the tables waiting for their noonday soup.

I took off my hat and hung it careful on a nail, but I didn't put on an apron. Today I had the job to entertain the people and I wanted to look nice. Zia Teresa and some of the other women who had come in would gladly help Mamma Lena.

All afternoon and far into the night the tables in the *osteria* were full. Even those young men from the church tower came in the evening and ordered wine so they could look at me and listen. The women sat on benches along the sides of the room and kept making me tell the same thing over and over. *Mamma mia*, but that was hard to believe—poor people in America eating meat every day! Tell about that again, Rosa. And about the streets of New York—show them how the people are always running and how they have to jump to get out of the way of the carriages and horses. And about those streetcars running right over the heads of people! No wonder the horses get frightened! And about the ships. And tell how that Bartini got all your money, Rosa. And the mustard oil. Tell about your nice bottles of mustard oil. I myself like to tell about that mustard oil. The men would laugh until they almost fell off the benches and slap each other on the back—to think of those high American men in all their gold braid trying to drink my mustard oil.

"And is it true, Rosa, that the *fiammetta*[18] comes in America too?"

"Yes," I said. "There too I saw the *fiammetta*. But in America the people are not afraid like here. In America the high people teach the poor people and tell them not to be scared." Then I told how Enrico had taken his lantern that night and made us poor Italians go there to the edge of the swamp where the little flame was and touch it, to show us that it wouldn't hurt anyone and how he had said that it was only some gas that comes out of the earth and not evil spirits at all.

"But if the *fiammetta* is not the evil spirit why does it come most in the cemetery?" said one old woman.

I didn't know, but I said, "I guess there's more grease in the cemetery and that's why."

18. *Fiammetta:* literally, little flame. Although the reference is not entirely clear, this may be burning swamp gas, or methane.

I could see those people didn't believe me—that they would go right on almost dying from the scare when the *fiammetta* appeared in their fields.

"And Enrico says there is no such thing as people witching you with the evil eye," I told them. "He says it's foolish to be scared of the *malocchio*. Nobody can make you sick just by looking at you." But even when I spoke the word *malocchio*,[19] some of the old women crossed themselves in fear.

The first day the savings bank was open I went there with the papers to get the money for Santino. What Santino wanted with all that money I didn't know. There was nothing to buy in the mining camp in Missouri. But he had told me to get it and so I was getting it. There were many people already in line at the window. And all the time more men kept coming and the women had to wait and let the men go first. I stood there waiting and waiting and I got tired. There were some nice chairs there on the other side of a little railing—chairs for the high people. But why should the high people have chairs and not the poor? The more I thought about those chairs, the more I wanted to go in there and sit down. Those chairs were doing nothing—why shouldn't I sit on one? So finally I did it; I pushed open the little gate and went in and sat down.

"Oh, Rosa!" gasped the other women in the line. "Come back! Come back! You'll get arrested. They'll put you in jail!"

"Well the chairs are here and nobody is sitting on them," I said. "You come too and sit down."

Soon the janitor came.

"*Che impertinenza!*"[20] he said. "Who gave you the permission to sit down?"

"Myself," I said and smiled at him because I was no longer afraid. "The chairs belong to the bank, isn't that so! And the people who have money in the bank have the right to use them, no?"

"You think you're smart because you come from America!"

"Yes," I said. "In America the poor people do get smart. We are not so stupid anymore."

And there the janitor could do nothing—he gave up and went away.

At last all the men had finished their business and only the women were left. So I got up and took my place before the window. And when it was my turn the officer smiled and bowed and didn't say anything at all about my sitting on the chair.

19. *Malocchio:* evil eye.
20. *Che impertinenza:* what impertinence (nerve).

"If you please," I said in English. "How do you do. Thank-you. Good-bye." That Italian officer wouldn't know that the words didn't fit and I wanted to show him that I was learning to speak English.

And there he was bowing and smiling so polite and the women were all looking and looking, with their mouths hanging open.

So I gave him my papers and told him what I wanted. And he was shaking his head yes and saying, "Si, signora. Si, si." And he arranged it so the bank would send the money to America for me, so I wouldn't have to carry it with me.

After all that good food I had had in America, I was no longer content with the sour-tasting black bread, or the thin onion-and-water soup, or a little polenta. I wanted to make thick soup with rice in it every day or cook the rice the way I had learned to cook it in America. "Whoever heard of such extravagance!" Mamma Lena would scold. "The people in America make pigs of themselves. They are like pigs!"

And if I turned up the lamp a little at night so I could see to clean the tables and do the knitting, Mamma Lena would scold, "You are all the time wasting! Don't waste the oil like that!"

Even when I played with Francesco and Domenico Mamma Lena would scold, "It's a sin to spoil the children like that!" Though she was always picking up Domenico and holding him.

"Rosa," she said one day when she was holding him. "When you go back to America with Francesco you can leave Domenico with me. He's younger. I can take care of him better."

"No!" I said. "No!"

Mamma Lena didn't say anything—she didn't even scold. Before I went to America I would have been afraid to say no.

Saturday night I went to confession. And on Sunday I went to mass and again to vespers. Mamma Lena and some of those other women thought I was not so religious, not so good, now that I came from America. I had to show them I had just as strong religion in America as in Italy. In the mining camp there wasn't any way to go to confession, except for those girls who were getting married, but that was not my fault.

Bianca, the cousin of Remo, with her straight hair and big nose was waiting for me outside the church after vespers. I left Zia Teresa and ran to see what Bianca wanted.

"Rosa," whispered Bianca, "I sent word to Remo[21] that you were back and he got leave and came home. He says for you to come to our house for supper tonight and he can see you there."

---

21. Remo had been Rosa's first love. Mamma Lena, however, had opposed their marriage and arranged for Santino to marry Rosa.

All week women had been asking me to come to their houses to eat so they could hear about America. But I had said no because I knew those people would have to go hungry a week after. Mamma Lena would think I said yes to Bianca because her family was not so poor. Mamma Lena would never know that Remo was there.

"Yes, Bianca," I said. "I'll go first to tell Mamma Lena, then I'll come."

Remo's mother and his uncle, Zio Ferdinando, and his aunt, Zia Chiara, had all come to the *osteria* with Bianca during the week and greeted me there. So when I came into their big room Sunday night they stood back and let Remo greet me alone.

There he was, dressed like a soldier, but looking just the same as he always had. He didn't even seem any older.

"*Benvenuto*, Rosa," he said. "Welcome!" And his eyes smiled, shy like, into mine.

"Hello, Remo," I said. But after that there seemed to be nothing to say or do.

"Well, let us eat," said Zio Ferdinando. "Let us go to the table and eat."

Bianca and her mother served the wine and the Sunday rice, the *minestra,* and we all sat down and ate. And after eating they all just sat there waiting for me to say something—waiting for me to entertain them. But what could I say? I couldn't think. It was in this room that Remo had said good-bye and run back to the army, afraid of the punishment. It was in this room that Mamma Lena had found me under the bed and dragged me home to marry Santino.

"Tell us about the mines, Rosa," said Zio Ferdinando. "Do the men work in tunnels down under the earth?"

"No, Zio Ferdinando," I said. "There is one tunnel—one big hole— but most of the men dig the iron right out of the open quarry."

I could feel Remo's eyes on me as I spoke. I should not have come. I was a married woman now and the mother of two children.

"No, Zio Ferdinando. They use hand drills and picks.... No, they load it on railway cars and it goes to the blast furnace near another town.... Yes, the single men all go together to eat.... Yes, I cook for twelve now. At first I had thirteen."

I wanted to tell about Gionin—about how Gionin couldn't stand it to see Santino beat me and beat the baby and that was why he had gone away. But what would Remo think if he knew about Gionin?

"Those men are good," I said. "At first I didn't know anything about cooking and I was feeding them plaster. But they didn't scold or anything. They just tried to help me."

When there was nothing more to say Zio Ferdinando asked when I was going back to America.

"I don't know," I said. "Some men are leaving next week for Missouri and my cousin Giuseppe, Zia Teresa's last son, is going with them. But Mamma Lena doesn't want me to go so soon."

At last the *lume* started flickering—the oil in that little lamp was almost gone.

"It's time I went home," I said. And as I got my shawl and chewed-up hat, Remo got his cap and coat and waited by the door.

"Better you go with them, Bianca," said Zio Ferdinando.

Bianca hesitated, looking first at Remo and then at me.

"Yes, Bianca," I said. "You come too." And I waited for her to get her shawl and headkerchief.

"Rosa," said Remo as soon as we were out in the darkness of the court. "Don't go next week! Please don't! Other men will be going to America later. Listen, Rosa. I'll tell you a secret. I think there is going to be a war. If war comes all those men in America will have to come back and fight. Santino too. Then maybe he will be killed. Maybe there will be a chance for me yet. Stay here, Rosa, and see if the war comes."

And Remo held my hand in his as we walked in silence across the square and back to the old *palazzo*.

"Addio, Remo," I said when we reached the gate to the court. Then I threw my arms around Bianca and kissed her on the cheek. "Dear, kind Bianca," I said. "I know how much you love him too!"

Then pushing open the gate I closed it quick behind me and stood there leaning against it. Mamma Lena had not gone to bed. There was still a light in the *osteria*. But I didn't want to go in just yet. I must decide what to do. Suppose the war did come and Santino got killed. Did I still want to marry Remo? I could dance all my life with Remo! But what about Gionin back there in Missouri? Gionin couldn't dance at all, but Gionin was ready to sit in jail the rest of his life to save me from Santino. He was even ready to die. Remo had been afraid—afraid of the punishment—when I wanted him to run away with me. Gionin was not pretty like Remo and he didn't care about the nice clothes. But Gionin was bigger, stronger, safer. Gionin had never even tried to touch my hand, but the gentleness that came into his fiery eyes when he looked into mine! Just the thought of Gionin made me stop shivering and feel more calm. And how Gionin loved my little Domenico! I smiled as I thought of the sympathy that strong man had for a helpless baby. And how happy he had been when he made the nice cradle. Gionin would love Francesco too. Gionin was crazy for the children.

Slow, slow, I took off my hat and walked on across the court. The *osteria* was empty except for Mamma Lena and one old drunk man who sat at the end of the second table. I went over to Mamma Lena and watched her for a while as she scrubbed the boards of the table with sand and a wet rag to make the rings of the wine glasses go away. "Mamma Lena," I said at last, "I think I will go back with those men who are going next week."

For a moment Mamma Lena let the rag rest on the table and just looked at me. Then she picked up the rag and an empty wine bottle and went on to the man at the end of the table. "Pay your bill and get out!" she said, shaking him by the shoulder.

The man looked up with sleepy eyes, then started feeling in his pockets. Finally he pulled out a little wallet, but couldn't untie the string. Mamma Lena did it for him, counted out what he owed, and gave the wallet back. Then she stood and waited as he got to his feet and staggered off across the room. When he had gone she came and sat down by the table across from me. For a long while we sat there together in silence. And when at last Mamma Lena spoke she was not like Mamma Lena at all. She was just like any other old woman who was alone and sad. "I wish you could stay a little longer with that new baby, Rosa," she said. "But you must do what you think best."

[Rosa returned to Missouri with her two children, but when Santino used his savings to purchase a brothel, Rosa refused to move in, feeling it would be a sin against God to support herself and her children through prostitution. Santino threatened to kill her, and fearing for her life, Rosa took the children and fled to Chicago, where she stayed at first with a cousin of Gionin from the mining camp. Gionin soon came to Chicago as well, and we pick up the story as Gionin helped Rosa move into her own place.—ed.]

Gionin found three little rooms for me in a big wooden house by the railroad. There were about ten Norwegian families in that house and two Italian men, Toni and his old father. Toni, he was North Italian like us but he was *Genovese*.[22] He was a nice young man—short, but he was pretty with black hair and gray eyes. He was one of those artists that put down the marble to make the *mosaico*. That old father had a hand-organ, but he was too old and sick to go very much on the street. They were in one of those three rooms when we came, so we let them stay and help pay the rent—we were all North Italian together.

22. *Genovese:* a native of the region around Genoa.

Gionin, he had a little money from the mine at Union so he could pay the rent. Then he bought a little secondhand stove and some wood and coal. The table he made himself from some boards he found in the street, and he made the bed too. But no chairs. For chairs we were sitting down on those big American Family Soap boxes. Then we had to buy some blankets. But Gionin was afraid to stay there with me—he was afraid the police would come. So he was sleeping by some of those other *Toscani* and by his cousin Tomaso.

The other people from *Toscana* were not religious, but Gionin never missed one Sunday to go to church. So here it was the first Sunday in Chicago and we didn't know where there was a church. Oh my goodness! We walked and walked and walked and walked and all the time asked somebody else, but everybody kept saying, "You're going right. It's far." We went way to that church on Franklin and Illinois. Me and my children froze to death walking. But we never even thought we could take the streetcar with the horse on. I was in America ten years and I never took the streetcar. We needed those five cents to eat. Five cents was enough to make the whole supper for the family in that time. Only the rich people could take the streetcar—not us poor people.

After not long Gionin found work. The first work he had in Chicago, he was carrying the bricks and mud for the new church they were making over past Chicago Avenue. It's a Polish church now but in that time it was Irish. He used to come by me with his shoulders all sore— all open—from carrying those bricks and I was making him some cotton-cloth pads to put on his shoulders so they don't get so cut. And every noon I used to carry him a little pail with the stuff to eat.

But sure enough! One day I was home doing the washing—I was bending over my tub scrubbing and rubbing those plaster shirts and with my foot rocking the cradle because my Domenico was sick and all the time crying—and here came the policeman to take me to jail. I couldn't understand much what he said so he talked to Toni. Toni told the police I was not the kind of woman he said and I didn't run around with no man. He said, "Don't take her to jail. She's an angel from heaven the way she works and takes care of her children!"

The police could see when he looked how I was doing all that heavy washing and taking care for my sick Domenico. So he said he didn't want to arrest me—he thought it would be a mistake. But then he told Toni I had to be in the court tomorrow morning. He said if I promised to be there and didn't run away he wouldn't put me in jail. He was good, that policeman. He didn't arrest me and he gave me fifteen cents to get some kind of medicine for Domenico. He wrote it on a paper what kind of medicine I must get from the drugstore.

So the next day I was in the court with my two children. Gionin and all his friends came there with me. Toni, too. There I was, a young Italian girl with a shawl over my head, and I couldn't understand nothing. When we went by the judge, there was Santino from Missouri! He was telling the judge that I was the worst kind of woman—that I ran away and was living with all the men, and this and that. He wanted the judge to punish me and put me to jail.

I can't tell you very much what happened, because the judge was talking English to all those friends of Gionin and to Toni. When he asked me the question Toni told me what it was and I answered the truth, that's all. In the end the judge told Santino to get out of town. He said if he was not gone by six o'clock the same day he would put *him* to jail instead of me. Then he said, "And don't you ever come back, either!"

Six o'clock night, when the train was supposed to leave for St. Louis, Gionin and all his friends and all his relatives in Chicago were in the depot with stones. If Santino didn't go they were going to stone him. When Santino saw all those people taking my part he had no intention to stay. He went back to Union. He went back there and got the divorce; then he married one of those women he was living with. But I heard later from his sister-in-law that that woman wouldn't take so much like me. When he started beating her she got him put in jail. He sat in jail twenty months for one beating he gave that new wife! That man, I have to leave him out of my story, that's all.

So after Santino had the divorce Gionin and me went to court in Chicago and got married together. The priest said he couldn't marry us in the church because I had the first husband living—only when he died we could be married in the church. Me, I was crying with tears coming down my eyes and praying God, "Oh God, why do You make it a sin for me to live with this good man Gionin? He's so good and so religious! My children will starve if he doesn't take care! Why do You make that a sin? How can that be a sin?"

Once a long time after, when Father Alberto came to America, I went by him and told him how I didn't say yes that time I was married with Santino in Bugiarno. I told him the priest was deaf but the people knew it that I didn't say yes. He said, "Well, if you can find all the people who were at your wedding and they sign their names on the paper that you didn't say yes, then I can marry you in the church."

But how am I going to find all those people? I can't, that's all!

(After Gionin and me were married together about ten years and have already three children, a missionary from Italy came in our church. He preached so strong against the divorce—what a sin it is against God, and the punishment God is going to give those people, and all and all—that Gionin got the scare and he went away and left me. About three months he left me alone to take care for all those children. Nobody but me knew why he went away that time, but I knew it was the *missionario*'s doing. So then one day he went to confession to Father Alberto and Father Alberto told him it's a sin to leave me alone like that with those children. Oh, Gionin was glad to hear that, so he could come back! He said he only left me because he didn't want to go to hell.)

My husband he was many months carrying the bricks and the mud for that new church. But then those other *Toscana* people—that little bunch of *Toscani* were all very friends together—they said to him, "Oh, you're foolish, Gionin. Why you don't get the horse and wagon and sell the bananas like us?"

So he did it—he got the horse and the wagon and he used to peddle the bananas. And when the cranberries came he sold the cranberries too.

Oh, now I remember another little thing to tell. One time Gionin bought a new horse and he came home and told me about it. He said he changed in the old one and he gave some money too for another one. He said, "Rosa, I bought a nice horse this time. But I don't know if I did right. There was another horse there for ten dollars more—it was still a nicer one. What d'you think?"

And I said, "Well, if you think it's worth ten dollars more you give it to him." But we didn't say no more about it. We went to sleep and we think no more. So in the morning my husband took the bananas and the horse and wagon and he went.

Then here came a *Toscana* man and he said, "Lady, you're the wife to Gionin?"

"Yes."

"Well Gionin, he said for you to give me the ten dollars because he wants to go by Guido and take that other horse."

And I said, "Why do *you* come for the ten dollars? Why did he send you and not come himself?"

"Well he sent me because he wanted to wait there on Franklin Street."

"Well," I said, "can't that other *Toscana* man give the horse, anyway, and trust my husband for ten dollars? If Guido won't even trust him one day, I don't have the ten dollars to give him!"

"Well," said the man, "don't get sore about it. I only do like he told me."

And I said, "Well I don't have one dollar—not one cent. I can't give it to you."

There I had all my husband's money in my underskirt pocket, but I told him I had not one penny.

So then my husband came home at night and I asked him why he sent that man for ten dollars, instead to come himself.

He said, "Why, Rosa, I didn't send nobody. I didn't go by Guido today. I didn't go."

"Oh, for the love of Mike!" I said. "That man came here and he said to give him the ten dollars. And he was a *Toscano* too." So then I told all about it.

Gionin said, "Well, God, He blessed you this time, Rosa, that you didn't give it!"

And nobody—nobody—knew where that man came from! I don't know yet who he was or how he could know about that other horse.

[After the depression of the 1890s, Rosa and her family had to move from their apartment because the building she lived in was purchased by the Chicago Commons, a settlement house.[23] Although Rosa was upset by the move, her life soon became closely entwined with the affairs of the settlement. She attended classes and eventually took a job as a cleaning woman for the settlement. It was there that she began telling the stories that eventually led Marie Hall Ets to record her life story.—ed.]

In the first beginning we always came in the club and made two circles in the room. One circle was for those ladies who could talk English and the other circle was for the ladies who talked German. Mis' Reuter talked German to the German ladies, and Miss Gray talked English to the other ladies. But I guess they both did the same preaching. They used to tell us that it's not nice to drink the beer, and we must not let the baby do this, and this. Me, I was the only Italian woman—where were they going to put me? I couldn't talk German, so I went in the English circle. So after we had about an hour, or an hour and a half of the preaching, they would pull up the circle and we'd play the games together. All together we played the games—the Norwegian, the German, the English, and me. Then we'd have some cake and coffee and the goodnight song. . . .

---

23. Chicago Commons: a major social settlement founded in Chicago's seventeenth ward in 1894. For a full description of the early years of the settlement, including the displacement of Italian families from the annex building, see Wade, *Graham Taylor*, chap. 5.

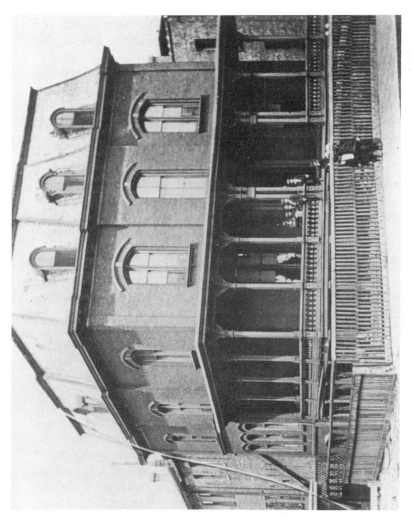

House of 140 North Union Street, where the Chicago Commons was founded, 1894. The building in the rear may have been the one from which Rosa was evicted. (From Louise C. Wade, *Graham Taylor: Pioneer for Social Justice, 1895–1938* [Chicago: University of Chicago Press, 1964], following p. 148)

Pretty soon they started the classes to teach us poor people to talk and write in English. The talk of the people in the settlement house was different entirely than what I used to hear. I used to love those American people, and I was listening and listening how they talked. That's how I learned to talk such good English. Oh, I was glad when I learned enough English to go by the priest in the Irish church and confess myself and make the priest understand what was the sin! But I never learned to do the writing in English. I all the time used to come to that class so tired and so sleepy after scrubbing and washing the whole day—I went to sleep when they started the writing. I couldn't learn it. They had the clubs for the children too; my little girls loved to go. And after a few years when they started the kindergarten, my Luie was one of the first children to go in. . . .

The year my Leo was born I was home alone and struggled along with my children. My husband went away because he was sick—he went by a doctor in St. Louis to get cured. That doctor said he must stay away from his home one year and gave him a job to do all the janitor work around his house for five dollars a month and his board. So me, I used to go all around to find the clothes to wash and the scrubbing. The city hall was helping me again in that time—they gave me a little coal and sometimes the basket of food. Bob, the sign painter downstairs, he helped me the most. He was such a good young man. He used to bring up a big chunk of coal and chop it up right in my kitchen and fix the stove.

I was to the end of my nine months, but the baby never came. So I went by one woman, Mis' Thomas, and I got part of the clothes washed. Then I said, "Oh, Mis' Thomas, I've got to go. I've got the terrible pains!"

She said, "You can go when you finish. You've got to finish first."

"No, I go. Otherwise I'll have to stay in your bed." When I said that she got scared I would have the baby there, so she let me go.

I went by the midwife, Mis' Marino, and told her to come; then I went home. When I saw it was my time, I told Domenico something and sent him with all the children to the wife of Tomaso. I told those people before, when they see the children come they must keep them all night—it's my time. It was really, really my time, and I had such a scare that I would be alone a second time. So when I heard a lady come in the building—she lived downstairs—I called to her. She said, "I have no time." And she didn't come up.

I was on my bed all alone by myself and then I prayed Sant' Antoni with all my heart. I don't know why I prayed Sant' Antoni—the Madonna put it in my mind. And then, just when the baby was born, I saw Sant' Antoni right there! He appeared in the room by me! I don't think it was really Sant' Antoni there, but in my imagination I saw him—all light like the sun. I saw Sant' Antoni there by my bed, and right then the door opened and the midwife came in to take care of the baby! It was February seventh and six below zero. There I had him born all alone, but Mis' Marino came when I prayed Sant' Antoni. She washed the baby and put him by me, but then she ran away. She didn't light the fire or nothing.

Oh, that night it was *so* cold! And me in my little wooden house in the alley with the walls all frosting—thick white frosting. I was crying and praying, "How am I going to live?" I said. "Oh, Sant' Antoni, I'll never live till tomorrow morning! I'll never live till the morning!"

And just as I prayed my door opened and a lady came in. She had a black shawl twice round her neck and head and that shawl came down to her nose. All I could see was half the nose and the mouth. She came in and lighted both the stoves. Then she came and looked at me, but I couldn't see her face. I said, "God bless you!"

She just nodded her head up and down and all the time she said not one word, only "Sh, sh."

Then she went down in the basement herself, nobody telling her nothing, and she got the coal and fixed the fire. Pretty soon she found that little package of camomile tea I had there on the dresser and she made a little tea with the hot water. And that woman stayed by me almost till daylight. But all the time she put her finger to her mouth to tell me to keep still when I tried to thank her. And I never knew where that lady came from! I don't know yet! Maybe she was the spirit of that kind girl, Annina, in Canaletto? I don't know. I really don't know! I was *so* sick and I didn't hear her voice or see her face. All the time she put her finger on her mouth and said, "Sh, sh." And when the daylight came she was gone.

About seven o'clock morning my children came home. And Mis' Marino, that midwife, she came at eight o'clock and said, "It's so cold I thought I'd find you dead!"

Then here came the city hall, or somebody, with a wagon. They wanted to take me and my new baby to the hospital. But how could I leave all my children? I started to cry—I didn't want to go. And my children cried too—they didn't want me to leave them. So then they didn't make me. They pulled my bed away from the frosting on the wall and put it in the front room by the stove. And my baby, I had him wrapped up in a pad I made from the underskirt like we do in *Italia*.

But the baby froze when he was born; he couldn't cry like other babies—he was crying weak, weak.

My Visella was bringing up the wood and the coal and trying to make that room warm. But she was only a little girl, she didn't know, and she filled the stove so full that all the pipes on the ceiling caught fire. I had to jump up from the bed and throw the pails of water so the house wouldn't burn down. Then God sent me help again. He sent that Miss Mildred from the settlement house. She didn't know about me and my Leo born; she was looking for some other lady and she came to my door and saw me. She said, "Oh, I have the wrong place."

I said, "No, lady, you find the right place."

So she came in and found out all. Then she ran away and brought back all those little things the babies in America have. She felt sorry to see my baby banded up like I had him. She didn't know then, Miss Mildred, that the women in *Italia* always banded their babies that way. And she brought me something to eat too—for me and for my children. That night another young lady from the Commons, Miss May, she came and slept in my house to take care of the fire. She was afraid for the children—maybe they would burn themselves and the house. Oh, that Miss Mildred and Miss May, they were angels to come and help me like that! Four nights Miss May stayed there and kept the fire going. They were high-up educated girls—they were used to sleeping in the warm house with the plumbing—and there they came and slept in my wooden house in the alley, and for a toilet they had to go down to that shed under the sidewalk. They were really, really friends! That time I had my Leo nobody knew I was going to have the baby—I looked kind of fat, that's all. Those women in the settlement house were so surprised. They said, "Why you didn't tell us before, Mis Cavalleri, so we can help you?"[24]

You know that Mis' Thomas—I was washing her clothes when the baby started to come—she wanted a boy and she got a baby girl right after my baby was born. When I went there the next week to do the washing I had to carry my baby with me. When she saw him she said, "Well better I have a girl than I have a boy that looks like your baby! He looks for sure like a monkey!"

In the first beginning he did look like a monkey, but in a few weeks he got pretty. He got so pretty all the people from the settlement house came to see him. After two or three months there was no baby in Chicago prettier than that baby.

24. Cavalleri is the fictitious surname that Marie Hall Ets gave to Rosa Cassettari to protect her anonymity.

When the year was over for him, my husband came home from St. Louis. He didn't send me the money when he was there—just two times the five dollars—so he brought me twenty-five dollars when he came back. Oh, he was so happy when he saw that baby with exactly, exactly his face and everything—the same dark gold hair and everything—and so beautiful. But he saw that baby was so thin and pale and couldn't cry like the other babies. "Better I go by a good doctor and see," he said. "I've got twenty-five dollars—I'm going to get a good doctor." So he did.

But the doctor said, "That baby can't live. He was touched in the lungs with the cold. Both lungs got froze when he was born."

And sure enough he was all the time sick and when it was nine months he died. My first Leo and my second Leo I lose them both. Oh, I was brokenhearted to lose such a beautiful baby! . . .

Pretty soon after my first Leo died that darling Miss May got me the job to come every day to do the cleaning in the settlement house. Then Gionin got the job sweeping the floor for the electric company. And after not long we got to be the janitor in that building where they didn't want the Italians. I had to scrub down the stairs once a week and do a little work like that, and we got the rent for half. We went along good that way. But I had a lot of worry too, because I was all the time gone to work and my children were alone on the street. My Visella was eight or nine years old and she had to be the mother to the other children. And I had more trouble because the landlord in that new building was so mean. He was all the time beating the children. One day he kicked Visella and beat her terrible because she was playing house in the back alley and moved some boxes he didn't want moved. I was afraid to tell Gionin because he would start fighting with that boss. . . .

Gionin, oh he was glad when I told the stories. So for practice I used to test them on him first. If he listened good—if I made him laugh or made his tears fall, then I knew I said them good. Sometimes he went with me to those parties in the settlement; but when I went up to tell the story, he went out of the room. He couldn't stay in, he was so afraid I'd make a mistake. He was more excited than me. But then after a while sometimes he used to stay in too. And he was proud how the people were enjoying to hear me tell.

Me, I was always crazy for a good story. That's why I love so much the dramatics. If somebody says to me, "Leave the supper and take the show," I'll take the show every time and let the eating go. I just love the drama! After I got the job to go every day to the settlement for the cleaning, and Gionin had the job with the electric company, we got along better. My children got bigger too. So then I used to hide a little money from the food so I can go to the shows. That one afternoon in the week I had home from the scrubbing I hurried up and did my washing and prepared the supper; then I'd run. But sometimes the show was long, and I'd see it start to get dark. I'd have such a scare I'd run all the way to get home before my husband came. I was going in the front door and quick put on the apron, because Gionin came in the back door—from the back street through the alley. Once he caught me. It was that time he was working in the night. As soon as he started for his work, I put on my shawl and I beat it. The snow was to my knees, but I didn't care, so long as I could see the show. But Gionin came back again—he forgot his little knife. He said, "Where's Ma? Where's Ma?"

Visella said, "Oh, she'll be right away back. Probably she ran to the store." . . .

Ten summers I took my children and I went to the Commons summer camp to cook for the boys. In the early time we had only the tents at camp. Every boy that came new had to go by the farmer and fill up his mattress with straw. When it rained those boys were in their bathing suits in the night. And in that big tent for the dining room it was raining down in the sugar bowl in the middle of the table. And when it stormed with the wind, all the boys—about seventy boys—were hanging on that post in the middle so the dining room wouldn't blow away. Oh boy, think of the joy I had in that camp when they made the wooden house for the dining room, and the big barrel for the water! Oh, I remember one summer, such a trouble I had cooking for sixty boys when I had only two little gasoline stoves! I had to put the oatmeal on the night before to be ready for breakfast. Then I couldn't sleep because when the wind came it all the time blew out the light. Mr. Witter, he was so sorry for me he went in town to the company to find out how much it would cost for a gas stove. The company said, "If you dig the ditch yourself, it will cost much less."

So here Mr. Witter came back and called all the boys together on the hill. When he told them, they were so glad if they can help me. They said, "Yes, we're going to do it!"

When I saw all those boys digging the ditch I said, "Why you do that? Somebody can fall in."

Mr. Witter said, "Well, we make the ditch so the water will run off."

When the ditch was made, here came some men with the pipe and in one-half hour they had in a big gas stove—not a really stove, but four nice burners. Wasn't that a grand surprise! I went by Mr. Witter with my two arms out like a cross and I said, "Oh, Mr. Witter, if you were not a man, I would kiss you!" And all the boys busted out laughing. I was so happy! In one hour I had the whole supper made.

Those boys liked me so much because I told them the stories, and they were tickled to death to dig the ditch for me. They all the time were begging me. They'd say, "Oh, Mis' Cavalleri tell us the story! We'll help you get through your work. We'll scrub the barrel! We'll bring the water! We'll wash the dishes! Come on, tell us the story!"

One summer Dr. Taylor let some Jew boys come to camp with the Italian boys. In the first beginning those boys were like the Devil and the Holy Ghost together! And such a war they put up! They pushed out the clothes to each other from the tents. But in the end they were worse than sweethearts. When it came the end of two weeks they could even kiss each other—Jacob and Luigi, Tony and Sam. But whether they were Jews or Italian they all begged me to tell them the stories. And they all busted out laughing.

Me, I can't tell the stories so good like those men in the barns in Bugiarno. And the American people can't laugh like the people of Bugiarno. When I heard that a lot of my *paesani* had come to America and were living in Joliet I wanted so much to go there. But I was afraid to go alone. So one day that darling Miss May she bought the tickets and went with me. And we saw all those girls from the silk mills—Caterina too—and the men who told stories in the barns.

FIVE

Rose Gollup: From Russia to the Lower East Side in the 1890s

Rose Gollup grew up in a small village in the part of western Russia known as the Pale of Settlement. In a swath running from northwest to southeast, from Lithuania on the Baltic through Byelorussia and the Ukraine to Odessa on the Black Sea, the Pale of Settlement contained a population of some 5 million Jews confined by Czarist edicts to densely populated villages, or shtetls, in a larger sea of Russians and other ethnic groups. The onset, in the early 1880s, of attacks on Jewish communities—known as pogroms—and the expulsion of Jews from numerous Russian towns and cities made life increasingly intolerable for the Jewish minority. These attacks, coupled with increasingly systematic discrimination against Jews in higher education and economic life, contributed to the growth of large-scale emigration of Russian Jews. About 2 million emigrated between 1880 and 1914, with the vast majority going to the United States.

The Gollup (sometimes spelled Gallup) family was part of this massive immigrant flow. Like many others, Rose Gollup's father migrated first, got a foothold for himself in New York City, and then sent prepaid steamship tickets to his family. In 1891, Rose and her unmarried aunt, Masha, made the trip that is described in *Out of the Shadow*.[1] Once in New York, Aunt Masha lived on her own, but all three family members worked to bring Rose's mother and siblings over. About a year after Rose arrived (just after the excerpts included below), the remainder of the family joined father and daughter in New York.

1. Rose Cohen, *Out of the Shadow* (New York: Jerome S. Ozer, 1971; originally published in 1918). A monograph that draws on Cohen's autobiography and employs numerous other memoirs to illuminate the experience of this generation of Russian Jewish immigrant women in urban America is Susan Glenn, *Daughters of the Shtetl: Life and Labor in the Immigrant Generation* (Ithaca, N.Y.: Cornell University Press, 1991). My thanks to Susan Glenn for directing me to Cohen's account.

The autobiography is unusually detailed, and the excerpts below give only a fraction of the events recorded. In later sections of the memoir, Rose Cohen (she wrote under her married name) describes a brief stint as a domestic servant, her rejection of a prospective suitor, and increasing health problems. During one illness, she was visited by the settlement worker Lillian Wald and soon discovered the world of the Nurses' Settlement on Henry Street. Through the settlement, she was referred to the uptown Presbyterian Hospital, where she met wealthy non-Jews who sponsored summer outings for children of the Lower East Side. She worked successive summers at a Connecticut retreat established for immigrant children and found herself torn between the world of her family in the immigrant ghetto and the broader American culture.

The autobiography gives the reader no clues as to Cohen's resolution of this conflict, but in an article subsequently published in a New York literary magazine, Cohen described in more detail the educational process by which she overcame her self-consciousness about the English language and became a writer after her marriage. She summed up her motivation, in words that capture the value of her autobiography for readers today: "My aim is to write, telling of the life among the Jews on Cherry Street from which I come, among the Russian peasants from whom I come, and among the Americans among whom I am."[2]

When I was about eleven years old there were five of us children.[3] One day father went to town and came back with a stranger, who, we were told, would teach us to read and write. Our teacher was a young man of middle height, thin, dark and pale. He had an agreeable voice, and when he sang it was pleasant to hear him. When we did our lessons well his eyes brightened and his tightly closed lips would relax a little. But when we did poorly he was angry and would scold us.

As soon as I learned how to read I would sit for hours and read to my grandmother. Besides the Bible, we had a few religious books.[4] I read

2. Rose Gollup Cohen, "To the Friends of 'Out of the Shadow,'" *Bookman* 55 (Mar. 1922): 40.

3. The date at this time is probably 1890 or 1891, judging from later events described in the memoir. Rose Cohen (Rahel in her autobiography) does not identify her hometown other than to describe it as a "small Russian village." *Out of the Shadow,* p. 9.

4. The Bible here means the Old Testament, as the Gollups were an orthodox Jewish family. Rose Gollup's first contact with the New Testament came in a Protestant hospital in New York City much later in life. *Out of the Shadow,* pp. 242–43.

these again and again, and became very devout. I read the morning, noon and evening prayers, and sometimes I fasted for half a day. Then I became less stubborn and the quarrels between sister and myself became less frequent.

One day father left home on a three days' journey. When he returned he did not look like himself. His face was pale and he seemed to be restless. During the three days that followed, father went out only at night. I also noticed that mother collected all of father's clothes, and, as she sat mending them, I often saw her tears fall on her work. On the third night I awoke and saw father bending over me. He wore his heavy overcoat, his hat was pulled well over his forehead and a knapsack was strapped across his shoulders. Before I had time to say a word he kissed me and went to grandmother's bed and woke her up. "I am going away, mother." She sat up, rubbed her eyes and asked in a sleepy voice. "Where?" "To America," father whispered hoarsely.

For a moment there was silence; then grandmother uttered a cry that chilled my blood. My mother, who sat in a corner weeping, went to her and tried to quiet her. The noise woke grandfather and the children. We all gathered around grandmother's bed, and I heard father explaining the reason for his going. He said that he could not get a passport (for a reason I could not understand at the time). And as no one may live in Russia even a week without a passport, he had to leave immediately. His explanation did not comfort grandmother; she still sat crying and wringing her hands. After embracing us all, father ran out of the house, and grandfather ran after him into the snow with his bare feet. When he returned he sat down and cried like a little child. I spent the rest of the night in prayer for a safe journey for my father.

As father's departure to America had to be kept secret until he was safe out of Russia, we had to bury our sorrow deep in our own hearts, and go about our works as if nothing unusual had happened. . . .

So the days passed.

One morning mother went to the postoffice and when she came back she looked as if she had suddenly aged. She took a postal card from her pocket and we all bent our heads over it and read: "I have been arrested while crossing the border and I am on my way home, walking the greater part of the way. If we pass through our village I shall ask the officer to let me stop home for a few minutes. Be brave and trust in God." At the news more tears were shed in our house than on the Day of Atonement. . . .

With the exception of grandmother, I was the most pious and the most superstitious member of the family. In sickness or trouble, while the others turned to do practical things, I appealed to God for help.

So it was on the day when father was led away to the next village. Knowing that he was to attempt an escape that very night, I felt that there was no time to be lost. Better to concentrate my mind on my prayers I climbed up on the stove and sat down in the darkest corner, facing the wall. To shut out the children's voices I stuck my fingers into my ears and began to pray. But I could not put any heart into it. I felt, however, that if I only could pray with all my heart and soul, God would hear me. . . .

I think it was the next day that a message came telling us that father had escaped from the constable in the next village. That was joy indeed though limited, for father was still on Russian soil and could be recaptured any minute. And so while we were waiting, fearing, hoping, another week or so passed.

. . . on Friday it cleared. The sun came out bright and warm. "It is a good sign that it cleared in honour of Sabbath," said grandmother, turning her pale, thin face hopefully to the window. That afternoon we saw the mistress of the inn and postoffice walking up to her waist in snow, coming toward our house. "Nothing but a letter would bring her here on a day like this," mother cried and rushed out of the house. When she came back she had a letter but she stood in the middle of the room holding it in her hand as though she feared to open it. "Look," said the post-mistress, pointing to the post mark. It was stamped Memel, Prussia.

Mother ran to grandmother and they embraced, and stood so long and so silently with their faces hidden from us, that we children were frightened and begged them to speak to us. Then mother turned and caught us all into her arms with a cry of joy, while grandmother raised her tear-stained face to Heaven in silent prayer.

Spring came. The snow which lay high all winter began to melt, and here and there green spots appeared. Then the dandelions began to show their yellow heads, and the storks came flying back to build their nests in the old stump in the cemetery. Hens, followed by groups of black and yellow headed chicks, walked about scratching in the soft warm earth and cackling cheerfully. . . .

Mother, who never sang except when rocking baby to sleep, and then only hummed, sang now as she went about her work. And grandmother spoke about America from morning till night. . . .

Now the chief part of the support of the family fell to mother, and the rest of us helped. Grandmother knitted stockings for the women of the village. Of course the stockings had to be looked over, the lost stitches found and mended carefully. That was my work. . . .

As soon as the warm weather came the women of the village gave all their time and thought to the work in the fields. And so now we had no stockings to knit, no sewing, and no pots for grandfather to mend. He would often come home from the village with his little bag empty and sadness in his eyes. Indeed, there were many days when we had not enough even of potatoes. But this hardship did not last long. Soon a letter and money came from father. This was the first letter from America. Father did not tell us much about his life out there. He just said that he was boarding with a nice Russian Jewish family and that he was already working and earning ten dollars a week. The rest of the letter was just good cheer and loving messages to each one of us. . . .[5]

Grandmother had two children besides father, both daughters. The elder was happily married and lived about two or three days' journey from us. . . .

The younger was twenty-one years of age now and was working in Mintck, a large city.[6] She left home when she was sixteen and being fond of children she became a nurse girl. As grandmother expected her to be a seamstress, this choice of occupation caused grandmother as many tears as father's becoming a tailor instead of a rabbi. For a nurse girl was thought to be as much below a seamstress as a tailor below a rabbi.

Father had been in America but a short time when grandmother realised that his emigration had lessened Aunt Masha's prospects of marriage. When she came to this conclusion her peace was gone. She wept night and day. "Poor Masha," she moaned, "what is to become of her? Her chances had been small enough without a dowry. And now, burdened with an aged father and a blind helpless mother, the best she can expect is a middle-aged widower with half a dozen children!" . . .

After dinner she said to mother, hesitating at every word as she spoke, "You know, I decided last night, that when you go to America Masha should go with you." This startled mother so that she almost dropped the baby whom she was swinging on her foot.

5. Rose's father was living in New York City, on the Lower East Side of Manhattan, home to the vast majority of Russian Jewish immigrants to the United States. He continued to follow the tailoring trade in New York City.

6. This was probably Minsk, a major city in the western Russian province of Byelorussia. Later, Rose and her mother and aunt traveled to this city, which served as a starting point for their trip to America. Cohen's spelling of the city is not consistent; she uses "Mintck" here and "Mintsk" in a later reference. *Out of the Shadow*, p. 192.

"What are you saying? Masha go to America and you left here alone?" . . .

Mother tried to dissuade her from this plan but she turned a deaf ear and insisted that we write to father at once. And we did.

About a month passed before we received an answer. The letter was heavier than usual. And when we opened it, two yellow tickets fell out from among the two closely-written sheets.

"What is this?" we all asked at once. "Not money. And this writing must be English."

We handed the tickets to grandmother who held out her hand for them. Suddenly her hand began to tremble and she said, "Perhaps these are steamer tickets. Quickly read the letter."

After the usual greetings father wrote, "Since Masha is to come to America she might as well start as soon as she can get ready. And Rahel had better come with her. I am sure she can earn at least three dollars a week. With her help I'll be able to bring the rest of the family over much sooner, perhaps in a year or so. And besides, now she can still travel on half a ticket, which I am enclosing with the one for Masha."

Quite bewildered, I looked at mother. Her lips were opening and closing without making a sound. Suddenly she caught me into her arms and burst into tears.

For many days mother could not look at the steamer tickets without tears in her eyes. And even then though she tried to speak cheerfully about my going to America, I noticed that the anxious look which came into her eyes while the letter was being read, never left them. Also I felt her eyes following me about on every step. But once only, she gave way to her feelings openly.

One morning while she was fastening the back of my dress I caught a few disconnected words, which she uttered low as though she were speaking to herself.

"Good Heavens! child twelve years old—care—herself." Then came those inward tearless sobs and I felt her hands tremble on my back. . . .

All through the Spring, while mother, grandmother and Aunt Masha were sewing and knitting stockings for Aunt Masha and me to take along to America, I wandered about in the fields, restless and unable to play at anything. . . .

"Rahel, promise me that you won't cry when you are starting. You hear? It is bad luck to cry when one is starting on a journey. And—I want you to write me whether there are any synagogues in America."

"I promise!"

Still holding my face between her hands she bent over it and looked at it intently. I saw a strained expression come into her face and the eyes move about restlessly under the heavy red lids, as though she were trying to see. Then came a pitiful moan, and tears rolled down her cheeks and fell on mine.

What happened after this I do not remember until the very minute of starting on the second of June. And even then, as I look back I can see nothing at first, but a thick grey mist. But the sounds I recall very distinctly.

There was Aunt Masha's voice crying, a crack of a whip, horses' hoofs striking against stones. Then there was a sudden jolt and I felt myself falling backwards. And now I remember what I saw, too.

When I rose I found myself sitting in a straw-lined wagon, with my back to the horse. Besides me were mother and the baby, who were coming to the city with us, and Aunt Masha who was lying with her face hidden in the straw, crying aloud.

I remembered grandmother's warning, "Nothing but bad luck could come to one who is crying while starting on a journey," and felt sorry for Aunt Masha. But as we were pulling out through the gate and I saw grandmother looking so lonely and forsaken, as she stood leaning against the house, and when I saw grandfather and the children who stood at the gate, looking after us and crying, I could not keep my own tears back, though I opened my eyes wide and blinked hard.

We were bound for Mintck. This was a large city about a day and a half hard travelling from our village. There mother was to see an agent about smuggling us across the border and buy a few necessary things for our journey. . . .

The dingy courtyard we passed through when we got out of the wagon, and the sunless room was the home of our cousins with whom we stayed as long as we remained in the city. These cousins were the children of father's and Aunt Masha's half-brother, who had died several years before. Aunt Masha knew them as well as she knew us, and mother knew them too, but to me they were strangers. . . .

During the three days that followed I stayed in the house and took care of baby while mother and Aunt Masha were doing their errands. There was quite some trouble with the agents. They found out that we had no local passport and could not get one. And so they demanded an unreasonable sum of money which mother finally had to pay. And even then, it was just as likely as not that we would be caught crossing the boundary and sent back.

"Your children had better take along plenty of money," the agent said with a smile, while he was pocketing the roll of bills, "for you never can tell how long they might have to wait in Hamburg for a steamer."[7] Mother wept, hearing this. There was so little left to take along. . . .

On the third morning Aunt Masha bought me a very pretty pair of black patent-leather slippers with two buttons. I remember that after I put them on, I sat most of the time. I wanted to keep the soles clean. And it was only to give baby the pleasure and myself, too, of hearing them squeak, that I walked across the room.

In the afternoon mother sewed the money that was left into the side lining of my little underwaist. "No one will suspect it there," she said. When she was through she spread the waist out on her knee and smoothed out the creases with great tenderness. While putting on the waist I noticed that there were many damp spots on it.

After that there was nothing more to do. Our new wicker basket was ready and stood corded at the door. And there was a small bag of zwieback and two new bright tin drinking cups. I remember how silently we all sat waiting for five o'clock, how white mother's face looked, how unnaturally cheerful Aunt Masha seemed, how attentive the boy was to all of us, how rapidly my heart beat as if I had been running a long distance.

A little before the hour my pale-faced cousin came in. And it seemed to me that he grew still paler when he looked at us and said, "The drosky is at the door."[8]

I don't remember how we left the house. But when we were in the drosky I saw that I had my tin cup in my hand and Aunt Masha had the bag of zwieback and the other cup. We were driven to the station at a speed that made baby's breath come and go in gasps.

The platform was crowded. "Here is the train," my cousin said. "Hurry!" Mother caught me into her arms with a cry that made me forget everything. Half unconscious now of what was going on, I held her around the neck with all my strength.

"A crowded train," I heard. "Hurry!" And again, "You will never get a seat now," and still later, "Oh, I thought you were such a brave girl"—"You will miss the train, Rahel!"

7. Hamburg, in northern Germany, was the most common port of departure for Russian Jewish emigrants in this period. For a similar account of border difficulties, the trip from western Russia to Hamburg, and the ocean crossing, see Mary Antin, *From Plotzk to Boston* (New York: Markus Wiener, 1986; originally published in 1899).

8. A drosky was a carriage for hire, in this case to take Rahel and Masha to their train to the border.

Some one pulled my hands apart. I was lifted from the back and carried into the train. I looked through the window into the crowd for mother. Just as I caught sight of her face the train began to move. I saw her fling out her arms wildly and run alongside of the train for a few steps. Then her arms dropped limply at her sides and she disappeared in the crowd. . . .

We were in the train two or three days. When we made long stops Aunt Masha used to leave me in the train and go to get food and drink. I remember the first time she went out I was trembling with fear lest the train should go off before she returned. Each time she went out I would get as near a window as possible and stand ready to jump out in case the train started.

I do not remember how or when we left the train, or how about twenty-five of us, two young men and the rest women and very small children, came to be travelling in a large, canvas-covered wagon, on a country road white with the heat and dust. . . .

Toward evening of that day we came to an empty little log house so much like ours at home that I could not restrain a cry of joy at the sight of it. The roof, however, was of shingles instead of straw.

When it grew quite dark a few wagons drove up to the door of the hut. There was a good deal of whispering and disputing about which Aunt Masha tried to keep me in ignorance. Her idea was to keep me from knowing everything that was unpleasant. . . .

. . . At last, after much talking and swearing on the part of the drivers, which I could not help overhearing, in spite of Masha's precaution, we were all placed. I was put flat on my face between Aunt Masha and her friend, into one of the wagons spread with ill-smelling hay. We were covered up with more of it, heads and all, then drove off, it seemed to me, each wagon in a different direction.

We might have been driving for an hour, though it seemed much longer for I could hardly breath, when I heard the driver's hoarse whisper, "Remember, people, you are not to make a sound, nor move a limb for the next half hour."

Soon after this I heard a rough voice in Russian, "Who is there?"

"It is Mushka," our driver answered.

"What have you in the wagon?" the Russian demanded.

"Oh, just some bags of flour," Mushka answered.

I felt a heavy hand laid on my back. At that moment it dawned on me that we were stealing across the border. My heart began to thump so that I was sure he heard it. And in my fear I began to pray. But I stopped at once, at a pinch from Aunt Masha and a nudge from her friend. Then I heard the clink of money. At last the rough voice called out loudly, "Flour? Go ahead."

As we started off again I heard the crying of children in the distance, and shooting.

One day, I don't remember how soon after we crossed the border, we arrived in Hamburg. We stopped in a large, red building run in connection with the steamship company. We were all shown (really driven) into a large room where many dirty, narrow cots stood along the walls. Aunt Masha shivered as she looked at the one in which we two were to sleep.

"The less we stay in these beds the better," she said. So, although we were dead tired we went to bed quite late. But before we were on our cot very long we saw that sleep was out of the question. . . .

Our breakfast, which was boiled potatoes and slices of white bread, was served on long bare tables in a room like the sleeping room. No sooner was the food put on the tables than it was gone, and some of us were left with empty plates. Aunt Masha and I looked at each other and burst out laughing. To see the bread grabbed up and the fingers scorched on the boiled potatoes was ugly and pathetic but also funny.

"To-morrow," Aunt Masha said, "we too shall have to grab. For the money sewed in your waist won't last if we have to buy more than one meal a day for a week." But the next day it was almost the same thing. Going hungry seemed easy in comparison with the shame we felt to put out our hands for the bread while there was such a struggle.

Aunt Masha managed to get one slice which she held out to me. "Here, eat it." When I refused she gave me a look that was as bad as a blow. "Take it at once," she said angrily. I took it. I found it hard to swallow the bread, knowing that she was hungry.

We stayed in Hamburg a week. Every day from ten in the morning until four in the afternoon we stayed in a large, bare hall waiting for our names to be called. On the left side of the hall there was a heavy door leading into the office, where the emigrants were called in one by one. . . .

One afternoon the door of the office opened wider than usual and a different clerk came out holding a paper in his hand. He told us that the English steamer for which we had been waiting was in. And then he read the names of those who were to go on it.

I'll never forget Aunt Masha's joy when she heard that we were to sail the next day. She ran from one to the other of her friends, crying and laughing at once.

"The scoundrel," she kept on saying, "he threatened to send us home. He said he had the power to send us home!" Then she ran over to me and in her joy almost smothered me in her embrace. . . .

We were deathly seasick the first three days. During that period I was conscious, it seems to me, only part of the time. I remember that once when I opened my eyes I seemed to see the steamer turn to one side and then disappear under water. Then I heard voices screaming, entreating, praying. I thought we were drowning, but I did not care. Nothing mattered now. On the fourth day, I became again interested in life. I heard Aunt Masha moaning. A long time seemed to have passed since I saw her face. I tried to lift my head. Finding it impossible, I lay quietly listening, but it hurt me to hear her moaning. At last it became so pitiful that I could not stand it.

"I'll die if I don't get a drop of water," she moaned, "just one drop to wet my throat."

And so as I lay flat on my face I felt about for my tin cup till I found it. Then I began to slip downward feet first until I reached the berth underneath.[9] From there I swung down to the floor. As I stood up the boat lunged to one side and I went flying to the door and fell in a heap, striking my head against the door post. I don't know how long I had been lying there, when I heard the cabin door open and a man's strong voice call out, "Up on deck." I opened my eyes and saw an enormous pair of black boots and the lower part of white trousers.

The man stooped down, looked at me and gently brushed the hair away from my eyes. As I was used now to being pushed about and yelled at, the kind touch brought tears to my eyes. For the first time since I left home I covered my face with my hands and wept heartily.

For a minute or so he stood looking down at me. Then he picked up my cup, which I had dropped in falling, and brought me water. I drank some, and pointed to Aunt Masha. He handed the cup to a woman who came tumbling out of her berth to go up on deck. Then picking me up as if I were a little infant, he again shouted, "Up on deck!" and carried me off.

I had heard that those who were very sick on the steamer and those who died were thrown into the ocean. There was no doubt in my mind, therefore, that that was where I was being carried. I clasped my arms tightly about the man's neck. I felt sick with fear. He climbed up a white staircase and propped me up in a corner on the floor. Then he went away, to fetch a rope, I thought. He returned in a few minutes. But instead of a rope there was half an orange in his hand.

9. Like the vast majority of immigrants in this period, Rahel and her aunt traveled in steerage. Bunks were typically stacked two or three high as young and old, men and women slept in cramped quarters below decks. Wealthier immigrants and tourists traveled in second-class or first-class cabins. For an interesting account of such a Russian Jewish immigrant in 1913, see Rose Pesotta, *Days of Our Lives* (Boston: Excelsior, 1958), pp. 236–44.

Above decks during the steamship crossing (by Walter Jack Duncan). (From Rose Cohen, *Out of the Shadow* [New York: George H. Doran, 1918], following p. 62)

He kneeled down in front of me, raised my chin, showed me how to open my mouth and squeezed a few drops of juice into it. A good-natured smile played about his lips as he watched me swallow. Three times between his work he went and came with the half orange, until it was dry.

After a while Aunt Masha came creeping up the steps on all fours, hugging our little bag of zwieback.

From that hour we improved quickly. All day we sat or walked about in the sun. Soon Aunt Masha's little round nose was covered with freckles and my hair was bleached a half dozen shades.

Sometimes while walking about on deck we passed the man who had fed me with orange juice. He always touched his cap and smiled to us.

A week passed.

One day, it was the first of July, Aunt Masha and I stood in Castle Garden.[10] With fluttering hearts yet patiently we stood scanning the faces of a group of Americans divided from us by iron gates.

"My father could never be among those wonderfully dressed people," I thought. Suddenly it seemed to me as if I must shout. I caught sight of a familiar smile.

"Aunt Masha, do you see that man in the light tan suit? The one who is smiling and waving his hand?"

"Why, you little goose," she cried, "don't you see? It's father!" She gave a laugh and a sob, and hid her face in her hands.

A little while later the three of us stood clinging to one another. . . .

From Castle Garden we drove to our new home in a market wagon filled with immigrants' bedding. Father tucked us in among the bundles, climbed up beside the driver himself and we rattled off over the cobbled stone pavement, with the noon sun beating down on our heads.

As we drove along I looked about in bewilderment. My thoughts were chasing each other. I felt a thrill: "Am I really in America at last?" But the next moment it would be checked and I felt a little disappointed, a little homesick. Father was so changed. I hardly expected to find him in his black long tailed coat in which he left

10. Castle Garden, located on the southern tip of Manhattan, was the immigrant depot in New York City between 1855 and 1890. In 1890 the depot was closed but entering immigrants continued to arrive at an adjacent Barge Office until the opening of Ellis Island in January 1892. That the Gollups disembarked at (or near) Castle Garden helps date their arrival to July 1891. Barbara Benton, *Ellis Island: A Pictorial History* (New York: Facts on File Publications, 1985), pp. 25, 37.

home. But of course yet with his same full grown beard and earlocks. Now instead I saw a young man with a closely cut beard and no sign of earlocks. As I looked at him I could scarcely believe my eyes. Father had been the most pious Jew in our neighbourhood. I wondered was it true then as Mindle said that "in America one at once became a libertine"?

Father's face was radiantly happy. Every now and then he would look over his shoulder and smile. But he soon guessed what troubled me for after a while he began to talk in a quiet, reassuring manner. He told me he would take me to his own shop and teach me part of his own trade. He was a men's coat finisher. He made me understand that if we worked steadily and lived economically we should soon have money to send for those at home. "Next year at this time," he smiled, "you yourself may be on the way to Castle Garden to fetch mother and the children." So I too smiled at the happy prospect, wiped some tears away and resolved to work hard.

From Mrs. Felesberg we learned at once the more serious side of life in America. Mrs. Felesberg was the woman with whom we were rooming. A door from our room opened into her tiny bedroom and then led into the only other room where she sat a great part of the day finishing pants which she brought in big bundles from a shop, and rocking the cradle with one foot. She always made us draw our chairs quite close to her and she spoke in a whisper scarcely ever lifting her weak peering eyes from her work. When she asked us how we liked America, and we spoke of it with praise, she smiled a queer smile. "Life here is not all that it appears to the 'green horn,'" she said. [11] She told us that her husband was a presser on coats and earned twelve dollars when he worked a full week. Aunt Masha thought twelve dollars a good deal. Again Mrs. Felesberg smiled. "No doubt it would be," she said, "where you used to live. You had your own house, and most of the food came from the garden. Here you will have to pay for everything; the rent!" she sighed, "for the light, for every potato, every grain of barley. You see these three rooms, including yours? Would they be too much for my family of five?" We had to admit they would not. "And even from these," she said, "I have to rent one out."

Perhaps it was due to these talks that I soon noticed how late my father worked. When he went away in the morning it was still dark, and when he came home at night the lights in the halls were out. It

11. Green horn was a colloquial term to describe immigrant newcomers fresh off the boat.

was after ten o'clock. I thought that if mother and the children were here they would scarcely see him.

One night when he came home and as he sat at the table eating his rice soup, which he and Aunt Masha had taught me to cook, I sat down on the cot and asked timidly, knowing that he was impatient of questions, "Father, does everybody in America live like this? Go to work early, come home late, eat and go to sleep? And the next day again work, eat, and sleep? Will I have to do that too? Always?"

Father looked thoughtful and ate two or three mouthfuls before he answered. "No," he said smiling. "You will get married."

So, almost a week passed and though life was so interesting, still no matter where I went, what I saw, mother and home were always present in my mind. Often in the happiest moments a pain would rise in my throat and my eyes burned with the tears held back. At these moments I would manage to be near Aunt Masha so that I could lean against her, touch her dress. . . .

On the following day father came home at noon and took me along to the shop where he worked. We climbed the dark, narrow stairs of a tenement house on Monroe Street and came into a bright room filled with noise. I saw about five or six men and a girl.[12] The men turned and looked at us when we passed. I felt scared and stumbled. One man asked in surprise:

"Avrom, is this your daughter? Why, she is only a little girl!"

My father smiled. "Yes," he said, "but wait till you see her sew."

He placed me on a high stool opposite the girl, laid a pile of pocket flaps on the little narrow table between us, and showed me how to baste.

All afternoon I sat on my high stool, a little away from the table, my knees crossed tailor fashion, basting flaps. As I worked I watched the things which I could see by just raising my eyes a little. I saw that the girl, who was called Atta, was very pretty.

A big man stood at a big table, examining, brushing and folding coats. There was a window over his table through which the sun came streaming in, showing millions of specks of dust dancing over the table and circling over his head. He often puffed out his cheeks and blew the dust from him with a great gust so that I could feel his breath at our table.

12. The description here suggests that Rahel's father was employed as a tailor in a tenement sweatshop. The garment industry was the major employer of Russian Jewish immigrants of both sexes in New York City in the period between 1890 and the outbreak of World War I.

A Lower East Side street scene (by Walter Jack Duncan). (From Rose Cohen, *Out of the Shadow* [New York: George H. Doran, 1918], following p. 100)

The machines going at full speed drowned everything in their noise. But when they stopped for a moment I caught the clink of a scissors laid hastily on a table, a short question and answer exchanged, and the pounding of a heavy iron from the back of the room. Sometimes the machines stopped for a whole minute. Then the men looked about and talked. I was always glad when the machines started off again. I felt safer in their noise.

Late in the afternoon a woman came into the shop. She sat down next to Atta and began to sew on buttons. Father, who sat next to me, whispered, "This is Mrs. Nelson, the wife of the big man, our boss. She is a real American."

She, too, was pretty. Her complexion was fair and delicate like a child's. Her upper lip was always covered with shining drops of perspiration. I could not help looking at it all the time.

When she had worked a few minutes she asked father in very imperfect Yiddish: "Well, Mr. ——— , have you given your daughter an American name?"

"Not yet," father answered. "What would you call her? Her Yiddish name is Rahel."

"Rahel, Rahel," Mrs. Nelson repeated to herself, thoughtfully, winding the thread around a button; "let me see." The machines were going slowly and the men looked interested.

The presser called out from the back of the room: "What is there to think about? Rahel is Rachel."

I was surprised at the interest every one showed. Later I understood the reason. The slightest cause for interruption was welcome, it broke the monotony of the long day.

Mrs. Nelson turned to me: "Don't let them call you Rachel. Every loafer who sees a Jewish girl shouts 'Rachel' after her. And on Cherry Street where you live there are many saloons and many loafers. How would you like Ruth for a name?"

I said I should like to be called Ruth. . . .

I liked my work and learned it easily, and father was pleased with me. As soon as I knew how to baste pocket-flaps he began to teach me how to baste the coat edges. This was hard work. The double ply of overcoat cloth stitched in with canvas and tape made a very stiff edge. My fingers often stiffened with pain as I rolled and basted the edges. Sometimes a needle or two would break before I could do one coat. Then father would offer to finish the edge for me. But if he gave me my choice I never let him. At these moments I wanted so to master the thing myself that I felt my whole body trembling with the desire. And with my habit of personifying things, I used to bend over the coat on my lap, force the obstinate and squeaking needle, wet with perspiration, in and out of the cloth and whisper with determination: "No, you shall not get the best of me!" When I succeeded I was so happy that father, who often watched me with a smile, would say, "Rahel, your face is shining. Now rest a while." He always told me to rest after I did well. I loved these moments. I would push my stool closer to the wall near which I sat, lean my back against it, and look about the shop. . . .

One evening in the Fall father came home with two brightly coloured frameless pictures and nailed one on the door leading into the Felesberg's rooms and the other on the door leading into the little old woman's. He explained to me that the pictures were of the two men, nominated for the presidential office. The prospective presidents in these pictures were herdsmen. Each one, dressed in fine black clothes and a high silk hat, stood in the midst of a herd of cattle. In one picture the herdsman was short, stout and clean shaven, the cattle were round and sleek and the pasture green and abundant. In the other it was just the reverse. The herdsman was tall, thin and bearded, the cattle had fallen-in sides, and the ground was brown and bare.

I looked at the pictures and took them literally and seriously. One meant four years of plenty, the other four years of famine. But after a while, noticing that no one else seemed at all worried over it, I merely wondered, "What happens on election day?"

Soon after this I saw the Gentile boys on our block begin to store away, into a cellar, all the barrels, boxes, broken couches, torn mattresses, and every stick of wood they could lay hands on. I understood that the preparations were for election night and I looked on silently with pleasant excitement.

At last election day came. In the shop the men were discussing the candidates and there was a cheerful holiday atmosphere. "I bet you a pint of beer Harrison will be elected." "I bet you two pints it will be Cleveland."[13] In the afternoon I heard the men say they would go home early. When I was leaving father too said he would be home before dark.

After supper I climbed out on Mrs. Felesberg's fire escape and looked down between the bars into the street. I saw the Jewish men hurrying home from work and noticed that very few of the Jewish

13. The presidential candidates described here, Benjamin Harrison and Grover Cleveland, ran against one another in 1888 and 1892. The proximity of this election and the onset of the depression of 1893 confirms that it is the 1892 contest described here.

children were out. The Gentile boys were busy dragging forth the
barrels and couches and mattresses and piling them up in a heap in
front of the four big tenements inhabited chiefly by Jews.

When it grew dark they lit the heaps of rubbish and in a moment
there was a great blaze. The sparks flew, the fire crackled and the re-
flections of the flames danced merrily on the small red brick houses
opposite, where the Gentiles lived. From the windows of these
houses groups of people were leaning out talking and laughing merrily. Mrs. Felesberg also stuck her head out of the window for a moment, looked down at the flame and said earnestly: "Thank God,
there is no wind. And if it comes I hope it will blow the other way." I
was beginning to feel uneasy and wished that father had come home
before dark, as he said he would. Scarcely any one passed through the
block now. I noticed with fear that not a Jew was to be seen on the
street. After a little while I saw some one coming from the Montgom-
ery Street side. Though I expected father to come through Clinton
Street it occurred to me that perhaps he had decided this other way
was safer, and I strained my eyes and watched. When the person came
nearer I saw that it was the son of the little old woman. He walked
slowly, hesitatingly and kept to the wall. The men and boys around the
fire seemed to pay no attention to his coming, but as soon as he was in
front of the fire they suddenly attacked him. There was a short tussle
and soon I saw him rushed into the hall.

I was beside myself with fear now. "Why doesn't father come? Why
did I leave him?" I could not help blaming myself.

Again Mrs. Felesberg came over and looked out of the window and
asked, "Isn't your father here yet, Rahel?"

"No," I shook my head. I could not answer her. I pressed my forehead to the iron bars and looked over to Clinton Street. Every time
the fire was poked the whole block was lit up and I could see all the
way over to the corner. I thought I saw a figure lurking away over in
the shadow. "Could that be father?" I thought. "Perhaps it is some
other Jewish man. Oh God, will he ever come!"

At last I saw him turn from Clinton into Cherry Street. The blaze
flared suddenly and I recognised his tan suit and hat. I jumped up,
leaned over the fire escape and watched him coming nearer and
nearer, keeping in the middle of the sidewalk. The boys and men
stood about the fire laughing, talking, pushing each other. One was
playing on a harmonica and a few were waltzing.

At last I saw father almost opposite the blaze. My heart stood still
and my eyes felt stretched so far apart that it seemed as though I
could never close them again.

"Will they let him pass? Oh, that is too good to be true." And indeed it was. The next moment I saw a black mass of bodies hurl itself at him.

"Father!" I screamed down. My voice struck terror into my own heart. The next moment I was rushing blindly through Mrs. Felesberg's rooms, lit only by the blaze from the outside, knocking myself against table and chairs. At last I was out in the hall and went falling and tumbling down stairs. On the first floor I met him coming up, pale and hatless. We stopped and looked at each other. I was beside myself with joy to see him alive but I heard myself say, "Father, your hat!" And he smiled and said pantingly, "That is nothing, I needed a new one."[14] . . .

Father began to strain all his energy to save the money to send for mother and the children. In the shop one morning I realised that he had been leaving out of his breakfast the tiny glass of brandy for two cents and was eating just the roll. So I too made my sacrifice. When as usual he gave me the apple and the roll, I took the roll but refused the apple. And he did not urge me. When a cold grey day at the end of November found him in his light tan suit quite worn and me in my thin calico frock, now washed out to a tan colour, we went to a second-hand clothing store on Division Street and he bought me a fuzzy brown coat reaching a little below my waist, for fifty cents, and for himself a thin threadbare overcoat. And now we were ready for the winter.

About the same time that the bitter cold came father told me one night that he had found work for me in a shop where he knew the presser. I lay awake long that night. I was eager to begin life on my own responsibility but was also afraid. We rose earlier than usual that morning for father had to take me to the shop and not be over late for his own work. I wrapped my thimble and scissors, with a piece of bread for breakfast, in a bit of newspaper, carefully stuck two needles into the lapel of my coat and we started.

The shop was on Pelem Street, a shop district one block long and just wide enough for two ordinary sized wagons to pass each other. We stopped at a door where I noticed at once a brown shining porcelain knob and a half rubbed off number seven. Father looked at his watch and at me.

14. The election night attacks on Jews described here are only one of many instances of anti-Semitism narrated by Cohen in her autobiography. See also *Out of the Shadow*, pp. 96–99, 104–7.

"Don't look so frightened," he said. "You need not go in until seven. Perhaps if you start in at this hour he will think you have been in the habit of beginning at seven and will not expect you to come in earlier. Remember, be independent. At seven o'clock rise and go home no matter whether the others go or stay."

He began to tell me something else but broke off suddenly, said "good-bye" over his shoulder and went away quickly. I watched him until he turned into Monroe Street.

Now only I felt frightened, and waiting made me nervous, so I tried the knob. The door yielded heavily and closed slowly. I was half way up when it closed entirely, leaving me in darkness. I groped my way to the top of the stairs and hearing a clattering noise of machines, I felt about, found a door, and pushed it open and went in. A tall, dark, beardless man stood folding coats at a table. I went over and asked him for the name (I don't remember what it was). "Yes," he said crossly. "What do you want?"

I said, "I am the new feller hand."[15] He looked at me from head to foot. My face felt so burning hot that I could scarcely see.

"It is more likely," he said, "that you can pull bastings than fell sleeve lining." Then turning from me he shouted over the noise of the machine: "Presser, is this the girl?" The presser put down the iron and looked at me. "I suppose so," he said, "I only know the father."

The cross man looked at me again and said, "Let's see what you can do." He kicked a chair, from which the back had been broken off, to the finisher's table, threw a coat upon it and said raising the corner of his mouth: "Make room for the new feller hand."

One girl tittered, two men glanced at me over their shoulders and pushed their chairs apart a little. By this time I scarcely knew what I was about. I laid my coat down somewhere and pushed my bread into the sleeve. Then I stumbled into the bit of space made for me at the table, drew in the chair and sat down. The men were so close to me on each side I felt the heat of their bodies and could not prevent myself from shrinking away. The men noticed and probably felt hurt. One made a joke, the other laughed and the girls bent their heads low over their work. All at once the thought came: "If I don't do this coat quickly and well he will send me away at once." I picked up the coat, threaded my needle, and began hastily, repeating the lesson father impressed upon me. "Be careful not to twist the sleeve lining, take small false stitches."

15. A feller hand is a stitcher who fells seams, that is, stitches the inside flaps of seams so that they lie flat. Rahel felled sleeve linings in this particular shop.

A tenement sweatshop (by Walter Jack Duncan). (From Rose Cohen, *Out of the Shadow* [New York: George H. Doran, 1918], following p. 230)

My hands trembled so that I could not hold the needle properly. It took me a long while to do the coat. But at last it was done. I took it over to the boss and stood at the table waiting while he was examining it. He took long, trying every stitch with his needle. Finally he put it down and without looking at me gave me two other coats. I felt very happy! When I sat down at the table I drew my knees close together and stitched as quickly as I could.

When the pedlar came into the shop everybody bought rolls. I felt hungry but I was ashamed and would not eat the plain, heavy rye bread while the others ate rolls.

All day I took my finished work and laid it on the boss's table. He would glance at the clock and give me other work. Before the day was over I knew that this was a "piece work shop," that there were four machines and sixteen people were working. I also knew that I had done almost as much work as "the grown-up girls" and that they did not like me. I heard Betsy, the head feller hand, talking about "a snip of a girl coming and taking the very bread out of your mouth." The only one who could have been my friend was the presser who knew my father. But him I did not like. The worst I knew about him just now was that he was a soldier because the men called him so. But a soldier, I had learned, was capable of anything. And so, noticing that he looked at me often, I studiously kept my eyes from his corner of the room.

Seven o'clock came and every one worked on. I wanted to rise as father had told me to do and go home. But I had not the courage to stand up alone. I kept putting off going from minute to minute. My neck felt stiff and by back ached. I wished there were a back to my chair so that I could rest against it a little. When the people began to go home it seemed to me that it had been night a long time.

The next morning when I came into the shop at seven o'clock, I saw at once that all the people were there and working as steadily as if they had been at work a long while. I had just time to put away my coat and go over to the table, when the boss shouted gruffly, "Look here, girl, if you want to to work here you better come in early. No office hours in my shop." It seemed very still in the room, even the machines stopped. And his voice sounded dreadfully distinct. I hastened into the bit of space between the two men and sat down. He brought me two coats and snapped, "Hurry with these!"

From this hour a hard life began for me. He refused to employ me except by the week. He paid me three dollars and for this he hurried me from early until late. He gave me only two coats at a time to do.

When I took them over and as he handed me the new work he would say quickly and sharply, "Hurry!" And when he did not say it in words he looked at me and I seemed to hear even more plainly, "Hurry!" I hurried but he was never satisfied. . . .

One day I noticed that there was a good deal of whispering among the men in the shop. At noon when all went out to lunch and I ran out to get a slice of cheese for mine, I saw that the men had gathered on the street before the door. They were eating sandwiches, stamping about over the snow and disputing in anxious earnest whispers.

In the shop the boss looked gloomier than ever.

"I'll not have any one coming into my shop and telling me what to do," he shouted to a strange man who came over to his table to talk to him. "This shop is mine. The machines are mine. If they are willing to work on my conditions, well and good, if not, let them go to the devil! All the tailors are not dead yet."

At our table Betsy whispered: "The men joined the union. The boss is in a hurry for the work." There was a twinkle in Betsy's usually lifeless eyes.

I had no idea what a union meant or what all this trouble was about. But I learned a little the next day. When I came in a little after six in the morning, I found only the three girls who were at my table. Not a man except the boss was in the shop. The men came in about five minutes to seven and then stood or sat at the presser's table talking and joking quietly. The boss stood at his table brushing coats furiously. Every minute or so he glanced at the clock and his face looked black with anger.

At the first stroke of seven the presser blew a whistle and every man went to his place. At the minute of twelve the presser again blew the whistle and the men went out to their noon meal. Those who remained in the shop ate without hurry and read their newspapers. The boss kept his eye on us girls. We began last, ate hurriedly and sat down to work at once. Betsy looked at the men reading their newspapers and grumbled in a whisper, "This is what it means to belong to a union. You get time to straighten out your bones." I knew that Betsy had been a feller hand for many years. Her back was quite bent over and her hands were white and flabby.

The men returned a little before one and sat waiting for the stroke of the clock and the presser's whistle. At seven in the evening when the presser blew his whistle the men rose almost with one movement, put away their work and turned out the lights over their tables and machines. We girls watched them go enviously and the boss turned his back towards the door. He did not answer their "Good-night." In the dark and quiet that followed his great shears clipped loudly and angrily.

One Saturday afternoon father came home and showed me a little book with a red paper cover which he took from his breast pocket. "This," he said, "is my union book. You too must join the union." He told me he had heard that a few of the feller hands had organized, and a mass meeting was to be held in a hall on Clinton Street that evening. He took me to the door of the building at eight o'clock, saw a young woman enter and told me to follow her. As I had no idea what a meeting was like or what to expect I was dazed and dazzled by the great number of lights, the red carpet covering the floor, and the crowd of people already seated on benches along the walls. The middle of the room was not used.

I glanced about from the doorway for a seat nearby. But the only ones I could see were in front. And for this I finally aimed, looking neither to right nor to left and feeling painfully conscious of my shabbiness. The seat I was forced to take was right in front and only about two yards away from the small square platform. I was so uneasy at being exposed from all sides that it was some time before I forgot my bare head, my red hands with the cracked and bleeding skin and my shoes with their turned up noses—already worn out and still too large for me. By that time a young man was standing on the platform speaking. I had seen this young man two or three times before. He lived on Cherry Street a few doors away from us, and Kate Felesberg had told me once that he was a "student." What he was saying now was something like this:

"Fourteen hours a day you sit on a chair, often without a back, felling coats. Fourteen hours you sit close to the other feller hand feeling the heat of her body against yours, her breath on your face. Fourteen hours with your back bent, your eyes close to your work you sit stitching in a dull room often by gas light. In the winter during all these hours as you sit stitching your body is numb with cold. In the summer, as far as you are concerned, there might be no sun, no green grass, no soft breezes. You with your eyes close to the coat on your lap are sitting and sweating the livelong day. The black cloth dust eats into your very pores. You are breathing the air that all the other bent and sweating bodies in the shop are throwing off, and the air that comes in from the yard heavy and disgusting with filth and the odour of the open toilets.

"If any of you know this, and think about it, you say to yourselves, no doubt, 'What is the use of making a fuss? Will the boss pay any attention to me if I should talk to him? And anyway it won't be for long. I won't stay in the shop all my life. I'll—perhaps this year, or next ———— .' Girls, I know your thought. You expect to get married! Not so quick! Even the man who works in a shop himself does not want to marry a white-faced dull-eyed girl who for years has been working fourteen hours a day. He realises that you left your strength in the shop, and that to marry you he would take on a bundle of troubles, and doctor's bills on his head. You know what he does most often? He sends to Russia for a girl he once knew, one who has never seen the inside of a shop. Or else he marries the little servant girl with the red cheeks and bright eyes.

"And even if you do marry, are you so secure? Don't forget that your husband himself is working in the shop fourteen hours and more a day, breathing the filthy air and the cloth dust. How long will he last? Who knows! You may have to go back to the shop. And even worse than this may be awaiting you. Your children may have to go to the shop! And unless you, now, change it, they may have to go back to the same dull shops, the filthy air and the fourteen hours. In the winter before daylight your little daughter may have to run through the streets in the rain and the snow in her worn little shoes, and thin coat. She will stand trembling before the boss in the same dull shop, perhaps, where you had once stood. She will sit in the same backless chair, rickety now, with her little back bent, for fourteen hours."

He seemed to be looking right at me. I tucked my feet far under my seat and bent my head to hide my tears. "Who is this man?" I wondered; "how does he know all this?"

He continued: "Each one of you alone can do nothing. Organise! Demand decent wages that you may be able to live in a way fit for human beings, not for swine. See that your shop has pure air and sun, that your bodies may be healthy. Demand reasonable hours that you may have time to know your families, to think, to enjoy. Organise! Each one of you alone can do nothing. Together you can gain everything."

For a moment the room was perfectly still. Then there was a storm of applause and the people rose and began to press close to the platform. I went to a vacant seat in an out-of-the-way corner and watched the people going out in groups and talking excitedly. When the hall was almost empty I went over to the secretary's desk. "I want to join the union," I said.

Our feller hands had not been at the meeting but they too had joined the union. And now our shop was a "strictly union shop." I'll always remember how proud I felt when the first evening at seven o'clock the presser blew the whistle and I with the other girls stood up with the men. But not many girls joined the union. And so, it was soon broken up.[16]

16. The strikes described by Cohen antedated by fifteen years the great uprisings that succeeded in unionizing the garment trades in New York City between 1909 and 1915. For a contemporary account of the later struggles, see Theresa Serber Malkiel, *The Diary of a Shirtwaist Striker* (Ithaca, N.Y.: ILR Press, 1990; originally published in 1910).

SIX

The Childhood of Mary Paik,
1905–1917

The occupation of Korea by Japanese forces in 1905 during the Russo-Japanese War prompted a flow of political refugees to Hawaii and the West Coast of the United States. Presbyterian missionary work had acquainted Koreans with the United States, and Christians were disproportionally represented in the refugee flow after 1905. Among these immigrants were Paik Sin Koo and his family.

In all only about 1,000 Koreans reached the mainland of the United States before Japanese pressure and a presidential order cut off this migrant flow.[1] Still, Mary Paik Lee's autobiography speaks to the broader experience of Asian Americans—primarily Chinese and Japanese—who found places in California agriculture in the first decades of the twentieth century.[2]

The Paik family immigrated first to Hawaii, where Paik Sin Koo worked on a plantation for a year before borrowing money and taking the family to San Francisco. Mary Paik was six when she arrived in the United States, and her autobiography, *Quiet Odyssey*, offers a poignant account of the hard work and exploitation that Korean immigrants faced in California in the early decades of the twentieth century.

Through the narrative, we follow the Paik family from town to town, as they worked in agricultural settlements near Los Angeles and in the Central Valley. Riverside, Claremont, Colusa, and Roberts Island provided the growing family's first homes, but they could never earn enough—even with the children doing laundry and housecleaning to

1. Mary Paik Lee, *Quiet Odyssey: A Pioneer Korean Woman in America*, ed. with an introduction by Sucheng Chan (Seattle: University of Washington Press, 1990), p. xlii.

2. For a slightly earlier period, see Sucheng Chan, *This Bittersweet Soil: The Chinese in California Agriculture, 1860–1910* (Berkeley: University of California Press, 1986).

supplement their father's earnings—to provide even a measure of economic security.[3] Paik Sin Koo finally found better paying work, but his job at the furnace of a quicksilver (mercury) mining operation so ruined his health that the oldest son had to give up his plans for high school to work and help support the family.

Much of the narrative focuses on Mary Paik's struggle to gain an education while earning enough money to cover the cost of room, board, and books. She repeatedly learned to cope with the racism that Asian Americans living in California faced in the 1910s and 1920s—from classmates, teachers, even fellow church members. Through the story, we learn of the strong will and family bonds that kept her going despite discriminatory treatment. We also learn of the human consequences of the virulent anti-Asian sentiment in California that eventually led to the almost total exclusion of Asian immigration with the passage of the Johnson-Reid Act in 1924.[4]

My maternal grandparents lived in Yangwu, a village some distance away. I do not remember them at all. Most people at that time traveled on foot only, so with the exception of very urgent matters, faraway relatives did not just drop by for visits. The marriage between my mother and father had been arranged by a paid matchmaker, as was the practice in those days. My mother's family were poor farmers; perhaps that is why they did not mind her, their only child, moving so far away to marry. Later on, my parents joked that her family had arranged the marriage because Father came from a family of ministers and teachers, so they thought her marrying him would be a step up; little did they realize that as soon as they came to the United States she would have to work on a farm again. Mother was sixteen and Father was twenty-two when they married.

One afternoon in 1905, as I was waiting on the front steps for Grandfather, I saw two men attired in strange-looking clothes walking towards our house. As they stopped at our gate, I ran into the house to call Grandmother. She came out to meet them. After a few minutes she returned, looking very serious, and said that we had to move out right away. This caused much talk and excitement during the evening

---

3. See the map on p. 178 for places where the Paik family lived during these years.

4. Sucheng Chan, ed., *Entry Denied: Exclusion and the Chinese Community in America, 1882–1943* (Philadelphia: Temple University Press, 1991); see also William S. Bernard, "Immigration: History of U.S. Policy," in Stephan Thernstrom, ed., *Harvard Encyclopedia of American Ethnic Groups* (Cambridge, Mass.: Harvard University Press, 1980), pp. 492–93.

meal. It turned out that the two strange men were Japanese officers, and they wanted everyone to move out so they could use our home to house their soldiers. As Grandmother told about the Japanese soldiers, my family sat in stunned silence. Although the news was no surprise to them, it must have felt as though the sky had fallen on us. Soon friends came over, asking what should be done. The only choice was to leave that night or to stay and live with the soldiers in our home, which no one wanted to do. I don't remember any of the details of what happened that night. It was so confusing. In the next few days, every evening as our family ate dinner they talked about all the disturbing rumors from other parts of our country. I felt a bit uneasy, but I was too young to realize the significance of these events and soon forgot about them in play. My family must have made a decision about what to do when the soldiers arrived, but I didn't know about it until later.

The family decided to go to Inchon, the nearest large city with a harbor, to see what we could do for a living there. It took several days and nights of walking with very little rest to reach our destination. We could only bring our bedding, clothes, and food for the journey. Father must have carried me on his back, but I must have slept most of the way because I don't remember anything about the trip. Many of our friends and neighbors came with us. Mother said that God must surely have been guiding us in the right direction.

There happened to be two ships in Inchon harbor, sent by owners of sugar cane plantations in Hawaii to recruit workers. People were told that if a man signed a contract to work for one year, he and his family would be given free passage to Hawaii. After that, he would be free to go wherever he wished. His wages were to be fifty cents per day, working from dawn to dusk. Father signed on, and that was how we went to Hawaii on the S.S. *Siberia*, arriving on May 8, 1905. . . .

Life in Hawaii was not much different from that in Korea because all the people I came in contact with were Orientals. I don't remember seeing white people, at least not face to face. There was a small group of Koreans in Oahu, where we lived, and a small church. Father preached there sometimes when he was not working on the plantations. He must have done hoeing or weeding: since he had not had any farming experience, he could not do specialized work such as picking. Mother wanted to work as well, but Father would not allow her to. He said, "Even if we have to starve, I don't want you working out in the fields."

When I asked Father years later if we had eaten bananas in Hawaii, he replied that although a big bunch of bananas sold for five cents, he could not afford to buy any. Since we had arrived with only the clothes on our backs and our bedding, we never had enough money left over to buy bananas. We lived in a grass hut, slept on the ground, and had to start from scratch to get every household item. Fortunately, the weather was warm, so we didn't need much clothing, but we never had enough money for a normal way of life.

While we were living in Hawaii, Mother didn't have much housework to do in the grass hut, so she had time to talk to us about why we were the only ones in our family to have left Korea. She told me that I had begged Grandmother to come with us, but she wouldn't leave her school. Grandmother had said that her students were depending on her to teach and guide them. She was certainly a very remarkable woman, with much courage in the face of danger. It is women like her who get things started in spite of opposition, and who accomplish what seem like impossibilities. I'm glad she lived to see her dream come true. She loved all of her students as though they were her own children, and she wouldn't desert them in their time of need. Uncle said the same thing about the young boys in his high school. Also, he had a wife and several children of his own to care for. Of course, Grandfather would not leave without Grandmother. So only my father had no obligations to anyone except his own wife and two children.

Mother told me there had been a lot of discussion for several days before the final decision was made for my parents, my brother, and me to leave Korea to find a better life elsewhere. Father was reluctant to leave, but his parents insisted, saying that his presence would not help them. They knew what would happen to them in the near future. They were prepared to face great hardship or worse, but they wanted at least one member of their family to survive and live a better life somewhere else. Such strong, quiet courage in ordinary people in the face of danger is really something to admire and remember always.

My second brother, Paik Daw Sun, was born on October 6, 1905, in Hawaii. Father was desperate, always writing to friends in other places, trying to find a better place to live. Finally, he heard from friends in Riverside, California, who urged him to join them: they said the prospects for the future were better in America; that a man's wages were ten to fifteen cents an hour for ten hours of work a day. After his year in Hawaii was up, Father borrowed enough money from friends to pay for our passage to America on board the S.S. *China*.

We landed in San Francisco on December 3, 1906. As we walked down the gangplank, a group of young white men were standing around, waiting to see what kind of creatures were disembarking. We must have been a very queer-looking group. They laughed at us and spit in our faces; one man kicked up Mother's skirt and called us names we couldn't understand. Of course, their actions and attitudes left no doubt about their feelings toward us. I was so upset. I asked Father why we had come to a place where we were not wanted. He replied that we deserved what we got because that was the same kind of treatment that Koreans had given to the first American missionaries in Korea: the children had thrown rocks at them, calling them "white devils" because of their blue eyes and yellow or red hair. He explained that anything new and strange causes some fear at first, so ridicule and violence often result. He said the missionaries just lowered their heads and paid no attention to their tormentors. They showed by their action and good works that they were just as good as or even better than those who laughed at them. He said that is exactly what we must try to do here in America—study hard and learn to show Americans that we are just as good as they are. That was my first lesson in living, and I have never forgotten it.

Many old friends came with us from Hawaii. Some stayed in San Francisco, others went to Dinuba, near Fresno, but most headed for Los Angeles. We ourselves went straight to the railroad depot nearby and boarded a train for Riverside, where friends would be waiting for us. It was our first experience on a train. We were excited, but we felt lost in such a huge country. When we reached Riverside, we found friends from our village in Korea waiting to greet us.

In those days, Orientals and others were not allowed to live in town with the white people. The Japanese, Chinese, and Mexicans each had their own little settlement outside of town. My first glimpse of what was to be our camp was rows of one-room shacks, with a few water pumps here and there and little sheds for outhouses. We learned later that the shacks had been constructed for the Chinese men who had built the Southern Pacific Railroad in the 1880s.

We had reached Riverside without any plans and with very little money, not knowing what we could do for a living. After much discussion with friends, it was decided that Mother should cook for about thirty single men who worked in the citrus groves. Father did not like her to work, but it seemed to be the only way we could make a living for ourselves. She would make their breakfast at 5 A.M., pack their lunches, and cook them supper at 7 P.M. But my parents did not have the cooking utensils we needed, so Father went to the Chinese settlement and told them of our situation. He could not speak Chinese but he wrote *hanmun*, the character writing that is the same

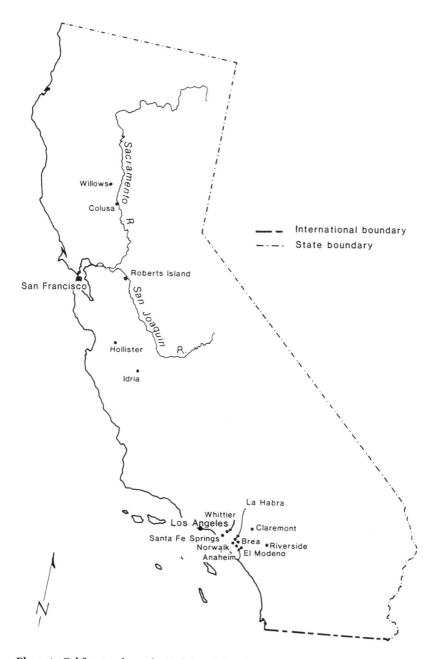

Places in California where the Paik family lived. (From Mary Paik Lee, *Quiet Odyssey* [Seattle: University of Washington Press, 1990], p. 10)

in Korean and Chinese. He asked for credit, promising to make regular payments from time to time. They trusted him and agreed to give us everything we needed to get started: big iron pots and pans, dishes, tin lunch pails, chopsticks, and so forth. They also gave us rice and groceries.

The Korean men went to the dumpyard nearby and found the materials to build a shack large enough for our dining area. They made one long table and two long benches to seat thirty men. Father made a large stove and oven with mud and straw, and he found several large wine barrels to hold the water for drinking and cooking. That was the start of our business. Mother had long, thick black hair that touched the ground. It became a nuisance in her work, so Father cut it short, leaving just enough to coil in a bun on the back of her head. It must have caused her much grief to lose her beautiful hair, but she never complained. We had already lost everything else that meant anything to us.

We lived in a small one-room shack built in the 1880s. The passing of time had made the lumber shrink, so the wind blew through the cracks in the walls. There was no pretense of making it livable—just four walls, one window, and one door—nothing else. We put mud in the cracks to keep the wind out. The water pump served several shacks. We had to heat our bath water in a bucket over an open fire outside, then pour it into a tin tub inside. There was no gas or electricity. We used kerosene lamps, and one of my chores was to trim the wicks, clean the glass tops, and keep the bowls filled with kerosene.

The Chinese men who had lived there in the 1880s must have slept on the floor. Father solved the problem of where we were going to sleep by building shelves along the four walls of our shack. Then he found some hay to put on each shelf. He put a blanket over the hay, rolled up some old clothes for a pillow—and that was a bed for a child. I used a block of wood for my pillow. It became such a habit with me that even to this day I do not like a soft pillow. My parents themselves slept on the floor.

After our shelter was taken care of, I looked around and found that all our immediate neighbors were old friends from Korea. Philip Ahn, who became a movie actor many years later, lived across from us. His father was Mr. Ahn Chang-ho. Mr. Ahn and my father, who had been boyhood friends in Korea, felt like brothers to each other and kept in touch through the years. It was good to see so many familiar faces again, and we felt happy to be there together.

Every day after school and on weekends, my older brother and I had to pile enough firewood up against the kitchen shack to last until the next day. Father found some wheels and boards at the dumpyard to make a long flatbed for carrying the wood, but we had to make several trips each day. An acre of trees grew some distance from us, where we found plenty of broken branches to gather up.

Meung's job was to keep the wine barrels filled with water so Mother could do her work. I cleaned the oil lamps, kept our shack in order, looked after my baby brother, and heated the bath water for the men at 6 P.M. so they could bathe before supper. The workers' bathhouse had just one large tub inside; I heated the water by building a fire under the floor. The men washed themselves with a hose before entering the tub.

Every Saturday Meung and I went to a slaughterhouse some distance away to get the animal organs that the butchers threw out—pork and beef livers, hearts, kidneys, entrails, tripe—all the things they considered unfit for human consumption. We were not alone—Mexican children came there also. They needed those things to survive just as we did. The butchers stood around laughing at us as we scrambled for the choice pieces. When I told Father I didn't want to go there anymore because they were making fun of us, he said we should thank God that they did not know the value of what they threw out; otherwise, we would go hungry.

Meung started school at the Washington Irving School, not far from our settlement. When I was ready to go, Father asked a friend who spoke a little English—a Mr. Song—to take me. My first day at school was a very frightening experience. As we entered the schoolyard, several girls formed a ring around us, singing a song and dancing in a circle. When they stopped, each one came over to me and hit me in the neck, hurting and frightening me. They ran away when a tall woman came towards us. Her bright yellow hair and big blue eyes looking down at me were a fearful sight; it was my first close look at such a person. She was welcoming me to her school, but I was frightened. When she addressed me, I answered in Korean, "I don't understand you." I turned around, ran all the way home, and hid in our shack. Father laughed when he heard about my behavior. He told me there was nothing to be afraid of; now that we were living here in America, where everything is different from Korea, we would have to learn to get along with everyone.

The next day when I went to school with my brother, the girls did not dance around us; I guess the teacher must have told them not to do it. I learned later that the song they sang was:

Ching Chong, Chinaman,
Sitting on a wall.

Along came a white man,
And chopped his head off.

The last line was the signal for each girl to "chop my head off" by giving me a blow on the neck. That must have been the greeting they
gave to all the Oriental kids who came to school the first day.

Because our Korean names were too difficult for them to remember,
the children at school always said "Hey you!" when they wanted our
attention. I told Meung that it was too late to change our names, but
we should give American names to our siblings. So we started with
Paik Daw Sun, who had been born in Hawaii, by calling him Ernest.
When another brother was born in Riverside on August 8, 1908, we
named him Stanford.

Meung was only three years older than I, but he was extremely ob-
servant and considerate for his age. He told me to stop playing around
and to notice how much work our mother had to do. He said that to
help her, every day before school he would wash the baby's diapers,
and I was to hang them on the line. After school, before going for firewood, I was to take them in, fold them, and put them away. Mean-
while he would fill the wine barrels with water from the pump. We
followed this routine from then on. I was always taking care of the babies, bathing them every night, changing their diapers, and feeding
them midnight bottles. He heated their bath water in a bucket outside
so I could give them baths in the tin tub inside our shack.

There was one large building for community meetings in Riverside,
where religious services were held on Sundays. We didn't have a minister, but several persons read the Bible and discussed it. Father
preached there whenever he had time. An American lady named Mrs.
Stewart, who lived in Upland, used to come to our church on Sundays. She was interested in the Korean people and brought presents
for everyone at Christmastime. She gave me the first and only doll I
ever had.

Meung and I had a special "gang" consisting of six members about
the same age. We ran to school together, ran home for lunch, back to
school, and home again. On the way to school there was a large mul-
berry bush growing in the front lawn of one house. Whenever we
passed, we noticed the big black berries that had fallen on the lawn.
They looked so tempting that we just had to stop and see what they
tasted like. They were so delicious we couldn't stop eating them. After
that, every time we passed that house we helped ourselves, but we
had an uneasy feeling about whether it was right or wrong to take the
fruit. We childishly decided that it was all right because the berries
were on the ground and weren't picked off the bush. We had a big

argument about it one day. When Meung said it was wrong to take something that belonged to someone else, my girlfriend got so angry she picked up a piece of firewood and hit him on the head. When we told Father about it, he said that the berries belonged to the owner of the bush, whether they were on the bush or on the ground. That settled our arguments. From then on we looked the other way every time we passed that house.

An old Chinese peddler used to come to our place once a week with fruits and vegetables on his wagon. I told Philip Ahn to climb up the front of his wagon and talk to him while I climbed up the back and filled my apron with small potatoes, lima beans, and corn, which we roasted in hot ashes. It was our first taste of such vegetables, and they were so good. But the old man got wise to us after a while, so whenever we approached his wagon, he used the horsewhip on us.

One evening, as I was helping Mother wash the lunch pails the men brought back, I asked her what kind of work the men were doing. She told me they were picking oranges, which gave me an idea, but I didn't dare to tell her about it. After breakfast the next day, as I passed out the lunch pails, I asked some of the men why they never brought me an orange. I said I had never seen or tasted one. That evening as I took in the lunch pails, they felt a bit heavy; when I opened one I saw a beautiful orange for the first time. I was so excited I told Father about it. He must have talked to the men, because there were only a few oranges after that. It helped make the work of washing the lunch pails seem less tiring to find a few. One night some time later, when I took in the lunch pails every single one felt heavy. I got really excited, but to my surprise, each pail had a rock in it. When I asked why, the men said they were afraid I would scold them if they didn't bring something, but there were no more oranges to be picked. Everybody had a good laugh about it.

After the orange season was over, the men picked lemons and grapefruit. In the fall there was work in the walnut groves. The men would shake the walnuts from the trees with long poles, then the women and children would gather them up in sacks, take them to a clearing, and peel off the outer shells [hulls]. They got paid by the sack for their labor. Between the walnut harvest and the time to prune the orange trees, the men got a short rest. When there was no work in the citrus groves, Father worked at the Riverside Cement Company on the edge of town.

Two incidents happened in Riverside that will always remain in my memory. The first was when I told Father I needed a coat to wear to school. He said that he would see what he could do about it. He rode to town on his bicycle to buy some material, and he made a coat for me. Since we did not have a sewing machine, he had to sew it by hand one evening. It was a beautiful red coat; I was so happy to wear it. All the girls at school wanted to know where I had purchased it. They couldn't believe my father had made it himself. When I asked Mother how Father could do such a wonderful thing, she smiled and said that, among other things, Father had been an expert tailor in Korea. He had studied to be a minister and had taught the Korean language to missionaries, but tailoring was how he made a living. . . .

We lived in Riverside for four or five years, but Father became concerned about Mother's health—the work of cooking for thirty men was too much for her. She was a small woman, only four feet eleven inches tall, and she was expecting another baby. So we paid off the Chinese merchants who had helped us get started, paid all our debts to friends, and moved to Claremont, not too far away. It was a quiet college town with many school buildings. We moved into a duplex building, where an old friend, Martha Kim, was living with her parents. It was across the street from the railroad station and a huge citrus-packing house. Those were the days before frozen fruit juices, so after the choice fruit was packed, the culls were piled up in boxes back of the buildings to be taken to the dump once a week. Because of this, we were fortunate that we could enjoy all the discarded fruit.

Our move to Claremont turned out to be our first experience with the American way of living. The new house seemed huge after our little shack. It had several rooms with beds, chairs, and other furniture. The kitchen had a gas stove, electric lights, and a sink with faucets for cold and hot water. But all that was as nothing compared with what we found in the bathroom. There was a big white tub with faucets at one end—I couldn't believe it was the place for taking our baths. And the biggest surprise of all was the toilet. Father flushed it to show us how it operated. He must have seen these wonders before somewhere, because he wasn't surprised at anything. For the first time, I felt glad that we had come to America.

Father found a job as a janitor in the nearby apartment buildings. He told Meung and me to ask the tenants if we could do their laundry, and also to ask our schoolteachers the same thing. On foot, Meung had to pick up the dirty laundry in a big basket and return it later. I helped with the laundry before and after school and with the ironing at night. In Claremont we had our first experience with an electric iron. Before this we had heated the old "sad irons," as they were called in those days, on the wood stove. It was such a relief to use the electric iron. No more going back and forth to the wood stove for a hot iron. No more kerosene lamps, hunting for firewood, and outhouses. Life was getting better. Every Saturday Father bought a beef roast, and every Sunday we had pot roast with mashed potatoes and bread. This was our introduction to American food, and it tasted wonderful. A small group of Koreans lived in Claremont. They came together to worship on Sundays in an old building. There was no minister, so Father preached there several times. Arthur was born in Claremont on December 2, 1910. The memory of our short stay there is a pleasant one.

Unfortunately Father's wages were so low in Claremont that it was difficult to make a living. So, a year later, we moved to Colusa in northern California, hoping to find work there. It turned out we had made a disastrous move. Father could not find any kind of work. There was a depression in 1911, and the situation was so bad the Salvation Army offered a bowl of soup and a piece of bread to each hungry person in town. But when I asked if we could go and get some, Father said no. He didn't want us to be humiliated by asking for help.

The feeling towards Orientals in southern California had not been friendly, but we had been tolerated. In the northern part of the state, we found the situation to be much worse. Although we found a house on the outskirts of town, the townspeople's attitude towards us was chilling. Father told Meung and me to ask our schoolteachers for their laundry. Once again, Meung had to fetch and deliver, carrying a basket on foot. Since we lived on the outskirts of town, it was a hard job for him, but he never complained. But because of the negative feeling towards Orientals in Colusa, we never got enough clothes to launder, and we could not earn enough money to meet our needs. . . .

While Father was working in Dinuba, he met a friend, a Mr. Kim, who was looking for someone to help him on a farm that raised potatoes. They made plans to grow Burbank potatoes on Roberts Island, a big island in the Sacramento–San Joaquin Delta. So in 1912 we took the train to Stockton, where we boarded a small motor boat and traveled for several hours to Roberts Island. We didn't have much to take with us, only our bedding and a few kitchen utensils and clothes. It was a relief to leave Colusa, even though we didn't know where we were going. But, as Mother always said, God was surely leading us to the right place. Moving to Roberts Island saved our lives and prevented our starving to death.

The motorboat ride was exciting. We saw many trees but very few houses along the banks of the river. After several hours, the boat stopped, and the crew put up a plank of wood so we could land. As I walked up the plank, I looked at a branch on a nearby tree and saw a green snake staring at me. That was our welcome to the farm, an indication of things to come.

We had never seen a vegetable farm before. It looked like a heavenly paradise to us. Fish jumped up and down in the river, and the banks were full of various vegetables growing wild from seeds scattered by former farmers. We had plenty to eat and to be really thankful for. The farmhouse was an ancient, wooden two-story building, barely standing. There was also a big old barn with some hay in it, a few chickens, rats, and numerous snakes. All of a sudden we were in a new world. We felt alive and eager to see everything. The younger children ran towards the barn, but they stopped suddenly. They just stood there, looking in. I wondered why and went to see for myself. Their noisy approach had startled the creatures living there: rats and snakes of all sizes and kinds were running around trying to avoid one another in their haste to leave the barn. It was our first look at such wildlife. The sight fascinated as well as frightened us. We backed off to join our parents, who were more interested in the old house. They were trying to figure out how to arrange things to make it comfortable for everyone. Father told us children that Mr. Kim would arrive in a day or two with twenty single men to work on the farm and all the groceries we needed for cooking. The kitchen and dining areas took about two-thirds of the ground floor of the house; the rest of the space became our bedroom. We were back to using kerosene lamps, a water pump outside, and outhouses, but the house was about twice the size of our old shack in Riverside.

We were so hungry that we pulled up the vegetables growing on the banks, washed them at the pump, then cooked and ate everything. It felt good to have something solid to chew on. Father found some white butcher string and some old fish hooks. He said he would show us how to catch fish. He cut a long, slim branch from the willow tree, tied the string to the branch's tip, and tied the hook to the other end of the string. Then he dug up enough worms to fill a coffee can and put one of the worms on the hook. An old rowboat belonging to the farm was tied with a long rope to a tree. He told us to sit in the boat and to let the worm fall into the river. In a few seconds there was a pull on the line. We saw a big grey-black catfish coming up at the end of the string. It was our first sight of a live fish—a very exciting moment. Father told Meung to take the fish off the hook and to put another worm on it. A large grey cat living on the farm jumped into the rowboat and sat on the back seat as we were fishing. When Meung pulled up his fish, the cat stood up, trying to grab it. Meung took the fish off the hook and put it in an old bucket that was in the boat. The cat tried to eat it. It must have been very hungry, because although there were plenty of rats around, they were so big and strong the cat was afraid of them and never went near the barn. When Meung took the fish out of the bucket and gave it to the cat, she ate it right away.

The river seemed to be crowded with fish that kept jumping up as though looking for something to eat. I didn't want to put my hand in a can full of worms, so Father made some dough with flour and water. He told me to make a small ball like a marble with it and press it over the hook. The fish didn't seem to care what they ate: they liked my bait just as well as the worms. It didn't take long to catch enough for our supper. Father made an open fire, put a piece of chicken wire over it, and cooked the fish for dinner. We also had lettuce, celery, and carrots that grew along the river banks. What a wonderful experience after our ordeal in Colusa! We all felt happy again.

Though vegetables grew wild on the property, the only trees in the area were the willow trees growing along the river banks, which were too green to use for firewood. Father said he would have to buy wood by the cord. Whenever we ordered wood, a loaded barge came by and threw the logs on the river bank. Then we had to pile them up outside the kitchen door.

Father solved the problem of our beds just as he had in Riverside. He built shelves along the walls, gathered hay from the barn, put blankets over the hay, rolled up some old clothes for pillows—and those became the children's beds. Our parents slept on the floor. We used a big old tin tub on the property for our bathtub. We had to heat the water in a bucket on a fire outside the house. We never had toothbrushes or toothpaste—just a spoonful of salt and our forefinger for a brush. Perhaps because we didn't have sugar in the house, no one ever had toothaches or any other dental problems.

There was no furniture in the house. Upstairs, where the men were going to sleep, there were no beds. Father said twenty men would have just enough room to sleep on the floor with their blankets. After all the excitement of the day, the little children were tired, so we heated the water for their baths and prepared for bed.

As I stretched my legs on my shelf bed, I felt a cold, rough object against my toes. I threw back the blanket and saw a red snake coiled up. It was as surprised as I was and slithered off outside. After that, we always pounded our beds with a long stick before jumping in. Then I woke up one night feeling a sharp pain on my nose and found myself staring at two black, beady eyes. I screamed. Father came run-

ning to see what was wrong. A big rat about the size of a baby kitten
had tried to eat my nose. No wonder the cat was afraid of the rats.

The morning after we arrived, Meung and I got up early and caught
enough catfish for our breakfast. Then we looked into the problem of
cooking for twenty men. The house evidently had been occupied by
Chinese before we came. There were big cast-iron pots, pans, and a
Chinese-style *wok*—all the heavy equipment they had not wanted to
take with them. It was our good fortune to find almost everything we
needed to get started. Mr. Kim and his friends arrived that afternoon
with the supplies we needed for cooking—rice, soy sauce, and so
forth. Suddenly there was a crowd. We had so much to do! Everyone
helped. We filled all the huge wine barrels with water from the pump
so the red clay from the river could settle before we drank it or cooked
with it. Some men went fishing so there would be enough to eat for
several days; others helped clean up everything around the house and
barn and chased all the rats and snakes away; yet others cleaned the
outhouse. There were a few chickens, so the men made a place for
them to lay their eggs; but we had to watch them and get their eggs
before the snakes did. After a while, the big rats and snakes stayed
away. Maybe they came back at night, but we seldom saw them during
the day. Some men started a garden, planting corn, cucumbers, Chinese cabbage, and watermelons.

To ensure a regular supply of fish, Father made a fish trap with a
bushel basket. He put chicken wire around it, made an opening on
top, then tied a rope around it and attached it to a tree. He put several
fish heads and scraps in the basket, stood in the rowboat, and threw it
into the river. I always got up early to pull it out, curious to see what
had been caught during the night. There were several other kinds of
fish besides catfish, small crabs, and lobsters. On weekends, some of
the men took the rowboat somewhere to dig clams. Once, Meung
caught a striped bass about a foot long. It tasted better than catfish,
but that species rarely came our way.

At harvest time, when more men were needed, the extra help
stayed in tents. I remember one man had a guitar; it was the first time
we ever had seen such a thing. Father sometimes hired twenty or so
Sikhs to help us with the harvest. They would sit around a large pot of
melted butter and garlic, dipping into it with tortillas made of flour
and water. The children had the job of weeding and irrigating plants
in the garden. Mother and I were relieved to find that she would not
have to pack lunches for the men. The field was close by, so they could
come home for lunch. Plenty of good food helped all of us to recover
our strength, and there was much to be thankful for.

Meung and I went to school on the other side of Roberts Island. One teacher taught all eight grades, and the whole school had only about thirty children. The teacher came to school on horseback. She looked very young, about eighteen or twenty years old. We noticed that the boys and some of the girls were barefoot, so we asked Father if we could go barefoot, too. We said our shoes were getting worn out. He told us it was all right if the others were also barefoot. The soft soil on the island, known as peat, didn't have rocks or anything in it to hurt our feet. It felt so good to walk without shoes.

One evening Father woke us up in the middle of the night and told us to hurry, put on our clothes, and come to the river bank. He wanted us to see something wonderful that happened only once a year, in June. We rushed up the bank and looked down at a mass of shining silver glittering in the moonlight. At first we were so startled we couldn't tell what we were looking at. A solid silvery mass completely covered the water. Our cat, who was with us, of course, seemed to know what it was. She went berserk at the sight. She ran down the bank, jumped on top of the silvery mass, and ran back and forth over to the little island in the middle of the river. Then we could see that a mass of very large fish were so jammed together that the water was hidden from view. Father said they were shad coming from the ocean to spawn in the river. He had brought a long pole with a chicken-wire basket that looked like a huge soup ladle tied to one end. The pressure of the fish had pushed our rowboat halfway up the bank. Father stood at the end of the boat and forced the pole into the water. He brought up several huge white fish and dropped them in the boat. He told us to go get some men to help us. He had evidently prepared everything for this occasion. The men laid the fish on a long board, rubbed off their scales and took out the roe, which was large and long. Then they filleted the fish and cut them into pieces about three inches wide. The roe and fish were carefully laid in wine barrels, where Mother salted them. This went on all night until several barrels were filled.

The salted roe is a favorite Korean delicacy, served with a special hot sauce. Before cooking, the fillets are soaked in water to reduce the salt content. Then they are drained dry and cooked over an open fire. They are very delicious, and we enjoyed them all that year on Roberts Island.

One day Ernest, who was six years old, became ill and refused to eat for several days. I knew he would not tell Mother what he wanted, so I asked him when no one else was in the room. He said he would like some canned peaches, which surprised me because we had never eaten such a thing. Mother gave me some money when I told her his desire; she sent me with Meung to a small store on the other side of the island. It took us a long time to find the store, asking people along the way how to get there. We bought a can of peaches and started for home. On the way back, we came to an irrigation ditch with just a narrow board across it. As we crossed, Meung dropped the can of peaches. We were scared stiff. The water was about six feet deep, and neither one of us could swim. We just stood there frozen with fear, staring at the can of peaches on the bottom of the ditch. Meung was fifteen years old then, but he acted like a man. He jumped into the water, grabbed the can of peaches, and struggled to the side, where I helped pull him out. We both gave a big sigh of relief and rested for a while. We did not dare say a word about what had happened, and we were relieved when Mother did not ask why we were so late or why Meung was all wet. She just said she had been worried and left it at that. Ernest was surprised and happy, and he ate the peaches. Maybe that was the medicine he needed, because he felt better the next day and got out of bed.

Another member of our family arrived about then. Ralph was born on Roberts Island on February 16, 1913.

Our potato plants that year were big and healthy looking. Instead of men digging them up with pitchforks, as they used to do, we now had a machine to make the work easier. As the horses pulled the machine, the plants were uprooted. All the potatoes were exposed, so it was easy to pick them up and put them into sacks. Almost as many snakes as potatoes came out of the ground. They were nonpoisonous, but we were afraid of them anyway. The men had to work longer hours at harvest time, so they needed a "snack" between meals. Mother made yeast doughnuts, which Meung and I took out to them with wine.

We had had a big harvest and were expecting a good profit from it, but Mr. Kim took a barge load to Stockton one morning and returned a week later with a sad story. He said the market price had dropped to ten cents for a hundred-pound sack of potatoes. He had not found even one buyer and had had to dump the load in the river. The depression that had caused us to move from Colusa was still in full force. We were so isolated from the rest of the world, we didn't know what was happening outside. No one came to Roberts Island and none of us went outside. Father had never farmed before, so he didn't know about watching the wholesale market prices. It was a heartbreaking situation. Everyone had worked so hard all year, only to find that no one wanted to buy our crop. We learned that just raising a good crop did not mean success.

Father became desperate. He wrote to friends everywhere, trying to find another place where we could make a living. We were sorry to see the men leave; we had all become good friends. A letter soon came from Mr. Byung Joon-lee, who was working for a quicksilver mining company in Idria, San Benito County, California. He said to come quickly, that a few jobs were available. Once again we had nothing to take with us, only our few clothes and blankets. The kitchen things did not belong to us, and we could not take the food. We left them so that whoever should come after us would find everything with which to start farming.

We were told that there were only a few quicksilver mines in the United States, the largest of which was in Idria. On the way to Idria, we had to stop in Sacramento, because Mother became very ill. We stayed at a boardinghouse owned by a Mr. and Mrs. Lee, where another brother, Young Sun, was born February 26, 1914. Mother was so weary and ill she almost died that night giving birth. Young Sun, also named (but never called) Lawrence, was born more dead than alive, a blue baby. Father and I had to place him in hot and cold water alternately and massage him vigorously. It took a long time to get his circulation going.

After a day or two of rest, we continued to Tres Piños, a very small village some distance south of San Jose, to catch a wagon to Idria. It was a big haywagon with benches on both sides, hitched to four large horses, which took us up the mountains. It took half a day to reach the place. We crossed several creeks and stopped to move big rocks that had rolled down the road from the mountain. The scenery was beautiful—tall pine trees and hilly country—with very few houses along the way. Every time we moved, we came to a different kind of world. This was the best so far. The pine trees smelled good, and the cool air made us feel refreshed.

Mr. Lee had found an old house for us. It had four small rooms, and a shack in the back served as a kitchen and dining area. There was a big oven in the shack and a picnic-style board table with benches on both sides. The house had a small wood stove for heat. The mines, the company buildings, the hotel, the store, the houses of a few Caucasian families, and the boardinghouse for Caucasian workers all had electricity, but there was no electricity in the shacks for the rest of the workers—mainly Mexicans, with a few Koreans. We were back to our old way of living, but we felt happy to be in such a beautiful, wild country. Meung and I had to hunt for firewood again. There was a water pump outside the house, and the outhouse was halfway down the hill.

Mr. Lee took Father to the company office and asked if he could work there. He was accepted and was given a card to record the supplies from the company store which we bought on credit. Father bought kerosene lamps, a sack of rice—and a big ham. It was the first time we children had ever seen such a luxury. The ham tasted wonderful, and we enjoyed it very much for several weeks.

Father got a basket and took us up in the hills to see what could be picked for food; he showed us what was good and what to avoid. In a shallow stream, we saw crayfish, which hurried to get under the rocks when they heard us coming, and soft green watercress, which grew on top of the water. All kinds of wild vegetables grew there. They had a light green color. The celery had thin stalks and smelled a bit like the celery we buy in the stores now. The lettuce looked like romaine, the same shape and size, but was soft green in color, with thin and very tender leaves. Little cucumbers on vines climbed on the tall bushes nearby. Also, gooseberries and blackberries took the place of other fruits that did not grow in that location. Nature had provided a great wild vegetable market for all the poor people living there. As we sat around the table for our supper that evening, Father thanked God for leading us to this place.

The short stay on Roberts Island had been a wonderful experience for us children. We learned a lot about all the wild creatures who share this world with us. This new place, Idria, was yet another exciting experience—an interesting new way of life.

Around the house of every Mexican family in Idria were two or three burros, one or two pigs, and some chickens. We found that burros were a necessity of life in those mountains. They were the only means of getting around because of the numerous rattlesnakes. We needed two of them to bring the firewood down from the mountains, so Father and I went to a neighbor who had several and asked if we could buy two. He brought the burros out to us and told them in Spanish that this man was to be their new owner, that they should go with him and should stay at his house and not come back. The burros just blinked their eyes and stood waiting while Father paid for them. The owner patted their backs and told them to go with us. I asked if we should tie them up. He said that was not necessary, that they knew what to do. Also, he said there was no need to feed them, that they would go up the mountains at night to feed on the grass there. I didn't believe him but waited to see what would happen. The burros followed us home. All my brothers were so excited and happy to see them. They brought water for them to drink and played with them all day. I thought the burros would run away at night and not come back, but the next morning I looked out the window and there they were, standing meekly by the kitchen shack. It was a wonderful surprise to see them there.

Meung and I took the burros up the mountains to look for firewood. There was plenty everywhere. We had to chop the wood into shorter lengths so we could pack bundles on both sides of the burros. We first put down a layer of sacks to protect the burros' bodies; then we tied the bundles of firewood tightly. The burros knelt down to let us tie the bundles with ropes around their bodies, but they would not get up when ordered. We were told this might happen, so we just left them there and returned home. They came home later when they felt like it. They must have received harsh treatment from others and expected the same from us. They were showing their feelings in the only way they knew. When they got home, we took off the loads, and the boys brought water for them and petted them. They seemed to enjoy the attention and love shown to them. After this happened a few times, they decided not to be so stubborn. They stood up after the loads were tied and walked home with us. It was a joy to have such cooperation from them. On weekends we made as many trips as possible to gather wood. We had to pile up a lot of wood by August, because our neighbors had told us that the winter might bring snow storms and that sometimes it might be impossible to get wood. We made a shelter for the woodpile so it would not be covered with snow or get soaked with rain.

Father worked in the furnace area of the mining company, stirring the rocks so they would burn evenly. He had to wear a piece of cloth over his nose so he would not breathe the poisonous fumes whenever the lid was opened. It was a hard, nasty job that few men wanted to do, even though the pay was five dollars a day, an unheard of amount in those times. But Father was desperate and felt compelled to take it.

The fumes from the furnace were poisonous not only to humans but to plant life as well. Nothing grew where the fumes went. Because quicksilver was used to make explosives, soldiers guarded the entrance to the mines. When the quicksilver was being shipped out, several soldiers accompanied the cargo to its destination. No one was allowed to walk around the mining areas or furnaces.

One day Mother asked me to see if the store had fresh meat to sell. The clerk said meat was sold at the back. A big hole had been made in the side of a hill and boarded up, just big enough to hang one side of beef and one of pork. An electric bulb was hanging in the back. It was a spooky place; I had to chase a snake away from the entrance. The so-called butcher asked how large a piece I wanted. I told him I wanted a small piece about the size of my fist. He just cut off a section from the side of beef, put it on a piece of paper and gave it to me. I told him to put it on my father's account.

When we were fairly settled, we looked around for the schoolhouse. It was on top of a low hill not far from our place. Meung and I discovered it was another one-room schoolhouse with a teacher who taught all eight grades. We registered and started going to school the next day. There were about thirty Mexican children at that school, mostly little ones, though some were big boys who looked about twelve to sixteen years old. They had never been to school before and spoke very little English. They were so noisy the teacher had a hard time. She didn't have time for Meung and me. She was forced to tell the boys to go home, but they couldn't understand what she said. I had picked up a few words of Spanish, so I told them what she had said. They were so startled to hear me speak Spanish that they got up and left. After that, the rest of us could learn our lessons.

There was a wood stove in the middle of the schoolroom. The teacher built a fire at noon and heated something in a small pot which smelled so good I asked her what it was. She said it was a can of Campbell's soup that she had bought at the store. That was my first introduction to Campbell's soups. I told Mother about the soup, and she bought one can at the store. She said it was good but that we couldn't afford to buy enough for the whole family.

I noticed that there was no one to sweep out the schoolroom, so I went to the company office and talked to the supervisor. He was a kindly man who listened to my story. I told him that I wanted to earn enough money to buy my books when I got to high school. He decided to hire me. My job was to clean the blackboards, sweep out the room, chop the wood for the stove, keep the outhouse clean, and ring the school bell at 8:30 A.M. so the children would know it was time for school. He would pay me twenty-five cents a day.

I had also been helping in the boardinghouse kitchen every evening. A couple there cooked and served about forty men every day. The wife paid me twenty-five cents every night and gave me leftover roast meat and rolls, which my family enjoyed. One evening while we were all busy in the kitchen, the couple started to argue about something. The wife said something that made her husband so angry he picked up a small can of lard and threw it at her. She

screamed and fell to the floor. I was so frightened, I dropped everything and ran home. Father told me not to go there anymore.

Instead, he wanted me to do something for him. He told me to look
for two stones of a certain size and thickness. He said he wanted to
make a millstone to grind beans, so we could make our kind of food to
eat. There were lots of big boulders around, but very few small ones
of the size he wanted. It took me several days to find the right kind.
When I did, I loaded them on the burros and brought them home.
Every day after work, Father would chip away at the stones with a
hammer and chisel. He made a beautiful two-piece mill. The top
stone had a small oblong hole on one side and a handle inserted on the
other side. On its bottom was a small hole, exactly in the middle. The
bottom stone had a metal bolt, which fitted into the hole of the top
stone. When the two stones were put together and the beans were put
into the hole, the upper stone was turned around. It ground the beans
into powder—a very ingenious machine. It must have been invented
by someone like my father in the ancient days. He was always thinking
up ways to improve our living conditions, always making things out of
materials other people had discarded. We never had much, but he always tried to make our lives as comfortable as possible—even though
harsh circumstances made that difficult most of the time. . . .

Whenever it rained on a school day, all the mothers of the Mexican
children in school got together and made big tamales with everything
good stuffed in them. One apiece was enough for each person. The
Mexican families were so generous—they always remembered to
make extra ones for Meung and me. They didn't have much, but they
were willing to share with others. Their generosity turned rainy days
into picnics.

I saw a motion picture for the first time in 1914. Some film company
showed a cowboy movie in front of the hotel. It was a free preview to
advertise the real picture at the dance hall that night. The movie
showed cowboys drinking in a saloon. They were staggering out,
laughing and firing their pistols. When they saw an old Chinese man
walking home on the other side of the road, they said they wanted to
see if he could dance. They started firing at his feet, and they laughed
as he kept jumping to avoid being hit. Of course, their aim was not
accurate, and he fell wounded. That made them laugh louder. They
told him to get up. When he could not, they kept shooting until he
was dead. Then they walked away, laughing as though it were a big
joke. I was so shocked, I vowed I would never go to see the pictures
again. That movie reflected the attitude toward Orientals in those

days. Our Mexican friends didn't like it, either. They remembered the days when their people were also treated that way. They had bitter memories of how their country lost California. . . .

Meung and I graduated from the school in Idria. The teacher said that we were the only students to have ever graduated there. She told us on the last day of school that we had passed the state tests and were now eligible to go to high school. So Meung and I talked about going to high school. We were so absorbed in our own plans, we had not noticed what was happening to Father. When we told him of our hopes, he said he was very sorry that he not only could not help us but also that he needed Meung to help him support the family. He had become quite ill and was unable to do much work. The effects of inhaling the poisonous quicksilver fumes had caused his teeth to turn dark, and they were so loose he could not chew his food. He had been losing a lot of weight, all of which we had not noticed because he never complained or talked about it. He said that he was unable to care for the family by himself and that he had been forced to give up his job in the furnace area to take a different job with half the pay. He said that there was work for Meung, repairing roads and cleaning up the work areas. That was what all the Mexican boys of his age were doing. Because Meung had such a generous nature, he could not refuse. He consented to go to work.

After Father had left that day, I looked all over for Meung. Finally I found him behind the kitchen shack, crying. I said I was very sorry, that I would stay and help, too, but there was nothing I could do in Idria. Meung had always dreamed of going to high school; not being able to go was a very bitter disappointment for him. That's why, later in life, he tried to educate himself by reading books as much as possible. Time and circumstances beyond our control were always against us poor people. Of course, he could have left home and made his own way, but his love and consideration for our family made him stay. He was that kind of man, even at that early age.

I had been planning to go to Hollister, the nearest town, about sixty miles away in the valley. During my year as janitor of the schoolhouse, I had saved some money to buy the books I needed. There wasn't much left to buy the other necessities, but I was determined to start school anyway. I asked my teacher what I should do. She said to get a "schoolgirl" job. That meant room and board in exchange for working before and after school and on weekends, with no pay. It sounded good to me because it was the only way I could ever go to high school.

I ordered two dresses from the Sears Roebuck catalog, one for work and one for school. I didn't have a sweater, coat, or umbrella. My undergarments were made from the sacks for rice and flour. I was naive enough to think that would be enough. I bought a pair of shoes at the company store and two pairs of stockings, and I packed everything in a little old suitcase we had at home. Father tried to discourage me from going. He said it would be too difficult to work so much while studying. He said I would not last more than three months before being forced to come back home. I made a bet with him that I would not come home until the end of the school year. My argument was that the children were all old enough to take care of themselves, and that Mother did not need me to help at home. I guess he was too sick to say any more.

Before I left, he gave me some advice about how I was to conduct myself in an American home. He said that I should eat in the kitchen and always watch the wife's reaction to whatever happened and try to please her. He also told me to go to a Presbyterian church on Sundays, if possible. Up to that time, none of us had gone to an American church, knowing that we would not be welcomed there. He gave one piece of advice I have never forgotten: although girls and women were supposed to be soft and obedient, they should also learn to think like men and make correct judgments. He told me to speak up when the occasion demanded and to stand up for what is right. That advice gave me strength in later life. . . .

After a long ride on an old hay wagon, we reached Hollister. I went straight to the newspaper office to advertise for a "schoolgirl" job. Luckily for me, the man I talked to at the newspaper office said his wife was hoping to find someone to help in their home. He said to wait a while and he would take me to his house. After a short wait, he drove me to a house not far away. His wife took one surprised look at me and pulled her husband aside and whispered to him. It was evident that she was not pleased with the queer-looking creature he had brought home. He must have told her there was no harm in trying me out for a few days, because, though she was angry, she gave in. She showed me a small room with a pile of boxes on one side and a cot on the other. . . .

I had to get up at 5 A.M. to make breakfast for Mr. Jenkins and fix his lunch. He had his own business, which was very successful, so he was quite busy. He had a large propane gas tank in his garage and, being a plumber, he had laid down long pipes to pump the gas into the kitchen stove for cooking. It took about fifteen minutes to pump the gas into the stove, but it made cooking easy. They also had a large water tank on the back porch. I saw my first washing machine on that back porch. It had to be operated by hand. A long upright handle on one side of the tub had to be thrust back and forth to stir the clothes around in the tub, but it was better than rubbing the clothes on the washboard and was certainly easier on one's hands.

Every day after Mr. Jenkins left for work, I cleaned the house a bit, cooked breakfast for the rest of the family, and made lunch for the two older boys. Since nothing was said about my lunch, I didn't dare take anything to school. A little after eight, I walked to school, which was about twenty blocks away.

The books I had bought were not enough, but I didn't have the money to buy any more, so I would copy the next day's lesson from a friend's book during the lunch hour. The principal happened to pass by one time while I was doing this. He said that students were not allowed to stay in the room during lunch hour, and he wanted to know why I was not eating my lunch. When I explained that I had no lunch, he told me to come to his office. He said that I was the first Oriental student in his school and he was very curious about my nationality. Of course, he had never heard of Korea. I gave him a brief summary of the kind of life all Oriental people had to live. He was amazed and shocked and said he had never heard of such conditions. He said he would talk to Mrs. Jenkins about me. I asked him not to do so and told him it would be difficult for me to find another place at this late date. He said not to worry, that he might be able to help me somehow. On the way home, my mind was troubled. I wondered what Mrs. Jenkins's reaction would be. As I entered the house, she acted friendly and said the principal had been there. She did not mention what he had said, but she told me in the future to take whatever I wanted for lunch.

She also gave me an umbrella and an old sweater of hers, as the result of another incident in school. One morning when it rained, I used a layer of newspapers to cover my head. Of course, that kind of protection didn't last too long, and I was very wet by the time I reached school. So, I went down to the basement to dry out near the furnace. The principal saw me and asked why I didn't wear a raincoat and use an umbrella. I had to tell him the facts of my life again.

During my early life, I had the very good fortune to meet kind people who helped me in times of dire need. When my family came here in 1906, the feeling towards all Orientals was hostile and cruel. "For Whites Only" signs were everywhere. We could not go to restrooms, theaters, swimming pools, barber shops, and so forth. But in the midst of all this, there were also kind and courageous persons, like the principal, who helped me in spite of their friends' disapproval. That was a wonderful experience. . . .

Near the end of the school year, I learned that Father was planning to move to Willows, Glenn County, California. World War I was still in progress, and all grain products were in great demand. Many Koreans were going to Willows to cultivate rice, in order to take advantage of the high market prices. Another brother, Edward, was born on March 21, 1917.

I managed to stay in Hollister until the end of the school year. I was glad that I had stuck it out and had won my bet with Father, but I felt weak and sick. I was very tired and weighed only ninety-eight pounds. I wanted to get back home before I collapsed. Mr. Jenkins was kind enough to buy my train ticket to Willows. I fell asleep as soon as I sat in a seat, and I don't remember anything about the train ride. I didn't wake up until the train was almost there. Father was waiting for me at the station. I found to my surprise that I couldn't remember the greeting in Korean, but the words all came back to me later.

I was surprised and shocked to see how much my father had aged during the short time I had been away. I guess he was just as surprised at my forlorn appearance. We just looked at each other without words. It was impossible to express our feelings then. We walked home in silence. Mother took one look at me and led me to a bed in a small room, where I fell asleep, relieved and thankful to be home again. It took days to relate all my experiences in Hollister. Father said that I had paid dearly for my education and that he was sorry he was unable to help me.

The day after I arrived in Willows, I went outside to see where our family was living. We were about a block from the railroad tracks outside the town limits. There were three old wooden buildings on one side of the dirt road. A sign on our building read "Chinese Food." A half block away were two other old buildings on one side. My family was living in a long building with one long hallway in the middle and several small rooms on each side. There was no bathroom and no hot water tank. A toilet was attached to the house outside the back door. The building had one small kitchen with a gas stove and a small dining area with benches and small tables. There was electricity for lights.

We were living in the so-called red light district. An old Chinese man owned the cafe and the buildings. He sold liquor and opium, which we could smell at night. Father said that it didn't matter where we lived, as long as we maintained our own way of life and tried to get along with everyone. We were in no position to judge what others did.

A large irrigation canal about half a block away brought water from the river to irrigate the rice fields and provided plenty of fish for us to catch. Willows was a small town with just a few stores, one of each kind. The attitude towards Orientals was rough and tough, a "take it or leave it" kind of treatment. Father and Meung worked in the rice fields.

Charlotte was two years old and Eddie was three months old at that time. Charlotte was afraid of me, this stranger who came to live in her house. When I resumed my old job of taking care of the younger children, she resented my supervision and thought of me as an outsider. That feeling persisted through the years. We never had the opportunity to get acquainted with each other.

On Sundays, about seven Korean families came to our house for services. We sang hymns, without music. Father preached a short sermon, then Mother served lunch. Everyone stayed and visited. We had a pleasant time together. It was good to see old friends again. No matter where we lived, Father always invited people to come to our house for a brief time of worship. He never asked for an offering, and Mother served whatever food we had for lunch. One Sunday, as Father was praying, I noticed that the little children were sneaking out. I followed them and found them eating whatever food they could find. The children could not help themselves; those were "hungry years" for all of us. Wages were low and work was hard to find. It was the custom among us to take some food as a gift whenever we went to visit friends. Father laughed when I told him not to make his prayers so long because the children would eat up everything in the kitchen.

My parents did not believe in whipping the children. I don't remember Father ever striking anyone, and Mother never raised her voice at us. She always spoke in a soft, calm voice, explaining why we should do this or that. She insisted that we keep our house clean, even if it was an old shack. Each child had a box for his personal things and a few clothes. We kept an orderly home no matter what the circumstances.

Since Father was a minister, friends always came to him for advice on different matters. He could not speak English, so he told me to interpret for them, and he told me what to say and how to say it. That's how I got started helping people with their problems. Mother gave me good advice about what my conduct should be in doing this. She said never to talk about a person's problems or sickness to anyone else, unless they were matters to be discussed with families. Each person's problems should be kept secret. Listening to my parents' philosophy has been a very interesting part of my life; I have learned a great deal about human beings and their peculiar notions. I learned early in life about all the ills of the older generation, which has helped me as I grew older. No matter how modern the world gets, human nature remains the same.

Mrs. Jenkins wrote twice asking me to come back to Hollister. She said she would pay me regular wages, but Father said no, it was too much for me. I started my second year of high school in Willows. The atmosphere in school was chilling: none of the students except one spoke to me, but my good luck was working for me again. The girl who sat across the aisle from me in several classes was very friendly and eager to talk to me. Her name was Margaret Finch. Strangely enough, although there were many Chinese, Japanese, and Koreans cultivating rice in Willows at that time, there were no Oriental students in the school, so I was an object of curiosity. During lunch and after school, Margaret always talked to me and we became friends.

One day she asked if I would like to go to her church with her. She said she went to the Presbyterian church, which was not far from our house. I asked Father about it. He said, "Why not? Maybe times are changing." He told me to go and find out. He was always the optimist. I told Margaret I would meet her at church the following Sunday. Something told me to go early and find out what kind of person the minister was, so I took three of my brothers and started out. As we neared the church, we saw a man standing in the doorway. As we were walking up the steps, he placed his arm across the door and said, "I don't want dirty Japs in my church." My reply was, "Would it make any difference if I told you we are not Japanese but Korean?" He said, "What the hell's the difference? You all look alike to me." He just glared at us with hatred in his eyes and told us to "go to hell." So we came back home and told Father about it. He just shook his head and didn't say a word.

Margaret was very annoyed with me for not meeting her at church. I told her what had happened. She said, "I don't believe it." I shrugged my shoulders and replied, "Well, it's the truth." The next day at school she said, "My father wants to talk to you after school." She led the way to the Glenn County Courthouse, which was a few blocks from school. At the end of the long hallway, she stopped. I looked up over the door from force of habit and saw a sign that read "Superior Judge Finch." As she opened the door, I saw a middle-aged man sitting behind a large desk. Margaret said, "Father, this is the girl I was telling you about." He told me to sit down and to tell him exactly what the minister had said to me that Sunday. He listened very intently, told me to go to church the next Sunday, and he guaranteed that I would be welcomed there. I said, "Thank you very much." We left his office and Margaret said, "You'd better not forget. I'll be there to meet you." Father was pleased when he heard. He said it often takes someone of courage and position to turn things around.

The following Sunday I went by myself, wondering what would happen. The minister was evidently waiting for me. He ran down the steps, shook my hand, and said, "You are welcome in this church." He was like a different person; he went out of his way to introduce me to a surprised congregation. The minister in Hollister was right; the congregation follows the leader whether they like it or not. In time they all became friendly and discovered that we, too, were human beings.

I have to match this story with another that involved Margaret's mother, the Judge's wife. Sometime after I started going to the church, Margaret said she had had a birthday party and had received a lot of presents that she wanted to show me. Father had told me a long time ago that I was not to enter my American friends' homes unless the mothers had invited me in. Margaret's house was a few blocks from school. As we entered the backyard, we saw her mother washing clothes in a tub on the washboard. She glared at me. I remembered my father's advice and asked Margaret to bring her presents outside. After Margaret went into the house, her mother turned to me and said in a very angry voice, "Don't you dare go into my house. I don't want dirty Japs walking around in my home." I felt a chill running down my back. What a difference between her and her husband!

My stay in school was a constant battle of wits. My English teacher was an old lady with a sour face. It was a common practice to give the nonwhite students lower grades than the whites, but one day she was so unfair, I protested. Her eyes were blazing with hatred as she said, "If you don't like it, get the hell out of here. We don't want you here anyway."

My history teacher was something else. He was a young man in his thirties, a "good looker" and a "smart aleck." When we came to the pages about China and Japan, he referred to them as the lands of "stinking Chinks and dirty Japs." Looking straight at me in a taunting manner, he said that Korea was a wild, savage country that had been civilized by the "Japs." That was the last straw. I was furious. I waited until the bell rang and all the students had left. I walked up to him and said, "Where did you learn Asian history? You don't know a thing about the subject. If you ever say such things again, I am going to stand up in class and in assembly meeting on Friday and tell everybody in school where you go every Friday and Saturday night." His face turned white, red, and purple, and he fell back in his chair. He finally managed to say, "What are you talking about?" I replied, "My family lives in an old building across the road from the Chinese place where you always go every weekend. I recognized the two girls with you, as one is from this class. I can ask them if you wish." His mouth fell open, he was speechless for a while, and then he asked, "What are *you* doing there?" I said, "My family and I are forced to live there because damned hypocrites like you think we are not fit to live in town. We are forced to live there, but what about you? You go there because you like it. That's the difference between us!" After that, he just turned past the pages about Asia; the class never learned about the subject.

SEVEN

The Galarza Family in the Mexican Revolution, 1910: From Mexico to Sacramento

More than any of the other sources reprinted here, *Barrio Boy*, the autobiography of Ernesto Galarza, offers a rich understanding of the destabilizing developments within the home country that could lead a family to migrate to the United States. In addition, it provides a sensitive depiction of the new life that opened up for the young Ernesto in the barrio neighborhood of Sacramento, which became his new home.

Ernesto Galarza grew up in Jalcocotán, a mountain village in central Mexico. There he received an education in the communal ways of the village. His was a life of poverty, but one marked by a rough equality among village residents that stood in sharp contrast to the class inequalities characterizing hacienda life down off the mountain.

The coming of the Mexican Revolution in 1910 profoundly disturbed rural life and set off a flood of migration northward within Mexico and then across the U.S. border. The overthrow of Porfirio Díaz did not bring an end to unrest, which continued until a new federal constitution was implemented in 1924. Mexican emigration between 1910 and 1929 totaled almost 700,000, as peasants fled the fighting and economic devastation that stalked the country in these years.[1]

Barrio Boy explores the impact of the Revolution on the Galarza family of central Mexico. Federal troops occupied Jalcocotán and conscripted any young men who remained there. The Galarzas fled their native village, moving from one town to another. After a life of independence in the countryside, they found urban living and wage labor

1. Carlos E. Cortés, "Mexicans," in Stephan Thernstrom, ed., *Harvard Encyclopedia of American Ethnic Groups* (Cambridge, Mass.: Harvard University Press, 1980), p. 699.

Ernesto Galarza, about ten, in a park in Sacramento. (Courtesy of Mae Galarza)

filled with uncertainties. Fighting between federal troops loyal to Porfirio Díaz and rebels under Francisco Madero and the class oppression felt by the poor in railroad towns lead them finally to migrate across the border to Tucson and then to Sacramento.

The final part of this excerpt picks up the story in the "lower part" of Sacramento, where Ernesto made a new life for himself in the Mexican barrio and eventually found that his high school diploma offered him a route out into broader American society. After the years covered by his biography, Galarza became a harvest hand, cannery worker, and labor organizer. He also earned a Ph.D. in economics from Columbia University, taught, and wrote about the plight of Mexican farmworkers in California. His most well-known work, *Merchants of Labor*, played a major role in the elimination of the Bracero Program, a policy that permitted the temporary importation and exploitation of Mexican laborers in U.S. agribusiness.[2]

The one and only street in Jalcocotán was hardly more than an open stretch of the mule trail that disappeared into the forest north and south of the pueblo. Crosswise, it was about wide enough to park six automobiles hub to hub. Lengthwise, you could walk from one end to the other in eight minutes, without hurrying, the way people walked in the village. The dirt surface had been packed hard by hundreds of years of traffic—people barefooted or wearing the tough leather sandals called huaraches; mule trains passing through on the way to the sea or to Tepic; burros carrying firewood and other products of the forest; *zopilotes*[3] hopping heavily here and there; pigs, dogs, and chickens foraging along the ditch.

There was a row of cottages on each side of the street, adobe boxes made of the same packed earth on which the houses stood. At one end of the street wall of every cottage there was a doorway, another in the wall standing to the back yard corral. There were no windows. The roofs were made of palm thatch, with a steep pitch, the ridge pole parallel to the street. Back of the houses were the *corrales*, fenced with stones piled about shoulder high to a man. Between the *corrales* there were narrow alleys that led uphill to the edge of the forest on the upper side of the village, and to the arroyo on the lower side. The eaves of the grass roofs hung well over the adobe walls to protect them

---

2. Ernesto Galarza, *Merchants of Labor: The Mexican Bracero Story* (Santa Barbara, Calif.: McNally and Loftin, 1978; originally published by the author in 1964).

3. *Zopilotes:* turkey vultures.

from the battering rains. In the summer time the overhang provided shade at midday, when it seemed as if all the suffocating heat of the heavens was pouring through a funnel with the small end pointed directly at Jalco.

Since there were no sidewalks, from the front door to the street was only a step. Our pueblo was too high up the mountain, the connecting trails were too steep and narrow to allow ox carts and wagons to reach it. Like the forest, our only street belonged to everybody—a place to sort out your friends and take your bearings if you were going anywhere.

Midway down the street, on the arroyo side, there was a small chapel, also of adobe, the only building in the town that had a front yard, a patch of sun-baked clay squeezed between two cottages. Back of the patio stood the squat adobe box of the chapel, with a red tile roof and a small dome in one corner topped with a wooden cross. Once upon a time the walls of the chapel had been plastered and whitewashed, but the rains and the sun had cracked and blistered them. The adobe was exposed in jagged patches with flecks of grey straw showing like wood grain on the ancient mud. The base of the walls, pelted by the rain, was chewed as if beavers had worked on it.

Directly across the street from the chapel, the row of cottages was interrupted by the plaza. In any pueblo of some importance this would have been the *zocalo*, or the *plaza mayor*, or more grandiloquently, the *plaza de armas*. In Jalco it was a square without a name, about forty steps wide along the street and as many deep.

In a village like Jalcocotán there was little use for either the chapel or the plaza. We had no resident priest. . . . There was no police, no fire department, no post office, no public library. No one was ever elected mayor or sheriff or councilman. There was no jail or judge or any other sort of *Autoridades*,[4] which explained why there was no city hall in Jalco. The shrunken, sun-beaten plaza was there nevertheless, solitary except when children played in it or passing mule drivers rested under the shade of its trees. It was a useless spot in our everyday life, but just by being there, the public square, like the chapel, gave our one and only street a touch of dignity, the mark of a proper pueblo.

Like the plaza, the street had no name. On a nameless street the houses, naturally, had no numbers. The villager was indoors and in bed after dark so there was no need for lights, of which our street had none. . . .

4. *Autoridades*: authorities, i.e., police or government officials.

Whatever happened in Jalcocotán had to happen on our street because there was no other place for it to happen. Two men, drunk with
tequila, fought with machetes on the upper edge of the village until
they were separated and led away by the neighbors. A hundred faces
peered around doorways watching the fight. When someone died
people joined the funeral procession as it passed by their doors. If a
stranger arrived on horseback, the clopping of horseshoes on the
rocks of the trail announced his arrival before he could turn into the
street. Arriving in Jalco was like stepping on a stage. The spectators
were already in the doorways, watching.

The narrow lanes between the corrals on the lower side of the street
led to the arroyo which ran the length of the village. The turbulent
waters, even in the dry season, twisted and churned among the boulders, slapping them and breaking into spray, or dividing around them
in serpentines of blue-green foam. Below the village the arroyo was
checked by a natural dam of rocks and silt, over which it dropped into
a quiet pond before rushing on to the sea. . . .

The arroyo was as much a part of the pueblo as the street. Like the
street, it had no name; it just tumbled into town from the timber
stands up the mountain that fed it the year round, and tumbled out
from the pond to pick up and carry to the ocean the seepage of the
forest below. . . .

Like the *monte*[5] and the street, the arroyo was common property.
Those who lived along the upper side of the street used the lanes
between the cottages on the lower side on their way to wash, to fill
their red clay *cántaros*,[6] or to water their stock. Going to the arroyo
from the street was called *bajar al agua*.[7] Going up the lanes to the
forest was called *subir al monte*.[8] Taking the trail to Tepic was *cuesta
arriba*.[9] Taking it down to Miramar was *cuesta abajo*.[10] These were
the four points of the compass for Jalcocotán. If you followed them you
could always find your way back home.

It was in the evening, when dusk was falling and supper was being
prepared, that Jalco shaded itself little by little into the forest, the arroyo, the sky, and the mountain to which it belonged. Westward toward the sea, a rose and purple mist nearly always lingered after
sunset.

---

5. *Monte:* the woods, a forest; in this case, uncultivated or wild land above the village.
6. *Cántaros:* clay jars for carrying water.
7. *Bajar al agua:* going down to the water.
8. *Subir al monte:* climbing to the forest.
9. *Cuesta arriba:* uphill.
10. *Cuesta abajo:* downhill.

The eastern slopes of the range became patches of black-blue. From the slant of the shadows and the signs in the sky, everyone knew when this would happen—almost to the minute. The men and the boys of working age came down or up the trail at about the right time to reach the street a few steps ahead of or a few steps behind the dusk. They walked, each man and his sons, to their cottages. On both sides of the street the doors were open. . . .

Through the doors, opened to receive the returning toilers and to freshen the air inside the cottages, came the sounds and sights of the street at sundown. There was the soft clapping of the women patting the ration of tortillas for the evening meal. The smoky light from the wicks of the *candiles* flickering through the doorways cast wobbling shadows on the threshold as people moved about. The air outside was a blend of the familiar smells of supper time—tortillas baking, beans boiling, chile roasting, coffee steaming, and kerosene stenching. The hens were clucking in their roosts in the corrals by the time the street was dark. . . .

Our adobe cottage was on the side of the street away from the arroyo. It was the last house if you were going to Miramar. About fifty yards behind the corral, the forest closed in.

It was like every other house in Jalco, probably larger. The adobe walls were thick, a foot or more, with patches of whitewash where the thatched overhang protected the adobe from the rain. There were no windows. The entrance doorway was at one end of the front wall, and directly opposite the door that led to the corral. . . .

All the living space for the family was in the one large room, about twelve feet wide and three times as long. Against the wall between the two doorways was the *pretil*, a bank of adobe bricks three feet high, three across, and two feet deep. In the center of the *pretil* was the main fire pit. Two smaller hollows, one on either side of the large one, made it a three-burner stove. On a row of pegs above the *pretil* hung the clay pans and other cooking utensils, bottom side out, the soot baked into the red clay. A low bench next to the *pretil*, also made of adobe, served as a table and shelf for the cups, pots, and plates.

The rest of the ground floor was divided by a curtain hung from one of the hand-hewed log beams, making two bedrooms. Above them, secured to the beams, was the *tapanco*, a platform the size of a double bed made of thin saplings tied together with pieces of rawhide. The top of a notched pole, braced against the foot of the back wall of the cottage, rested against the side of the *tapanco*, serving as a ladder. Along the wall opposite the *pretil*, in the darkest and coolest part of the house, were the big *cántaros*, the red clay jars, the *canastos*, tall

baskets made of woven reeds; the rolled straw *petates* to cover the dirt
floor where people walked or sat; and the hoes and other work
tools. . . .

The corral was the other important part of a Jalco home. Ours was
enclosed on three sides by stone walls and shut off from the street by
the house. The only entrance to the corral was through the back door
of the cottage. The ground sloped up toward the edge of the monte. A
ditch along the back wall stopped the runoff water and sluiced it toward the lane between our house and our neighbor's. Close to the
house, there was a corncrib built like a miniature adobe cottage with
the walls sloping inward at the bottom. It was raised on stilts and covered with a grass roof. . . .

I never thought to count them, but there could have been forty such
homes in Jalcocotán when I lived there. Some cottages were deeper
and longer than others, some corral walls were patched with poles
and adobe bricks, some roofs rested on straight-up gables and others
on slanting ones. But every cottage seemed built and placed to look
like every other one. There were no building codes in the pueblo
about where to set the walls, or how high they must be or as to the
pitch of the roof. The houses made an almost solid front on either
side of the street except for the breaks of the lanes, the plaza, and
the chapel.

We moved to Jalco—my mother, my uncle Gustavo, my uncle José
and I—several weeks before I was born. They walked, with a few
clothes and some food, from Miramar, about twenty miles away down
the mountain. Under the circumstances, the journey was no problem
for me.

My father, Don Ernesto, senior, was not in the small caravan. He
had stayed in Miramar, where he kept books and supervised the peons
of an hacienda. My mother and he had been married in San Blas, but
only *por lo civil*, not *por la iglesia*[11] because my father was a Lutheran
and my mother a Catholic, and he would not have a priest. As it
turned out, and as often happened in such a place as Miramar and
such times as I am telling about, my father got around to thinking that
a civil wedding was not much more for keeps than one in church. The
divorce was a simple matter. He wrote my mother a letter and she
wrote one in return. Aunt Esther and Uncle Gustavo went to Miramar
to talk the matter over. It was arranged that the ring which my father

---

11. *Por lo civil*, not *por la iglesia*: Galarza's parents had been married in a civil, not a
religious, ceremony.

had given my mother was to be kept by her. She was also to keep the sewing machine he had given her for a wedding present. And as part of the property settlement, I was to remain with my mother. . . .

The move to Jalcocotán was the only way out of Miramar for the four of us. My grandfather, Don Felix, and his wife, Doña Isabel, had died. Their few possessions had been sold to pay off debts, out of which Don Felix did not seem able to keep. We had relatives in San Blas, but none with room enough for three people and possibly four.

Aunt Esther had married Don Catarino López, one of a numerous family of Jalco. Don Catarino, his father, and brothers worked the corn patches and the *milpas*[12] on the mountain, tilled and harvested bananas deep in the forest and earned a living in other ways from the countryside. Don Catarino had brought his bride, Esther, to the pueblo where they were living with their two boys—Jesús, a year older than myself and Catarino junior, a year younger. The four of them hardly filled the one big room of the cottage. The extra beds behind the curtain and the *tapanco* could accommodate us all, cramped or cozy, depending on how you looked at it. . . .

Like many other mountain pueblos, Jalcocotán had no school. . . .

Reading, writing, and arithmetic were held in great esteem by the jalcocotecanos. A few adults in the town had finished the third or fourth grade somewhere else. They taught their own children the *a, b, c's* and simple arithmetic with the abacus. . . .

Books were rare. My mother had one, which she kept in the cedar box. It had a faded polychrome drawing on the cover with the title *La Cocinera Poblana,* a cookbook which had belonged to Grandmother Isabel. . . .

For me and my cousins until we were six, book learning was limited to a glimpse now and then of my mother's cookbook. Our school was the corral, the main street of Jalco, the arroyo, and the kitchen. . . .

It was in the cultivated patches in the forest that boys grew into men. With machetes they cleared the steep slopes and the hollows, setting fire to the brush and the stumps. In the ashes they planted corn, beans, peppers, *jitomate,*[13] and bananas. Under the shade of a tall tree they grew coffee bushes. The forest provided the rest of Jalcocotán's living—timber, charcoal, wild fruit, herbs, boars, deer, and hides from alligators and cougars. . . .

12. *Milpas:* cornfields.
13. *Jitomate:* tomatoes.

The world of work into which Jacinto and the other seven-year-olds were apprenticed was within sight and sound of the pueblo. It was work under blazing suns, in rainstorms, in pitch-black nights. It was work that you were always walking to or walking from, work without wages and work without end. It was work that gave you a bone-tired feeling at the end of the day, so you learned to swing a machete, to tighten a cinch, and to walk without lost motion. Between seven and twelve you learned all this, each lesson driven home when your *jefe*,[14] said with a scowl: "Así no, hombre; así." And he showed you how.

But he knew that there was another world of work beyond Jalco. Over in Miramar, Los Cocos, Puga and such places there were haciendas where peasants from the pueblos could work for money. Some *jalcocotecanos*[15] did this kind of hiring out. They cut sugarcane, herded cattle, butchered steers, tended the crops, gathered coconuts for the soap works, and cleared land *a puro machetazo*—with your bare hands and a machete.

Boys who went with their fathers to the haciendas soon learned the differences between making a living on the mountain and working for the *patrónes*.[16] One was that on the mountain you took home corn, bananas, peppers, coffee, and anything else you had raised, but never money. From the hacienda, when your contract ended, you never took anything to eat or wear except what you paid for at the *tienda de raya*, the company store. A peon could make as much as ten pesos a month at hard labor working from dawn to dusk, seven days a week, four weeks every month. It came to about two or three centavos per hour, plus your meals and a place to spread your straw sleeping mat. . . .

[THE REVOLUTION COMES TO RURAL MEXICO]

In the beginning it was mostly rumors. A family received a letter from a son who had left Jalco and had gone to work somewhere in the north. My mother read the letter to the family and she said it was from Sonora where they had public letter writers in the plazas and her son, who himself did not know how to read or write, had the letter written for him. In it he said he was going to the United States because in Sonora there had been a strike in the mines where he worked, and men had been killed.

14. *Jefe:* literally, chief; in this case, one's employer or, more likely, one's father.
15. *Jalcocotecanos:* residents of Jalcocotán.
16. *Patrónes:* bosses or, in this case, landowners.

Arrieros[17] who passed through the village said that the government was rounding up young men in the towns and drafting them into the army. The *varillero*[18] told us that Don Francisco Madero had been in Mazatlán campaigning for president of the Republic against Don Porfirio. Everybody in Jalco knew about Don Porfirio, although nobody had ever seen him, and only the old men could remember a time when General Porfirio Díaz had not been president. Nobody knew Don Francisco Madero.

News always reached us in bits and pieces—when the *arrieros* passed through the town, when the *varillero* appeared with his gee-gaws or when *jalcocotecanos* returned from their long hikes to Tepic or San Blas to buy and sell. The news spread without newspapers or telephones. In the village no one ever kept news to himself; while you were telling it you were paid attention to, especially if you added comments of your own.

It was over this grapevine that our family heard of the first stirrings of trouble through the countryside. It was said that the *maderistas*[19] had formed a party against the *porfiristas*.[20] The farmhands of the haciendas were running away and gathering in bands in the mountains. One of these bands had held up a stage coach bound for Mazatlán. A regiment of soldiers had arrived in Tepic to defend it from attack by the peasant guerillas. The *administrador* of Las Varas had packed his goods and he and his family had disappeared. Young men were leaving the *milpas* to join the guerillas, which they called "bolas." A *bola* could start in any pueblo and take off for the hills, to join other *bolas* and form a command under a *jefe revolucionario*.

In Jalco a new fear was growing in the village. It came home to all of us the day José brought word that the *rurales*[21] were riding toward our town. He had met a peasant on the trail who told him they had been seen moving out of Ixtapa the day before.

We heard José telling the family the news. Then, without waiting for their supper, the three men left the cottage. The rest of us stood at

17. *Arrieros:* drivers of pack animals—mules, burros, or horses.

18. *Varillero:* peddler.

19. *Maderistas:* supporters of Francisco Madero, recently defeated candidate for president of Mexico. Madero and his supporters launched an insurrection that forced President Porfirio Díaz to resign in May 1911. Unrest persisted—with coups, two U.S. interventions, rigged elections, and more fighting—and the Mexican Revolution lasted until a new constitution was put into place in 1924. See Charles C. Cumberland, *Mexico: The Struggle for Modernity* (New York: Oxford University Press, 1968), chap. 9.

20. *Porfiristas:* supporters of longtime Mexican president Porfirio Díaz.

21. *Rurales:* rural guards of the Mexican federal government known for their violence and terror.

the front door, watching as they stopped to chat with other men in the street or in the doorways. Some of Don Catarino's *compadres* and their *compadre's compadres* came to our house and stepped into the corral, murmuring to the women as they passed "Con su permiso." They carried machetes. There was quiet talk for a while, like all the conversation in Jalco—someone saying something, a silence to think it over, a question.

It was pitch dark when our visitors left. The women served supper. My mother packed tortillas, a pot of beans, some salt, and a few strings of jerked meat into José's shoulder bag. The same rations were prepared for Gustavo. They picked up their sarapes and machetes, and stepped out the front door without a word. José turned into the lane towards the woods, Gustavo heading up the street toward the trail for Tepic. Except for Don Catarino, who squatted under the eaves to smoke, the rest of us stood in the doorway looking into the darkness where Gustavo and José had disappeared.[22]

The *rurales* rode into Jalco before Coronel crowed the next morning. We heard the clopping of the horses' hooves as they crossed the arroyo below the pond, and the jingling of spurs and the rattle of sabers as the troops passed by. The ponies whinnied and somebody cursed in front of our house. Jalco was occupied before the men would be starting out for the *milpas*.

It was barely light outside when Don Catarino unbarred the front door to answer a knock. Doña Esther and my mother and we three boys stood well back in the shadows of the room. By the light of the lamp we saw a *rural* standing in the doorway, in the uniform of Don Porfirio's mounted police—peaked sombrero, tight pants, bolero jacket, riding shoes.

"Good morning," he said, his thumbs hooked on his ammunition belt. "By order of my Sergeant, no one is to leave the pueblo." He paused. "The Sergeant requests, if you will be so good, to prepare breakfast for the troop." The *rural* turned on his heel, his spurs jingling as he walked away.

On the spot, Jesús, Catarino, and I were given our own orders. We were to stay in the house unless called. Coronel and the hens were to be kept in the corral. We were to answer no questions whatsoever.

While Doña Esther busied herself with breakfast for the *rurales*, my mother opened the cedar box and brought out the clay pig bank

22. Gustavo and José were of age for military service, and the family helped them disappear in advance of the *rurales*, who would probably have conscripted them into the military. In this respect, Mexican peasants shared similar experiences with Jews and Slavs in Eastern Europe and Russia, who often migrated to escape tsarist military service.

and a leather wallet. "Help me," she commanded. We stepped into the back yard. She handed me the pig bank and the wallet. Straining, she lifted a geranium planted in a five-gallon tin. Beneath it was a hollow in the ground. "Quick, in the hole." I put the wallet down and the pig on top. She lifted the can so as not to drag it over the ground and leave marks and set it over the hole carefully. My mother bent over me. "Not a word. To any one. Do you understand?" The sharpness in her whisper not only bound me to a secret; it also made me understand that I was taking part in dangerous events.

The troop of some twenty *rurales* went about the business of taking over a pueblo. We saw them walking their ponies down the lanes to the arroyo to water them. The mounts were tethered in the plaza and given grain provided by the *jalcocotecanos* on orders from the Sergeant. The women served the soldiers, who squatted or sat in the shade of the trees. The Sergeant and two *rurales* rode up and down the street, noticing everything. They turned up our lane and rode back to the street, looking over the walls into our corral.

We were at the back door, watching intently. The Sergeant rode by our door. He was on a black pony not nearly as big as the horse of the *administrador* of Los Cocos, and uniformed like all the *rurales*—gray jacket like a bull fighter's, tight pants with two rows of buttons down each leg, and a felt hat with a tall pointed crown and wide brim. A rifle in a sheath hung from the saddle. The bullets inserted in his belt showed with their round brass bottoms up and their tiny gray teeth down. Besides his rifle and pistol, the commander of the troop carried a saber dangling from his belt.

Half of the *rurales* remained in the plaza while the others searched the houses one by one. They asked us. "Arms?" "No, sir, we have none." "How many people live here?" "Five, not counting the children." "Where are the others?" "They are working." It was no use for us to lie about how many of us lived there. The police could easily tell from the beds, the *tapanco*, the pots and pans and other telltale details. But we could lie about Gustavo and José. At that moment nobody could have found them.

The search of our house ended with a short speech by the *rural*. "We have orders to protect the pueblos. The government desires the cooperation of the citizens to maintain peace and tranquility."

"Si, señor."

"You will be so kind as to prepare a lunch for one man and bring it to the plaza."

"Si, señor."

Toward noon the *rurales* rode out of Jalco, taking the trail down the mountain. After the last invader had disappeared the talk went the rounds of the village, mixed with jokes, a kind of quiet celebration over the defeat of the *rurales*. They had not found what they most wanted—arms and young men. Nor had the *rurales* found *aguardiente* in the cottages on which they could get drunk and shoot up the town.

The men prepared to go to the *milpas*, but some did not go to work that day. Along the *veredas*[23] that short-cut the trail to the villages and the homesteads up and down the mountain they hurried ahead of the *rurales*, to pass the word that they were coming.

"Malditos," my mother said that night at supper.

I knew the word. When we played war on the pasture, we drew straws to choose sides of good *jalcocotecanos* and bad *rurales*. When it was my turn to be a *campesino*[24] chasing *rurales* and killing them, I yelled "malditos" adding the worst insult of all: "aquí está su padre," like Catalino.

José came back to the village a day or two after the *rurales* left. He had circled the mountain, talking with the peasants. He said that the *bolas* were forming, and that people were asking whether there would be one in Jalcocotán. Gustavo had not returned. It had been decided that he would go to Tepic and let us know what was happening there.

The villagers were still talking about the occupation by the mounted police when Halley's comet appeared.[25] Only old Don Cleofas claimed that he had seen anything like it before, when he was a boy.

Every man, woman, and child gathered in the plaza to stare at the heavenly kite with the bushy tail. Shooting stars we saw every night, streaking across the most unexpected places of the sky. They came in a wink and were gone in another. A comet was something else. Don Cleofas said it was bigger than the earth and that the tail was so long nobody could guess how many millions of kilometers it was from tip to tip. Jesús and Catarino and I were called down from the *tapanco* the first night the comet appeared. I caught the awe of the older people who were listening to Don Cleofas tell that a comet foretold something important, and serious. He said that this one meant *La Revolución*.

23. *Veredas:* footpaths.

24. *Campesino:* peasant.

25. The appearance of Halley's comet helps date these events to May 1910; on the night of May 18–19, Halley's comet reached its closest point to earth. Richard Flaste, Holcomb Noble, Walter Sullivan, and John Noble Wilford, *The New York Times Guide to the Return of Halley's Comet* (New York: Times Books, 1985), chap. 4.

Gustavo returned from Tepic a few days later. He, too, had seen the comet. He said that soldiers had arrived in Tepic, that guards were traveling with the stage coaches, and that the *rurales* were taking young men to the regimental barracks to be drafted into Don Porfirio's army. The rumors about Don Francisco Madero were true; in the marketplace he had heard that the *maderistas* had already fought the *porfiristas* in the north. A peasant from Escuinapa said that he had himself seen the *rurales* set fire to a village.

Evenings after supper the conversation was about these matters, and important decisions were made. It was agreed that Gustavo was to leave for Tepic. José, my mother, and I would follow him. The four of us would find work and a place to live for the whole family in the city.

Doña Henriqueta made a bundle of Gustavo's belongings and he said good-bye to his friends in town. We three were still asleep in the *tapanco* when he left one morning before dawn. . . .

[After leaving Jalcocotán, the Galarzas never stayed put for long, moving first to Tepic, then to Santiago, Acaponeta, Urías, and Mazatlán. Work was scarce, and the Revolution and its fighting were always close by. Once separated from their rural village, class inequalities pressed upon them with a greater immediacy. They finally traveled to Nogales on the Sonora-Arizona border and crossed over into the United States. After a brief period in Tucson, the Galarza family was reunited in Sacramento, California, where the narrative picks up their life in the "lower part of town."—ed.]

They paid our hotel bill and we gathered our things. We stepped into the cold drizzly street, my uncles carrying the suitcases and tin trunk and holding me by the hands. With the two of them on either side and Doña Henriqueta behind me I trotted confidently through the scurrying crowd on the sidewalks, the rumbling drays and the honking automobiles. I was beginning to lose my fear of Sacramento.

It was a short walk from the hotel to the house where we turned in, the tallest I had ever seen. A wide wooden stairway went up from the sidewalk to a porch on the second story, and above that another floor, and still higher a gable as wide as the house decorated with carvings and fretwork. The porch balustrade was in the same gingerbread style of lattice work and the wooden imitation of a fringe between the round pillars. We walked up the stairway and the three of us waited while José went inside.

He came back with the landlady. She was certainly a gringo lady— two heads taller than Gustavo, twice as wide as José, square-jawed, rosy-faced, a thin nose with a small bulge on the end and like all Americans, with rather large feet. She had a way of blinking when she smiled at us.

Standing as straight as the posts of the porch and holding her shoulders square and straight across she seemed to me more like a general than a lady.

Mostly with blinks and hand motions and a great many ceremonial smiles, we were introduced to Mrs. Dodson, who led us into the house, down some narrow, dark stairs and to the back of the first floor where she left us in our new apartment. . . .

Since Gustavo and José were off to work on the track early the next morning after our arrival, it was up to us to tidy the apartment and get the household into shape. As usual when we moved into a new place, we dusted and swept and scrubbed floors, doors, woodwork, windows, and every piece of furniture. Mrs. Dodson provided us with cans of a white powder that was sprinkled on everything that needed cleaning—cans with the picture of an old lady dressed in wooden shoes, a swinging skirt, and white bonnet.

The Americans, we discovered, put practically everything in cans on which they pasted fascinating labels, like *La Vieja Dotch Klen-ser*. Doña Henriqueta admired the bright colors and the delicious pictures of fruits and vegetables. We spelled and sounded out as well as we could the names of unfamiliar foods, like corn flakes and Karo syrup. On the kitchen shelf we arranged and rearranged the boxes and tins, with their displays of ingenious designs and colors, grateful that the Americans used pictures we knew to explain words that we didn't.

Once the routine of the family was well started, my mother and I began to take short walks to get our bearings. It was half a block in one direction to the lumber yard and the grocery store; half a block in the other to the saloon and the Japanese motion picture theater. In between were the tent and awning shop, a Chinese restaurant, a secondhand store, and several houses like our own. We noted by the numbers on the posts at the corners that we lived between 4th and 5th streets on L.

Once we could fix a course from these signs up and down and across town we explored farther. On Sixth near K there was the Lyric Theater with a sign that we easily translated into Lírico. It was next to a handsome red stone house with high turrets, like a castle. Navigating by these key points and following the rows of towering elms along L Street, one by one we found the post office on 7th and K; the cathedral, four blocks farther east; and the state capitol with its golden dome.

It wasn't long before we ventured on walks around Capitol Park which reminded me of the charm and the serenity of the Alameda in Tepic. In some fashion Mrs. Dodson had got over to us that the capitol was the house of the government. To us it became El Capitolio or, as more formally, the Palacio de Gobierno. Through the park we walked into the building itself, staring spellbound at the marble statue of Queen Isabel and Christopher Columbus. It was awesome, standing in the presence of that gigantic admiral, the one who had discovered America and Mexico and Jalcocotán, as Doña Henriqueta assured me.

After we had thoroughly learned our way around in the daytime we found signs that did not fail us at night. From the window of the projection room of the Lyric Theater a brilliant purple light shone after dark. A snake of electric lights kept whipping round and round a sign over the Albert Elkus store. K Street on both sides was a double row of bright show windows that led up to the Land Hotel and back to Breuner's, thence down one block to the lumber yard, the grocery store, and our house. We had no fear of getting lost.

These were the boundaries of the lower part of town, for that was what everyone called the section of the city between Fifth Street and the river and from the railway yards to the Y-street levee. Nobody ever mentioned an upper part of town; at least, no one could see the difference because the whole city was built on level land. We were not lower topographically, but in other ways that distinguished between Them, the uppers, and Us, the lowers. Lower Sacramento was the quarter that people who made money moved away from. Those of us who lived in it stayed there because our problem was to make a living and not to make money. A long while back, Mr. Howard, the business agent of the union told me, there had been stores and shops, fancy residences, and smart hotels in this neighborhood. The crippled old gentleman who lived in the next room down the hall from us, explained to me that our house, like the others in the neighborhood, had been the home of rich people who had stables in the back yards, with back entrances by way of the alleys. Mr. Hansen, the Dutch carpenter, had helped build such residences. When the owners moved uptown, the back yards had been fenced off and subdivided, and small rental cottages had been built in the alleys in place of the stables. Handsome private homes were turned into flophouses for men who stayed one night, hotels for working people, and rooming houses, like ours.

Among the saloons, pool halls, lunch counters, pawnshops, and poker parlors was skid row, where drunk men with black eyes and unshaven faces lay down in the alleys to sleep.

The lower quarter was not exclusively a Mexican *barrio* but a mix of many nationalities. Between L and N Streets two blocks from us, the Japanese had taken over. Their homes were in the alleys behind shops, which they advertised with signs covered with black scribbles. The women walked on the street in kimonos, wooden sandals, and white stockings, carrying neat black bundles on their backs and wearing their hair in puffs with long ivory needles stuck through them. When they met they bowed, walked a couple of steps, and turned and bowed again, repeating this several times. They carried babies on their backs, not in their arms, never laughed or went into the saloons. On Sundays the men sat in front of their shops, dressed in gowns, like priests.

Chinatown was on the other side of K Street, toward the Southern Pacific shops. Our houses were old, but those in which the Chinese kept stores, laundries, and restaurants were older still. In black jackets and skullcaps the older merchants smoked long pipes with a tiny brass cup on the end. In their dusty store windows there was always the same assortment of tea packages, rice bowls, saucers, and pots decorated with blue temples and dragons.

In the hotels and rooming houses scattered about the *barrio* the Filipino farm workers, riverboat stewards, and houseboys made their homes. Like the Mexicans they had their own poolhalls, which they called clubs. Hindus from the rice and fruit country north of the city stayed in the rooming houses when they were in town, keeping to themselves. The Portuguese and Italian families gathered in their own neighborhoods along Fourth and Fifth Streets southward toward the Y-street levee. The Poles, Yugo-Slavs, and Koreans, too few to take over any particular part of it, were scattered throughout the *barrio*. Black men drifted in and out of town, working the waterfront. It was a kaleidoscope of colors and languages and customs that surprised and absorbed me at every turn.

Although we, the foreigners, made up the majority of the population of that quarter of Sacramento, the Americans had by no means given it up to us. Not all of them had moved above Fifth Street as the *barrio* became more crowded. The bartenders, the rent collectors, the insurance salesmen, the mates on the river boats, the landladies, and most importantly, the police—these were all gringos. So were the craftsmen, like the barbers and printers, who did not move their shops uptown as the city grew. The teachers of our one public school were all Americans. On skid row we rarely saw a drunk wino who was not a gringo. The operators of the pawnshops and secondhand stores were white and mostly Jewish.

For the Mexicans the barrio was a colony of refugees. We came to know families from Chihuahua, Sonora, Jalisco, and Durango.[26] Some had come to the United States even before the revolution, living in Texas before migrating to California. Like ourselves, our Mexican neighbors had come this far moving step by step, working and waiting, as if they were feeling their way up a ladder. They talked of relatives who had been left behind in Mexico, or in some far-off city like Los Angeles or San Diego. From whatever place they had come, and however short or long the time they had lived in the United States, together they formed the *colonia mexicana*. In the years between our arrival and the First World War, the *colonia* grew and spilled out from the lower part of town. Some families moved into the alley shacks east of the Southern Pacific tracks, close to the canneries and warehouses and across the river among the orchards and rice mills.

The *colonia* was like a sponge that was beginning to leak along the edges, squeezed between the levee, the railroad tracks, and the river front. But it wasn't squeezed dry, because it kept filling with newcomers who found families who took in boarders: basements, alleys, shanties, run-down rooming houses and flop joints where they could live.

Crowded as it was, the *colonia* found a place for these *chicanos*, the name by which we called an unskilled worker born in Mexico and just arrived in the United States. The *chicanos* were fond of identifying themselves by saying they had just arrived from *el macizo*, by which they meant the solid Mexican homeland, the good native earth. Although they spoke of *el macizo* like homesick persons, they didn't go back. They remained, as they said of themselves, *pura raza*.[27] So it happened that José and Gustavo would bring home for a meal and for conversation workingmen who were *chicanos* fresh from *el macizo* and like ourselves, *pura raza*. Like us, they had come straight to the *barrio* where they could order a meal, buy a pair of overalls, and look for work in Spanish. They brought us vague news about the revolution, in which many of them had fought as *villistas*, *huertistas*, *maderistas*, or *zapatistas*.[28] As an old *maderista*, I imagined our *chicano* guests as battle-tested revolutionaries, like myself.

As poor refugees, their first concern was to find a place to sleep, then to eat and find work. In the *barrio* they were most likely to find

26. These are four Mexican states from which many immigrants came during the Mexican Revolution.

27. *Pura raza:* literally, pure race; in this context, all Mexican.

28. *Villistas, huertistas, maderistas,* or *zapatistas:* supporters of major leaders in the revolutionary struggle, Francisco Villa, Victoriano Huerta, Francisco Madero, and Emiliano Zapata, respectively.

all three, for not knowing English, they needed something that was even more urgent than a room, a meal, or a job, and that was information in a language they could understand. This information had to be picked up in bits and pieces—from families like ours, from the conversation groups in the poolrooms and the saloons.

Beds and meals, if the newcomers had no money at all, were provided—in one way or another—on trust, until the new *chicano* found a job. On trust and not on credit, for trust was something between people who had plenty of nothing, and credit was between people who had something of plenty. It was not charity or social welfare but something my mother called *asistencia*, a helping given and received on trust, to be repaid because those who had given it were themselves in need of what they had given. *Chicanos* who had found work on farms or in railroad camps came back to pay us a few dollars for *asistencia* we had provided weeks or months before.

Because the *barrio* was a grapevine of job information, the transient *chicanos* were able to find work and repay their obligations. The password of the barrio was *trabajo*[29] and the community was divided in two—the many who were looking for it and the few who had it to offer. Pickers, foremen, contractors, drivers, field hands, pick and shovel men on the railroad and in construction came back to the *barrio* when work was slack, to tell one another of the places they had been, the kind of *patrón* they had, the wages paid, the food, the living quarters, and other important details. Along Second Street, labor recruiters hung blackboards on their shop fronts, scrawling in chalk offers of work. The grapevine was a mesh of rumors and gossip, and men often walked long distances or paid bus fares or a contractor's fee only to find that the work was over or all the jobs were filled. Even the chalked signs could not always be relied on. Yet the search for *trabajo*, or the *chanza*, as we also called it, went on because it had to.

We in the *barrio* considered that there were two kinds of *trabajo*. There were the seasonal jobs, some of them a hundred miles or more from Sacramento. And there were the closer *chanzas* to which you could walk or ride on a bicycle. These were the best ones, in the railway shops, the canneries, the waterfront warehouses, the lumber yards, the produce markets, the brick kilns, and the rice mills. To be able to move from the seasonal jobs to the close-in work was a step up the ladder. Men who had made it passed the word along to their relatives or their friends when there was a *chanza* of this kind.

29. *Trabajo:* work.

It was all done by word of mouth, this delicate wiring of the grape-vine. The exchange points of the network were the places where men gathered in small groups, apparently to loaf and chat to no purpose. One of these points was our kitchen, where my uncles and their friends sat and talked of *el macizo* and of the revolution but above all of the *chanzas* they had heard of.

There was not only the everlasting talk about *trabajo*, but also the never-ending action of the *barrio* itself. If work was action the *barrio* was where the action was. Every morning a parade of men in oily work clothes and carrying lunch buckets went up Fourth Street to-ward the railroad shops, and every evening they walked back, grimy and silent. Horse drawn drays with low platforms rumbled up and down our street carrying the goods the city traded in, from kegs of beer to sacks of grain. Within a few blocks of our house there were smithies, hand laundries, a macaroni factory, and all manner of places where wagons and buggies were repaired, horses stabled, bicycles fixed, chickens dressed, clothes washed and ironed, furniture re-paired, candy mixed, tents sewed, wine grapes pressed, bottles washed, lumber sawed, suits fitted and tailored, watches and clocks taken apart and put together again, vegetables sorted, railroad cars unloaded, boxcars iced, barges freighted, ice cream cones molded, soda pop bottled, fish scaled, salami stuffed, corn ground for masa, and bread ovened. To those who knew where these were located in the alleys, as I did, the whole *barrio* was an open workshop. The peo-ple who worked there came to know you, let you look in at the door, made jokes, and occasionally gave you an odd job.

This was the business district of the *barrio*. Around it and through it moved a constant traffic of drays, carts, bicycles, pushcarts, trucks, and high-wheeled automobiles with black canvas tops and honking horns. On the tailgates of drays and wagons, I nipped rides when I was going home with a gunnysack full of empty beer bottles or my gleanings around the packing sheds.

Once we had work, the next most important thing was to find a place to live we could afford. Ours was a neighborhood of leftover houses. The cheapest rents were in the back quarters of the rooming houses, the basements, and the run-down clapboard rentals in the al-leys. Clammy and dank as they were, they were nevertheless one level up from the barns and tents where many of our *chicano* friends lived, or the shanties and lean-to's of the migrants who squatted in the "jungles" along the levees of the Sacramento and the American rivers.

Barrio people, when they first came to town, had no furniture of their own. They rented it with their quarters or bought a piece at a time from the secondhand stores, the *segundas*, where we traded. We cut out the ends of tin cans to make collars and plates for the pipes and floor moldings where the rats had gnawed holes. Stoops and porches that sagged we propped with bricks and fat stones. To plug the drafts around the windows in winter, we cut strips of corrugated cardboard and wedged them into the frames. With squares of cheesecloth neatly cut and sewed to screen doors holes were covered and rents in the wire mesh mended. Such repairs, which landlords never paid any attention to, were made *por mientras*, for the time being or temporarily. It would have been a word equally suitable for the house itself, or for the *barrio*. We lived in run-down places furnished with seconds in a hand-me-down neighborhood all of which were *por mientras*.

We found the Americans as strange in their customs as they probably found us. Immediately we discovered that there were no *mercados* and that when shopping you did not put the groceries in a *chiquihuite*.[30] Instead everything was in cans or in cardboard boxes or each item was put in a brown paper bag. There were neighborhood grocery stores at the corners and some big ones uptown, but no *mercado*. The grocers did not give children a *pilón*,[31] they did not stand at the door and coax you to come in and buy, as they did in Mazatlán. The fruits and vegetables were displayed on counters instead of being piled up on the floor. The stores smelled of fly spray and oiled floors, not of fresh pineapple and limes.

Neither was there a plaza, only parks which had no bandstands, no concerts every Thursday, no Judases exploding on Holy Week, and no promenades of boys going one way and girls the other. There were no parks in the *barrio;* and the ones uptown were cold and rainy in winter, and in summer there was no place to sit except on the grass. When there were celebrations nobody set off rockets in the parks, much less on the street in front of your house to announce to the neighborhood that a wedding or a baptism was taking place. Sacramento did not have a *mercado* and a plaza with the cathedral to one side and the Palacio de Gobierno on another to make it obvious that there and nowhere else was the center of the town.

It was just as puzzling that the Americans did not live in *vecindades*,[32] like our block on Leandro Valle. Even in the alleys, where people knew one another better, the houses were fenced apart,

30. *Chiquihuite:* a wicker basket used for shopping.
31. *Pilón:* a sweet.
32. *Vecindades:* neighborhoods.

Ernesto Galarza, about nine, with his Uncle José at a photo studio in Sacramento. (Courtesy of Mae Galarza)

without central courts to wash clothes, talk and play with the other children. Like the city, the Sacramento *barrio* did not have a place which was the middle of things for everyone.

In more personal ways we had to get used to the Americans. They did not listen if you did not speak loudly, as they always did. In the Mexican style, people would know that you were enjoying their jokes tremendously if you merely smiled and shook a little, as if you were trying to swallow your mirth. In the American style there was little difference between a laugh and a roar, and until you got used to them you could hardly tell whether the boisterous Americans were roaring mad or roaring happy.

It was Doña Henriqueta more than Gustavo or José who talked of these oddities and classified them as agreeable or deplorable. It was she also who pointed out the pleasant surprises of the American way. When a box of rolled oats with a picture of red carnations on the side was emptied, there was a plate or a bowl or a cup with blue designs. We ate the strange stuff regularly for breakfast and we soon had a set of the beautiful dishes. Rice and beans we bought in cotton bags of colored prints. The bags were unsewed, washed, ironed, and made into gaily designed towels, napkins, and handkerchiefs. The American stores also gave small green stamps which were pasted in a book to exchange for prizes. We didn't have to run to the corner with the garbage; a collector came for it.

With remarkable fairness and never-ending wonder we kept adding to our list the pleasant and the repulsive in the ways of the Americans. It was my second acculturation.

The older people of the *barrio*, except in those things which they had to do like the Americans because they had no choice, remained Mexican. Their language at home was Spanish. They were continuously taking up collections to pay somebody's funeral expenses or to help someone who had had a serious accident. Cards were sent to you to attend a burial where you would throw a handful of dirt on top of the coffin and listen to tearful speeches at the graveside. At every baptism a new *compadre* and a new *comadre* joined the family circle.[33] New Year greeting cards were exchanged, showing angels and cherubs in bright colors sprinkled with grains of mica so that they glistened like gold dust. At the family parties the huge pot of steaming tamales was still the center of attention, the *atole*[34] served on the side with chunks of brown sugar for sucking and crunching. If the party

33. *Compadre, comadre:* godfather, godmother.
34. *Atole:* thick drink made from corn meal.

lasted long enough, someone produced a guitar, the men took over and the singing of *corridos*[35] began.

In the *barrio* there were no individuals who had official titles or who were otherwise recognized by everybody as important people. The reason must have been that there was no place in the public business of the city of Sacramento for the Mexican immigrants. We only rented a corner of the city and as long as we paid the rent on time everything else was decided at City Hall or the County Court House, where Mexicans went only when they were in trouble. Nobody from the *barrio* ever ran for mayor or city councilman. For us the most important public officials were the policemen who walked their beats, stopped fights, and hauled drunks to jail in a paddy wagon we called *La Julia*.

The one institution we had that gave the *colonia* some kind of image was the *Comisión Honorífica*, a committee picked by the Mexican Consul in San Francisco to organize the celebration of the *Cinco de Mayo* and the Sixteenth of September, the anniversaries of the battle of Puebla and the beginning of our War of Independence. These were the two events which stirred everyone in the *barrio*, for what we were celebrating was not only the heroes of Mexico but also the feeling that we were still Mexicans ourselves. On these occasions there was a dance preceded by speeches and a concert. For both the *cinco* and the sixteenth queens were elected to preside over the ceremonies.

Between celebrations neither the politicians uptown nor the *Comisión Honorífica* attended to the daily needs of the *barrio*. This was done by volunteers—the ones who knew enough English to interpret in court, on a visit to the doctor, a call at the county hospital, and who could help make out a postal money order. By the time I had finished the third grade at the Lincoln School I was one of these volunteers. My services were not professional but they were free, except for the IOU's I accumulated from families who always thanked me with "God will pay you for it."

My clients were not *pochos*, Mexicans who had grown up in California, probably had even been born in the United States. They had learned to speak English of sorts and could still speak Spanish, also of sorts. They knew much more about the Americans than we did, and much less about us. The *chicanos* and the *pochos* had certain feelings about one another. Concerning the *pochos*, the *chicanos* suspected that they considered themselves too good for the *barrio* but were not, for some reason, good enough for the Americans. Toward the *chicanos*, the *pochos* acted superior, amused at our confu-

35. *Corridos*: popular ballads.

sions but not especially interested in explaining them to us. In our family when I forgot my manners, my mother would ask me if I was turning *pochito*.

Turning *pocho* was a half-step toward turning American. And America was all around us, in and out of the *barrio*. Abruptly we had to forget the ways of shopping in a *mercado* and learn those of shopping in a corner grocery or in a department store. The Americans paid no attention to the Sixteenth of September, but they made a great commotion about the Fourth of July. In Mazatlán Don Salvador had told us, saluting and marching as he talked to our class, that the *Cinco de Mayo* was the most glorious date in human history. The Americans had not even heard about it.

In Tucson, when I had asked my mother again if the Americans were having a revolution, the answer was: "No, but they have good schools, and you are going to one of them." We were by now settled at 418 L Street and the time had come for me to exchange a revolution for an American education.

The two of us walked south on Fifth Street one morning to the corner of Q Street and turned right. Half of the block was occupied by the Lincoln School. It was a three-story wooden building, with two wings that gave it the shape of a double-T connected by a central hall. It was a new building, painted yellow, with a shingled roof that was not like the red tile of the school in Mazatlán. I noticed other differences, none of them very reassuring.

We walked up the wide staircase hand in hand and through the door, which closed by itself. A mechanical contraption screwed to the top shut it behind us quietly.

Up to this point the adventure of enrolling me in the school had been carefully rehearsed. Mrs. Dodson had told us how to find it and we had circled it several times on our walks. Friends in the *barrio* explained that the director was called a principal, and that it was a lady and not a man. They assured us that there was always a person at the school who could speak Spanish.

Exactly as we had been told, there was a sign on the door in both Spanish and English: "Principal." We crossed the hall and entered the office of Miss Nettie Hopley.

Miss Hopley was at a roll-top desk to one side, sitting in a swivel chair that moved on wheels. There was a sofa against the opposite wall, flanked by two windows and a door that opened on a small balcony. Chairs were set around a table and framed pictures hung on the walls of a man with long white hair and another with a sad face and a black beard.

The principal half turned in the swivel chair to look at us over the pinch glasses crossed on the ridge of her nose. To do this she had to duck her head slightly as if she were about to step through a low doorway.

What Miss Hopley said to us we did not know but we saw in her eyes a warm welcome and when she took off her glasses and straightened up she smiled wholeheartedly, like Mrs. Dodson. We were, of course, saying nothing, only catching the friendliness of her voice and the sparkle in her eyes while she said words we did not understand. She signaled us to the table. Almost tiptoeing across the office, I maneuvered myself to keep my mother between me and the gringo lady. In a matter of seconds I had to decide whether she was a possible friend or a menace. We sat down.

Then Miss Hopley did a formidable thing. She stood up. Had she been standing when we entered she would have seemed tall. But rising from her chair she soared. And what she carried up and up with her was a buxom superstructure, firm shoulders, a straight sharp nose, full cheeks slightly molded by a curved line along the nostrils, thin lips that moved like steel springs, and a high forehead topped by hair gathered in a bun. Miss Hopley was not a giant in body but when she mobilized it to a standing position she seemed a match for giants. I decided I liked her.

She strode to a door in the far corner of the office, opened it and called a name. A boy of about ten years appeared in the doorway. He sat down at one end of the table. He was brown like us, a plump kid with shiny black hair combed straight back, neat, cool, and faintly obnoxious.

Miss Hopley joined us with a large book and some papers in her hand. She, too, sat down and the questions and answers began by way of our interpreter. My name was Ernesto. My mother's name was Henriqueta. My birth certificate was in San Blas. Here was my last report card from the Escuela Municipal Numero 3 para Varones of Mazatlán, and so forth. Miss Hopley put things down in the book and my mother signed a card.

As long as the questions continued, Doña Henriqueta could stay and I was secure. Now that they were over, Miss Hopley saw her to the door, dismissed our interpreter and without further ado took me by the hand and strode down the hall to Miss Ryan's first grade.

Miss Ryan took me to a seat at the front of the room, into which I shrank—the better to survey her. She was, to skinny, somewhat runty me, of a withering height when she patrolled the class. And when I least expected it, there she was, crouching by my desk, her blond radiant face level with mine, her voice patiently maneuvering me over the awful idiocies of the English language.

During the next few weeks Miss Ryan overcame my fears of tall, energetic teachers as she bent over my desk to help me with a word in the pre-primer. Step by step, she loosened me and my classmates from the safe anchorage of the desks for recitations at the blackboard and consultations at her desk. Frequently she burst into happy announcements to the whole class. "Ito can read a sentence," and small Japanese Ito, squint-eyed and shy, slowly read aloud while the class listened in wonder: "Come, Skipper, come. Come and run." The Korean, Portuguese, Italian, and Polish first graders had similar moments of glory, no less shining than mine the day I conquered "butterfly," which I had been persistently pronouncing in standard Spanish as boo-ter-flee. "Children," Miss Ryan called for attention. "Ernesto has learned how to pronounce *butterfly!*" And I proved it with a perfect imitation of Miss Ryan. From that celebrated success, I was soon able to match Ito's progress as a sentence reader with "Come, butterfly, come fly with me."

Like Ito and several other first graders who did not know English, I received private lessons from Miss Ryan in the closet, a narrow hall off the classroom with a door at each end. Next to one of these doors Miss Ryan placed a large chair for herself and a small one for me. Keeping an eye on the class through the open door she read with me about sheep in the meadow and a frightened chicken going to see the king, coaching me out of my phonetic ruts in words like *pasture, bow-wow-wow, hay,* and *pretty,* which to my Mexican ear and eye had so many unnecessary sounds and letters. She made me watch her lips and then close my eyes as she repeated words I found hard to read. When we came to know each other better, I tried interrupting to tell Miss Ryan how we said it in Spanish. It didn't work. She only said "oh" and went on with *pasture, bow-wow-wow,* and *pretty.* It was as if in that closet we were both discovering together the secrets of the English language and grieving together over the tragedies of Bo-Peep. The main reason I was graduated with honors from the first grade was that I had fallen in love with Miss Ryan. Her radiant, no-nonsense character made us either afraid not to love her or love her so we would not be afraid, I am not sure which. It was not only that we sensed she was with it, but also that she was with us.

Like the first grade, the rest of the Lincoln School was a sampling of the lower part of town where many races made their home. My pals in the second grade were Kazushi, whose parents spoke only Japanese; Matti, a skinny Italian boy; and Manuel, a fat Portuguese who would never get into a fight but wrestled you to the ground and just sat on you. Our assortment of nationalities included Koreans, Yugoslavs, Poles, Irish, and home-grown Americans.

Miss Hopley and her teachers never let us forget why we were at Lincoln: for those who were alien, to become good Americans; for those who were so born, to accept the rest of us. Off the school grounds we traded the same insults we heard from our elders. On the playground we were sure to be marched up to the principal's office for calling someone a wop, a chink, a dago, or a greaser. The school was not so much a melting pot as a griddle where Miss Hopley and her helpers warmed knowledge into us and roasted racial hatreds out of us.

At Lincoln, making us into Americans did not mean scrubbing away what made us originally foreign. The teachers called us as our parents did, or as close as they could pronounce our names in Spanish or Japanese. No one was ever scolded or punished for speaking in his native tongue on the playground. Matti told the class about his mother's down quilt, which she had made in Italy with the fine feathers of a thousand geese. Encarnación acted out how boys learned to fish in the Philippines. I astounded the third grade with the story of my travels on a stagecoach, which nobody else in the class had seen except in the museum at Sutter's Fort. After a visit to the Crocker Art Gallery and its collection of heroic paintings of the golden age of California, someone showed a silk scroll with a Chinese painting. Miss Hopley herself had a way of expressing wonder over these matters before a class, her eyes wide open until they popped slightly. It was easy for me to feel that becoming a proud American, as she said we should, did not mean feeling ashamed of being a Mexican.

The Americanization of Mexican me was no smooth matter. I had to fight one lout who made fun of my travels on the *diligencia*,[36] and my barbaric translation of the word into "diligence." He doubled up with laughter over the word until I straightened him out with a kick. In class I made points explaining that in Mexico roosters said "qui-qui-ri-qui" and not "cock-a-doodle-doo," but after school I had to put up with the taunts of a big Yugoslav who said Mexican roosters were crazy. . . .

In our musty apartment in the basement of 418 L, ours remained a Mexican family. I never lost the sense that we were the same, from Jalco to Sacramento. There was the polished cedar box, taken out now and then from the closet to display our heirlooms. I had lost the rifle

36. *Diligencia:* stagecoach.

shells of the revolution, and Tio Tonche, too, was gone. But there was the butterfly sarape, the one I had worn through the Battle of Puebla; a black lace mantilla Doña Henriqueta modeled for us; bits of embroidery and lace she had made; the tin pictures of my grandparents; my report card signed by Señorita Bustamante and Don Salvador; letters from Aunt Esther; and the card with the address of the lady who had kept the Ajax for us. When our mementos were laid out on the bed I plunged my head into the empty box and took deep breaths of the aroma of *puro cedro,* pure Jalcocotán mixed with camphor.

We could have hung on the door of our apartment a sign like those we read in some store windows—*Aqui se habla espanol.* We not only spoke Spanish, we read it. From the *Libería Española,* two blocks up the street, Gustavo and I bought novels for my mother, like *Genoveva de Brabante,* a paperback with the poems of Amado Nervo and a handbook of the history of Mexico. The novels were never read aloud, the poems and the handbook were. Nervo was the famous poet from Tepic, close enough to Jalcocotán to make him our own. And in the history book I learned to read for myself, after many repetitions by my mother, about the deeds of the great Mexicans Don Salvador had recited so vividly to the class in Mazatlán. She refused to decide for me whether Abraham Lincoln was as great as Benito Juarez, or George Washington braver than the priest Don Miguel Hidalgo. At school there was no opportunity to settle these questions because nobody seemed to know about Juarez or Hidalgo; at least they were never mentioned and there were no pictures of them on the walls.

The family talk I listened to with the greatest interest was about Jalco. Wherever the conversation began it always turned to the pueblo, our neighbors, anecdotes that were funny or sad, the folk tales and the witchcraft, and our kinfolk, who were still there. I usually lay on the floor those winter evenings, with my feet toward the kerosene heater, watching on the ceiling the flickering patterns of the light filtered through the scrollwork of the chimney. As I listened once again I chased the *zopilote* away from Coronel, or watched José take Nerón into the forest in a sack. Certain things became clear about the *rurales* and why the young men were taken away to kill Yaqui Indians, and about the Germans, the Englishmen, the Frenchmen, the Spaniards, and the Americans who owned the haciendas, the railroads, the ships, the big stores, the breweries. They owned Mexico because President Porfirio Díaz had let them steal it, José explained as I listened. Now Don Francisco Madero had been assassinated for trying to get it back. On such threads of family talk I followed my own recollection of the years from Jalco—the attack of Mazatlán, the captain of Acaponeta, the camp at El Nanchi and the arrival at Nogales on the flatcar.

Only when we ventured uptown did we feel like aliens in a foreign land. Within the *barrio* we heard Spanish on the streets and in the alleys. On the railroad tracks, in the canneries, and along the riverfront there were more Mexicans than any other nationality. And except for the foremen, the work talk was in our language. In the secondhand shops, where the *barrio* people sold and bought furniture and clothing, there were Mexican clerks who knew the Mexican ways of making a sale. Families doubled up in decaying houses, cramping themselves so they could rent an extra room to *chicano* boarders, who accented the brown quality of our Mexican *colonia*.

It was at the family parties that the world of the Americans was completely shut off. Usually they were arranged by families from the same part of Mexico who considered themselves *paisanos*.[37] The host family prepared the tamales or the enchiladas and everyone brought something for the feast. But these occasions were mainly for talking and not for eating. They were long parties, from late afternoon to midnight, the men in the front room, the mothers in the kitchen, the young women serving and whispering in the hall, the boys playing on the porch and the babies put to bed all over the house.

When the case of beer arrived the singing began. A guitar came down from a peg on the wall and those who could sing took turns with the ballads and the country love songs, the girls crowding the door to listen, the boys at the windows. As the singers warmed up there were duets and the fighting songs of the revolution, like "La Valentina" and "Adelita."

When the party was at the Duran's, a family from Sonora, the singing drifted into talk of the revolution. Duran had been a miner in Cananea, had taken part in the great strike there that was put down by gringo soldiers, and knew the Flores Magon brothers, who had stirred the miners to revolt. Duran's face was a burnt brown, the dark shade of an olive skin turned nearly charcoal by the sun. He had a slightly hawked nose and powerful black eyes. His talk turned into a passionate lecture on the sufferings of the Mexican people, with detailed accounts of great events, like the massacre of the mill workers of Rio Blanco. Duran had been crippled in an accident and he limped slightly, something about him suggesting a crippled man even when he fidgeted in his chair denouncing Porfirio Díaz and the rich despots who owned the country.

---

37. *Paisanos:* fellow countrymen and women.

It was Duran, also, who brought us up to date on the revolution at our doors, for that was how he explained the Industrial Workers of the World, who were holding meetings on sandlots and in out-of-the way spots along the river. He snorted now and then as he talked, to clear his throat, and to bear down on his contempt for the capitalists who were breaking up meetings of the I.W.W. and sending them to jail. The circle of brown faces in the room caught some of the glow in Duran's face, and after we said good-bye and walked home across town I kept thinking of him.[38]

We invited friends for New Year's supper, preparing for which I spent the day running to the store and in the kitchen grinding corn in the coffee mill, hammering cones of brown sugar into powder, and pounding herbs in the pestle. Somehow we crowded our guests into the living room where my mother served *atole* and the tissue-thin *buñuelos*[39] dunked in syrup. We had no guitar so José, on his new mouth organ named *La Filarmónica*, provided the music.

In the family parties, the funerals, the baptisms, the weddings and the birthdays, our private lives continued to be Mexican.

38. This early experience with a union activist may have been formative for young Ernesto Galarza and contributed to his lifelong concern for Mexican farmworkers in California.

39. *Buñuelos:* crullerlike pastry.

EIGHT

Kazuko Itoi: A Nisei Daughter's Story 1925–1942

Unlike most of the other authors of the diaries, letters, and reminiscences brought together in this volume, Kazuko Itoi was not herself an immigrant. She was born in Seattle of immigrant parents (*Issei*, or first generation in the Japanese usage). As a second-generation, American-born member of the Japanese community, she was a *Nisei*.[1]

As a Nisei, she held a position intermediate between her immigrant parents and Seattle's native-born white majority. She was a "child of Skidrow" and even thought of herself as a Yankee, but she soon came to understand what it meant to have "Japanese blood." It meant that she and her family could not rent an apartment wherever they chose; it meant that after the Japanese attack on Pearl Harbor she and her family would be shipped to an internment camp away from the West Coast.

Nisei Daughter, her autobiography, speaks to the differing attitudes of immigrants and their children toward mainstream American culture. While the Itois were determined to send their children to a Japanese cultural school, the children resented the imposition of what they felt to be an "alien" culture. The parents prevailed, however, and their children learned Japanese language and culture in an after-school program.

The distinct orientations of the Issei and Nisei generations became particularly significant when they were interned together during World War II. In the camps, Nisei were particularly advantaged since they had more education than their parents did and they spoke En-

---

1. Monica Sone, *Nisei Daughter* (Seattle: University of Washington Press, 1988; originally published in 1953). Born Kazuko Monica Itoi, the author used her middle name and marital surname after her marriage; hence, Monica Sone and the Kazuko Itoi of her narrative are the same person.

glish. Issei and Nisei attitudes toward internment and their ability to maneuver within American culture were very different. At the assembly center in Puyallup, outside of Seattle, for instance, the Itoi children were given jobs of considerable responsibility and modest salaries, while their parents were not. Henry worked in the camp hospital and Kazuko did clerical work. Taking upon themselves the responsibility of enforcing camp regulations, other Nisei were sometimes harsh toward their Issei elders.[2] Camp life and the aging process tipped the balance of power within the Japanese-American community irreversibly toward the Nisei generation.

A SHOCKING FACT OF LIFE

The first five years of my life I lived in amoebic bliss, not knowing whether I was plant or animal, at the old Carrollton Hotel on the waterfront of Seattle. One day when I was a happy six-year-old, I made the shocking discovery that I had Japanese blood. I was a Japanese.

Mother announced this fact of life to us in a quiet, deliberate manner one Sunday afternoon as we gathered around for dinner in the small kitchen, converted from one of our hotel rooms. Our kitchen was cozily comfortable for all six of us as long as everyone remained in his place around the oblong table covered with an indestructible shiny black oilcloth; but if more than Mother stood up and fussed around, there was a serious traffic jam—soy sauce splattered on the floor and elbows jabbed into the pot of rice. So Father sat at the head of the table, Kenji, Henry, and I lined up on one side along the wall, while Mother and baby Sumiko occupied the other side, near the kitchen stove.

Now we watched as Mother lifted from a kettle of boiling water a straw basket of steaming slippery noodles. She directed her information at Henry and me, and I felt uneasy. Father paid strict attention to his noodles, dipping them into a bowl of fragrant pork broth and then sprinkling finely chopped raw green onion over them.

Japanese blood—how is it I have that, Mama?" I asked, surreptitiously pouring hot tea over my bowl of rice. Mother said it was bad manners to wash rice down with tea, but rice was delicious with *obancha*.[3]

2. Sone, *Nisei Daughter*, pp. 187–88.
3. *Obancha:* coarse tea.

Kazuko Itoi (right) and her sister in front of the Hotel Rainier in Seattle, 1932. (Courtesy of Monica Sone)

"Your father and I have Japanese blood and so do you, too. And the same with Henry, Ken-chan, and Sumi-chan."

"Oh." I felt nothing unusual stirring inside me. I took a long cool sip of milk and then with my short red chopsticks I stabbed at a piece of pickled crisp white radish.

"So, Mama?" Henry looked up at her, trying to bring under control with his chopsticks the noodles swinging from his mouth like a pendulum.

"So, Papa and I have decided that you and Ka-chan will attend Japanese school after grammar school every day." She beamed at us.

I choked on my rice.

Terrible, terrible, terrible! So that's what it meant to be a Japanese—to lose my afternoon play hours! I fiercely resented this sudden intrusion of my blood into my affairs.

"But, Mama!" I shrieked. "I go to Bailey Gatzert School already. I don't want to go to another!"

Henry kicked the table leg and grumbled, "Aw gee, Mama, Dunks and Jiro don't have to—why do I!"

"They'll be going, too. Their mothers told me so."

My face grew hot with anger. I shouted, "I won't, I won't!"

Father and Mother painted glowing pictures for me. Just think you'll grow up to be a well-educated young lady, knowing two languages. One of these days you'll thank us for giving you this opportunity.

But they could not convince me. Until this shattering moment, I had thought life was sweet and reasonable. But not any more. Why did Father and Mother make such a fuss just because we had Japanese blood? Why did we have to go to Japanese school? I refused to eat and sat sobbing, letting great big tears splash down into my bowl of rice and tea.

Henry, who was smarter and adjusted more quickly to fate, continued his meal, looking gloomy, but with his appetite unimpaired.

Up to that moment, I had never thought of Father and Mother as Japanese. True, they had almond eyes and they spoke Japanese to us, but I never felt that it was strange. It was like one person's being red-haired and another black.

Father had often told us stories about his early life. He had come from a small village in the prefecture of Tochigi-ken.[4] A third son from

4. Tochigi-ken: Japan is divided into administrative districts known as prefectures. Tochigi is located north of Tokyo on the main island of Honshu. Most emigrants from Japan between 1890 and 1924 came from the southern Honshu prefectures of Hiroshima and Wakayama.

among five brothers and one sister, Father had gone to Tokyo to study law, and he practiced law for a few years before he succumbed to the fever which sent many young men streaming across the Pacific to a fabulous new country rich with promise and opportunities.

In 1904 Father sailed for the United States, an ambitious young man of twenty-five, determined to continue his law studies at Ann Arbor, Michigan. Landing in Seattle, he plunged into sundry odd jobs with the hope of saving enough money to finance his studies. Father worked with the railroad gang, laying ties on virgin soil, he toiled stubbornly in the heat of the potato fields of Yakima, he cooked his way back and forth between Alaska and Seattle on ships of all sizes and shapes, but fortune eluded him. Then one day he bought a small cleaning and pressing shop on Tenth and Jackson Street, a wagon and a gentle white dobbin, "Charlie." The years flew by fast, but his savings did not reflect his frenzied labor. With each passing year, his dream of Ann Arbor grew dimmer.

At last Father's thoughts turned toward marriage. About this time the Reverend Yohachi Nagashima—our grandfather—brought his family to America. Grandfather Nagashima was a minister of a Congregational church in Sanomachi, about twenty miles north of Tokyo in Tochigi-ken prefecture. He had visited the United States twice before on preaching missions among the Japanese. Grandfather had been impressed with the freedom and educational opportunities in America. He arrived in Seattle, with his wife, Yuki, three daughters, Yasuko, my mother Benko, and Kikue, twenty-two, seventeen and sixteen years of age respectively, and two little round-eyed sons, Shinichi and Yoshio, six and four years. . . .

Father heard of the Nagashimas' arrival. He immediately called to pay his respects. Seeing three marriageable daughters, Father kept going back. Eventually he sent a mutual friend to act as go-between to ask for the hand of the first daughter, Yasuko, but the friend reported that Mr. Nagashima had already arranged for Yasuko's marriage to a Mr. Tani. Undaunted, Father sent his friend back to ask for the second daughter, Benko. Mother said that when her father called her into his study and told her that a Mr. Itoi wanted to marry her, she was so shocked she fled to her room, dived under her bed and cried in protest, "I can't, Otoh-san, I can't. I don't even know him!"

Her father had got down on his hands and knees and peered at her under the bed, reprimanding her sternly. "Stop acting like a child, Benko. I advise you to start getting acquainted with Mr. Itoi at once."

And that was that. Finally Mother gave her consent to the marriage, and the wedding ceremony was performed at the Japanese mission branch of the Methodist Episcopal Church on Fourteenth and Washington Street. Years later, when Henry and I came upon their wedding picture in our family album, we went into hysterics over Mother's face which had been plastered white and immobile with rice powder, according to Japanese fashion. . . .

In January, 1918, their first child was born, Henry Seiichi—son of truth. Shortly after, Father sold his little shop and bought the Carrollton Hotel on Main Street and Occidental Avenue, just a stone's throw from the bustling waterfront and the noisy railroad tracks. . . .

When Father took over the hotel in 1918, the building fairly burst with war workers and servicemen. They came at all hours of the day, begging to sleep even in the chairs in the lobby. Extra cots had to be set up in the hallways.

Father and Mother loved to tell us how they had practically rejuvenated the battered, flea-ridden Carrollton by themselves. Father had said firmly, "If I have to manage a flophouse, it'll be the cleanest and quietest place around here." With patience and care, they began to patch the aches and pains of the old hotel. The tobacco-stained stairways were scrubbed, painted and lighted up. Father varnished the floors while Mother painted the woodwork. New green runners were laid out in the corridors. They repapered the sixty rooms, one by one. Every day after the routine room-servicing had been finished, Mother cooked up a bucket of flour and water and brushed the paste on fresh new wallpaper laid out on a long makeshift work table in the hall. . . .

Shortly after the Armistice of World War I was signed, I was born and appropriately named Kazuko Monica, the Japanese name meaning "peace." (Mother chose Monica from her reading about Saint Augustine and his mother, Saint Monica.) Two years later Kenji William arrived, his name meaning "Healthy in body and spirit." Mother added "William" because she thought it sounded poetic. And two years after that, Sumiko, "the clear one," was born.

For our family quarters, Mother chose three outside rooms looking south on Main Street, across an old and graying five-story warehouse, and as the family increased, a fourth room was added. Father and Mother's small bedroom was crowded with a yellow brass bed that took up one wall. Mother's dainty white-painted dresser and a small square writing table piled with her books and papers occupied another wall. Father's brown dresser stood off in another corner, its only ornament a round, maroon-lacquered collar box. A treadle sewing machine squatted efficiently in front of the window where Mother sat in the evenings, mending torn sheets and pillowcases. Their closet was a pole slung against the fourth wall, covered with a green, floral-print curtain.

The living room was large, light and cheerful-looking, with a shiny mahogany-finished upright piano in one corner. Right above it hung a somber picture of Christ's face which looked down upon me each time I sat in front of the piano. Depending on my previous behavior, I felt restless and guilty under those brooding eyes or smugly content with myself. Against another wall, next to the piano, stood an elegant-looking, glass-cased secretary filled with Father's Japanese books, thick hotel account books, a set of untouched, glossy-paged encyclo-pedias, and the back numbers of the *National Geographic*. In the corner, near the window, was a small square table, displaying a mon-strous, iridescent half of an abalone shell and a glass ball paperweight filled with water, depicting an underwater scene with tiny corals and sea shells lying on the ocean bottom. In front of the other two win-dows was a long, brown leather davenport with a small gas heater nearby. A round dining table in the center of the room was sur-rounded by three plain chairs. . . .

At first glance, there was little about these simple, sparse furnish-ings to indicate that a Japanese family occupied the rooms. But there were telltale signs like the *zori* or straw slippers placed neatly on the floor underneath the beds. On Mother's bed lay a beautiful red silk comforter patterned with turquoise, apple-green, yellow and purple Japanese parasols. And on the table beside the local daily paper were copies of the *North American Times*, Seattle's Japanese-community paper, its printing resembling rows of black multiple-legged insects. Then there was the Oriental abacus board which Father used once a month to keep his books.

Our kitchen was a separate room far down the hall. The kitchen window opened into an alley, right above the Ace Café. An outdoor icebox, born of an old apple crate, was nailed firmly to our kitchen window sill.

Father had put in a gas stove next to the small sink. The huge stove took up nearly all the floor space. He had nailed five layers of shelves against the opposite wall almost up to the ceiling, and next to this, he installed a towering china cabinet with delicate, frosted glass win-dows. A large, oblong table was wedged into the only space left, in a corner near the door. Here in the kitchen were unmistakable Oriental traces and odors. A glass tumbler holding six pairs of red and yellow lacquered chopsticks, and a bottle of soy sauce stood companionably among the imitation cut-glass sugar bowl and the green glass salt and pepper shakers at the end of the table. The tall china cabinet bulged with bright hand-painted rice bowls, red lacquered soup bowls, and Mother's precious *somayaki* tea set.

The tea set was stunningly beautiful with the uneven surface of the gray clay dusted with black and gold flecks. There was a wisp of soft green around the rim of the tiny cups, as if someone had plucked off grass from the clay and the green stain had remained there. At the bottom of each teacup was the figure of a galloping, golden horse. When the cup was filled with tea, the golden horse seemed to rise to the surface and become animated. But the tea set was only for special occasions and holidays, and most of the time we used a set of dinnerware Americana purchased at the local hardware store and a drawerful of silver-plated tableware.

In the pantry, the sack of rice and gallon jug of *shoyu*[5] stood lined up next to the ivory-painted canisters of flour, sugar, tea and coffee. From a corner near the kitchen window, a peculiar, pungent odor emanated from a five-gallon crock which Mother kept filled with cucumbers, *nappa* (Chinese cabbage), *daikon* (large Japanese radishes), immersed in a pickling mixture of *nuka*, consisting of rice polishings, salt, rice and raisins. The fermented products were sublimely refreshing, delicious, raw vegetables, a perfect side dish to a rice and tea mixture at the end of a meal.

Among the usual pots and pans stood a dark red stone mixing bowl inside of which were cut rows and rows of minute grooves as on a record disc. The bowl was used to grind poppy seeds and *miso* (soybeans) into soft paste for soups and for flavoring Japanese dishes. I spent many hours bent over this bowl, grinding the beans into a smooth, fine paste with a heavy wooden club. For all the work that went into making *miso shiru*, soybean soup, I thought it tasted like sawdust boiled in sea brine. Mother told me nothing could be more nutritious, but I could never take more than a few shuddering sips of it.

In our family we ate both Western and Oriental dishes. Mother had come to America just fresh out of high school and had had little training in Japanese culinary art. In the beginning, Father taught Mother to cook all the dishes he knew. Father had a robust, mass-cooking style which he had learned in the galleys of Alaska-bound ships and he leaned heavily toward ham and eggs, steak and potatoes, apple and pumpkin pies. Later Mother picked up the technique of authentic

5. *Shoyu:* soy sauce.

Japanese cooking herself and she even learned to cook superb Chinese dishes. Although we acquired tastes for different types of food, we adhered mostly to a simple American menu.

So we lived in the old Carrollton. Every day, amidst the bedlam created by four black-eyed, jet-propelled children, Father and Mother took care of the hotel. Every morning they went from room to room, making beds and cleaning up. To help speed up the chores, we ran up and down the corridors, pounding on doors. We brutally woke the late sleepers, hammering with our fists and yelling, "Wake up, you sleepyhead! Wake up, make bed!" Then someone would think of pushing the linen cart for Father and the rest of us would rush to do the same. We usually ended up in a violent tussle. . . .

I thought the whole world consisted of two or three old hotels on every block. And that its population consisted of families like mine who lived in a corner of the hotels. And its other inhabitants were customers—fading, balding, watery-eyed men, rough-tough bearded men, and good men like Sam, Joe, Peter and Montana who worked for Father, all of whom lived in these hotels.

It was a very exciting world in which I lived. . . . And when I finally started grammar school, I found still another enchanting world. Every morning I hurried to Adams Hotel, climbed its dark flight of stairs, and called for Matsuko. Together we made the long and fascinating journey—from First Avenue to Twelfth Avenue—to Bailey Gatzert School. We always walked over the bridge on Fourth Avenue where we hung over the iron rails, waiting until a train roared past under us, enveloping us completely in its hissing, billowing cloud of white, warm steam. We meandered through the international section of town, past the small Japanese shops and stores, already bustling in the early morning hour, past the cafés and barber shops filled with Filipino men, and through Chinatown. Then finally we went up a gentle sloping hill to the handsome low-slung, red-brick building with its velvet green lawn and huge play yard. I felt like a princess walking through its bright, sunny corridors on smooth, shiny floors. I was mystified by a few of the little boys and girls. There were some pale-looking children who spoke a strange dialect of English, rapidly like gunfire. Matsuko told me they were "hagu-jins," white people. Then there were children who looked very much like me with their black hair and black eyes, but they spoke in high, musical singing voices. Matsuko whispered to me that they were Chinese.

And now Mother was telling us we were Japanese. I had always thought I was a Yankee, because after all I had been born on Occidental and Main Street. Montana, a wall-shaking mountain of a man who lived at our hotel, called me a Yankee. I didn't see how I could be a Yankee and Japanese at the same time. It was like being born with two heads. It sounded freakish and a lot of trouble. Above everything, I didn't want to go to Japanese school.

THE STUBBORN TWIG

The inevitable, dreaded first day at Nihon Gakko arrived. Henry and I were dumped into a taxicab, screaming and kicking against the injustice of it all. When the cab stopped in front of a large, square gray-frame building, Mother pried us loose, though we clung to the cab door like barnacles. She half carried us up the hill. We kept up our horrendous shrieking and wailing, right to the school entrance. Then a man burst out of the door. His face seemed to have been carved out of granite and with turned-down mouth and nostrils flaring with disapproval, his black marble eyes crushed us into a quivering silence. This was Mr. Ohashi, the school principal, who had come out to investigate the abominable, un-Japanesey noise on the school premises.

Mother bowed deeply and murmured, "I place them in your hands."

He bowed stiffly to Mother, then fastened his eyes on Henry and me and again bowed slowly and deliberately. In our haste to return the bow, we nodded our heads. With icy disdain, he snapped, "That is not an *ojigi*." He bent forward with well-oiled precision. "Bow from the waist, like this."

I wondered, if Mr. Ohashi had the nerve to criticize us in front of Mother, what more would he do in her absence.

School was already in session and the hallway was empty and cold. Mr. Ohashi walked briskly ahead, opened a door, and Henry was whisked inside with Mother. I caught a glimpse of little boys and girls sitting erect, their books held upright on their desks. . . .

I was ushered into a brightly lighted room which seemed ten times as brilliant with the dazzling battery of shining black eyes turned in my direction. I was introduced to Yasuda-sensei, a full-faced woman with a large, ballooning figure. She wore a long, shapeless cotton print smock with streaks of chalk powder down the front. She spoke kindly to me, but with a kindness that one usually reserves for a dull-witted child. She enunciated slowly and loudly, "What is your name?"

I whispered, "Kazuko," hoping she would lower her voice. I felt that our conversation should not be carried on in such a blatant manner.

"*Kazuko-san desuka?*" she repeated loudly. "You may sit over there." She pointed to an empty seat in the rear and I walked down an endless aisle between rows of piercing black eyes.

"Kazuko-san, why don't you remove your hat and coat and hang them up behind you?"

A wave of tittering broke out. With burning face, I rose from my seat and struggled out of my coat.

When Mother followed Mr. Ohashi out of the room, my throat began to tighten and tears flooded up again. I did not notice that Yasuda-sensei was standing beside me. Ignoring my snuffling, she handed me a book, opened to the first page. I saw a blurred drawing of one huge, staring eye. Right above it was a black squiggly mark, resembling the arabic figure one with a bar across the middle. Yasuda-sensei was up in front again, reading aloud, "*Meh!*" That was "eye." As we turned the pages, there were pictures of a long, austere nose, its print reading "*hana,*" an ear was called "*mi-mi,*" and a wide anemic-looking mouth, "*ku-chi.*" Soon I was chanting at the top of my voice with the rest of the class, "*Meh! Hana! Mi-Mi! Ku-chi!*"

Gradually I yielded to my double dose of schooling. Nihon Gakko was so different from grammar school I found myself switching my personality back and forth daily like a chameleon. At Bailey Gatzert School I was a jumping, screaming, roustabout Yankee, but at the stroke of three when the school bell rang and doors burst open everywhere, spewing out pupils like jelly beans from a broken bag, I suddenly became a modest, faltering, earnest little Japanese girl with a small, timid voice. I trudged down a steep hill and climbed up another steep hill to Nihon Gakko with other black-haired boys and girls. On the playground, we behaved cautiously. Whenever we spied a teacher within bowing distance, we hissed at each other to stop the game, put our feet neatly together, slid our hands down to our knees and bowed slowly and sanctimoniously. In just the proper, moderate tone, putting in every ounce of respect, we chanted, "*Konichi-wa, sensei.* Good day."

For an hour and a half each day, we were put through our paces. At the beginning of each class hour, Yasuda-sensei punched a little bell on her desk. We stood up by our seats, at strict attention. Another "ping!" We all bowed to her in unison while she returned the bow solemnly. With the third "ping!" we sat down together.

There was *yomi-kata* time when individual students were called upon to read the day's lesson, clear and loud. The first time I recited I stood and read with swelling pride the lesson which I had prepared the night before. I mouthed each word carefully and paused for the proper length of time at the end of each sentence. Suddenly Yasuda-sensei stopped me.

"Kazuko-san!"

I look up at her confused, wondering what mistakes I had made.

"You are holding your book in one hand," she accused me. Indeed, I was. I did not see the need of using two hands to support a thin book I could balance with two fingers.

"Use both hands!" she commanded me.

Then she peered at me. "And are you leaning against your desk?" Yes, I was, slightly. "Stand up straight!"

"*Hai!* Yes, ma'am!" . . .

As time went on, I began to suspect that there was much more to Nihon Gakko than learning the Japanese language. There was a driving spirit of strict discipline behind it all which reached out and weighed heavily upon each pupil's consciousness. That force emanated from the principal's office.

Before Mr. Ohashi came to America, he had been a zealous student of the Ogasawara Shiko Saho, a form of social conduct dreamed up by a Mr. Ogasawara. Mr. Ohashi himself had written a book on etiquette in Japan. He was the Oriental male counterpart of Emily Post. Thus Mr. Ohashi arrived in America with the perfect bow tucked under his waist and a facial expression cemented into perfect samurai control. He came with a smoldering ambition to pass on this knowledge to the tender Japanese saplings born on foreign soil. The school-teachers caught fire, too, and dedicated themselves to us with a vengeance. It was not enough to learn the language. We must talk and walk and sit and bow in the best Japanese tradition.

As far as I was concerned, Mr. Ohashi's superior standard boiled down to one thing. The model child is one with deep *rigor mortis*...no noise, no trouble, no back talk.

We understood too well what Mr. Ohashi wanted of us. He yearned and wished more than anything else that somehow he could mold all of us into Genji Yamadas. Genji was a classmate whom we detested thoroughly. He was born in Seattle, but his parents had sent him to Japan at an early age for a period of good, old-fashioned education. He returned home a stranger among us with stiff mannerisms and an arrogant attitude. . . .

. . . Every time Mr. Ohashi came into our room for a surprise visit to see if we were under control, he would stop at Genji's desk for a brief chat. Mr. Ohashi's eyes betrayed a glow of pride as he spoke to

Genji, who sat up erect, eyes staring respectfully ahead. All we could make out of the conversation was Genji's sharp staccato barks, *"Hai!... Hai!... Hai!"*

This was the response sublime to Mr. Ohashi. It was real man to man talk. Whenever Mr. Ohashi approached us, we froze in our seats. Instead of snapping into attention like Genji, we wilted and sagged. Mr. Ohashi said we were more like *"konyaku,"* a colorless, gelatinous Japanese food. If a boy fidgeted too nervously under Mr. Ohashi's stare, a vivid red stain rose from the back of Mr. Ohashi's neck until it reached his temple and then there was a sharp explosion like the crack of a whip. *"Keo-tsuke!* Attention!" It made us all leap in our seats, each one of us feeling terribly guilty for being such an inadequate Japanese.

I asked Mother, "Why is Mr. Ohashi so angry all the time? He always looks as if he had just bitten into a green persimmon. I've never seen him smile."

Mother said, "I guess Mr. Ohashi is the old-fashioned schoolmaster. I know he's strict, but he means well. Your father and I received harsher discipline than that in Japan...not only from schoolteachers, but from our own parents."

"Yes, I know, Mama." I leaned against her knees as she sat on the old leather davenport, mending our clothes. I thought Father and Mother were still wonderful, even if they had packed me off to Nihon Gakko. "Mrs. Matsui is so strict with her children, too. She thinks you spoil us." I giggled, and reassured her quickly, "But I don't think you spoil us at all."

Mrs. Matsui was ten years older than Mother, and had known Mother's father in Japan. Therefore she felt it was her duty to look after Mother's progress in this foreign country. . . .

Mrs. Matsui thought Mother's relationship with her children was chaotic. She clucked sympathetically at Mother, "Do they still call you, 'Mama' and 'Papa'?"

"Oh, yes," Mother smiled to hide her annoyance. "You know how it is. That's all they've ever heard around here. In fact, my husband and I have been corrupted, too. We call each other 'Mama' and 'Papa.' It just seems natural in our environment."

Mrs. Matsui drew herself up stiffly. "I taught my young ones to say 'Otoh-san' and 'Okah-san' from the very beginning."

"That's wonderful, Mrs. Matsui, but I'm afraid it's too late for us."

"Such a pity! You really ought to be more firm with them, too, Itoi-san. When I say 'no,' my children know I mean it. Whenever I feel they're getting out of hand, my husband and I take steps."

Mother looked interested.

"We give 'okyu' quite often." Mrs. Matsui folded her hands neatly together. Okyu was an old-country method of discipline, a painful and lasting punishment of applying a burning punk on a child's bare back. "Believe me, after okyu, we don't have trouble for a long, long time."

Henry, Kenji, Sumiko and I eyed each other nervously. We wished Mrs. Matsui would stop talking about such things to Mother.

Mr. Ohashi and Mrs. Matsui thought they could work on me and gradually mold me into an ideal Japanese ojoh-san, a refined young maiden who is quiet, pure in thought, polite, serene, and self-controlled. They made little headway, for I was too much the child of Skidrow. As far as I was concerned, Nihon Gakko was a total loss. I could not use my Japanese on the people at the hotel. Bowing was practical only at Nihon Gakko. If I were to bow to the hotel patrons, they would have laughed in my face. Therefore promptly at five-thirty every day, I shed Nihon Gakko and returned with relief to an environment which was the only real one to me. Life was too urgent, too exciting, too colorful for me to be sitting quietly in the parlor and contemplating a spray of chrysanthemums in a bowl as a cousin of mine might be doing in Osaka. . . .

WE ARE OUTCASTS

A gray gloom settled down over our family. Sumiko was ill. Always during the winter she had asthmatic attacks, but this particular winter was the worst. The little black kitten, Asthma, which Mrs. Matsui had given her because, she said, black cats could cure asthma, mewed all day long and rubbed its back against the bed. Almost every day Dr. Moon climbed the long flight of stairs and walked through the hotel without a glance at our rough-looking hotel guests who stared rudely at him. . . .

That evening Dr. Stimson came. We stood, gray-lipped, quietly waiting to hear the verdict. Dr. Stimson's eyes twinkled as he told us that Sumiko did not have tuberculosis. We cried with relief as we hugged Sumiko, swathed in a heavy flannel nightgown and smelling of camphor oil. Like a thin little sparrow burrowed deep in its nest, Sumiko cocked her Dutch-bobbed head at us and spoke carefully so as not to wheeze or cough. "I'm glad I don't have to go on that vacation!"

Dr. Stimson said Sumiko must have plenty of milk, rest and sunshine. So Father and Mother decided to rent a cottage by the sea for the summer. Father said, "Yes, we must do it this summer. We'll start looking right away for a suitable place near Alki Beach."

Early one day, Mother and I set out to Alki to find a cottage near the beach where we always picnicked. We found a gray house with a FOR RENT sign on its window, just a block from the beach. One side of the house was quilted with wild rambler roses and the sprawling green lawn was trim behind a white-painted picket fence. When I pressed the doorbell, musical chimes rang softly through the house. A middle-aged woman wearing a stiffly starched apron opened the door. "Yes, what can I do for you?" she asked, looking us over.

Mother smiled and said in her halting English, "You have nice house. We like to rent this summer." Mother paused, but the woman said nothing. Mother went on, "How much do you want for month?"

The woman wiped her hands deliberately on her white apron before she spoke, "Well, I'm asking fifty dollars, but I'm afraid you're a little too late. I just promised this place to another party."

"Oh," Mother said, disappointed. "That's too bad. I'm sorry. We like it so much."

I swallowed hard and pointed to the sign on the window. "You still have the sign up. We thought the house was still open."

"I just rented it this morning. I forgot to remove it. Sorry, I can't do anything for you," she said sharply.

Mother smiled at her, "Thank you just the same. Good-by." As we walked away, Mother said comfortingly to me, "Maybe we'll find something even nicer, Ka-chan. We have a lot of looking to do yet."

But we scoured the neighborhood with no success. Every time it was the same story. Either the rent was too much or the house was already taken. We had even inquired at a beautiful new brick apartment facing the beach boulevard, where several VACANCY signs had been propped against empty windows, but the caretaker told us unsmilingly that these apartments were all taken.

That night I went to bed with burning feet. From my darkened bedroom, I heard Mother talking to Father in the living room. "Yes, there were some nice places, but I don't think they wanted to rent to Japanese."

I sat bolt upright. That had not occurred to me. Surely Mother was mistaken. Why would it make any difference? I knew that Father and Mother were not Americans, as we were, because they were not born here, and that there was a law which said they could not become naturalized American citizens because they were Orientals. But being Oriental had never been an urgent problem to us, living in Skidrow.

A few days later, we went to Alki again. This time I carried in my purse a list of houses and apartments for rent which I had cut out from the newspaper. My hands trembled with a nervousness which had nothing to do with the pure excitement of house-hunting. I wished that I had not overheard Mother's remark to Father.

We walked briskly up to a quaint, white Cape Cod house. The door had a shiny brass knocker in the shape of a leaping dolphin. A carefully marcelled, blue-eyed woman, wearing a pince-nez on her sharp nose, hurried out. The woman blinked nervously and tapped her finger on the wall as she listened to Mother's words. She said dryly, "I'm sorry, but we don't want Japs around here," and closed the door. My face stiffened. It was like a sharp, stinging slap. Blunt as it was, I had wanted to hear the truth to wipe out the doubt in my mind. Mother took my hand and led me quickly away, looking straight ahead of her. After a while, she said quietly, "Ka-chan, there are people like that in this world. We have to bear it, just like all the other unpleasant facts of life. This is the first time for you, and I know how deeply it hurts; but when you are older, it won't hurt quite as much. You'll be stronger."

Trying to stop the flow of tears, I swallowed hard and blurted out, "But, Mama, is it so terrible to be a Japanese?"

"Hush, child, you mustn't talk like that." Mother spoke slowly and earnestly. "I want you, Henry, and Sumi-chan to learn to respect yourselves. Not because you're white, black or yellow, but because you're a human being. Never forget that. No matter what anyone may call you, to God you are still his child. Mah, it's getting warm. I think we had better stop here and get some refreshment before we go on."

I wiped my eyes and blew my nose hastily before I followed Mother into a small drugstore. There I ordered a towering special de luxe banana split, and promptly felt better.

The rest of the day we plodded doggedly through the list without any luck. They all turned us down politely. On our way home, Mother sat silent, while I brooded in the corner of the seat. All day I had been torn apart between feeling defiant and then apologetic about my Japanese blood. But when I recalled the woman's stinging words, I felt raw angry fire flash through my veins, and I simmered.

We found Sumiko sitting up in bed, waiting for us with an expectant smile. Mother swung her up into the air and said gaily, "We didn't find a thing we liked today. The houses were either too big or too small or too far from the beach, but we'll find our summer home yet! It takes time." I set my teeth and wondered if I would ever learn to be as cheerful as Mother.

Later in the evening, Mr. Kato dropped in. Father told him that we were looking for a cottage out at Alki and that so far we had had no luck. Mr. Kato scratched his head, "Yahhh, it's too bad your wife went to all that trouble. That district has been restricted for years. They've never rented or sold houses to Orientals and I doubt if they ever will."

My face burned with shame. Mother and I had walked from house to house, practically asking to be rebuffed. Our foolish summer dream was over.

Somehow word got around among our friends that we were still looking for a place for the summer. One evening, a Mrs. Saito called on the phone. She lived at the Camden Apartments. She said, "My landlady, Mrs. Olsen, says there is a small apartment in our building for rent. She is a wonderful person and has been kind to us all in the apartments, and we're practically all Japanese. You'd like it here."

Mother said to me afterwards, "See, Ka-chan, I told you, there are all kinds of people. Here is a women who doesn't object to Orientals."

The Camden Apartments was a modest, clean building in a quiet residential district uptown, quite far from Alki. . . .

The modest apartment on the top fourth floor was just large enough to accommodate Mother and Sumiko in the one bedroom while I occupied the sofa in the living room. Father and Henry, we decided, would stay at the hotel, but join us every evening for dinner. Marta assured us that by winter we would all be together in a larger apartment which would be vacated.

Of course, we were grateful for even this temporary arrangement, especially when we found the Olsens to be such warm, friendly folks. Marta and her husband were a middle-aged childless couple; but they apparently looked upon all the children living in the apartments as their own. . . .

That summer Sumiko and I pretended we were living in the turret of a castle tower. We made daily swimming trips to Lake Washington, surrounded by cool green trees and beautiful homes. But deep in our hearts we were still attached to Alki Beach. We kept comparing the mud-bottom lake and its mosquitoes to the sparkling salt water of Puget Sound, its clean, hot sands and its fiery sunsets. . . .

PEARL HARBOR ECHOES IN SEATTLE

On a peaceful Sunday morning, December 7, 1941, Henry, Sumi and I were at choir rehearsal singing ourselves hoarse in preparation for the annual Christmas recital of Handel's "Messiah." Suddenly Chuck Mizuno, a young University of Washington student, burst into the chapel, gasping as if he had sprinted all the way up the stairs.

"Listen, everybody!" he shouted. "Japan just bombed Pearl Harbor...in Hawaii! It's war!" . . .

A shocked silence followed. Henry came for Sumi and me. "Come on, let's go home," he said.

We ran trembling to our car. Usually Henry was a careful driver, but that morning he bore down savagely on the accelerator. Boiling angry, he shot us up Twelfth Avenue, rammed through the busy Jackson Street intersection, and rocketed up the Beacon Hill bridge. We swung violently around to the left of the Marine Hospital and swooped to the top of the hill. Then Henry slammed on the brakes and we rushed helter-skelter up to the house. . . .

Mother was sitting limp in the huge armchair as if she had collapsed there, listening dazedly to the turbulent radio. Her face was frozen still, and the only words she could utter were, "*Komatta neh, komatta neh.* How dreadful, how dreadful."

Henry put his arms around her. She told him she first heard about the attack on Pearl Harbor when one of her friends phoned her and told her to turn on the radio. . . .

Father rushed home from the hotel. He was deceptively calm as he joined us in the living room. Father was a born skeptic, and he believed nothing unless he could see, feel and smell it. He regarded all newspapers and radio news with deep suspicion. He shook his head doubtfully, "It must be propaganda. With the way things are going now between America and Japan, we should expect the most fantastic rumors, and this is one of the wildest I've heard yet." But we noticed that he was firmly glued to the radio. It seemed as if the regular Sunday programs, sounding off relentlessly hour after hour on schedule, were trying to blunt the catastrophe of the morning. . . .

Late that night Father got a shortwave broadcast from Japan. Static sputtered, then we caught a faint voice, speaking rapidly in Japanese. Father sat unmoving as a rock, his head cocked. The man was talking about the war between Japan and America. Father bit his lips and Mother whispered to him anxiously, "It's true then, isn't it, Papa? It's true?"

Father was muttering to himself, "So they really did it!" Now having heard the news in their native tongue, the war had become a reality to Father and Mother. . . .

Next morning the newspapers fairly exploded in our faces with stories about the Japanese raids on the chain of Pacific islands. We were shocked to read Attorney General Biddle's announcement that 736

Japanese had been picked up in the United States and Hawaii.[6] Then Mrs. Tanabe called Mother about her husband's arrest, and she said at least a hundred others had been taken from our community. Messrs. Okayama, Higashi, Sughira, Mori, Okada—we knew them all.

"But why were they arrested, Papa? They weren't spies, were they?"

Father replied almost curtly, "Of course not! They were probably taken for questioning."

The pressure of war moved in on our little community. The Chinese consul announced that all the Chinese would carry identification cards and wear "China" badges to distinguish them from the Japanese. Then I really felt left standing out in the cold. The government ordered the bank funds of all Japanese nationals frozen. Father could no longer handle financial transactions through his bank accounts, but Henry, fortunately, was of legal age so that business could be negotiated in his name. . . .

It made me positively hivey the way the FBI agents continued their raids into Japanese homes and business places and marched the Issei men away into the old red brick immigration building, systematically and efficiently, as if they were stocking a cellarful of choice bottles of wine. At first we noted that the men arrested were those who had been prominent in community affairs, like Mr. Kato, many times president of the Seattle Japanese Chamber of Commerce, and Mr. Ohashi, the principal of our Japanese language school, or individuals whose business was directly connected with firms in Japan; but as time went on, it became less and less apparent why the others were included in these raids.

We wondered when Father's time would come. We expected momentarily to hear strange footsteps on the porch and the sudden demanding ring of the front doorbell. Our ears became attuned like the sensitive antennas of moths, translating every soft swish of passing cars into the arrival of the FBI squad.

. . . Mrs. Matsui became an expert on the FBI, and she stood by us, rallying and coaching us on how to deal with them. She said to Mother, "You must destroy everything and anything Japanese which may incriminate your husband. It doesn't matter what it is, if it's printed or made in Japan, destroy it because the FBI always carries off those items for evidence."

6. In all, the FBI arrested and detained about 1,500 Japanese as "enemy aliens" in the aftermath of Pearl Harbor. See Roger Daniels, *Concentration Camps USA: Japanese Americans and World War II* (Hinsdale, Ill.: Dryden Press, 1971), p. 34.

In fact all the women whose husbands had been spirited away said the same thing. Gradually we became uncomfortable with our Japanese books, magazines, wall scrolls, and knickknacks. When Father's hotel friends, Messrs. Sakaguchi, Horiuchi, Nishibue and a few others vanished, and their wives called Mother weeping and warning her again about having too many Japanese objects around the house, we finally decided to get rid of some of ours. We knew it was impossible to destroy everything. The FBI would certainly think it strange if they found us sitting in a bare house, totally purged of things Japanese. But it was as if we could no longer stand the tension of waiting, and we just had to do something against the black day. We worked all night, feverishly combing through bookshelves, closets, drawers, and furtively creeping down to the basement furnace for the burning. I gathered together my well-worn Japanese language schoolbooks which I had been saving over a period of ten years with the thought that they might come in handy when I wanted to teach Japanese to my own children. I threw them into the fire and watched them flame and shrivel into black ashes. But when I came face to face with my Japanese doll which Grandmother Nagashima had sent me from Japan, I rebelled. It was a gorgeously costumed Miyazukai figure, typical of the lady in waiting who lived in the royal palace during the feudal era. The doll was gowned in an elegant purple silk kimono with the long, sweeping hemline of its period and sashed with rich-embroidered gold and silver brocade. With its black, shining coiffed head bent a little to one side, its delicate pink-tipped ivory hand holding a red lacquer message box, the doll had an appealing, almost human charm. I decided to ask Chris if she would keep it for me. Chris loved and appreciated beauty in every form and shape, and I knew that in her hands, the doll would be safe and enjoyed.

Henry pulled down from his bedroom wall the toy samurai sword he had brought from Japan and tossed it into the flames. Sumi's contributions to the furnace were books of fairy tales and magazines sent to her by her young cousins in Japan. We sorted out Japanese classic and popular music from a stack of records, shattered them over our knees and fed the pieces to the furnace. Father piled up his translated Japanese volumes of philosophy and religion and carted them reluctantly to the basement. Mother had the most to eliminate, with her scrapbooks of poems cut out from newspapers and magazines, and her private collection of old Japanese classic literature.

It was past midnight when we finally climbed upstairs to bed. Wearily we closed our eyes, filled with an indescribable sense of guilt for having destroyed the things we loved. This night of ravage was to haunt us for years. As I lay struggling to fall asleep, I realized that we hadn't freed ourselves at all from fear. We still lay stiff in our beds, waiting. . . .

Then a new menace appeared on the scene. Cries began to sound up and down the coast that everyone of Japanese ancestry should be taken into custody. For years the professional guardians of the Golden West had wanted to rid their land of the Yellow Peril, and the war provided an opportunity for them to push their program through. As the chain of Pacific islands fell to the Japanese, patriots shrieked for protection from us. A Californian sounded the alarm: "The Japanese are dangerous and they must leave. Remember the destruction and the sabotage perpetrated at Pearl Harbor. Notice how they have infiltrated into the harbor towns and taken our best land." . . .

In February, Executive Order No. 9066 came out, authorizing the War Department to remove the Japanese from such military areas as it saw fit, aliens and citizens alike. Even if a person had a fraction of Japanese blood in him, he must leave on demand.

A pall of gloom settled upon our home. We couldn't believe that the government meant that the Japanese-Americans must go, too. We had heard the clamoring of superpatriots who insisted loudly, "Throw the whole kaboodle out. A Jap's a Jap, no matter how you slice him. You can't make an American out of little Jap Junior just by handing him an American birth certificate." But we had dismissed these remarks as just hot blasts of air from an overheated patriot. We were quite sure that our rights as American citizens would not be violated, and we would not be marched out of our homes on the same basis as enemy aliens.

In anger, Henry and I read and reread the Executive Order. Henry crumpled the newspaper in his hand and threw it against the wall. "Doesn't my citizenship mean a single blessed thing to anyone? Why doesn't somebody make up my mind for me. First they want me in the army. Now they're going to slap an alien 4-C on me because of my ancestry. What the hell!"[7]

Once more I felt like a despised, pathetic two-headed freak, a Japanese and an American, neither of which seemed to be doing me any good. . . .

---

7. Henry is referring to a nondraftable classification with the U.S. Selective Service here. Eventually Japanese American young men (native-born who were American citizens) were permitted to volunteer for an all-Japanese-American combat unit that fought in Europe. Later the draft was extended to Japanese Americans. Daniels, *Concentration Camps USA*, pp. 123–29.

LIFE IN CAMP HARMONY

General DeWitt kept reminding us that E day, evacuation day, was drawing near. "E day will be announced in the very near future. If you have not wound up your affairs by now, it will soon be too late."

Father negotiated with Bentley Agent and Company to hire someone to manage his business. Years ago Father had signed a long-term lease with the owner of the building and the agent had no other alternative than to let Father keep control of his business until his time ran out. He was one of the fortunate few who would keep their businesses intact for the duration.

And Mother collected crates and cartons. She stayed up night after night, sorting, and re-sorting a lifetime's accumulation of garments, toys and household goods. Those were pleasant evenings when we rummaged around in old trunks and suitcases, reminiscing about the good old days, and almost forgetting why we were knee-deep in them. . . .

Henry went to the Control Station to register the family. He came home with twenty tags, all numbered "10710," tags to be attached to each piece of baggage, and one to hang from our coat lapels. From then on, we were known as Family #10710. . . .

The front doorbell rang. It was Dunks Oshima, who had offered to take us down to Eighth and Lane in a borrowed pickup truck. Hurriedly the menfolk loaded the truck with the last few boxes of household goods which Dunks was going to take down to the hotel. He held up a gallon can of soy sauce, puzzled, "Where does this go, to the hotel, too?"

Nobody seemed to know where it had come from or where it was going, until Mother finally spoke up guiltily, "Er, it's going with me. I didn't think we'd have shoyu where we're going."

Henry looked as if he were going to explode. "But Mama, you're not supposed to have more than one seabag and two suitcases. And of all things, you want to take with you—shoyu!"

I felt mortified. "Mama, people will laugh at us. We're not going on a picnic!"

But Mother stood her ground. "Nonsense. No one will ever notice this little thing. It isn't as if I were bringing liquor!" . . .

We climbed into the truck, chattering about the plucky little swallow. As we coasted down Beacon Hill bridge for the last time, we fell silent, and stared out at the delicately flushed morning sky of Puget Sound. We drove through bustling Chinatown, and in a few minutes arrived on the corner of Eighth and Lane. This area was ordinarily

lonely and deserted but now it was gradually filling up with silent, la-
beled Japanese, standing self-consciously among their seabags and
suitcases. . . .

Newspaper photographers with flash-bulb cameras pushed busily
through the crowd. One of them rushed up to our bus, and asked a
young couple and their little boy to step out and stand by the door for
a shot. They were reluctant, but the photographers were persistent
and at length they got out of the bus and posed, grinning widely to
cover their embarrassment. We saw the picture in the newspaper
shortly after and the caption underneath it read, "Japs good-natured
about evacuation."

Our bus quickly filled to capacity. All eyes were fixed up front, waiting. The guard stepped inside, sat by the door, and nodded curtly to
the gray-uniformed bus driver. The door closed with a low hiss. We
were now the Wartime Civil Control Administration's babies.[8] . . .

About noon we crept into a small town. Someone said, "Looks like
Puyallup, all right."[9] Parents of small children babbled excitedly,
"Stand up quickly and look over there. See all the chick-chicks and fat
little piggies?" One little city boy stared hard at the hogs and said
tersely, "They're *bachi*—dirty!"

Our bus idled a moment at the traffic signal and we noticed at the
left of us an entire block filled with neat rows of low shacks, resembling chicken houses. Someone commented on it with awe, "Just look
at those chicken houses. They sure go in for poultry in a big way
here." Slowly the bus made a left turn, drove through a wire-fenced
gate, and to our dismay, we were inside the oversized chicken farm.
The bus driver opened the door, the guard stepped out and stationed
himself at the door again. Jim, the young man who had shepherded us
into the busses, popped his head inside and sang out, "Okay, folks, all
off at Yokohama, Puyallup."

We stumbled out, stunned, dragging our bundles after us. It must
have rained hard the night before in Puyallup, for we sank ankle deep
into gray, gluttinous mud. The receptionist, a white man, instructed
us courteously, "Now, folks, please stay together as family units and
line up. You'll be assigned your apartment."

8. This was the agency formed within the army to handle evacuation and resettlement of
West Coast Japanese and Japanese Americans.

9. Puyallup was one of a number of West Coast assembly centers established at former
fairgrounds or race tracks to accommodate Japanese and Japanese Americans until more
permanent inland facilities were constructed. For a detailed description of another family's
experience at a similar assembly center, see John Modell, ed., *The Kikuchi Diary: Chronicle
from an American Concentration Camp* (Urbana: University of Illinois Press, 1973).

An internee and the baggage of several families at assembly center, Salinas, California, March 1942. (Courtesy of the Library of Congress)

We were standing in Area A, the mammoth parking lot of the state fairgrounds. There were three other separate areas, B, C and D, all built on the fair grounds proper, near the baseball field and the race tracks. This camp of army barracks was hopefully called Camp Harmony.

We were assigned to apartment 2-1-A, right across from the bachelor quarters. The apartments resembled enlongated, low stables about two blocks long. Our home was one room, about 18 by 20 feet, the size of a living room. There was one small window in the wall opposite the one door. It was bare except for a small, tinny wood-burning stove crouching in the center. The flooring consisted of two by fours laid directly on the earth, and dandelions were already pushing their way up through the cracks. Mother was delighted when she saw their shaggy yellow heads. "Don't anyone pick them. I'm going to cultivate them." . . .

Mother and Father wandered out to see what the other folks were doing and they found people wandering in the mud, wondering what other folks were doing. Mother returned shortly, her face lit up in an ecstatic smile, "We're in luck. The latrine is right nearby. We won't have to walk blocks."

We laughed, marveling at Mother who could be so poetic and yet so practical. Father came back, bent double like a woodcutter in a fairy tale, with stacks of scrap lumber over his shoulder. His coat and trouser pockets bulged with nails. Father dumped his loot in a corner and explained, "There was a pile of wood left by the carpenters and hundreds of nails scattered loose. Everybody was picking them up, and I hustled right in with them. Now maybe we can live in style with tables and chairs." . . .

We felt fortunate to be assigned to a room at the end of the barracks because we had just one neighbor to worry about. The partition wall separating the rooms was only seven feet high with an opening of four feet at the top, so at night, Mrs. Funai next door could tell when Sumi was still sitting up in bed in the dark, putting her hair up. "*Mah, Sumi-chan,*" Mrs. Funai would say through the plank wall, "are you curling your hair tonight again? Do you put it up every night?" Sumi would put her hands on her hips and glare defiantly at the wall. . . .

All through the night I heard people getting up, dragging cots around. I stared at our little window, unable to sleep. I was glad Mother had put up a makeshift curtain on the window for I noticed a powerful beam of light sweeping across it every few seconds. The lights came from high towers placed around the camp where guards with Tommy guns kept a twenty-four hour vigil. I remembered the

wire fence encircling us, and a knot of anger tightened in my breast.
What was I doing behind a fence like a criminal? If there were accu-
sations to be made, why hadn't I been given a fair trial? Maybe I
wasn't considered an American anymore. My citizenship wasn't real,
after all. Then what was I? I was certainly not a citizen of Japan as my
parents were. On second thought, even Father and Mother were
more alien residents of the United States than Japanese nationals for
they had little tie with their mother country. In their twenty-five years
in America, they had worked and paid their taxes to their adopted
government as any other citizen.

Of one thing I was sure. The wire fence was real. I no longer had
the right to walk out of it. It was because I had Japanese ancestors. It
was also because some people had little faith in the ideas and ideals of
democracy. They said that after all these were but words and could not
possibly insure loyalty. New laws and camps were surer devices. I finally buried my face in my pillow to wipe out burning thoughts and
snatch what sleep I could.

———

Kazuko Itoi and her family remained at Puyallup from May until
August, when they were transferred to the Minidoka relocation camp
in south central Idaho. After a year there, her older brother, Henry,
married his Seattle sweetheart (also a camp inmate).

War Relocation Authority regulations permitted Nisei to leave the
internment camps, provided they had jobs or attended college away
from the West Coast. Henry and his wife moved to St. Louis. Kazuko
was permitted to leave the camp and take work as a dental assistant in
suburban Chicago; shortly thereafter, she moved to Indiana, enrolling
in Wendell College. Finally, her younger sister, Sumi, volunteered for
the Cadet Nurses Corp, leaving only the Itoi parents interned at
Minidoka until the war's end.

NINE

Piri Thomas, Puerto Rican or Negro? Growing Up in East Harlem during World War II

*D*own These Mean Streets, portions of which are excerpted here, is the autobiography of Piri Thomas, a dark-skinned child of Puerto Ricans who grew up in the 1930s and 1940s in the streets of East Harlem, an ethnically mixed New York City neighborhood of Blacks, Puerto Ricans, and Italians. The memoir chronicles Thomas's search for a sense of identity and his descent into drugs and street crime. It ends with his release from prison and his first steps toward rehabilitation.

Thomas's story reveals the interconnections of race and ethnicity in American society. Wanting to be accepted as an American of Puerto Rican heritage, Thomas finds that people around him see nothing but his color. In one episode after another, a sometimes subtle, sometimes brutal racism meets him at every step. From a beating administered by a neighborhood Italian gang, to the racism of a high school classmate, to discrimination when he and a white friend search for jobs, Thomas cannot escape the consequences of his color.[1] Color differences among members of his family leave him questioning who he is and his own worth. He begins to accept the judgment that denies his worth in the broader society. His story is a moving tale of the pain and suffering inflicted by a racism that stymies his repeated attempts to assimilate into the broader American society. It reminds readers of the persisting barriers that American society has erected for immigrants of color and their descendants.

1. The last of these incidents is not included in the excerpt that follows. See *Down These Mean Streets* (New York: Alfred A. Knopf, 1967), chap. 11.

PUERTO RICAN PARADISE

Poppa didn't talk to me the next day. Soon he didn't talk much to anyone. He lost his night job—I forget why, and probably it was worth forgetting—and went back on home relief. It was 1941, and the Great Hunger called Depression was still down on Harlem.

But there was still the good old WPA.[2] If a man was poor enough, he could dig a ditch for the government. Now Poppa was poor enough again.

The weather turned cold one more time, and so did our apartment. In the summer the cooped-up apartments in Harlem seem to catch all the heat and improve on it. It's the same in the winter. The cold, plastered walls embrace that cold from outside and make it a part of the apartment, till you don't know whether it's better to freeze out in the snow or by the stove, where four jets, wide open, spout futile, blue-yellow flames. It's hard on the rats, too.

Snow was falling. "My *Cristo*," Momma said, "*qué frío*.[3] Doesn't that landlord have any *corazón*?[4] Why don't he give more heat?" I wondered how Pops was making out working a pick and shovel in that falling snow.

Momma picked up a hammer and began to beat the beat-up radiator that's copped a plea from so many beatings. Poor steam radiator, how could it give out heat when it was freezing itself? The hollow sounds Momma beat out of it brought echoes from other freezing people in the building. Everybody picked up the beat and it seemed a crazy, good idea. If everybody took turns beating on the radiators, everybody could keep warm from the exercise.

We drank hot cocoa and talked about summertime. Momma talked about Puerto Rico and how great it was, and how she'd like to go back one day, and how it was warm all the time there and no matter how poor you were over there, you could always live on green bananas, *bacalao*,[5] and rice and beans. "*Dios mío*,"[6] she said, "I don't think I'll ever see my island again."

"Sure you will, Mommie," said Miriam, my kid sister. She was eleven. "Tell us, tell us all about Porto Rico."

"It's not *Porto* Rico, it's *Puerto* Rico," said Momma.

---

2. WPA: Works Progress Administration, the New Deal agency that offered employment on public works projects during the Roosevelt Administration.

3. *Qué frío:* what cold.

4. *Corazón:* heart.

5. *Bacalao:* salt cod.

6. *Dios mío:* my God.

Card players in Spanish Harlem, circa 1946. (Courtesy of Victor Laredo)

"Tell us, Moms," said nine-year-old James, "about Puerto Rico."

"Yeah, Mommie," said six-year old José.

Even the baby, Paulie, smiled.

Moms copped that wet-eyed look and began to dream-talk about her *isla verde*, Moses' land of milk and honey.

"When I was a little girl," she said, "I remember the getting up in the morning and getting the water from the river and getting the wood for the fire and the quiet of the greenlands and the golden color of the morning sky, the grass wet from the *lluvia*[7]...Ai, Dios, the *coquís*[8] and the *pajaritos*[9] making all the *música*..."

"Mommie, were you poor?" asked Miriam.

"*Sí, muy pobre*,[10] but very happy. I remember the hard work and the very little bit we had, but it was a good little bit. It counted very much. Sometimes when you have too much, the good gets lost within and you have to look very hard. But when you have a little, then the good does not have to be looked for so hard."

"Moms," I asked, "did everybody love each other—I mean, like if everybody was worth something, not like if some weren't important because they were poor—you know what I mean?"

"*Bueno hijo*,[11] you have people everywhere who, because they have more, don't remember those who have very little. But in Puerto Rico those around you share *la pobreza*[12] with you and they love you, because only poor people can understand poor people. I like *los Estados Unidos*,[13] but it's sometimes a cold place to live—not because of the winter and the landlord not giving heat but because of the snow in the hearts of the people."

"Moms, didn't our people have any money or land?" I leaned forward, hoping to hear that my ancestors were noble princes born in Spain.

"Your grandmother and grandfather had a lot of land, but they lost that."

"How come, Moms?"

"Well, in those days there was nothing of what you call *contratos*,[14] and when you bought or sold something, it was on your word and a

---

7. *Lluvia:* rain.
8. *Coquís:* crickets.
9. *Pajaritos:* little birds.
10. *Muy pobre:* very poor.
11. *Bueno hijo:* good son.
12. *La pobreza:* poverty.
13. *Los Estados Unidos:* United States.
14. *Contratos:* contracts.

handshake, and that's the way your *abuelos*[15] bought their land and then lost it."

"Is that why we ain't got nuttin' now?" James asked pointedly.

"Oh, it—"

The door opened and put an end to the kitchen yak. It was Poppa coming home from work. He came into the kitchen and brought all the cold with him. Poor Poppa, he looked so lost in the clothes he had on. A jacket and coat, sweaters on top of sweaters, two pairs of long johns, two pairs of pants, two pairs of socks, and a woolen cap. And under all that he was cold. His eyes were cold; his ears were red with pain. He took off his gloves and his fingers were stiff with cold.

"*Cómo está?*"[16] said Momma. "I will make you coffee."

Poppa said nothing. His eyes were running hot frozen tears. He worked his fingers and rubbed his ears, and the pain made him make faces. "Get me some snow, Piri," he said finally.

I ran to the window, opened it, and scraped all the snow on the sill into one big snowball and brought it to him. We all watched in frozen wonder as Poppa took that snow and rubbed it on his ears and hands.

"Gee, Pops, don't it hurt?" I asked.

"*Sí,* but it's good for it. It hurts a little first, but it's good for the frozen parts."

I wondered why.

"How was it today?" Momma asked.

"Cold. My God, ice cold."

Gee, I thought, *I'm sorry for you, Pops. You gotta suffer like this.*

"It was not always like this," my father said to the cold walls. "It's all the fault of the damn depression."

"Don't say 'damn,' " Momma said.

"Lola, I say 'damn' because that's what it is—*damn.*"

And Momma kept quiet. She knew it was "damn."

My father kept talking to the walls. Some of the words came out loud, others stayed inside. I caught the inside ones—the damn WPA, the damn depression, the damn home relief, the damn poorness, the damn cold, the damn crummy apartments, the damn look on his damn kids, living so damn damned and his not being able to do a damn thing about it.

And Momma looked at Poppa and at us and thought about her Puerto Rico and maybe being there where you didn't have to wear a

15. *Abuelos:* grandparents.
16. *Cómo está:* how are you.

lot of extra clothes and feel so full of damns, and how when she was a little girl all the green was wet from the *lluvias.*

And Poppa looking at Momma and us, thinking how did he get trapped and why did he love us so much that he dug in damn snow to give us a piece of chance? And why couldn't he make it from home, maybe, and keep running?

And Miriam, James, José, Paulie, and me just looking and thinking about snowballs and Puerto Rico and summertime in the street and whether we were gonna live like this forever and not know enough to be sorry for ourselves. . . .

ALIEN TURF

Sometimes you don't fit in. Like if you're a Puerto Rican on an Italian block. After my new baby brother, Ricardo, died of some kind of germs, Poppa moved us from 111th Street to Italian turf on 114th Street between Second and Third Avenue. I guess Poppa wanted to get Momma away from the hard memories of the old pad.

I sure missed 111th Street, where everybody acted, walked, and talked like me. But on 114th Street everything went all right for a while. There were a few dirty looks from the spaghetti-an'-sauce cats, but no big sweat. Till that one day I was on my way home from school and almost had reached my stoop when someone called: "Hey, you dirty fuckin' spic."

The words hit my ears and almost made me curse Poppa at the same time. I turned around real slow and found my face pushing in the finger of an Italian kid about my age. He had five or six of his friends with him.

"Hey, you," he said. "What nationality are ya?"

I looked at him and wondered which nationality to pick. And one of his friends said, "Ah, Rocky, he's black enuff to be a nigger. Ain't that what you is, kid?"

My voice was almost shy in its anger. "I'm Puerto Rican," I said. "I was born here." I wanted to shout it, but it came out like a whisper.

"Right here inna street?" Rocky sneered. "Ya mean right here inna middle of da street?"

They all laughed.

I hated them. I shook my head slowly from side to side. "Uh-uh," I said softly. "I was born inna hospital—inna bed."

"Umm, *paisan*—born inna bed," Rocky said.

I didn't like Rocky Italiano's voice. "Inna hospital," I whispered, and all the time my eyes were trying to cut down the long distance from this trouble to my stoop. But it was no good; I was hemmed in by Rocky's friends. I couldn't help thinking about kids getting wasted for moving into a block belonging to other people.

"What hospital, *paisan?*" Bad Rocky pushed.

"Harlem Hospital," I answered, wishing like all hell that it was 5 o'clock instead of just 3 o'clock, 'cause Poppa came home at 5. I looked around for some friendly faces belonging to grown-up people, but the elders were all busy yakking away in Italian. I couldn't help thinking how much like Spanish it sounded. Shit, that should make us something like relatives.

"Harlem Hospital?" said a voice. "I knew he was a nigger."

"Yeah," said another voice from an expert on color. "That's the hospital where all them black bastards get born at."

I dug three Italian elders looking at us from across the street, and I felt saved. But that went out the window when they just smiled and went on talking. I couldn't decide whether they had smiled because this new whatever-he-was was gonna get his ass kicked or because they were pleased that their kids were welcoming a new kid to their country. An older man nodded his head at Rocky, who smiled back. I wondered if that was a signal for my funeral to begin.

"Ain't that right, kid?" Rocky pressed. "Ain't that where all black people get born?"

I dug some of Rocky's boys grinding and pushing and punching closed fists against open hands. I figured they were looking to shake me up, so I straightened up my humble voice and made like proud. "There's all kinds of people born there. Colored people, Puerto Ricans like me, an'—even spaghetti-benders like you."

"That's a dirty fuckin' lie"—*bash*, I felt Rocky's fist smack into my mouth—"you dirty fuckin' spic."

I got dizzy and more dizzy when fists started to fly from everywhere and only toward me. I swung back, *splat, bish*—my fist hit some face and I wished I hadn't, 'cause then I started getting kicked.

I heard people yelling in Italian and English and I wondered if maybe it was 'cause I hadn't fought fair in having hit that one guy. But it wasn't. The voices were trying to help me.

"Whas'sa matta, you no-good kids, leeva da kid alone," a man said. I looked through a swelling eye and dug some Italians pushing their kids off me with slaps. One even kicked a kid in the ass. I could have loved them if I didn't hate them so fuckin' much.

"You all right, kiddo?" asked the man.

"Where you live, boy?" said another one.

"Is the *bambino* hurt?" asked a woman.

I didn't look at any of them. I felt dizzy. I didn't want to open my mouth to talk, 'cause I was fighting to keep from puking up. I just hoped my face was cool-looking. I walked away from that group of strangers. I reached my stoop and started to climb the steps.

"Hey, spic," came a shout from across the street. I started to turn to the voice and changed my mind. "Spic" wasn't my name. I knew that voice, though. It was Rocky's. "We'll see ya again, spic," he said.

I wanted to do something tough, like spitting in their direction. But you gotta have spit in your mouth in order to spit, and my mouth was hurt dry. I just stood there with my back to them.

"Hey, your old man just better be the janitor in that fuckin' building."

Another voice added, "Hey, you got any pretty sisters? We might let ya stay onna block."

Another voice mocked, "Aw, fer Chrissake, where ya ever hear of one of them black broads being pretty?"

I heard the laughter. I turned around and looked at them. Rocky made some kind of dirty sign by putting his left hand in the crook of his right arm while twisting his closed fist in the air.

Another voice said, "Fuck it, we'll just cover the bitch's face with the flag an' fuck er for old glory."

All I could think of was how I'd like to kill each of them two or three times. I found some spit in my mouth and splattered it in their direction and went inside.

Momma was cooking, and the smell of rice and beans was beating the smell of Parmesan cheese from the other apartments. I let myself into our new pad. I tried to walk fast past Momma so I could wash up, but she saw me.

"My God, Piri, what happened?" she cried.

"Just a little fight in school, Momma. You know how it is, Momma, I'm new in school an'..." I made myself laugh. Then I made myself say, "But Moms, I whipped the living—outta two guys, an' one was bigger'n me."

"*Bendito*,[17] Piri, I raise this family in Christian way. Not to fight. Christ says to turn the other cheek."

"Sure, Momma." I smiled and went and showered, feeling sore at Poppa for bringing us into spaghetti country. I felt my face with easy

17. *Bendito:* blessing.

fingers and thought about all the running back and forth from school that was in store for me.

I sat down to dinner and listened to Momma talk about Christian living without really hearing her. All I could think of was that I hadda go out in that street again. I made up my mind to go out right after I finished eating. I had to, shook up or not; cats like me had to show heart.

"Be back, Moms," I said after dinner, "I'm going out on the stoop." I got halfway to the stoop and turned and went back to our apartment. I knocked.

"Who is it?" Momma asked.

"Me, Momma."

She opened the door. "*Qué pasa?*"[18] she asked.

"Nothing, Momma, I just forgot something," I said. I went into the bedroom and fiddled around and finally copped a funny book and walked out the door again. But this time I made sure the switch on the lock was open, just in case I had to get back real quick. I walked out on that stoop as cool as could be, feeling braver with the lock open.

There was no sign of Rocky and his killers. After awhile I saw Poppa coming down the street. He walked like beat tired. Poppa hated his pick-and-shovel job with the WPA. He couldn't even hear the name WPA without getting a fever. *Funny,* I thought, *Poppa's the same like me, a stone Puerto Rican, and nobody in this block even pays him a mind. Maybe older people get along better'n us kids.*

Poppa was climbing the stoop. "Hi, Poppa," I said.

"How's it going, son? Hey, you sure look a little lumped up. What happened?"

I looked at Poppa and started to talk it outta me all at once and stopped, 'cause I heard my voice start to sound scared, and that was no good.

"Slow down, son," Poppa said. "Take it easy." He sat down on the stoop and made a motion for me to do the same. He listened and I talked. I gained confidence. I went from a tone of being shook up by the Italians to a tone of being a better fighter than Joe Louis and Pedro Montanez lumped together, with Kid Chocolate thrown in for extra.

"So that's what happened," I concluded. "And it looks like only the beginning. Man, I ain't scared, Poppa, but like there's nothin' but Italianos on this block and there's no me's like me except me an' our family."

18. *Qué pasa:* what's the matter.

Poppa looked tight. He shook his head from side to side and mumbled something about another Puerto Rican family that lived a coupla doors down from us.

I thought, *What good would that do me, unless they prayed over my dead body in Spanish?* But I said, "Man! That's great. Before ya know it, there'll be a whole bunch of us moving in, huh?"

Poppa grunted something and got up. "Staying out here, son?"

"Yeah, Poppa, for a little while longer."

From that day on I grew eyes all over my head. Anytime I hit that street for anything, I looked straight ahead, behind me and from side to side all at the same time. Sometimes I ran into Rocky and his boys—that cat was never without his boys—but they never made a move to snag me. They just grinned at me like a bunch of hungry alley cats that could get to their mouse anytime they wanted. . . .

BABYLON FOR THE BABYLONIANS

In 1944 we moved to Long Island. Poppa was making good money at the airplane factory, and he had saved enough bread for a down payment on a small house.

As we got our belongings ready for the moving van, I stood by watching all the hustling with a mean feeling. My hands weren't with it; my fingers played with the top of a cardboard box full of dishes. My face tried hard not to show resentment at Poppa's decision to leave my streets forever. I felt that I belonged in Harlem; it was my kind of kick. I didn't want to move out to Long Island. My friend Crutch had told me there were a lot of paddies[19] out there, and they didn't dig Negroes or Puerto Ricans.

"Piri," Momma said.

"Yeah, Moms." I looked up at Momma. She seemed tired and beat. Still thinking about Paulie all the time and how she took him to the hospital just to get some simple-assed tonsils out. And Paulie died. I remember she used to keep repeating how Paulie kept crying, "Don't leave me, Mommie," and her saying, "Don't worry, *nene*, it's just for a day." Paulie—I pushed his name out of my mind.

"*Dios mío,* help a little, *hijo*," Momma said.

"Moms, why do we gotta move outta Harlem? We don't know any other place better'n this."

---

19. *Paddies:* white people.

"*Caramba!*[20] What ideas," Momma said. "What for you talk like that? Your Poppa and I saved enough money. We want you kids to have good opportunities. It is a better life in the country. No like Puerto Rico, but it have trees and grass and nice schools."

"Yeah, Moms. Have they got Puerto Ricans out there?"

"*Si,* I'm sure, Señora Rodriguez an' her family, an' Otelia—remember her? She lived upstairs."

"I mean a lotta *Latinos,* Moms. Like here in the *Barrio.*[21] And how about *morenos?*"[22]

"*Muchacho,*[23] they got all kind." Momma laughed. "Fat and skinny, big and little. And—"

"Okay, Momma," I said. "You win. Give me a kiss."

So we moved to Babylon, a suburb on the south shore of Long Island. Momma was right about the grass and trees. And the school, too, was nice-looking. The desks were new, not all copped up like the ones in Harlem, and the teachers were kind of friendly and not so tough-looking as those in Patrick Henry.

I made some kind of friends with some paddy boys. I even tried out for the school baseball team. There were a lot of paddy boys and girls watching the tryouts and I felt like I was the only one trying out. I dropped a fly ball in the outfield to cries of "Get a basket," but at bat I shut everybody out of my mind and took a swing at the ball with all I had behind it and hit a home run. I heard the cheers and made believe I hadn't.

I played my role to the most, and the weeks turned into months. I still missed Harlem, but I didn't see it for six months. *Maybe,* I thought, *this squeeze livin' ain't as bad as Crutch said.* I decided to try the lunchtime swing session in the school gym. The Italian paddy, Angelo, had said they had hot music there. I dug the two-cents admission fee out of my pocket and made it up the walk that led to the gym.

"Two cents, please," said a little *muchacha blanca.*

"Here you are."

"Thank you," she smiled.

I returned her smile. Shit, man, Crutch was wrong.

The gym was whaling. The music was on wax, and it was a mambo. I let myself react. It felt good to give in to the natural rhythm. Maybe there were other worlds besides the mean streets, I thought. I looked

---

20. *Caramba:* damn it.
21. *Barrio:* colloquial term for Spanish Harlem where Piri Thomas had grown up.
22. *Morenos:* dark-skinned ones.
23. *Muchacho:* boy.

around the big gym and saw some of the kids I knew a little. Some of them waved; I waved back. I noticed most of the paddy kids were dancing the mambo like stiff. Then I saw a girl I had heard called Marcia or something by the other kids. She was a pretty, well-stacked girl, with black hair and a white softness which set her hair off pretty cool. I walked over to her. "Hi," I said.

"Huh? Oh, hi."

"My first time here."

"But I've seen you before. You got Mrs. Sutton for English."

"Yeah, that's right. I meant this is my first time to the gym dance."

"I also was at the field when you smashed that ball a mile."

"That was *suerte*," I said.

"What's that?" she asked.

"What?"

"What you said—'swear-tay.' "

I laughed. "Man, that's Spanish."

"Are you Spanish? I didn't know. I mean, you don't look like what I thought a Spaniard looks like."

"I ain't a Spaniard from Spain," I explained. "I'm a Puerto Rican from Harlem."

"Oh—you talk English very well," she said.

"I told you I was born in Harlem. That's why I ain't got no Spanish accent."

"No-o, your accent is more like Jerry's."

What's she tryin' to put down?" I wondered. Jerry was the colored kid who recently had moved to Bayshore.

"Did you know Jerry?" she asked. "Probably you didn't get to meet him. I heard he moved away somewhere."

"Yeah, I know Jerry," I said softly. "He moved away because he got some girl in trouble. I know Jerry is colored and I know I got his accent. Most of us in Harlem steal from each other's language or style or stick of living. And it's *suerte*, s-u-e-r-t-e. It means 'luck.' " *Jesus, Crutch, you got my mind messed up a little. I keep thinking this broad's trying' to tell me something shitty in a nice dirty way. I'm gonna find out.* "Your name is Marcia or something like that, eh?" I added.

"Ahuh."

"Mine's Piri. Wanna dance?"

"Well, this one is almost over."

"Next one?"

"Well, er—I, er—well, the truth is that my boyfriend is sort of jealous and—well, you know how—"

I looked at her and she was smiling. I said, "Jesus, I'm sorry. Sure, I know how it is. Man, I'd feel the same way."

She smiled and shrugged her shoulders pretty-like. I wanted to believe her. I did believe her. I had to believe her. "Some other time, eh?"

She smiled again, cocked her head to one side and crinkled her nose in answer.

"Well, take it easy," I said. "See you around."

She smiled again, and I walked away not liking what I was feeling, and thinking that Crutch was right. I fought against it. I told myself I was still feeling out of place here in the middle of all these strangers, that paddies weren't as bad as we made them out to be. I looked over my shoulder and saw Marcia looking at me funny-like. When she saw me looking, her face changed real fast. She smiled again. I smiled back. I felt like I was plucking a mental daisy:

> You're right, Crutch
> You're wrong, Crutch
> You're right, Crutch
> You're wrong, Crutch.

I wanted to get outside and cop some sun and I walked toward the door.

"Hi, Piri," Angelo called. "Where you going? It's just starting."

"Aw, it's a little stuffy," I lied. "Figured on making it over to El Viejo's—I mean, over to the soda fountain on Main Street."

"You mean the Greek's?"

"Yeah, that's the place."

"Wait a sec till I take a leak and I'll go over with you."

I nodded okay and followed Angelo to the john. I waited outside for him and watched the kids dancing. My feet tapped out time and I moved closer to the gym and I was almost inside again. Suddenly, over the steady beat of the music, I heard Marcia say, "Imagine the nerve of that black thing."

"Who?" someone asked.

"That new colored boy," said another voice.

They must have been standing just inside the gym. I couldn't see them, but I had that for-sure feeling that it was me they had in their mouths.

"Let's go, Piri," Angelo said. I barely heard him. "Hey fella," he said, "what's the matter?"

"Listen, Angelo. Jus' listen," I said stonily.

"...do you mean just like that?" one of the kids asked.

"Ahuh," Marcia said. "Just as if I was a black girl. *Well!* He started to talk to me and what could I do except be polite and at the same time not encourage him?"

"Christ, first that Jerry bastard and now him. We're getting invaded by niggers," said a thin voice.

"You said it," said another guy. "They got some nerve. My dad says that you give them an inch them apes want to take a yard."

"He's not so bad," said a shy, timid voice. "He's a polite guy and seems to be a good athlete. And besides, I hear he's a Puerto Rican."

"Ha—he's probably passing for Puerto Rican because he can't make it for white." said the thin voice. "Ha, ha, ha."

I stood there thinking who I should hit first. *Marcia. I think I'll bust her jaw first.*

"Let's go, Piri," Angelo said. "Those creeps are so fuckin' snooty that nobody is good enough for them. Especially that bitch Marcia. Her and her clique think they got gold-plated assholes."

"...no, *really!*" a girl was saying. "I heard he's a Puerto Rican, and they're not like Neg—"

"There's no difference," said the thin voice. "He's still black."

"Come on, Piri, let's go," Angelo said. "Don't pay no mind to them."

"I guess he thought he was another Jerry," someone said.

"He really asked me to dance with him," Marcia said indignantly. "I told him that my boyfriend..."

The rest of the mean sounds faded as I made it out into the sun. I walked faster and faster. I cut across the baseball field, then ran as fast as I could. I wanted to get away from the things running to mind. My lungs were hurting—not from running but from not being able to scream. After a while I sat down and looked up at the sky. How near it seemed. I heard a voice: "Piri! Holy hell, you tore up the ground running." I looked up and saw Angelo. He was huffing and out of wind. "Listen, you shouldn't let them get you down," he said, kneeling next to me. "I know how you feel."

I said to him very nicely and politely, "Do me a favor, you motherfuckin' paddy, get back with your people. I don't know why the fuck you're here, unless it's to ease your—oh, man, just get the fuck outta here. I hate them. I hate you. I hate all you white motherjumps."

"I'm sorry, Piri."

"Yeah, *blanco*[24] boy, I know. You know how I feel, ain't that right? Go on, paddy, make it."

24. *Blanco:* white.

Angelo shook his head and slowly got up. He looked at me for a second, then walked away. I dug the sky again and said to it, "I ain't ever goin' back to that fuckin' school. They can shove it up their asses." I plucked the last mental daisy: *You was right, Crutch.*

TEN

The Nguyen Family: From Vietnam to Chicago, 1975–1986

With the fall of Saigon in 1975, the evacuation of the U.S. military, and the reunification of Vietnam under Communist rule, a new wave of Southeast Asian migration began. By 1990, 2 million Asian refugees had uprooted themselves. Almost a million of them came to the United States; another half million remained in refugee camps in Thailand, Malaysia, Singapore, and Hong Kong, awaiting resettlement or repatriation.[1] Coupled with renewed Chinese, Korean, and Filipino migration, these newcomers have made Asian Americans the fastest growing ethnic group in the United States today.[2]

Among the first emigrants who left South Vietnam with departing U.S. troops in 1975 was the family of Trong and Thanh Nguyen, who eventually settled in the "Uptown" neighborhood of Chicago and were interviewed by Al Santoli in 1989. Their experience as refugees was more unsettling than that of others who emigrated with more advance planning. Still, their path was far smoother than that of Vietnamese who escaped by boat five or ten years later and spent lengthy periods in refugee holding camps before gaining admission to the United States.

At the time of the following interview, the Nguyen family had resided in Chicago for ten years. The parents had made considerable accommodation to the demands of the broader American society. Trong Nguyen worked as a social worker for Travelers and Immigrants Aid, helping more recent immigrants adjust to their new lives. The family had recently opened up a restaurant, which drew on the labor

---

1. John Tenhula, *Voices from Southeast Asia: The Refugee Experience in the United States* (New York: Holmes and Meier, 1991), pp. 1–2, 83, 234–35.

2. "Immigration Brings New Diversity to Asian Population in the U.S.," *New York Times,* June 12, 1991.

of parents and children alike. The interview focuses principally on Trong Nguyen but includes comments by his wife, Thanh; their nineteen-year-old son, Tran; and their fourteen-year-old daughter, Thahn Tram. In the differing perspectives of parents and children, we gain a sense of the diversity of the Vietnamese immigrant experience in contemporary America. We sense as well strong links between the history of one immigrant family in the United States today and the experiences of earlier immigrants, such as the Hollingworths, the Gollups, and Itois, whose stories we have already read in this collection.

TRONG: I have always believed that, if you just stay home and do nothing you are not a person whom others will respect. Since I came to Chicago in 1976, I've been involved in building the Vietnamese community. Of the twelve thousand Vietnamese who live in this city, more than half live in a fourteen-block area around the Argyle Street business strip, between Broadway and Sheridan roads.

Uptown is called the Ellis Island of Chicago. Some thirty languages are spoken in the area. Besides the Vietnamese, there are a thousand Cambodians, two hundred Laotians, and some Hmong. But most of the people are American blacks, Appalachian whites who came from the coal mines of Kentucky and West Virginia, Mexicans, and some American Indians.

In 1975, when the refugees first began arriving, the area was a dumping ground for derelicts, mental patients, and everyone else the city didn't want. Drug addicts, gangs, and prostitutes hung out in abandoned buildings owned by absentee landlords. Some refugee families with children live in transient hotels alongside winos. Large multistory housing projects like on the corner of Argyle and Sheridan were very dangerous. Refugees were constantly robbed and beaten.

The Argyle Street business strip had only a few struggling businesses, like small Chinese restaurants, a mom-and-pop bakery, and a tavern with naked dancers. Most storefronts were empty, with a lot of threatening people on the street.

When my wife and I came to Chicago, our major concern was to feed our five small children. We had Vietnamese pride and did not want to take public aid. We wanted the American community and authorities to respect us.

In Uptown, we felt like we were thrust from one war zone to another. Local community organizations strongly opposed the refugees. People talked about a "Yellow Horde invasion." They started a lawsuit

Little Saigon in Chicago's Uptown. (Courtesy of Al Santoli)

campaign against the city for bringing Indochinese into their area. They said, "Because the refugees are moving in, rents are going higher."

The absentee landlords in the neighborhood were horrible. The [community] organizations had started a boycott against them before the refugees arrived. This created a lot of vacancies in some of the run-down buildings. The voluntary agencies who sponsored the refugees saw the cheap rents and placed refugee families in those apartments. That allowed slumlords to stay in business.

At the height of the tension, the city brought the community associations, some refugee leaders, and voluntary agency representatives into a room to talk. Commander Howard Patinkin of the police department moderated the session, because it was getting to the point of violence. At the meeting, the community groups realized that the refugees were good people, and an agreement was made for the voluntary agencies to coordinate with local residents.

Just trying to begin a new life here, we had so many difficulties. When I worked as a janitor at Water Tower Place, a co-worker told me, "Trong, do you know that America is overpopulated? We have more than two hundred million people. We don't need you. Go back where you belong." I was shocked to hear people trying to chase us out. I thought, "Who is going to feed the children?" In America, a single income can never feed the family. Even though our youngest was just a baby, my wife had to find work.

THANH: When we first came to Chicago, I cried a lot. In the factory where I worked, there weren't many Americans. Most were Mexicans, some legal, but also many illegal aliens. They acted like, as Vietnamese say, "Old ghosts bully new ghosts." They cursed our people.

Some Mexicans said, "You come here and take our jobs. Go back wherever you came from." I was very upset and cried. They said so many things. Then one day some of them said, "You come here to make money, then go back home and live like kings." That was too much. I couldn't hold it in any more.

I told them in a very soft voice, "We are Vietnamese people. You don't have enough education to know where our country is. Vietnam is a small country, but we did not come to America to look for jobs. We're political refugees. We can't go back home." I didn't call them bad names or anything, but I said, "You are the ones who come here to make money to bring back to your country. We spend our money here." After that, they didn't bother us very much.

TRONG: In 1978, just before the boat-people crisis began, I found a job as a caseworker with Travelers and Immigrants Aid. My goal was to help those in need. After seven years in that job, when the Vietnamese community had become stabilized, I decided to open a restaurant. For my wife, working in a factory was such a heavy job. She tried so hard to stay with that type of work to help feed our family, but she was laid off on different occasions. When friends sometimes came to our home, they enjoyed my wife's cooking. They said, "Maybe one day open a restaurant, so we can eat your cooking more often."

They were joking, but it gave us the idea to open our own business. In June 1985, we opened this restaurant. We named it Song Huong, after the Perfume River in my home area of central Vietnam.

As a social worker, I've never made much money. I didn't qualify to borrow from the bank. To open the restaurant, we had to borrow from friends. To keep our operating expenses down, my son and two oldest daughters help out. I know that isn't professional in terms of building a reputation for a good restaurant, but we have no other choice.

My life here has been working for the community. I never thought about making a lot of money for my own use. Sometimes my wife says, "It seems that you care more about the community than your own family."

My children here are my nineteen-year-old son and my fifteen-, fourteen-, twelve-, and eleven-year-old daughters. Sometimes the children have expressed disappointment that I'm not home very often. I explain to them that when you have a bowl of rice, no matter how small, you have to think about those people who don't have any rice to eat.

In Vietnam, I was involved in social activity since I was sixteen years old. As a student in Saigon, I saw many war victims, especially children in orphanages, who were abandoned by society. So I organized a group of students to visit the orphans. The girls in our group gave the little ones a bath and took care of their clothes. The boys played with the kids and contributed our pocket money to buy them milk, candy, and toys. We wanted to give these kids at least a short period of happiness.

My father was a soldier from the time I was born, in 1940. He was recruited by the anti-Japanese resistance to go to England for military training. He was then sent to China on a secret mission. In Kunming, which was the headquarters of the Free Chinese fighting against the Japanese occupation, he met my future father-in-law, Vu Van Bach, who had been a revolutionary leader in northern Vietnam since the 1920s.

As a member of the non-Communist Vietnam Quoc Dan Dang [VNQDD] he was imprisoned by the French for taking part in the Yen

Bay uprising in 1929. That event is known as the beginning of Vietnam's modern struggle for independence. When he was released from prison, he went to China to work on the railroad. In Kunming in 1942, he learned that the Allied army was trying to recruit Vietnamese to go back home to fight the Japanese.

Bach saw an Asian soldier in a British uniform. Bach addressed him in Chinese. The soldier said, "I am Vietnamese, I don't speak Chinese," and they became like brothers. The man in uniform was my father. The Vietnamese group was moved by the British from China to Calcutta, India, for training. I believe it was funded by the American OSS. At the same time, the OSS also set up a secret zone in China to train Ho Chi Minh's Communist forces.

My father had had no idea I was born. When he left Vietnam at the outset of the war, he and my mother were just married. She hadn't yet realized that she was pregnant. During the war, they lost contact. When I was two or three years old, my father parachuted into Laos as part of a twelve-man reconnaissance team to scout Japanese positions. The Vietnamese Liberation Forces working out of Calcutta were like the Special Forces. They did many secret missions for the Allies.

Somebody told my mother that my father was in Laos. She left me with my grandparents and went to search for her husband. Unfortunately, my father's mission was to march through Laos into Burma. He never found out about my mother's trip, and, in the chaos of the war, she disappeared.

In 1945, the Allies appointed Chinese General Lu Han to oversee the Japanese surrender in northern Vietnam, while the British went into southern Vietnam. While Ho Chi Minh took power in Hanoi, my father, Mr. Bach, and other non-Communist resistance leaders came back to Saigon. But the British dissolved the Liberation Army. And, the final blow, the British invited the French colonialists back.

In Hue, my home area, Emperor Bao Dai began to build an army. My father knew how Ho Chi Minh had betrayed and assassinated many nationalist leaders, so he accepted an invitation to join this new army. His idea was first to defeat the Communists and then drive out the French.

When my father came back to Hue, my mother was still missing. I was living like an orphan with my mother's parents in the countryside. It was an area where my father sometimes fought. But he did not know that I existed until I was nine years old. In November 1949, during an operation against the Communists, my father found me.

My father brought me to Hue, where I lived with his new wife and began going to school. And in 1950, when my father was transferred to Saigon, I went with him. We finally found my real mother in 1955.

She had been living in Laos, remarried with a couple of children. I continued living with my stepmother and her parents in Saigon. I spent most of my time studying.

When the French prepared to leave Vietnam in 1954, my father, a lieutenant colonel, gave a lot of help to the emerging leader of South Vietnam, Ngo Dinh Diem. He helped to protect Diem from both the Communists and French loyalists. After Diem became chief of state, my father was loyal to him. . . .

The political climate in South Vietnam was very unstable, with many rival personalities and factions competing for power. And in 1959, the Communists organized a Liberation Front. . . . When I graduated from high school in 1962, the Viet Cong had already stepped up military activities. Because of the growing war, I knew that sooner or later I would be drafted. So I decided to join the army.

I graduated from the Military Academy at Thu Duc in November 1963. . . .

At the end of 1965, I was transferred to the 81st Airborne Ranger Battalion, based in Nha Trang. We were moved anywhere in the country where there was serious trouble. . . .

Nineteen sixty-six was also the year that my wife, Thanh, and I were married. We had been good friends since childhood, like brother and sister, because our fathers were so close. When our parents decided that marriage would be a good thing for us, we obeyed. But immediately after the wedding, my Ranger battalion was again continually sent on missions anywhere the Allied Command decided was urgent. . . .

In late 1968, after attending Officer Leadership and Pathfinder training in the United States, I became very sick with an enlarged heart. I took a less physically demanding position as aide-de-camp to General Lam Son, the head of special forces. But my health got worse. In January 1970, I was medically discharged from the army. I returned to Nha Trang.

My wife was happy to have me home. But I felt torn, because I liked military life. Our two sons were three and four years old. To support the family, we opened a bakery at Cam Ranh Bay, near the sea.

Our business did well. I did the baking at night, and my wife ran the shop during the day. But I weakened from working long hours and continued to suffer from my illness. So my doctor advised me to stop. We had to close the bakery at the end of 1971.

A friend came to see me and said, "I understand you have a lot of time on your hands. There is a new military team called Special Missions Advisory Group that is recruiting former Special Forces." I became the head translator for the Americans who trained the group.

After the year of training, they were moved to Da Nang. I didn't want to be separated from my family, so I took a job with the province administration in Nha Trang.

I was made the community-development officer. My responsibility was to visit villages to study the needs of the people. Then I would make a report and suggest a budget to USAID to assist local self-help projects. After a year, I was promoted to the regional office. Then USAID hired me as a livestock specialist and in 1973–74 I became an agricultural-program manager. We introduced strong new strains of rice that were being developed in the Philippines and Thailand.

Our area in II Corps was pretty peaceful, and the agricultural programs were very successful. For the first time, the people could grow two crops in a year, which made them more prosperous. This made them very happy.

In the spring of 1975, the North Vietnamese broke the Paris Peace Agreement and began a major offensive in the South. I stayed in Nha Trang until the Communist army was advancing on the city. On April 2, my family joined a crowd of two to three hundred people who planned to evacuate to Saigon. But at Nha Trang Airport, the planes were already taken by the air force.

We telephoned the American embassy in Saigon. They promised to send an aircraft for us. So we camped at the air terminal and waited until midnight. The plane didn't come. Most of the people were panicked, because they had all been American employees. At the last minute, the Americans were abandoning them and their families. So they began to chant anti-American slogans.

I stood before them and said, "Look, even if you are anti-American now, you cannot save your heads. The Communists will still punish you for working with the U.S. government."

They shouted, "How are we going to find a way out? We cannot take the road, we cannot fly."

I told them, "See that C 130 airplane unloading supplies? When it is empty and ready to return to Saigon, we'll rush into it. Many trucks and cars have been left here without keys. I'll cross the ignition wires of one and start it up. We need someone to slowly drive the car behind a procession to the commander's headquarters at the radar station. Children and women in front, so the guards won't shoot at us."

When we approached the radar station, the guard shot into the air, and shouted, "Stop." But the general agreed to transport us to Saigon. We all fit, but we had to leave our luggage behind.

In Saigon, the AID headquarters asked me to help with a feasibility study for planting vegetables and raising livestock around the city in case of a long siege. For several days, our group drove out to surrounding areas. But each day the team became smaller as members fled the country.

My wife and I didn't wish to leave Vietnam, especially if we had to leave our parents behind. We had five children with us. Our youngest daughter was just an infant. And my oldest son, who was nine, was separated from us: he was with my mother outside of the Saigon area. When I realized that the situation was hopeless, I reluctantly prepared evacuation documents. An American friend said, "Trong, your extended family is so large, sixteen people. How can you make it in America?"

On April 28, 1975, my extended family group was driven to Tan Son Nhut Air Base. There was a large crowd of maybe ten thousand people waiting at the terminal. The evacuation was planned for five the following morning. We kept the kids close to us and tried to get a little sleep on the ground.

Around midnight, the North Vietnamese bombed the airstrip. Everyone panicked. People were crying and some began running to escape. So I stood up and shouted, "Please, listen." I kept shouting and shouting. People looked at me like I was strange. When it became quiet, I said, "Panic kills people more than guns. We have to cooperate."

I called for young men to help keep order in the crowd. And I asked the people, "Please, throw away your luggage. The evacuation will be very fast, like lightning. We don't want people left behind because of suitcases."

Around 5:00 A.M., C 46 helicopters landed in front of us. U.S. Marines checked out the landing zone and took security positions. A man spoke Vietnamese through a loudspeaker in his hand. People hurried to the helicopters. My own family was divided onto three different aircraft.

We landed on the huge boat, the *Pioneer Contender*. I had mixed emotions. I felt that we were going to heaven—the United States. But I already missed my country. I realized that I would never see Vietnam again.

After a short period on the island of Guam, we were brought to a refugee camp in Fort Chaffee, Arkansas, near Little Rock. There were quite a few Vietnamese already there. Everybody was asking about "sponsors."

Many Americans visited the camp, just like a slave market. Many were rice farmers in Arkansas who wanted Vietnamese as cheap laborers. They would invite refugees into the coffee shop and talk with them. If these Americans thought, "Oh, this or that person is good," they went to the office to fill out sponsorship papers.

My former USAID boss wanted to sponsor my family to Washington. I said, "No, I don't want to bother a good friend. My family is too large." I was afraid he would have to feed all sixteen of us.

To make resettlement easier, I divided the extended family into three groups: my wife and kids, my parents' group, and my in-laws' family. My sponsor was the pastor of a Methodist church in central Ohio. He owned sixteen hundred acres of land, with around a million pine trees that needed trimming. He also had chestnuts, blueberries, and grapevines.

I helped him draw a plan to improve his property. But that wasn't what he wanted—he expected me to be a simple laborer. And we had misunderstandings about religion. I am a Catholic, and my wife is a Buddhist. I told him, "In front of God we are equal. I believe in God the same as you. But I want to keep my own religion."

Every week his wife, Elizabeth, would drive us to the supermarket. My wife is a good cook, but she didn't know anything about American food, like ground beef. Thanh wanted to buy pork, but Elizabeth said, "No. You are limited to a twenty-five-dollar budget a week." And the sponsor wanted me to talk English with my children. I said, "No, they will learn bad speaking habits from me. It's better for them to learn correct American English at school."

We were lucky that the town's Catholic pastor, Father Ron, allowed us to live in his rectory. But, after two months, the sponsor wanted to send us back to Fort Chaffee. I was afraid to go back to the camp. If we returned, as many others had, it would look bad for the refugee program. So I asked the sponsor, "Sir, please wait one more month. I will look for another sponsor."

Father Ron didn't want to create a problem with the Methodists, so he took me to his native town, a short drive away. The church agreed to sponsor my family. Our first day in Lancaster, Ohio, I found a job as a donut baker. I worked twelve hours a day, six days a week. The shop owner trained me and paid $100 a week. My kids enrolled in school, and my wife stayed home with the baby.

I was still coming out of shock from leaving our homeland. My emotions were very unstable. I was constantly dreaming of Vietnam. I had a lot of nightmares. My boss had very much sympathy for me. But I felt too much stress.

After nine months of working in the shop, one day in mid-1976, I made ten dozen donuts that didn't rise enough. One of my co-workers yelled at me. She said, "If you don't want to work, get out. We don't want you here." I said, "I'm sorry. I quit tomorrow."

I drove to Chicago, where my in-laws were living. The second day, I found a job as a janitor at Water Tower Place, the most luxurious shopping mall. My wife and children came to join me a week later.

The majority of the janitors at the mall were Vietnamese. The company liked to hire us, because we did the job well. But sometimes the superintendent of the building came to my supervisor and said, "We want these gooks out of here tomorrow." So some Vietnamese went to the Department of Labor, who ruled that the superintendent's prejudice was illegal.

Uptown was the area where many Vietnamese refugees were sent by the voluntary agencies. My wife and I found a place to live in the Albany Park neighborhood, which had a lot of Koreans and other Asians. We found that my income was not enough to meet the family's needs. So although Thanh's English was not good, she found a second shift job at a factory making plastic cups. We rotated responsibility for the children.

My son, Tran, was nine years old, and my daughters were five, four, three, and one. My two oldest children had a lot of problems with their classmates in Chicago. The school in Albany Park was a mixture of white, black, Asian, everything. Tran was beaten sometimes, and his teacher wasn't patient with him, because he didn't know English. I went to the school and told the principal that I thought the teacher was being unfair. The principal was sympathetic and said, "I understand." After that there was no more problem.

After one year at the mall, I was appointed supervisor. My responsibility was the Continental Bank. But the next year, in 1978, I realized that there were a few thousand Vietnamese refugees in Chicago who needed assistance. When I heard that Travelers and Immigrants Aid was looking to hire a caseworker, I took the job.

I found an apartment large enough for all of my children in Uptown, on Argyle and Sheridan, right in the center of the Vietnamese refugee community. Robberies and crime throughout the neighborhood were severe. My cousin, who lived one floor below me, was robbed twice. Thieves came into his apartment, tied up his family, and robbed them.

Every day, after finishing at my office, I would go on the street and ask people about their needs. To improve the area, the first thing we had to deal with were the community associations, who wanted the refugees to leave. So we worked with the church, the police, and local officials. As a caseworker, I served as a mediator between the refugees and the authorities. Many problems occurred at the medical center and in the schools. Small issues were magnified by language and cultural differences.

For instance, in Vietnam, when both parents work, their older children take care of the babies. But in America, that creates problems. The schools would call the homes to ask why students weren't attending class. In many cases, neither the parents nor the children could speak English. Since I was the one who registered the kids in school, the authorities would call me to help.

I would visit the families at night to explain the law to them. They would respond, "But I need them to watch the little children." I'd emphasize, "If you don't obey the law, they'll take away your children." There were no day-care centers. That put extra pressure on families working in low-paying jobs who were trying to be self-supportive and stay off welfare.

The older kids attend Senn High School, which is considered the most ethnically diverse in America. Some seventy-eight languages are spoken there. There weren't many problems with the white American kids, but other ethnic groups really gave the Vietnamese children a hard time. Especially the blacks, Mexicans, and Chinese.

Chinese kids from Hong Kong chased the refugee children. "Go home. Go back where you came from." Usually the refugee children kept quiet. They listened to their parents: "Go to school to learn and study—not to fight." But the children couldn't be patient any more.

A fight began between a Vietnamese-Chinese and a Hong Kong Chinese boy. It quickly expanded to four, six, twelve kids, then became a big battle. Some of the Hong Kong kids were hospitalized. The first response was a lot of prejudice toward the refugees. In the newspaper, an authority said, "Because Vietnamese kids grew up in wartime, what they know is killing, nothing else." It became a hot issue in the community. And the parents of the Chinese kids tried to sue the refugee parents. So I called a lawyer. I told him, "I need your help. I don't have money to pay the fee for the children. And most of their parents are on welfare." The lawyer said, "Okay, I'll see what I can do." We had a long conversation about refugee life here and our culture. The lawyer adapted well. He used all the facts I gave him and won the case.

That was a small victory compared to other problems in the community. Crime threatened everyone's daily life. Muggers robbed refugees on the street, in the lobby of apartment buildings, in the elevators, in the stairwells, everywhere. In Vietnam, people seldom had locks on their doors. We had to teach them to bolt the door or hook the chain on the lock.

Whenever an incident happened, the refugees would call my office. One day there were more than thirty robberies. We needed to develop a strategy to deal with all the crime. So I called the police, the church (which has Vietnamese priests), the voluntary agencies, and community leaders.

We decided to organize what Chicago police call "beat representatives." These are citizens' groups that watch the neighborhood and call police if there's trouble. And among the refugees, we developed an "ambush" strategy.

Refugee men organized committees to catch robbers. One notorious building was a twenty-four-floor high-rise on West Lakeside. Muggers very badly tormented the refugees who lived there. And there were a few other large buildings where crimes occurred every day.

Our strategy was to set up ambushes from the high-rise buildings. Refugees opened their windows to look onto the street. One person acted as bait and walked alone. When a robber started to follow her, the watchers from one building would signal the other buildings, just like a military operation. When the robber grabbed her neck and took her purse, which had phony money inside, the citizens' patrols began to follow. They converged on him from all directions until he was surrounded. The refugees kept him cornered until the police arrived to take him away.

The police were very supportive and stopped many robberies. When word went out around the neighborhood that the police were active and the refugees were organized and defending themselves, much of the crime stopped.

During 1980, at the height of the Vietnamese boat-people crisis, my wife quit her job at the cup factory to work for the Intergovernmental Committee for Migration to greet refugees at O'Hare Airport. She helped transfer them to connecting flights. Her job was very tough, because the refugees were arriving at all hours of day or night. It was dangerous for her to come home alone after dark. There were still problems in the neighborhood—a lot of rapes—and I was afraid that, if we stayed, the children would grow up with a bad influence. So I decided to move.

I looked for a home close to the neighborhood, but no landlords wanted a family our size. Sometimes I thought, "Is having a lot of children a crime in America?" Finally, a friend in Des Plaines, on the North Side, close to the airport, was selling a home for $50,000 with a very low down payment. I didn't have enough savings, so I borrowed money from friends. I just closed my eyes and bought it.

I continued working in Uptown every day at my Travelers Aid job. We were resettling a lot of refugees into the area, and I worried about their future. Uptown was still a disaster, and the Vietnamese boat people, the Cambodians who survived the holocaust, and the Laotians and Hmong were less educated than the Indochinese who arrived in 1975. Many refugees came from rural areas, unprepared for city life. They didn't have a higher education or any skills except farming. I couldn't move them into apartments considered good, or even livable. The families were usually large.

I felt hurt, because I did not want my family to live in that neighborhood, so how could I tell other people to live there? I was determined to improve the neighborhood, but how to do that was the big question.

The business strip on Argyle Street was a disaster area. Around sixty percent of the buildings were owned by a Chinese association, Hip Sing, which had a vision in the late 1960s of turning the area into a new Chinatown. But they had little success, because of crime and the depressed environment. Still, the Vietnamese thought that maybe it could be a good place to start our business area.

We asked the Hip Sing to rent us some abandoned storefronts. They said, "No, you're not Chinese. This is the New Chinatown." But I began to work closely with a Chinese manager of one of the buildings. I said, "If you can help us, we can all benefit. There aren't that many Chinese living in the area. If you let the Vietnamese rent spaces, this area can be developed. And I can place new refugees in apartment buildings that the Hip Sing owns, that have a low occupancy rate. They will shop here on Argyle and the area will grow and develop." He agreed.

I didn't know anything about business in America; I could only advise refugees on social issues. But we were able to provide a translation service so they could obtain business permits. The neighborhood began to grow.

Nearly all the businesses owned by refugees were started by families pooling their money together or borrowing from friends. The first places were restaurants and small supermarkets. As more refugees moved into the neighborhood and new businesses were springing up, the gangs, the drug addicts, and the winos had fewer and fewer abandoned buildings to hang out in. And as the neighborhood began to come back to life, the police sent more security. But in the alleys and side streets it was still something else.

Argyle Street became a kind of a beachhead where people could have a semblance of ordinary life. From my Travelers Aid office I began sending a newsletter to teach the refugees about American life and personal safety. But the refugees needed a community center staffed by their own people. There is more pride in a community when an ethnic group can take care of their own. It takes pressure off the welfare system when successful members of an ethnic community help others to find jobs. People can adapt to their new society without having to be ashamed of their own culture.

In 1980, I heard that the U. S. Department of Health and Human Services planned to contribute grants for Mutual Assistance Associations. I gathered friends, and we wrote a proposal that was awarded a federal grant to develop a Vietnamese Community Service Center through the Vietnamese Association of Illinois. We found office space on Broadway, a few blocks from Argyle. We searched for a good director, and we trained a small staff.

The Center opened in the winter of 1980 with only two donated desks and a dozen folding chairs. A group of volunteers built plywood tables and benches to furnish classrooms. Sometimes the heater broke down and the staff had to work in many sweaters, scarves, and gloves.

Despite conditions in the office, the Center grew very quickly. After a year, the Center was awarded a state grant, so there was enough money to continue services as the Vietnamese population blossomed. Now the Vietnamese Association has expanded the center to twenty staff members. The director is a very talented young woman, Ngoan Le, who has great initiative. And Mr. Zung Dao, who owns a successful restaurant business in the neighboring Edgewater area, runs the Center's Community Economic Development Project. That is the only program in our area to teach refugees how to do business in America. And we are helping other refugees, like the Ethiopians who just opened a restaurant on Argyle Street.

Argyle has become an international area. There are more than fifty Vietnamese family-owned businesses on the strip. There are also stores owned by Khmer, Lao, Chinese, Ethiopians, a Jewish kosher butcher, two Hispanic grocers, a black record shop, and an American bar. There are Japanese, Thai, Indian, and Mexican restaurants in the area. And a McDonald's.

I remember in 1978–79, when I worked with American sponsors from the suburbs, if I said, "Why don't you come to Uptown to work with the refugees?" they would say, "No way, it's too dangerous." Now people from many areas like to come to Argyle Street to shop, and enjoy coming to community activities like the annual Argyle Street Festival or Lunar New Year Celebration.

The Vietnamese restaurants do a lot of their business from tourists on weekends. Many don't earn a lot, but they survive by family manpower. For example, Mr. and Mrs. Phan, who own the Nha Tang Restaurant, had a simple dream. They came here as boat people in 1979, worked in a factory to save enough to make a $700 lease payment on a small storefront to open a twelve-table restaurant. His wife is a very good cook, and they charge low prices. Since they opened in 1981, they stay open seven days a week from 9:00 A.M. until 10:00 P.M. They earn enough to keep the family well fed and have a little profit left over for saving.

The most famous place in the neighborhood is the Mekong Restaurant, on the corner of Argyle and Broadway, which attracts many people from the suburbs and other states. The owner, Mr. Lam Ton, worked with the U.S. State Department in Vietnam.

The first year his restaurant opened, in 1983, Lam Ton lost money. The neighborhood's reputation was still very rough. But, all of a sudden, his business turned around after some Chicago newspaper people wrote very favorably about the restaurant. The Mekong brought Uptown into the limelight, especially in 1985, when a lot of media attention was given to the tenth anniversary of the fall of Saigon.

Newspeople saw a lot of new stores with posterboards written in Vietnamese. They wrote stories emphasizing how the refugees revitalized Uptown and turned the slum area into a more beautiful place. They began calling Argyle Street "Little Saigon."

But as the neighborhood's good reputation began to grow, that created a problem. The Chinese Hip Sing organization, who dreamed that the area would become the "New Chinatown," started to feel like second-class citizens.

The Hip Sing office building is right next to the el train station on Argyle, and they still own a lot of property that the Vietnamese lease. So they consider themselves the ones who control the area.

On one occasion, the Vietnamese organized a big Mid-Autumn Festival for the children, and we had a Lion Dance on Argyle Street. One Chinese man came out of the Hip Sing building and said, "Did you ask our permission to dance on this street?" I said to him, "Why do I have to ask your permission? This is America. The streets are built by the taxpayers, not you guys."

He said, "I don't want to see you people, because the Lion Dance is for Chinese." I said, "The kids enjoy it, even if they don't do the dance properly. Their joy is our goal."

The Hip Sing, under Jimmy Wong and Charley Soo, did work hard to develop the area. Improvements like the sidewalk renovation by the city were made thanks to their lobbying. But they never had enough population for a New Chinatown. It was the Southeast Asian refugees who decided that, even if we were put into a slum, we would improve the neighborhood. And we had enough people to support new businesses on Argyle.

The small family-owned businesses can only employ a limited number of people. So refugees travel to jobs on the South Side of Chicago or in the suburbs. Many are unskilled factory workers, like machine operators. Other refugees work as painters or mechanics. During the past couple years, Chicago has turned into a service-based city. In a lot of new hotels, refugees work in housekeeping or maintenance jobs. And many of the earlier, better-educated refugees went to school to become electronics technicians at places like GTE or AT&T.

At first, some Vietnamese refuse to work at menial jobs because they don't want a lower social standing than they had in Vietnam. Others take welfare because they are lazy or don't have the right encouragement to study English. I try to motivate them. But sometimes I'm told, "Forget about being a social worker. Who are you to tell me what to do? You are Vietnamese, just like us. You have no right to push me."

The Vietnamese Community Center has been instrumental in changing people's attitudes from being so negative. The Center now has five programs: Employment, Social Adjustment, Youth, Women, and Economic Development. Within a few years, the Vietnamese welfare dependency rate declined from eighty-seven percent to fifty-five percent, and now only around twenty-five percent are unemployed or on public assistance.

After I saw the neighborhood begin to turn around and living conditions for the refugees improve, I thought, "How about their moral and cultural life?" There are family conflicts, because the children are learning so quickly in school to adopt American culture. The parents might learn a little English at work, but it is a very slow process. They have to rely a lot on the children. The kids watch television and forget about the Vietnamese cultural values. The parents are shocked. They feel they have lost authority. There are arguments. The children want to move out or run away.

To deal with the generation gap, we started counseling sessions for the parents and children at the school, to keep them from drifting apart. There are boys who have both parents working or who escaped from Vietnam alone. They have a lot of unsupervised time and begin to get into trouble. I try to work very closely with the schools to follow the progress of students and develop strategies for teachers to work better with the children. . . .

At the Community Center we try to create activities for kids. There are three main youth clubs: Boy Scouts, the Buddhist Family Club, and Catholic Youth. Sometimes we organize sports. And to reduce the generation gap with their parents, we have Vietnamese language classes for the kids while their parents study English at a nearby public agency.

My own children like the new fashions, the New Wave. I've tried to stay with the Asian Confucian tradition. As a father, I have to be strict. But in this society, you can't force children to do what you say. They have their own lives.

THANH: Our children were very young when we came here. So we have adjusted and let them have some freedom. We realize that we can't live the way we did in Vietnam. But we try to teach them to respect family life. I tell my children, "The U.S. is liberal. You have the right to drive a car. But when you see a 'One Way' sign, you can't ignore it and say, 'this is a free country, nobody can tell me what to do.' That will lead to a bad accident where you can get hurt. You must also think that way in terms of family rules."

TRONG: Our oldest daughter is fifteen. I wouldn't be happy if a boy asked her to a dance at school or for a date, but it would be okay to go to a party at school, because it would be under supervision. Sometimes we compromise and allow her to go to a party at a friend's house if we know the parents.

Vietnamese tradition is not as strict with boys. I gave my son more freedom when he was in high school, but I had to know where he was going and who he was associating with. I told him, "I give you freedom, but you have to be home by 10:00 P.M., or midnight." If he didn't come home at the time limit—"Sorry," the next time he asks. But sometimes, when he was having a lot of fun and wanted to stay out a little longer, if he called me to ask permission, that was fine.

Last year, after Tran graduated from high school, he moved out on his own. That was a great shock for me. We didn't have enough money to send him to college, so he started working full-time to save for tuition. His high-school grades were average, but he is very artistic, a good drummer. In his free times, he practices a lot with his band. During days he works at a company downtown, and in the evenings he comes into our restaurant to help.

This first year of the restaurant business was miserable. Little by little, our customers have been building up. Our location, on the border of the Uptown and Edgewater neighborhood, is not the greatest.

Promotion and advertising cost money that we don't have. My son and two oldest daughters help to keep our costs down. Another reason I have the girls working here is to learn how to communicate with people. If they can handle serving customers, it will help them to handle a lot of other situations in the future. My oldest daughter is very shy, but she's becoming more relaxed and talks with the customers a little more. My second daughter, Thanh Tram, is more outgoing and enjoys dealing with customers.

THAHN TRAM: When most Americans first meet me, they think that I'm seventeen or eighteen and was born here. When they find out that I'm only fourteen and was born in Vietnam, they are surprised.

I don't work at the restaurant on weekdays during the school year. But if I don't have any homework, I'll call the restaurant and see if my mom and dad need me. I come in all day on weekends and during the summer.

The best thing about working here is that I've gotten better at speaking Vietnamese. Where I go to school in Des Plaines, there aren't Vietnamese to talk with. I only talk Vietnamese if I talk on the phone with friends in Uptown. But by working here, I've learned how to talk and write better.

I became a citizen with my parents two years ago. The whole family took the oath of citizenship together. Now most of my friends at school say that, because I have my citizenship, I am American, no longer Vietnamese. I always tell them, "I'm still Vietnamese, no matter what. I'm never going to be all American. I always have to stick to my country."

I cried one time in school when they were talking about Vietnam in class...the war and everything. Some kids saw me crying and said, "Why are you crying?" I said, "No, my eyes are tearing." They said, "If you want to cry, why don't you go outside, like a little baby?" I said to them, "If you lost your country, wouldn't you cry?" They said, "No. Not if you can't even go back." I told them, "I wish that I was over there rather than here." They said, "Do you want to die?" I said, "Even though I like it here, I also want to be in my own country." So a boy shrugged his shoulders and said, "Whatever you say."

Most of the kids call me "stuck up." I don't mean to get them upset. I just can't express my feelings. No one at my school thinks about what it's like to be a refugee. No one ever cares, unless I have a real close friend who tries to help me through these problems. Otherwise I never tell anyone about my feelings.

I was very young when I came here. But I still remember what my house in Vietnam looked like, and the beach. One time in Des Plaines, I was sitting by the small lake near my home. It was getting dark, the sun was orange. I sat down on a bench and closed my eyes. I saw myself on the beach in Vietnam. I started crying. I opened my eyes and saw the sun setting over the lake. I cried even more and began talking to myself.

My sister and her American friends came up to me and asked what was wrong. I didn't want to tell them. When I told my sister, she said I was stupid. She asked, "Why are you still thinking of that?" Her attitude is that we're American now; we shouldn't think of the past.

This year, I started ninth grade. It's not worse than junior high, except the homework is a little harder. The only thing I don't like this year is that my parents won't let me play the sports that I like. They say the volleyball will ruin my hands, but that's a sport I'm good at. They don't want me playing basketball, because it's too rough, but I played in seventh and eighth grade. They say, "Why don't you play tennis?" But I don't even know how to play. And I don't want to do swimming because sometimes I have trouble holding my breath.

My sisters and I do volunteer work at school. And I like my counselor a lot. At first I was shy and wouldn't tell her anything. But once I got to know her, I've seen her as a real close friend and I tell her everything about my life. I know what I want to be when I grow up. I want to be a doctor, like a specialist in the laboratory.

Now that I'm in high school, I can take more classes like science and labs. I'm just starting to learn computers. I'm not that good on them yet. I'm looking forward to starting biology classes.

TRONG: Thanh Tram has a very nice dream to become a doctor. I only hope that I will be able to support her education. To become a doctor takes a long time and a lot of money. She gets mostly A's in school and graduated from middle school in the Honor Society.

She is very mature for a fourteen-year-old. But I worry a lot about my son, Tran. I want him to go further in his education. His high-school grades were kind of average—B's. He's still deciding what he wants to do.

TRAN: I didn't know what I wanted after I finished high school last year. My dad wanted me to go to college, but first I wanted to support myself. I moved out on my own because I wanted to have more life experience. Now I live in this neighborhood, on the street next to the restaurant. A guy from my band rooms with me.

I don't expect playing the drums will be my profession. I just love music. It's a way for me to forget my problems. When I get home from work at night, I listen to mostly Vietnamese music, because you can concentrate on the lyrics and feel the music better. But when I get up

Trong and Tran Nguyen. (Courtesy of Al Santoli)

in the morning or go to parties, I like New Wave. For a while in high school, I only listened to heavy metal. That drove my parents crazy.

The band I'm with plays all different kinds. Some Vietnamese music, some rock songs like "Jump" by Van Halen. But we play mostly New Wave, because at parties that's what a lot of kids expect. We play only on weekends, because most of the guys in the band work or go to school.

I work downtown at a hearing-aid company, doing shipping and receiving from nine to five. Then I take a bus to Uptown and work in the restaurant until eleven o'clock. I would like to start school this winter semester, so I have to work full-time. But I don't take any money for helping my parents. I do it because I have a responsibility as their son.

There has been some conflict in my family because I want to establish myself on my own. But my loyalty to them hasn't changed. When I lived at home, I argued with my parents a lot. I had an attitude just like American kids. But once I left, I realized how much I respect them.

Before I moved back to the Uptown area, I practically forgot the Vietnamese language. I was eight or nine years old when we left Vietnam. When we came to America, I had to concentrate on learning the new language. In high school there were only two Vietnamese kids, so I hung out with American kids. There were a lot of different groups that kids hung around in. There were the jocks; the wimps, who always studied; the burnouts, who partied all the time. Each group never associated with the others. I like to hang around with all groups. I don't care if they're the wimps or the Melvins. But some kids' attitudes were, "You be with my group only, or we don't want you around." So I said, "Forget it. I don't need no one."

For all four years of high school, what I mostly did was go to school and come straight home. I'd listen to music, study, and play my drums. At that time, I really hated the Vietnamese—I don't know why. I played with only American kids, even though I didn't have many friends. Now that I'm back in Uptown, I like the Vietnamese better. Friendships with people here are a lot easier, even though the neighborhood is rough.

There is a problem with drugs in Uptown. Whether you like it or not, some people are going to press you: "Hey, do you want to try some good weed?" I don't do it, because I think it's really stupid. You just ruin your health.

Some Vietnamese kids adopt a punk style of dressing and wearing their hair. The way they dress is called New Wave. When I go to work, I dress normal. But when I go out, I dress that way, too. There are two groups in Chicago that are called New Wave. One group causes trouble and the other doesn't. Most kids that dress New Wave are decent; they just go with the style. But a few kids in Uptown, mostly without parents here, really cause trouble. They harass and beat people up, anything to get into trouble.

I can't stand some of the punks around here. Not only the Vietnamese—there are a lot of American punks. On the subway, they harass people and steal their money. The other day, on my way home from work, I saw three black kids beating up this one old guy in downtown Chicago.

I think, "Maybe I can do something about it. Fight them, get rid of them." But what's that going to do? You can't take the law into your own hands. Ever since I was a little kid, I never started any fights. I don't like violence at all.

I can remember some things about the war, when we left Vietnam. It was hard...terrible. Men were fighting, pushing children and women to the ground, so they could get a place on the plane. People were panicking to get out of the country, because the Communist army was coming. There was shooting. My parents said, "Follow us, we have to go." I didn't realize that we were going to a new country.

Among refugees in the U.S., each age group has their own point of view. From what I see in Uptown, I wouldn't say that everyone is keeping a positive attitude. Some people don't care about their old culture any more.

I'm almost twenty years old. I don't have enough money saved yet, so I'll start at a community college in the neighborhood, Truman College. When I have enough money, I'll transfer to a better school.

I don't like seeing kids my age who are messing around real bad. They're hurting people and hurting our reputation. I want to do something about it. So I decided to study law enforcement in college for two years and then join the police academy.

TRONG: I was very upset when my son went out on his own. I was worried about his well-being. In the Vietnamese community, I saved a lot of families from the generation gap, but when the problem came to my own family, I couldn't solve it.

My children were very young when they came here, so their values have become much more American. I try to behave as an American too, but in my heart I am always Vietnamese. I dream that one day I can get back to Vietnam. I was born there, grew up there.... I still remember that, in the past, my father and father-in-law worked for our people's freedom. What I am doing now is very different from what they did. We have freedom here, and sixty million people in Vietnam still do not have that. I still dream of somehow helping them to win their freedom.

Selected Bibliography of
First-Person Immigrant Accounts

This bibliography is intended to permit readers who have been tantalized by the excerpts contained in this reader to explore more fully the vast literature of immigrant first-person accounts. It is a selective bibliography that has grown as I worked on this book, but it entails a conscious effort to include accounts from all groups of immigrants and relatively equal numbers of men and women.

Bibliographies that were particularly helpful in constructing this listing include W. Ralph Janeway, *Bibliography of Immigration in the United States, 1900–1930* (Columbus, Ohio: H. L. Hendrick, 1934); Research Institute of Immigration and Ethnic Studies, *Recent Immigration to the United States: The Literature of the Social Sciences* (Washington, D.C.: Smithsonian Institution Press, 1976); John D. Buenker and Nicholas C. Burckel, *Immigration and Ethnicity: A Guide to Information Sources* (Detroit: Gale Research Company, 1977); and Donna R. Gabaccia, *Immigrant Women in the United States: A Selectively Annotated Multidisciplinary Bibliography* (New York: Greenwood, 1989). Also rich in bibliographical citations was William Boelhower, *Immigrant Autobiography in the United States* (Verona, Italy: Essedue Edizioni, 1982).

I have included published books only, although many fine first-person accounts appear only in scholarly journals or in manuscript form in archives. I have also excluded works of fiction, although in many cases the line between autobiography and fiction is a thin one. That is another area of immigrant writing that readers may want to investigate after exploring this collection. Useful guides to this literature include Joseph S. Roucek, *The Immigrant in Fiction and Biography* (New York: New York Bureau for Intercultural Education, 1945); Babette F. Inglehart and Anthony R. Mangione, *The Image of Pluralism in American Literature: An Annotated Bibliography on the American Experience of European Ethnic Groups* (New York: Institute for Pluralism and Group Identity of the American Jewish Committee, 1974); David Fine, *The City, the Immigrant, and American Fiction, 1880–1920* (Metuchen,

N.J.: Scarecrow Press, 1977); and Wesley Brown and Amy Ling, eds., *Imagining America: Stories from the Promised Land* (New York: Persea Books, 1991).

I have cited the most recent edition of titles for which more than one edition exists, on the assumption that generally more recent editions will be easier to find. I do note the date of original publication for all books and the ethnic group involved where it is not evident from the title or publisher of the work.

Abinader, Elmaz. *Children of the Roojme: A Family's Journey.* New York: W. W. Norton, 1991. (Lebanese)

Abramson, Paul R. *A Case for Case Studies: An Immigrant's Journal.* Newbury Park, Calif.: Sage Publications, 1992. (Russian Jewish)

Acosta, Oscar Zeta. *The Autobiography of a Brown Buffalo.* San Francisco: Straight Arrow Books, 1972. (Mexican American)

Adamic, Louis. *Laughing in the Jungle: The Autobiography of an Immigrant in America.* New York: Arno Press, 1969; originally published in 1932. (Slovenian)

———. *My America.* New York: Harper, 1938. (Slovenian)

Adler, Polly. *A House Is Not a Home.* New York: Rinehart, 1953. (Jewish)

Albert, Félix. *Immigrant Odyssey: A French-Canadian Habitant in New England.* Introduction by Francis H. Early; translation by Arthur L. Eno, Jr. Orono: University of Maine Press, 1991.

Alvarado, Arturo. *Chronicle of Aztlan.* Berkeley, Calif.: Quito Sol, 1974. (Mexican American)

Anderson, Mary Jane Hill. *Autobiography.* Minneapolis: University of Minnesota Press, 1934. (Irish)

Anderson, Mary, and Mary Winslow. *Woman at Work: The Autobiography of Mary Anderson.* Minneapolis: University of Minnesota Press, 1951. (Swedish)

Andres, Chaya R. *Years Have Sped By: My Life Story.* Edited by Jeanett Cohen. Dallas: Chaya R. Andres, 1981. (Jewish)

Anid, Reverend Cyril. *I Grew with Them.* Jounich, Lebanon: Paulist Press, 1967. (Syrian)

Antin, Mary. *At School in the Promised Land, or the Story of a Little Immigrant.* Boston: Houghton Mifflin, 1912. (Russian Jewish)

———. *From Plotzk to Boston.* New York: Markus Wiener, 1986; originally published in 1899. (Russian Jewish)

———. *The Promised Land.* Princeton, N.J.: Princeton University Press, 1985; originally published in 1912. (Russian Jewish)

Arrighi, Antonio A. *The Story of Antonio the Galley-Slave: A Romance of Real Life, in Three Parts.* New York: Fleming H. Revell, 1910. (Italian)

Avakian, Arlene. *Lion Woman's Legacy: An Armenian-American Memoir.* New York: Feminist Press, 1991.

Axford, Roger W., ed. *Too Long Been Silent: Japanese Americans Speak Out.* Lincoln, Nebr.: Media Publishing and Marketing, 1986.

Barton, H. Arnold, ed. *Letters from the Promised Land: Swedes in America, 1840–1914.* Minneapolis: University of Minnesota Press, 1975.

Beaumont, Betty Bentley. *Twelve Years of My Life: An Autobiography.* Philadelphia: T. B. Peterson, 1887. (English)

Behrman, S. N. *The Worcester Account.* New York: Random House, 1954. (Jewish)

Berg, Rebecca Himber. "Childhood in Lithuania." In *Memoirs of My People,* edited by Leo Schwartz. Philadelphia: Jewish Publication Society of America, 1943.

Berky, Andres S., ed. and trans. *The Journals and Papers of David Schultze.* 2 vols. Pennsburg, Pa.: Schwenkfelder Library, 1952 and 1953. (German)

Billigmeier, Robert H., and Fred Altschuler Picard, eds. *The Old World and the New: The Journals of Two Swiss Families in America in the 1820's.* Minneapolis: University of Minnesota Press, 1965.

Bisno, Abraham. *Abraham Bisno, Union Pioneer.* Madison: University of Wisconsin Press, 1967. (Russian Jewish)

Bjerke, Erik, and Erthe Marie Bjerke. *Bjerke Family History, 1818–1967.* Hatton, N.D.: n.p., n.d. (Norwegian)

Blegen, Theodore, ed. *Frontier Parsonage: The Letters of Olaus Fredrick Duus, Norwegian Pastor in Wisconsin, 1855–1858.* New York: Arno Press, 1979; originally published in 1947.

———. *Land of Their Choice: The Immigrant Writes Home.* Minneapolis: University of Minnesota Press, 1954. (Norwegian)

Bok, Edward William. *The Americanization of Edward Bok: The Autobiography of a Dutch Boy Fifty Years After.* New York: Charles Scribner's Sons, 1922.

Bost, Theodore. *A Frontier Family in Minnesota: Letters of Theodore and Sophie Bost, 1851–1920.* Edited and translated by Ralph H. Bowen. Minneapolis: University of Minnesota Press, 1981. (Swiss)

Boyle, Kay, comp. *The Autobiography of Emanuel Carnevali.* New York: Horizon Press, 1967. (Italian)

Buaken, Manuel. *I Have Lived with the American People.* Caldwell, Idaho: Caxton, 1948. (Filipino)

Buechler, Hans, and Judith-Maria Buechler, eds. *Carmen: The Autobiography of a Spanish Galician Woman.* Cambridge, Mass.: Schenkman, 1981.

Bulosan, Carlos. *America Is in the Heart.* Seattle: University of Washington Press, 1973; originally published in 1946. (Filipino)

Burland, Rebecca, and Edward Burland. *A True Picture of Emigration, or Fourteen Years in the Interior of North America.* New York: Citadel Press, 1968; originally published in 1848. (English)

Buss, Fran Leeper. *La Partera: Story of a Midwife.* Ann Arbor: University of Michigan Press, 1980. (Mexican American)

Byer, Etta. *Transplanted People.* Chicago: M. J. Aron, 1955. (Jewish)

Cade, Winnifred, ed. *I Think Back: Being the Memoirs of Grandma Gruen.* San Antonio: privately printed, 1937. (German)

Cahan, Abraham. *The Education of Abraham Cahan*. Translated by Leon Stein, Abraham P. Conan, and Lynn Davison. Philadelphia: Jewish Publication Society of America, 1969; 5 vols. originally published in Yiddish, 1926–31.

Cain, Betty Swanson. *American from Sweden: The Story of A. V. Swanson*. Carbondale: Southern Illinois University Press, 1987.

Campon, Peter F. *The Evolution of an Immigrant*. Brooklyn: Gaus' Sons, n.d. (Italian)

Chao, Buwei Yang. *Autobiography of a Chinese Woman*. New York: John Day, 1947.

Chao, Thomas Ming-Heng. *Shadow Shapes: Memoirs of a Chinese Student in America*. Peking: Peking Leader Press, 1928.

Chernin, Kim. *In My Mother's House*. New Haven, Conn.: Ticknor and Fields, 1983. (Russian Jewish)

Chotzinoff, Samuel. *A Lost Paradise: Early Reminiscences*. New York: Alfred A. Knopf, 1955. (Jewish)

Christowe, Stoyan. *My American Pilgrimage*. Boston: Little, Brown, 1947. (Macedonian Bulgarian)

———. *This Is My Country*. Philadelphia: J. B. Lippincott, 1938. (Macedonian Bulgarian)

Clausen, C. A., ed. *The Lady with the Pen: Elise Waerenskjold in Texas*. Northfield, Minn.: Norwegian-American Historical Association, 1951.

Clausen, Clarence A., and Andreas Elviken, trans. and eds. *A Chronicle of Old Muskego: The Diary of Soren Bache, 1839–1847*. Northfield, Minn.: Norwegian-American Historical Association, 1951.

Cohen, David Steven, ed. *America, the Dream of My Life: Selections from the Federal Writers' Project's New Jersey Ethnic Survey*. New Brunswick, N.J.: Rutgers University Press, 1990.

Cohen, Morris Raphael. *A Dreamer's Journey*. Boston: Beacon Press, 1949. (Russian Jewish)

Cohen, Rose. *Out of the Shadow*. New York: Jerome S. Ozer, 1971; originally published in 1918. (Russian Jewish)

Colón, Jesús. *A Puerto Rican in New York and Other Sketches*. New York: Arno Press, 1975; originally published in 1961.

Conway, Alan. *The Welsh in America: Letters from the Immigrants*. Minneapolis: University of Minnesota Press, 1961.

Corsi, Edward. *In the Shadow of Liberty: The Chronicle of Ellis Island*. New York: Macmillan, 1935. (Italian)

Cournos, John. *Autobiography*. New York: Putnam, 1935. (Russian Jewish)

Covello, Leonard. *The Heart Is the Teacher*. New York: McGraw-Hill, 1958. (Italian)

Cowen, Philip. *Memories of an American Jew*. New York: Arno Press, 1975; originally published in 1932. (German Jewish)

Cruz, Nicki, with Jamie Buckingham. *Run, Baby, Run*. New York: Jove, 1978; originally published in 1968. (Puerto Rican)

Cruz, Philip Vera. *Philip Vera Cruz: A Personal History of Filipino Immigrants and the Farmworkers Movement*. Los Angeles: UCLA Labor Center, Institute of Industrial Relations and UCLA Asian American Studies Center, 1992.

Cusack, May. *Nun of Kenmare: An Autobiography*. Boston: Ticknor, 1888. (Irish)

D'Angelo, Pascal. *Pascal D'Angelo, Son of Italy*. New York: Arno Press, 1975; originally published in 1924.

Davis, Marilyn P. *Mexican Voices/American Dreams: An Oral History of Mexican Immigration to the United States*. New York: Henry Holt, 1990.

Dessler, Julia Shapiro. *Eyes on the Goal*. New York: Vantage, 1954. (Lithuanian)

Di Donato, Pietro. *Three Circles of Light*. New York: Julian Messner, 1960. (Italian)

Doty, C. Stewart. *The First Franco-Americans: New England Life Histories from the Federal Writers' Project, 1938–1939*. Orono: University of Maine at Orono Press, 1985.

Edelman, Fannie. *The Mirror of Life: The Old Country and the New*. New York: Exposition Press, 1961. (Jewish)

Embrey, Sue Kunitomi, Arthur A. Hansen, and Betty Kulberg Mitson, eds. *Manzanar Martyr: An Interview with Harry Y. Ueno*. Fullerton, Calif.: Oral History Program, California State University, Fullerton, 1986. (Japanese American)

Erickson, Charlotte, ed. *Invisible Immigrants: The Adaptation of English and Scottish Immigrants in Nineteenth-Century America*. Ithaca, N.Y.: Cornell University Press, 1990; originally published in 1972.

Ets, Marie Hall. *Rosa: The Life of an Italian Immigrant*. Minneapolis: University of Minnesota Press, 1970.

Farseth, Pauline, and Theodore C. Blegen, eds. *Frontier Mother: The Letters of Gro Svendsen*. Northfield, Minn.: Norwegian-American Historical Association, 1950.

Fisher, Minnie. *Born One Year before the Twentieth Century: Minnie Fisher/ An Oral History*. New York: Community Documentation Workshop, St. Mark's Church on the Bowery, 1976. (Jewish)

Flores, Juan, ed. *Divided Arrival: Narratives of the Puerto Rican Migration, 1920–1950* (New York: Centro de Estudios Puertorriqueños, n.d.).

Frank, Louis F., comp. *German-American Pioneers in Wisconsin and Michigan: The Frank-Kerler Letters, 1849–1864*. Translated by Margaret Wolff; edited by Harry H. Anderson. Milwaukee, Wis.: Milwaukee County Historical Society, 1989; originally published in 1971.

Freeman, James M. *Hearts of Sorrow: Vietnamese-American Lives*. Stanford, Calif.: Stanford University Press, 1989.

Freund, Max, ed. and trans. *Gustav Dresel's Houston Journal: Adventures in North America and Texas, 1837–1841*. Austin: University of Texas Press, 1954. (German)

Fukuzawa, Yukichi. *The Autobiography of Yukichi Fukuzawa*. New York: Columbia University Press, 1966. (Japanese)

Galarza, Ernesto. *Barrio Boy*. South Bend, Ind.: University of Notre Dame Press, 1971. (Mexican)

Gamble, Lillian M. *Mor's New Land*. New York: Exposition Press, 1951. (Norwegian)

Gamio, Manuel. *The Mexican Immigrant: His Life Story*. New York: Arno Press, 1969; originally published in 1931.

Ganz, Marie. *Rebels: Into Anarchy—And Out Again*. New York: Dodd, Mead, 1920. (Jewish)

Geannopulos, James Nicholas. *Mother's Wish*. St. Louis: Smith, 1936. (Greek)

Gehle, Frederick W. *Our Dubbledam Journey: An Account of How a Family Came to America, 1891–1941*. New York: John Costello and Sons, 1941. (English)

Goldman, Abraham. *The Goldman Family Saga*. Rochester, N.Y.: privately printed, 1961. (Lithuanian Jewish)

Goldman, Emma. *Living My Life*. 2 vols. New York: Dover Publications, 1970; originally published in 1931. (Russian Jewish)

Gompers, Samuel. *Eighty Years of Life and Labor: An Autobiography*. New York: E. P. Dutton, 1925. (English Jewish)

Gonzales, Ramon, as told to John Poggie, Jr. *Between Two Cultures: The Life of an American-Mexican*. Tucson: University of Arizona Press, 1973.

Gustorf, Fred, ed. *The Uncorrupted Heart: Journals and Letters of Frederick Julius Gustorf, 1800–1845*. Columbia: University of Missouri Press, 1969. (German)

Hale, Frederick, ed. *Danes in North America*. Seattle: University of Washington Press, 1984.

Handlin, Oscar, ed. *Children of the Uprooted*. New York: Braziller, 1966.

Hannula, Reino Kikolai. *Blueberry God: The Education of a Finnish-American*. San Luis Obispo, Calif.: Quality Hill Books, 1981.

Hansen, Arthur A., ed. *Japanese American World War II Evacuation Oral History Project. Part I: Internees*. Westport, Conn.: Meckler, 1991.

Hareven, Tamara K., and Randolph Langenbach, eds. *Amoskeag: Life and Work in an American Factory-City*. New York: Pantheon, 1978.

Hasanovitz, Elizabeth. *One of Them: Chapters from a Passionate Autobiography*. Boston: Houghton Mifflin, 1918. (Jewish)

Hendrickson, Dyke. *Quiet Presence: Dramatic, First-Person Accounts—True Stories of Franco-Americans in New England*. Portland, Maine: Guy Gannett, 1980.

Herscher, Uri D., ed. *The East European Jewish Experience in America: A Century of Memories*. Cincinnati: American Jewish Archives, 1983.

Heyslip, Le Ly, with Jay Wurts. *When Heaven and Earth Changed Places*. New York: Doubleday, 1989. (Vietnamese)

Higa, Thomas Taro. *Memoirs of a Certain Nisei, 1916–1985*. Kaneohe, Hawaii: Higa Publications, 1988 (Okinawan American)

Hirabayashi, Gordon. *Good Times, Bad Times: Idealism Is Realism*. Argenta, B.C.: Argenta Friends Press, 1985. (Japanese American)

Hoffman, Eva. *Lost in Translation: A Life in a New Language*. New York: E. P. Dutton, 1989. (Polish Jewish)

Hoflund, Charles J. *Getting Ahead: A Swedish Immigrant's Reminiscences, 1834–1887*. Edited by H. Arnold Barton. Carbondale: Southern Illinois University Press, 1989.

Holt, Hamilton, ed. *The Life Stories of Undistinguished Americans as Told by Themselves*. New York: Routledge, 1990; originally published in 1906.

Hom, Marlon K. *Songs of Golden Mountain: Cantonese Rhymes from San Francisco Chinatown*. Berkeley: University of California Press, 1987.

Horwich, Bernard. *My First Eighty Years*. Chicago: Argues, 1939. (Lithuanian Jewish)

Houston, Jean W., and D. Houston. *Farewell to Manzanar: A True Story of Japanese American Experience during and after the World War II Internment*. Boston: Houghton Mifflin, 1973.

Hyun, Peter. *Man Sei! The Making of a Korean American*. Honolulu: University of Hawaii Press, 1986.

Iamurri, Gabriel A. *The True Story of an Immigrant*. Rev. ed. Boston: Christopher, 1951. (Italian)

Ifkovic, Edward. *American Letters: Immigrants and Ethnic Writing*. Englewood Cliffs, N.J.: Prentice Hall, 1975.

Ige, Tom. *Boy from Kahaluu: An Autobiography*. Honolulu: Kin Cho Jim Kai, 1989. (Japanese American)

Imahara, James M., as told to Anne Butler Poindexter. *James Imahara: Son of Immigrants*. N.p: James M. Imahara, 1982. (Japanese)

Isely, Elise Dubach, as told to Bliss Isely. *Sunbonnet Days*. Caldwell, Idaho: Caxton, 1935. (Swiss)

Ishikawa, Yoshimi. *Strawberry Road: A Japanese Immigrant Discovers America*. Tokyo: Kodansha, 1992.

Ito, Kazuo. *Issei: A History of Japanese Immigrants in North America*. Seattle, Wash.: Japanese Community Center, 1973.

Jannopoulo, Helen P. *And across Big Seas*. Caldwell, Idaho: Caxton, 1949. (Greek)

Jastrow, Marie. *Looking Back: The American Dream through Immigrant Eyes, 1907–1918*. New York: W. W. Norton, 1986. (Serbian Jewish)

——. *A Time to Remember: Growing up in New York before the Great War*. New York: W. W. Norton, 1979. (Serbian Jewish)

Joe, Jeanne. *Ying-Ying: Pieces of a Childhood*. San Francisco: East/West Publishing, 1982.

Kalergis, Mary Motley. *Home of the Brave: Contemporary American Immigrants*. New York: E. P. Dutton, 1989.

Kamphoefner, Walter D., Wolfgang Helbich, and Ulrike Sommer, eds. *News from the Land of Freedom: German Immigrants Write Home*. Translated by Susan Carter Vogel. Ithaca, N.Y.: Cornell University Press, 1991.

Kang, Younghill. *East Goes West*. New York: Charles Scribner's Sons, 1937. (Korean)

——. *The Grass Roof*. New York: W. W. Norton, 1975; originally published in 1931. (Korean)

Katzman, David, and William M. Tuttle, Jr., eds. *Plain Folk: The Life Stories of Undistinguished Americans.* Urbana: University of Illinois Press, 1982.

Kessner, Thomas, and Betty Boyd Caroli. *Today's Immigrants, Their Stories: A New Look at the Newest Americans.* New York: Oxford University Press, 1981.

Kikumura, Akemi. *Promises Kept: The Life of an Issei Man.* Novato, Calif.: Chandler and Sharp, 1991. (Japanese American)

―――. *Through Harsh Winters: The Life of a Japanese Immigrant Woman.* Novato, Calif.: Chandler and Sharp, 1981.

Kimball, Gussie. *Gitele.* New York: Vantage, 1960. (Jewish)

Kingston, Maxine Hong. *The Woman Warrior: Memoir of a Girlhood among Ghosts.* New York: Random House, 1976. (Chinese)

Klepp, Susan E., and Billy G. Smith, eds. *The Infortunate: The Voyage and Adventures of William Moraley, an Indentured Servant.* University Park: Pennsylvania State University Press, 1992.

Knaplund, Paul. *Moorings Old and New: Entries in an Immigrant's Log.* Madison: State Historical Society of Wisconsin, 1963. (Norwegian)

Kodama-Nishimoto, Michi, Warren S. Nishimoto, and Cynthia A. Oshiro, eds. *Hanahana: An Oral History Anthology of Hawaii's Working People.* Honolulu: Ethnic Studies Oral History Project, University of Hawaii at Manoa, 1984.

Kohut, Rebekah. *More Yesterdays: An Autobiography.* New York: Bloch, 1950. (Hungarian Jewish)

―――. *My Portion.* New York: Thomas Seltzer, 1925. (Hungarian Jewish)

Koren, Else Hysing. *The Diary of Elisabeth Koren, 1853–1855.* Translated and edited by David T. Nelson. Northfield, Minn.: Norwegian-American Historical Association, 1955.

Kramer, Sydelle, and Jenny Masur, eds. *Jewish Grandmothers.* Boston: Beacon Press, 1976.

Kula, Witold. *Writing Home: Immigrants in Brazil and the United States, 1890–1891.* New York: Columbia University Press, 1986. (Polish)

Kumarappa, Bharatan. *My Student Days in America.* Bombay, India: Padma, 1945.

Kune, Julian. *Reminiscences of an Octogenarian Hungarian Exile.* Chicago: n.p., 1911.

LaGuardia, Fiorello H. *The Making of an Insurgent: An Autobiography, 1882–1919.* New York: Capricorn, 1961. (Italian)

La Gumina, Salvatore J. *The Immigrants Speak: Italian Americans Tell Their Story.* Staten Island, N.Y.: Center for Migration Studies, 1979.

Lai, H. Mark, Genny Lim, and Judy Yung. *Island: Poetry and History of Chinese Immigrants on Angel Island, 1910–1940.* Seattle: University of Washington Press, 1991.

Lang, Lucy Robins. *Tomorrow Is Beautiful.* New York: Macmillan, 1948. (Jewish)

Larson, Laurence M. *Logbook of a Young Immigrant.* Northfield, Minn.: Norwegian-American Historical Association, 1939.

Leavitt, Thomas W., ed. *The Hollingworth Letters: Technical Change in the Textile Industry, 1826–1837*. Cambridge, Mass.: M.I.T. Press, 1969. (English)

Lee, Joann Faung Jean. *Asian American Experiences in the United States: Oral Histories of First to Fourth Generation Americans from China, the Philippines, Japan, India, the Pacific Islands, Vietnam and Cambodia*. Jefferson, N.C.: McFarland, 1991.

Lee, Mary Paik. *Quiet Odyssey: A Pioneer Korean Woman in America*. Edited by Sucheng Chan. Seattle: University of Washington Press, 1990.

Lee, Yan Phou. *When I Was a Boy in China*. Boston: Lothrop, 1887.

Lewisohn, Ludwig. *Mid-Channel*. New York: Harper and Brothers, 1929. (German Jewish)

———. *Up Stream: An American Chronicle*. New York: Boni and Liveright, 1922. (German Jewish)

Li, Ling-Ai. *Life Is for a Long Time: A Chinese Hawaiian Memoir*. New York: Hastings House, 1972.

Lin, Alice. *Grandmother Had No Name*. San Francisco: China Books, 1988. (Chinese)

Lisitzky, Ephraim E. *In the Grip of Cross-Currents*. New York: Bloch, 1959. (Russian Jewish)

Lorde, Audre. *Zami: A New Spelling of My Name*. Freedom, Calif.: Crossing Press, 1982. (Grenadan American)

Lowe, Pardee. *Father and Glorious Descendant*. Boston: Little, Brown, 1943. (Chinese American)

McKay, Claude. *A Long Way from Home*. New York: Arno Press, 1969; originally published in 1937. (Jamaican)

Mangione, Jerre. *An Ethnic at Large: A Memoir of America in the Thirties and Forties*. New York: Putnam, 1978. (Italian)

———. *Mount Allegro*. New York: Perennial Library, 1989; originally published in 1943. (Italian)

Marchello, Maurice R. *Black Coal for White Bread: Up From the Prairie Mines*. New York: Vantage, 1972. (Italian)

Masaoka, Mike, with Bill Hosokawa. *They Call Me Moses Masaoka: An American Saga*. New York: William Morrow, 1987. (Japanese American)

Masumoto, David Mas. *Country Voices: The Oral History of a Japanese American Family Farm Community*. Del Rey, Calif.: Inaka Countryside Publications, 1987.

Mathabane, Mark. *Kaffir Boy in America: An Encounter with Apartheid*. New York: Charles Scribner's Sons, 1989. (Black South African)

Matsui, Haru. *Restless Wave: My Life in Two Worlds*. New York: Modern Age Books, 1940. (Japanese)

Matsumoto, Toru, and Marion Olive Lerrigo. *A Brother Is a Stranger*. New York: John Day, 1946. (Japanese)

Mattson, Hans. *Reminiscences: The Story of an Emigrant*. St. Paul, Minn.: Merrill, 1891. (Swedish)

Meir, Golda. *My Life*. New York: Putnam, 1975. (Russian Jewish)

Metzker, Isaac, comp. *A Bintel Brief: Letters to the Jewish Daily Forward, 1950–1980*. New York: Viking Penguin, 1981.

――――. *A Bintel Brief: Sixty Years of Letters from the Lower East Side to the Jewish Daily Forward*. Garden City, N.Y.: Doubleday, 1971.

Meyer, Ernest Louis. *Bucket Boy: A Milwaukee Legend*. New York: Hastings, 1947. (German)

Minatoya, Linda Yuri. *Talking to High Monks in the Snow*. New York: HarperCollins, 1992.

Mittelberger, Gottlieb. *Journey to Pennsylvania*. Edited and translated by Oscar Handlin and John Clive. Cambridge, Mass.: Harvard University Press, 1960.

Morgan, Ted. *On Becoming American*. Boston: Houghton Mifflin, 1978. (French)

Morrison, Joan, and Charlotte Fox Zabusky, eds. *American Mosaic: The Immigrant Experience in the Words of Those Who Lived It*. New York: New American Library, 1980.

Morse, Dean W. *Pride against Prejudice: Work in the Lives of Older Blacks and Younger Puerto Ricans*. Montclair, N.J.: Allanheld, Osmun, 1980. (Oral histories)

Mukerji, Dhan Gopal. *Caste and Outcast*. New York: E. P. Dutton, 1923. (Indian)

Mullen, Barbara. *Life Is an Adventure*. London: Faber and Faber, 1937. (Irish American)

Mullen, Pat. *Man of Aran*. London: Faber and Faber, 1934. (Irish)

Murata, Kiyoaki. *An Enemy among Friends*. Tokyo: Kodansha, 1991. (Japanese)

Namias, June. *First Generation: In the Words of Twentieth-Century American Immigrants*. Boston: Beacon Press, 1978.

Nelson, Teresa Leopando Lucero. *White Cap and Prayer*. New York: Vantage, 1955. (Filipino)

Newby, Elizabeth. *A Migrant with Hope*. Nashville, Tenn.: Broadman Press, 1977. (Mexican)

Ngor, Haing. *A Cambodian Odyssey*. New York: Macmillan, 1987.

Nguyen-Hong-Nhiem, Lucy, and Joel Martin Halpern. *The Far East Comes Near: Autobiographical Accounts of Southeast Asian Students in America*. Amherst: University of Massachusetts Press, 1989.

Nielsen, Thomas M. *How a Dane Became an American, or Hits and Misses of My Life*. Cedar Rapids, Iowa: Torch, 1935.

Nord, Sverre. *A Logger's Odyssey*. Caldwell, Idaho: Caxton, 1943. (Swedish)

Norelius, Eric. *The Journals of Eric Norelius: A Swedish Missionary on the American Frontier*. Translated and edited by G. Everett Arden. Philadelphia: Fortress, 1967.

Okubo, Miné. *Citizen 13660*. New York: Columbia University Press, 1946. (Japanese)

Okumura, Takie. *Seventy Years of Divine Blessing*. Honolulu: n.p., 1940. (Japanese)

Olseth, O. H. *Mama Came from Norway.* New York: Vantage, 1955.

O'Neal, Mary T. *These Damn Foreigners.* Hollywood, Calif.: Minerva, 1971. (Welsh)

Otero, Miguel Antonio. *Otero: An Autobiographical Trilogy.* New York: Arno Press, 1974; 3 vols. originally published in 1935–40. (Mexican American)

Panunzio, Constantine M. *The Soul of an Immigrant.* New York: Arno Press, 1969; originally published in 1921. (Italian)

Park, No Yong. *Chinaman's Chance.* Boston: Meador, 1940.

Pellegrini, Angelo. *An Immigrant's Quest: American Dream.* San Francisco: North Point Press, 1986. (Italian)

Perez, Joseph F. *Tales of an Italian-American Family.* New York: Gardner Press, 1991.

Pesotta, Rose. *Bread upon the Waters.* Ithaca, N.Y.: ILR Press, 1987; originally published in 1945. (Russian Jewish)

————. *Days of Our Lives.* Boston: Excelsior, 1958. (Russian Jewish)

Plotkin, Sara. *Full-Time Active: Sara Plotkin, an Oral History.* Edited by Arthur Tobier. New York: Community Documentation Workshop, 1980. (Jewish)

Poggie, John J., Jr. *Between Two Cultures: The Life of an American-Mexican.* Tucson: University of Arizona Press, 1973.

Polacheck, Hilda Satt. *I Came a Stranger: The Story of a Hull-House Girl.* Edited by Dena J. Polacheck Epstein. Urbana: University of Illinois Press, 1989. (Polish Jewish)

Polasek, Emily M. K. *A Bohemian Girl in America.* Edited by Edward Hayes. Winter Park, Fla.: Rollins Press, 1982.

Preus, Caroline Dorothea Margarethe (Keyser). *Linka's Diary on Land and Sea, 1845–1864.* Translated and edited by Johan Carl Keyser Preus and Diderikke Margrethe Brandt Preus. Minneapolis: Augsburg, 1952. (Norwegian)

Prisland, Marie. *From Slovenia—to America, Recollections and Collections.* Chicago: Slovenian Women's Union of America, 1968.

Pupin, Michael I. *From Immigrant to Inventor.* New York: Charles Scribner's Sons, 1923. *(Hungarian)*

Raaen, Aagot. *Grass of the Earth: Immigrant Life in Dakota Country.* Northfield, Minn.: Norwegian-American Historical Association, 1950.

Ravage, Marcus Eli. *An American in the Making: The Life Story of an Immigrant.* New York: Harper, 1917. (Rumanian)

Reinhart, Herman Francis. *The Golden Frontier: The Recollections of Herman Francis Reinhart, 1854–1869.* Austin: University of Texas Press, 1962. (German)

Rihani, Ameen. *The Book of Khalid.* New York: Dodd, Mead, 1911. (Syrian)

Rihbany, Abraham Mitre. *A Far Journey.* New York: Houghton Mifflin, 1914. (Syrian)

Riis, Jacob. *The Making of an American.* New York: Macmillan, 1953; originally published in 1901. (Danish)

Riley, Edward Miles, ed. *The Journal of John Harrower: An Indentured Servant in the Colony of Virginia, 1773–1776*. Williamsburg, Va.: Colonial Williamsburg, 1963. (Shetland Islander)

Rivera, Edward. *Family Installments: Memories of Growing Up Hispanic*. New York: Morrow, 1982.

Rizk, Salom. *Syrian Yankee*. Garden City, N.Y.: Doubleday, Doran, 1943.

Rodrigues, Luis Javier. *Barrio Expressions*. Berkeley, Calif.: Quito Sol, 1974. (Mexican American)

Rodriquez, Richard. *Hunger of Memory: The Education of Richard Rodriguez*. Boston: David R. Godine, 1982. (Mexican American)

Roskolenko, Harry. *The Time that Was Then: The Lower East Side, 1900–1914, an Intimate Chronicle*. New York: Dial Press, 1971. (Jewish)

———. *When I Was Last on Cherry Street*. New York: Stein and Day, 1965. (Jewish)

Roth, Kelly. *Experiences and Travels of an Immigrant Boy*. Los Angeles: n.p., 1944. (Hungarian)

Rouillard, Jacques. *Ah les Etats! Les travailleurs Canadiens-Français dans l'industrie textile de la Nouvelle-Angleterre d'après le témoinage des dernier migrants*. Montreal: Boréal Express, 1985. (French Canadian; for those who read French)

Rubin, Steven J., ed. *Writing Our Lives: Autobiographies of American Jews, 1890–1990*. Philadelphia: Jewish Publication Society of America, 1991.

Sanjek, Louis. *In Silence*. New York: Fortuny's, 1938. (Croatian)

Santoli, Al. *New Americans, an Oral History: Immigrants and Refugees in the U.S. Today*. New York: Ballantine Books, 1988.

Sarasohn, Eileen Sunada, ed. *The Issei: Portrait of a Pioneer, an Oral History*. Palo Alto, Calif.: Pacific Books, 1983. (Japanese)

Saroff, Sophie. *Stealing the State: An Oral History*. New York: Community Documentation Workshop, 1983. (Jewish)

Schneiderman, Rose, with Lucy Goldthwaite. *All for One*. New York: Paul S. Eriksson, 1967. (Russian Jewish)

Schroeder, Adolf E., and Carla Schulz-Geisberg, eds. *Hold Dear, as Always: Jette, an Immigrant Life in Letters*. Columbia: University of Missouri Press, 1988. (German)

Schurz, Carl. *Autobiography: An Abridgement in One Volume*. New York: Charles Scribner's Sons, 1961; 3 vols. originally published in 1907–8. (German)

Simon, Kate. *Bronx Primitive: Portraits in a Childhood*. New York: Viking Press, 1982. (Polish Jewish)

———. *A Wider World: Portraits in an Adolescence*. New York: Harper and Row, 1986. (Polish Jewish)

Siwundhla, Alice (Princess Msumba). *Alice Princess: An Autobiography*. Montain View, Calif.: Pacific Press, 1965. (African)

———. *My Two Worlds*. Montain View, Calif.: Pacific Press, 1965. (African)

Sone, Monica. *Nisei Daughter*. Seattle: University of Washington Press, 1979; originally published in 1953. (Japanese American)

Soto, Pedro Juan. *Hot Land, Cold Season*. New York: Dell, 1973. (Puerto Rican)

Steiner, Edward A. *From Alien to Citizen: The Story of My Life in America*. New York: Fleming H. Revell, 1914. (Austro-Hungarian)

Stern, Elizabeth G., pseud., Leah Morton. *I Am a Woman—and a Jew*. New York: Arno Press, 1969; originally published in 1926. (German Jewish)

———. *My Mother and I*. New York: Macmillan, 1917. (German Jewish)

Stone, Goldie. *My Caravan of Years: An Autobiography*. New York: Bloch, 1945. (Jewish)

Sugimoto, Etsu Inagaki. *A Daughter of the Samurai*. Garden City, N.Y.: Doubleday, Page, 1925. (Japanese)

Surmelian, Leon Z. *I Ask You, Ladies and Gentlemen*. New York: E. P. Dutton, 1945. (Armenian)

Tateishi, John. *And Justice for All: An Oral History of the Japanese-American Detention Camps*. New York: Random House, 1984.

Tenhula, John. *Voices from Southeast Asia: The Refugee Experience in the United States*. New York: Holmes and Meier, 1991.

Thomas, Piri. *Down These Mean Streets*. New York: Vintage, 1974; originally published in 1967. (Puerto Rican)

———. *Savior, Savior, Hold My Hand*. New York: Doubleday, 1972. (Puerto Rican)

———. *Seven Long Times*. New York: Praeger, 1974. (Puerto Rican)

Thomas, William I., and Florian Znaniecki. *The Polish Peasant in Europe and America*. Edited by Eli Zaretsky. Urbana: University of Illinois Press, 1985; 5 vols. originally published in 1920.

Thomson, Gladys Scott. *A Pioneer Family: The Birkbecks in Illinois, 1818–1827*. London: Jonathan Cape, 1953. (English)

Trupin, Sophie. *Dakota Diaspora: Memoirs of a Jewish Homesteader*. Lincoln: University of Nebraska Press, 1984.

Uchida, Yoshiko. *Desert Exile: The Uprooting of a Japanese American Family*. Seattle: University of Washington Press, 1982.

Unonius, Gustaf Elias Marius. *A Pioneer in Northwest America, 1841–1858: The Memoirs of Gustaf Unonius*. 2 vols. Minneapolis: University of Minnesota Press, 1950 and 1960. (Swedish)

Vanzetti, Bartolomeo. *The Story of a Proletarian Life*. Boston: New Trial League, 1923. (Italian)

Vecoli, Rudolph, ed. *American Immigrant Autobiographies*. Frederick, Md.: University Publications of America, 1988. (Microfilm—Italian and Finnish are most frequent among unpublished autobiographies reprinted here)

———. *Voices from Ellis Island: An Oral History of American Immigration*. Frederick, Md.: University Publications of America, 1988. (Microfilm or microfiche)

Vega, Bernardo. *Memoirs of Bernardo Vega: A Contribution to the History of the Puerto Rican Community in New York*. Translated by Juan Flores. New York: Monthly Review Press, 1984.

Ventresca, Francesco. *Personal Reminiscences of a Naturalized American.* New York: Ryerson, 1937. (Italian)

Walther, Anna H. *A Pilgrimage with a Milliner's Needle.* New York: Frederick A. Stokes, 1917. (Danish)

Wheeler, Thomas, ed. *The Immigrant Experience: The Anguish of Becoming American.* New York: Dial Press, 1971.

Wiesenfeld, Leon. *Jewish Life in Cleveland in the 1920's and 1930's: The Memoirs of a Jewish Journalist.* Cleveland: Jewish Voice Pictorial, 1965.

Wong, Jade Snow. *Fifth Chinese Daughter.* New York: Harper and Row, 1950.

———. *No Chinese Stranger.* New York: Harper and Row, 1975.

Yep, Laurence. *The Lost Garden.* New York: Julian Messner, 1991. (Chinese American)

Yezierska, Anzia. *Red Ribbon on a White Horse.* New York: Charles Scribner's Sons, 1950. (Polish Jewish)

Yoneda, Karl G. *Ganbatte: Sixty-year Struggle of a Kibei Worker.* Los Angeles: Asian American Studies Center, 1983. (Japanese)

Yung, Wing. *My Life in China and America.* New York: Arno Press, 1978; originally published in 1909.

Zaimi, Nexhmie. *Daughter of an Eagle: The Autobiography of an Albanian Girl.* New York: Ives Washburn, 1937.

Zakrewska, Marie E. *A Memoir.* Boston: New England Hospital for Women and Children, 1903. (Polish)

———. *A Woman's Quest.* Edited by Agnes C. Vietor. New York: Appleton, 1924. (Polish)

Zempel, Solveig, ed. and trans. *In Their Own Words: Letters from Norwegian Immigrants.* Minneapolis: University of Minnesota Press, 1991.

Index

Thomas Dublin is a professor of history at the State University of New York at Binghamton, where he teaches courses in U.S. ethnic, labor, and women's history. He is the author of *Women at Work* (1979), editor of *Farm to Factory* (1981), and coeditor (with Kathryn Kish Sklar) of *Women and Power in American History* (1991).